Conquering Demons

The "Kirishitan," Japan, and the World in Early Modern Japanese Literature

JAN C. LEUCHTENBERGER

CENTER FOR JAPANESE STUDIES
THE UNIVERSITY OF MICHIGAN
ANN ARBOR   2013

Copyright © 2013 by The Regents of the University of Michigan

All rights reserved.

Published by the Center for Japanese Studies,
The University of Michigan
1007 E. Huron St.
Ann Arbor, MI 48104-1690

Library of Congress Cataloging-in-Publication Data

Leuchtenberger, Jan C., 1964–
  Conquering Demons : the "Kirishitan," Japan, and the World in Early Modern Japanese Literature / Jan C. Leuchtenberger.
    pages cm. -- (Michigan Monograph Series in Japanese Studies ; Number 75)
  Includes bibliographical references and index.
  ISBN 978-1-929280-77-3 (hardback : alk. paper) -- ISBN 978-1-929280-78-0 (pbk. : alk. paper) -- ISBN 978-1-929280-79-7 (ebook)
  1. Japanese literature--Edo period, 1600-1868--History and criticism. 2. Christianity and literature--Japan. 3. Literature and society--Japan. I. Title.

PL726.45.C45L48 2013
895.6'09003--dc23

2013033257

This book was set in Palatino Macron.
The *kanji* were set in MS Mincho.

This publication meets the ANSI/NISO Standards for Permanence of Paper for Publications and Documents in Libraries and Archives (Z39.48—1992).

Printed in the United States of America

In memory of my parents,
Martin and Jean Leuchtenberger

Conquering Demons

MICHIGAN MONOGRAPH SERIES IN JAPANESE STUDIES
NUMBER 75

CENTER FOR JAPANESE STUDIES
THE UNIVERSITY OF MICHIGAN

Contents

List of Illustrations ... ix

List of Tables ... x

Acknowledgments ... xi

1   Building the Barbarian Kirishitan Other and a Sacred Japan ... 1

2   Romans and Demons: Kirishitan Villains in *Baterenki* and *Kirishitan monogatari* ... 32

3   Imagining the Kirishitan, Japan, and the World in *Kirishitan shūmon raichō jikki* ... 70

4   Conjurers and Conquerors: The Kirishitan Figure in Other Late Edo Discourses ... 107

Epilogue ... 132

Translations

Baterenki: "History of the Padres" ... 137

Nanbanji monogatari: "Tale of the Southern Barbarian Temple" ... 161

Appendix: Extant Copies and Variants of the *Raichō jikki* Narrative ... 199

Bibliography 214

Index 228

Illustrations

Figure 1. Map of the entire three realms cosmology   26

Figure 2. Detail of the three realms cosmology   27

Figure 3. Urugan Bateren arrives in Nagasaki   53

Figure 4. Urugan Bateren presents his gifts to Oda Nobunaga   54

Figure 5. Map of India   100

Figure 6. 1710 *Nansenbushū bankoku shōka no zu*   102

Figure 7. 1645 *Bankoku sōzu* (World Map)   104

Tables

Table 1. *Kabuki* and *jōruri* plays featuring a Kirishitan villain   111

Table A1. Extant manuscripts of *Raichō jikki* variants   209

Table A2. Texts that include the *Raichō jikki* narrative in full   213

Table A3. Manuscripts of the *Shimabara jitsuroku* text   213

Acknowledgments

There are many people to whom I am grateful for their guidance and assistance on this project as it grew from dissertation to book. At the University of Michigan, I was fortunate to have as my advisor Esperanza Ramirez-Christensen, whose insightful critiques guided me through this and many other projects at the university. Ken Ito and Hitomi Tonomura also gave generously of their time to critique my work and advise me both during my time at Michigan and since. I was also fortunate to benefit from the advice and shared interests of Jonathan Zwicker and Stephanie Seigmund. Watanabe Kenji and Komine Kazuaki of Rikkyō University in Tokyo both have guided me in my research and supported it for several years. Special thanks also go to Niwa Misato, who patiently helped me read some of the more difficult manuscripts.

Initial research for this project was supported by grants from the Center for Japanese Studies at the University of Michigan, and dissertation research was carried out with a generous fellowship from The Japan Foundation. A year as an associate fellow at the Michigan Society of Fellows supported me while I wrote the dissertation. Additional research and revisions for the book project were made possible by a Martin Nelson Junior Sabbatical and other research grants provided by the University of Puget Sound.

The bulk of the early research involved consulting manuscripts in at least twenty libraries in Japan as well as two archives in Rome, and there were many people who helped me gain access to those collections. For his invaluable assistance with all of the Japanese libraries I am very grateful to Michigan Asia Librarian Emeritus Kenji Niki. Without his countless letters of introduction and, on occasion, personal intervention, none of this research could have been accomplished. I would also like to thank Kate Nakai of Sophia University in Tokyo and Ueda Hiroyasu of Dōshisha University in Kyoto for their assistance in making the collections of those libraries available. I am grateful to Aileen Gatten, not only for her introduction to the Vatican Library, but also for her encouragement at the beginning of this project, without which it never would have come to fruition.

My time at Michigan was greatly enriched by the friendship of my colleagues in the department. For their unwavering support and unfailing sense of humor I am grateful to Robert Rama, Jason Herlands, Kristina Vassil, Shawn Walker, Tim Van Compernolle, Mimi Plauche, Jeremy Robinson and Jocelyn Flint, Alex and Amy Bates, Hoyt and Mea Long, David Henry, and Chisato Murakami. Special thanks go to Alex and Jeremy for rescuing me from a number of potential computer disasters. I have had the great fortune to move from one supportive environment at Michigan to a new one at Puget Sound, where the boundless energy and enthusiasm of my colleagues in Asian Studies have inspired me to live up to their example. Special thanks go to Mikiko Ludden, Lotus Perry, Judy Tyson, Elizabeth Chen, Lorraine Toler, and Karl Fields for creating a program that is a joy to work in, and to Lisa Ferrari and Aaron Taylor for always listening.

The book has undergone a number of revisions thanks to the encouraging and very helpful comments of the reviewers as well as the patient guidance of Bruce Willoughby at CJS Publications. I thank all of them for making the process a relatively painless one.

Finally, my family has been a solid pillar of support, and I would like to thank my siblings for listening and for the help that took so many forms. My mother was my best friend and most enthusiastic supporter throughout the dissertation process, and I am most grateful for her love and her friendship. Though neither she nor my father was able to see the dissertation become a book, it only happened because of the love of reading, writing, and learning that they both instilled in me. I dedicate this work to their memory.

Chapter One

Building the Barbarian Kirishitan Other and a Sacred Japan

In November of 1614, a large group of Christian missionaries and lay people boarded ships in Nagasaki bound for Macao and Manila, bringing an official end to the Japanese missions of several European orders.[1] Despite the bakufu's ban on Christianity and the order of expulsion that had prompted the exodus, a few dozen missionaries remained in hiding to minister to their converts, while others continued to enter Japan as stowaways on European trade ships. Over the next several decades, enforcement of the ban grew increasingly harsh and broadened to encompass native believers as well as foreign missionaries. Countless converts and some hidden missionaries were killed, while others were forced to apostatize or go underground. By the early 1630s the "Kirishitan"[2]

---

1. The Society of Jesus (Jesuits) was the first order to establish itself in Japan when Francis Xavier arrived with a small group of fathers in 1549, and therefore was the longest running mission in the country. Other orders whose representatives had arrived in Japan in the 1590s or later included the Dominicans, Franciscans, and Augustinians.
2. The word "Kirishitan" was derived from the Portuguese word for Christian and was originally used by Japanese people to refer to both the Christian missionaries and their converts (but not to Christ), and also to the religion of Christianity. Nobody knows how much the Japanese converts really understood about the Christianity they were taught, so the term "Kirishitan" is used to refer to what was understood as Christians/Christianity by the Japanese, though it could have been quite different from what the Western Christians thought of themselves and their religion. That gap between what the missionaries represented and taught and what was understood by the Japanese only widens with time, so the term Kirishitan is a shifting one. In this study, when the plural, Kirishitans, is used, it usually refers to multiple Kirishitan characters in a text, and when the singular is used it refers to the overall figure or cultural construct of the Kirishitan represented in the text.

religion and its adherents appeared to have been eradicated. However, in 1637, rebels in the Shimabara area of Kyushu marched under Kirishitan banners and proved alarmingly tenacious in their fight, raising concerns that the foreign missionaries still held influence over their converts. The rebels were eventually defeated and killed in 1638, and no foreigners were found among the dead, but the experience prompted the bakufu to take further measures to prevent any missionaries from entering the country. The final expulsion edict of 1639 broke off all trade with Iberian countries and prohibited Spanish and Portuguese ships from landing in Japan. Though arrests of Kirishitan converts and even a few hidden missionaries continued off and on until the late seventeenth century, historical accounts of the Christian missions in Japan generally cite the year of this edict as the end of what has sometimes been called "the Christian century" in Japan.

Practicing Kirishitan may have disappeared from public view by the middle of the seventeenth century, but the figure of the Kirishitan lived on for more than two centuries in pseudohistorical narratives that continually replayed his abjection and expulsion. Beginning with *Baterenki* (History of the Padres, circa 1610), in which the Kirishitan are expelled at a regional level from the Ōmura domain, the theme of the thwarted Kirishitan conquest grew to become a story of national peril and salvation, as the tale was expanded and repeated in two printings of *Kirishitan monogatari* (Tale of the Kirishitan, 1639 and 1665) and in the narrative of the later *Kirishitan shūmon raichō jikki* (A True Account of the Arrival of the Kirishitan Sect in Japan, Kyōhō period, 1716–35).[3] Despite increased censorship after 1665 of works on the Kirishitan, the latter work was copied and circulated widely under different titles through private hands and the lending library system for well over a century in quantities large enough that more than 150 manuscript copies are still extant today.[4]

Their endurance and popularity over such a long period of time indicate that these narratives were more than just good entertainment; their topic struck a nerve. As several versions of the tales point out, the arrival and expulsion of the Kirishitan affected the entire country in the form of the Shimabara Rebellion and other institutions intended to eradicate the religion, such as the practice of *fumie* and temple registration.[5] For these

3. The second printing of *Kirishitan monogatari* bore the title *Kirishitan taiji monogatari* (Tale of the Defeat of the Kirishitan) and contained illustrations. See chapter 2 for more on both texts.
4. See the appendix for a list of some of those manuscripts and where they are held.
5. To show the sincerity of their change of heart Kirishitan apostates were required first to step on an image of Mary or Jesus (*fumie*), and then were required to register with a Buddhist temple. Though this kind of temple registration began in 1614 in Kyoto for apostates, it later became government policy that all people register and that each

reasons alone, it is not surprising that the accounts were widely read. But the narratives also chronicle what Ronald Toby has called the "Iberian Irruption"—a moment when one of Japan's Others was consistently *within* its boundaries rather than outside, and when new information brought by that Other forced a reconsideration of Japanese identity and its place in the world.[6] The moment produced a cultural anxiety that clearly influenced the increased concern in seventeenth- and eighteenth-century texts with Japan and its Others, and the growing discourse on national and cultural identity in the Edo period. As one part of that discourse, the anti-Kirishitan narratives not only record the arrival of a significant new Other, but also offer anxious readers one way to grapple with issues raised by Japan's initial engagement with the West by representing Japan as the victor in a battle for political and cultural dominance. New maps brought by the Iberians had challenged the traditional three-realms cosmology and Japan's place in it. But within the narratives, Japan expels the Kirishitan *and* the new world they brought with them, reasserting a more traditional world order in which it maintains a significant and sacred position.

Considerable research has been devoted to historical events surrounding the Western missions and their aftermath, with a focus on the effect those events and Christianity had on Japanese religion, politics, trade, and intellectual history.[7] These studies sometimes mention the anonymous narratives about the arrival and expulsion of the Kirishitan, but the texts are usually dismissed as fiction that is more useful to a study

---

    temple perform a yearly examination of all its members. By 1640, the system became an official part of bakufu administration of the country. While the registration was required of everyone, descendants of apostate Kirishitan were singled out for special examination for up to seven generations for men and up to four generations for women. See Ikuo Higashibaba, *Christianity in Early Modern Japan: Kirishitan Belief and Practice* (Leiden: Brill, 2001), 158.

6. Ronald P. Toby, "Three Realms/Myriad Countries: an 'Ethnography' of Other and the Re-Bounding of Japan, 1550-1750," in *Constructing Nationhood in Modern East Asia*, edited by Kai-wing Chow, Kevin M. Doak, Poshek Fu (Ann Arbor: The University of Michigan Press, 2001), 15–45.

7. Basic histories of the period include Charles F. Boxer, *The Christian Century in Japan 1549-1650* (Berkeley: University of California Press, 1951); Anesaki Masaharu, *Kirishitan shūmon no hakugai to senpuku* (Tokyo: Dōbunkan, 1925); idem, *Kirishitan dendō no kōhai* (Tokyo: Dōbunkan, 1930); Ebisawa Arimichi, *Nihon kirishitanshi* (Tokyo: Hanawa shobō, 1966); and Michael Cooper, *Rodrigues the Interpreter: an Early Jesuit in Japan and China* (New York: Weatherhill, 1974). Books that deal with the implications of Christianity in Japanese culture and ideology include Ebisawa Arimichi, *Kirishitanshi no kenkyū* (Tokyo: Unebi shobō, 1942); idem, *Kirishitan no shakai katsudō oyobi nanban igaku* (Tokyo: Fuzanbō, 1944); George Elison, *Deus Destroyed: the Image of Christianity in Early Modern Japan* (Cambridge, Mass.: Harvard University Press, 1973); Higashibaba, *Christianity in Early Modern Japan*; and Kiri Paramore, *Ideology and Christianity in Japan* (London: Routledge, 2009).

of propaganda methods than to one of Christianity in Japan.[8] In fact, the Kirishitan figure of the pseudohistorical narratives had little to do with its original referent, the Christian missionary or convert. Rather, it was a construct that represented simultaneously that first point of contact with the West and ongoing anxiety about its influence and about Japan's place in a new world whose dimensions only became known with that contact. Timon Screech has demonstrated the importance and influence of Ran as another construct that served as one symbol of Europe and the West in Edo-period culture.[9] Circulating at the same time but under more restrictions due to the censorship of Christianity, the Kirishitan can be seen as the alter ego of Ran, representing a darker, more sinister side of the West. If Ran was associated with "precision," "sobriety," and "impeccable inter-personal mannerliness," the Kirishitan were portrayed as grotesque, uncanny tricksters who's sole purpose was to usurp other countries and steal their wealth.[10] By the eighteenth century, "Kirishitan" had come to signify more than a religion and its adherents; it was implicated with the uncanny, the threat of conquest, questions of religious, national, and racial identity, and the degradation of traditional culture by contact with new Others. In fact, Kirishitan was a "cluster of concepts" that encompassed all that was fearful about the changes brought by the Iberian Irruption.[11]

This study traces the construction of the Kirishitan figure in *Kirishitan shūmon raichō jikki* (hereafter *Raichō jikki*) and its predecessors, *Baterenki* and *Kirishitan monogatari*, and examines the figure's significance as a new Other in discourses on Japan's identity and on the world in the eighteenth and nineteenth centuries. The development of the figure from a relentless would-be

---

8. Early scholarship on all three narratives by Anesaki Masaharu, Ebisawa Arimichi, and George Elison has been most concerned with historical inaccuracies in what is read as a direct representation of the Christian missionaries, and often has looked to political forces to explain the narratives' existence and popularity. The texts generally have been characterized as propaganda that served the purposes of the bakufu by spreading the anti-Christian message to the lower classes, though research by Peter Kornicki has shown that the bakufu was relatively slow to realize the social and ideological power of the print industry and did not make great use of it to support its ideological positions. See Peter Kornicki, *The Book in Japan: a Cultural History From the Beginnings to the Nineteenth Century* (Honolulu: University of Hawai'i Press, 2001), 331. It is important to note that contemporary readers of the narratives did not appear to distinguish them as less truthful than other works on the Kirishitan. Though scholars of the eighteenth and nineteenth centuries clearly read the narratives critically, they also appear to have viewed them as legitimate sources for knowledge on the Kirishitan and the West. See chapter 4 for more on this topic.
9. Timon Screech, *The Lens Within the Heart: The Western Scientific Gaze and Popular Imagery in Later Edo Japan* (Honolulu: University of Hawai'i Press, 2002).
10. Ibid., 31–34.
11. The phrase "cluster of concepts" was used by Timon Screech to describe Ran. Ibid., 7.

conqueror in *Baterenki* to a grotesque and uncanny foreigner in *Raichō jikki*, who uses money, magic, and medicine to lure the gullible into giving up their country to him, reflects not only changing views of the Kirishitan but also evolving discourses on Japan and its Others. By the eighteenth century, the terms "Kirishitan" and "Nanbanjin," which had originally referred to a religious group and Westerners, respectively, came to be synonymous with a kind of universal Western threat.[12] Where Nanbanjin, or "southern barbarian," had originally described people whose ships came from the South (Macao and Manila) and from outside of the Sino-centric sphere of civilization, the Nanbanjin of the Kirishitan tales were from the mythical country of "Nanban," which represented an indistinct outside world perpetually bent on the conquest of Japan. In fact, though the image of the Kirishitan evolved over the years, common to all of the representations was the threat he posed to Japanese sovereignty and identity, and the constant repetition of the cycle of penetration and expulsion—the dogged insistence at the end of each narrative that the Kirishitan had been expelled seemingly negated by the next one again chronicling his arrival. Despite the insistence in each of the tales on Japan's victory over the barbarian, the curious result of the continuous reproduction of the narratives from the seventeenth through the nineteenth century is that the Kirishitan was never actually expelled from the discursive space and the imagination of Edo-period Japan. The apparent need to repeat the expulsion story continually throughout the Edo period points to the importance of the Kirishitan figure as a repository for anxiety about Japan's vulnerability to influences and powers from outside of its borders. *Baterenki*, *Kirishitan monogatari*, and the *Raichō jikki* narrative all reflect that anxiety, but they also work to allay it not only in the tale of expulsion, but also in the degradation of the Kirishitan through his representation as a grotesque and barbaric Other. In doing so, they also reassert a sacred identity for Japan within the traditional three-realms cosmology that had been displaced by new maps brought with Western traders and missionaries.

CONSTRUCTING AND DOMINATING THE KIRISHITAN OTHER

The Kirishitan figure evolved considerably in the hundred years that passed between the production of *Baterenki*, close to the time of the first

---

12. Nanbanjin originally referred primarily to the Portuguese and Spanish, because they came from the south (Manila and Macao) and from outside the Sino-centric civilized realm. As Screech has pointed out, the term was replaced by "Ranjin" in Ran discourse of the eighteenth and nineteenth centuries, but it continued to be used in anti-Kirishitan texts into the nineteenth century to refer to subjects of the king of Nanban, a country that appears to stand for the West in general. Screech, *The Lens Within the Heart*, 34.

expulsion, and the publication of the eighteenth-century *Raichō jikki*. While the Kirishitan of *Baterenki* are priests sent by the Pope in Rome, the villains of *Raichō jikki* are adepts sent by the king of the vast but mythical land of "Nanban." The greater part of *Baterenki* narrates the many unsuccessful attempts of the Kirishitan to enter Japan, with only the last few pages chronicling his activities once he arrives. Thus, the Kirishitan of *Baterenki* are primarily outside, trying to get in. Conversely, though the Kirishitan of *Kirishitan monogatari* and *Raichō jikki* come to Japan from Nanban, the narratives are mostly concerned with what they do *in* Japan. Finally, the Kirishitan figure of *Baterenki* is primarily characterized by his religion and a thirst for conquest, and not by his physical appearance or behavior, whereas the Kirishitan of the two later tales is portrayed as a grotesque degenerate. This later Kirishitan's appearance is compared to that of animals and demons, his religious practice includes bloody sacrifice, and he recruits the lowest in society by tricking them with magic or bribing them with money. This evolution of the Kirishitan figure shows the passage of time between the time of the missionaries and the production of *Raichō jikki*, but it also shows a change in the purpose that the Kirishitan figure served in literature and society. Clearly, by the eighteenth century, he had become the repository for anxiety about more than just the arrival and expulsion of the European missionaries.

Significantly, *Raichō jikki* is remarkably concerned with the distinguishing characteristics of the foreign Kirishitan figure and how his appearance and practices differ from those of Japan, despite the fact that over half a century had passed since the final expulsion edict. While this may reflect anxiety about the earlier penetration of the West and about the continuing discovery of hidden Kirishitan converts, it also clearly demonstrates a growing desire to clarify a Japanese identity in opposition to the Kirishitan/Nanban Other. In fact, at the time that *Raichō jikki* was produced, a number of media show increasing concern with defining and organizing the peoples of the world, and Japan among them. In popular maps and encyclopedias of the time, those peoples were often organized according to their perceived level of civilization, with Japan and China always at the top.[13] Similarly, the *Raichō jikki* narrative places great em-

13. Perhaps the most popular of the maps was the *Bankoku sōzu* (Map of the Myriad Realms), which first appeared in 1645 and was reproduced many times by printers in Nagasaki and Kyoto. Encyclopedias included Nakamura Tekisai's *Kinmō zui* (Encyclopedia Primer, 1666), which outlined the various occupations and status levels of Japanese people, in addition to describing a wide range of foreign peoples, including the Nanbanjin. Nishikawa Jōken was one of the more prolific writers of this genre in the early eighteenth century. His *Ka'i tsūshō kō* (Thoughts on Trade between China and Barbarians),

phasis on a civilized, sacred Japan in contrast to the barbarian Kirishitan/ Nanbanjin. In doing so, it calls upon tropes from Japanese literature to imagine that barbarian Other in opposition to traditional views of what was civilized and sacred. In light of this, it is perhaps not surprising that the Kirishitan figure of the later tales more closely resembles a villain from medieval *setsuwa* than a Western padre. Not only was there less information in the eighteenth century about the historical padres, but whether the Kirishitan resembled them or not was irrelevant; they merely needed to be the barbarian counterpart to a civilized Japan.

This kind of preoccupation with an Other who serves as the repository for cultural anxiety during a time of upheaval is common in many cultures, and early modern England's deep concern with Jews and "Jewishness" is one case that shows surprising parallels with that of Japan and the Kirishitan. James Shapiro points out that the question of who was a Jew was rarely brought up in medieval England, but with the expansion of travel and exploration, and in the wake of the Reformation and the Spanish and Portuguese Inquisitions, growing concern about identifying the racial and physical differences of Jews substituted for what was fundamentally a concern about "the nature of Englishness itself and who has the right to stake a claim in it."[14] England's early modern discourse on the Jews shows concern for how to perceive the difference between Jews and Englishmen, and anxiety about a "hidden and insidious" Jewish crime, as well as the potential for Jewishness to "reassert itself from within."[15] This concern, which Shapiro traces in the works of Shakespeare and other famous authors of the period, came at a time when there were, in fact, few Jews in England.

The Kirishitan tales also show a transition from a knowable and relatively uncomplicated Kirishitan Other to one whose difference is constantly examined and asserted precisely at the time when Kirishitan were no longer visible in public life. In *Baterenki*, there is little attempt to explain

---

an encyclopedia about the countries of the world, which first came out in 1695 and was revised and reissued in 1709, was an important source on world countries for writers throughout the eighteenth century. His later *Shijūnikoku jinbutsu zusetsu* (The Peoples of the Forty-two Counties, 1720) also was influential, and many subsequent works on the subject continued to represent a world outside of Japan made up of forty-two countries. A contemporary of Jōken's, Terajima Ryōan, spent thirty years beginning in 1712 compiling an 80-volume encyclopedia named the *Wakan sansai zue* (Sino-Japanese Encyclopedia of the Three Realms). Modeled after the Chinese *Sancai tuhui* (Encyclopedia of the Three Realms, 1607), Terajima's work was divided into the categories of "heaven, man, and earth" and included a section on foreign peoples. For more on these maps and encyclopedias, see Ronald Toby, "Three Realms/Myriad Countries," 26–33.

14. James Shapiro, *Shakespeare and the Jews* (New York: Columbia University Press, 1996), 4.

the Kirishitan figure's difference—the fact of his foreignness seems to be sufficient to express it. But in the eighteenth-century *Raichō jikki*, the appearance and behavior of the Kirishitan figure are constantly brought up as signs of his barbarian nature, with the narrator sometimes observing how different those features are from Japanese appearance and practice. Also in the later narrative, there is a greater emphasis on an insidious and hidden Kirishitan influence that needs to be identified and eradicated. This can be seen in the addition of accounts of Japanese converts who change their names and move to other communities but continue to practice their "magic" until they are discovered by the authorities. The blurring of Kirishitan/Nanbanjin identities, and the resulting representation of the Kirishitan as an indeterminate Western threat, also show that they had become much more than a religious threat. In the case of England, Shapiro writes:

> Even as England could be defined in part by its having purged itself of Jews, English character could be defined by its need to exclude "Jewishness." In the decades following the Reformation, the English began to think of the Jews not only as people who almost three centuries earlier had been banished from English territory but also as a potential threat to the increasingly permeable boundaries of their own social and religious identities.[16]

As in the case of England, "Japaneseness" is defined in the tales not only by the fact of the expulsion, but also by the need to exclude the Kirishitan, who in their expanded role as a Western Other represent a threat to Japanese religious, social, and national identity. And it is clear that in the expulsion tales, as in early modern English representations of Jews, discourses on race, nation, and theology were inextricably intertwined.[17]

Europe's earliest discourses on the Orient illustrate a similar cultural anxiety about permeable borders and identities but also demonstrate how literary production of the Other can work to allay that anxiety. In *Orientalism*, Edward Said describes perceptions of the Orient formed during the military, cultural, and religious expansion of Islam from the seventh through the fourteenth centuries, when it had spread as far north as Spain and parts of France and as far east as Indonesia and China. To the Europeans of this time, Islam represented the constant threat of barbarian hordes with the potential to conquer any one of the Christian kingdoms.

15. Ibid., 8–9.
16. Ibid., 7.
17. Ibid., 226.

"For Europe, Islam was a lasting trauma. Until the end of the seventeenth century the 'Ottoman peril' lurked alongside Europe to represent for the whole of Christian civilization a constant danger...."[18]

European representations of Islam and the Ottoman empire dealt with the anxiety of the threat by trying to control it within the framework of familiar language and images. From a vast and complex history a few figures and events were chosen, and these were narrated again and again in literature and on stage in symbolic rituals of control. An important factor in that control was the use of language and images with which the audience was familiar, diminishing the threat by showing it to be mundane. One result of that process was the portrayal of Islam as just a "misguided version of Christianity."[19] Mohammed was assumed to be at the center of Islam, just as Christ was at the center of Christianity. From there, he came to be labeled the "Imposter," a prophet who preached a false doctrine. "Similarly, since Mohammed was viewed as the disseminator of a false Revelation, he became as well the epitome of lechery, debauchery, sodomy, and a whole battery of assorted treacheries, all of which derived 'logically' from his doctrinal impostures."[20] Through this process the exotic and threatening was rendered recognizable and almost prosaic in its evil, and "the Orient at large, therefore, vacillates between the West's contempt for what is familiar and its shivers of delight in—or fear of—novelty."[21]

In *Kirishitan monogatari* and *Raichō jikki* we see the same combination of contempt and fear at the figure of the Kirishitan. He is on the one hand exotic in his difference, both in appearance and practice, and on the other hand completely familiar in his heresy. The Kirishitan sect is just a misguided form of Buddhism—its grounding in heresy embodied in the grotesque appearance of its followers and demonstrated by their preoccupation with money and magic. The reader alternates between the thrill of novelty inspired by his grotesque features and exotic-sounding Portuguese words, and contempt for the most common of Buddhist conmen. In this way the Kirishitan menace is dominated on two levels in the tales: through narrative, with the expulsion and persecution ordered by the authorities, but also through representation, with a thoroughly domesticated image of Otherness. That domestication is performed by constructing the Kirishitan as recognizably base or Other using the familiar images of popular literature, including the subhuman character

---

18. Edward Said, *Orientalism* (New York: Penguin, 2003), 59.
19. Ibid., 61.
20. Ibid., 62.
21. Ibid., 59.

of the demon or animal villain, the taboo figure of the *yamabushi*, and the degenerate Buddhist priest tempted by desires of the world.

Animals and Demons

The opening paragraph of *Kirishitan monogatari* features a physical description of the padres that compares some of their features to those of horses and owls, and also questions the humanity of the foreigners by saying that they resemble such demons as the *tengu* (a long-nosed, birdlike creature) or *mikoshi nyūdō* (a long-necked figure dressed in priestly garb). *Raichō jikki* copies that physical description nearly verbatim, though it adds that the padres have nails on their hands and feet as long as those of bears. In addition, it features a description of another padre whose unnatural height and green face add to the pantheon of grotesque features on the foreign Kirishitan. In one change between the descriptions in *Kirishitan monogatari* and *Raichō jikki*, the references to demons are left out in the latter, though the otherworldly, uncanny nature of the Kirishitan figure is preserved in the more developed magical skills attributed to him in the later text. The equation of the padres with animals in *Raichō jikki* extends to their behavior as well in the scene when Nobunaga consults his counselors on whether he should allow them to spread their "Buddhist" teachings. The passage comes soon after the grotesque physical description and questions the intelligence and culture of a man of such appearance. When Nobunaga asks for his lords' opinions, the Buddhist priest Bunkyōin Hokkyō points to the foreigner's manner of greeting the leader, with his leg(s) stretched in front of him, his arms crossed over his chest and his head raised, as proof that he is uncivilized and therefore incapable of knowing the true path. After explaining that proper forms of obeisance are integral to all of the accepted religions and modes of thought, Bunkyōin remarks, "These are the ways of men. But this Padre Urugan stretches his leg(s) out before him and does not lower his head. Raising one's head does not show reverence; it is the way of animals. His appearance is vulgar, like the people of Ebisu or Mongolia.[22] It seems unlikely he would know any Buddhist teachings that we would want."[23] Here we see the grotesque appearance linked to a lack of civility and knowledge, all pointing to a base nature that is questionably human.

Animals and demons appear frequently in Japanese *setsuwa* literature of the medieval period and later, often taking human form at some point

---

22. The words used here are *mōko* and *ebisu*. *Mōko* refers to Mongolia, but *ebisu* could be either Ezo, which referred to present-day Hokkaido, or it could also mean Mongolia. Later in the text, Ezo clearly refers to Mongolia.
23. Washio Junkei, ed., *Nihon shisō tōsō shiryo*, vol. 10 (Tokyo: Meichō kankyōkai, 1969), 328.

in the tale. In some cases, a human being will turn into an animal because of bad karma or forbidden desire, as in the tale of Dōjōji, in which the woman who lusts after a priest turns into a giant snake and dies.[24] In other cases, an animal or demon will take human form in order to deceive people. Foxes will often appear to be human and lie in wait for unsuspecting passersby whom they will lead into liaisons or lure into other worlds. In these tales, the fox's motive is purely to torment the humans, who are terrified when they discover what has happened, though they are generally unharmed.[25] The demons in *setsuwa* literature, however, often want to eat people, and they take human form in order to lure in their prey. In most of these stories, the animals and demons encounter their victims on deserted roads or in abandoned buildings far from the centers of civilization. In this way, their status as Other is reinforced by the physical space they occupy as well as by the nonhuman features they display in their natural state. In the Buddhist hierarchy within the cycle of birth and rebirth, animals and demons rank below humans, who are poised before the ultimate goal of nirvana. And as can be seen in many of the tales, the wrong path in life could condemn a human being to rebirth in these lower ranks.

The descriptions of their grotesque features and the association with animals and demons work to abject the Kirishitan on a number of different levels. Certainly the comparison to bears and demons raises the fear of a sinister and predatory nature. The remark in *Kirishitan monogatari* about how the padre "appears to be human" though also looks like a demon implies that he could be shape shifting like the animals and demons of popular literature. These references support the image of the Kirishitan as predators trying to steal the people's allegiance and, ultimately, their country, and as deceivers who use magic and lies to achieve their aims. The suggestion that they are, in fact, not human also emphasizes the argument in both narratives that they are not merely barbarians from outside of the civilized realm but perhaps animals or demons taking human form. This status could be punishment for misdeeds in this life or a previous one,

---

24. This story appears in *Konjaku monogatarishū*. An English translation of the story is "How a Monk of the Dōjōji in the Province of Kii Copied the Lotus Sutra and Brought Salvation to Serpents"; see Marian Ury, *Tales of Times Now Past: Sixty-Two Stories From a Medieval Japanese Collection*, Michigan Classics in Japanese Studies, vol. 9 (Ann Arbor: Center for Japanese Studies, University of Michigan, 1979), 93–96.
25. The exception seems to be when a human ends up having sexual relations with a transformed fox. An example of a fox merely playing tricks on a human can be seen in *Konjaku monogatarishū*, "How the Fox of Kōyagawa Turned into a Woman and Rode on Horses' Croups"; Ury, *Tales*, 167–71. Reference to the fate of those who have sex with foxes can be found in "About a Man Who Copied the Lotus Sutra to Save the Soul of a Fox"; Ury, *Tales*, 96–98.

and certainly could be the result of leading people down the wrong path. In fact, the similarly grotesque features of the Kirishitan converts in *Raichō jikki* are attributed to bad karma resulting from their own behavior earlier in life. Though the Japanese converts are not compared to animals or demons, the fact that they and the foreign Kirishitan share these physical characteristics implies that they and their teachings are all equally flawed and not only barbaric, but also straying from the correct Buddhist path.

The grotesque features of the Kirishitan and their comparison to animals and demons in the tale are easily recognizable as forms of debasement even outside of Japanese cultural references. But an understanding of all of the levels of meaning implied by them requires knowledge of contemporary Buddhist thought on karma and the cycle of birth and rebirth. It also rests on familiarity with the common literary representation of animals and demons as sinister beings whose purpose often is to deceive, and of the features of well-known demons. Readers in the Edo period would have easily recognized all of the ways in which the Kirishitan are Other in the tales, but also probably found them to be familiar Others. The exotic appearance that might have been fearsome in its foreign difference becomes that of the recognizable demon of *setsuwa* literature, or the more mundane animals of everyday life. At their worst, the Kirishitan are no better than the uncivilized "barbarians" of the north, or the unclean outcasts living under bridges and in fields. The Kirishitan threat thus domesticated is dominated figuratively, even as the padres of the tale are expelled from the country.

Magic and Medicine: The Padre as Yamabushi
The figure of the Kirishitan in the tales also resembles another familiar Other of Japanese *setsuwa* literature—the *yamabushi*, or mountain ascetic. *Yamabushi*, also called *shugenja*, were practitioners of Shugendō, a folk religion that combines elements of Shinto, Buddhism, and Daoism and is known for its ascetic practices. Those practices were thought to endow the *yamabushi* with special powers, especially healing ones. While the *yamabushi* figure of *setsuwa* literature was invariably a mountain-dwelling hermit or an itinerant traveler, by the sixteenth century actual practitioners of Shugendō had begun to settle in villages, changing their focus from their own austerities to that of ministering to the people. The populace believed them to have mystical powers and sought relief from "evil" manifest as illness or bad fortune in the incantations and amulets that the *shugenja* offered for sale.[26]

26. Higashibaba, *Christianity in Early Modern Japan*, 43–49.

The resemblance of the Kirishitan in the tales to the *yamabushi* may, in fact, have been inspired by perceived similarities in their religious practices. Reports from the period show that the European missionaries were often viewed as simply another kind of Shugendō practitioner, and that people sought help from them when their *shugenja* charms had failed, and vice versa.[27] Ikuo Higashibaba points out that the movement of the *shugenja* into the villages, accompanied by a secularization and militarization of institutional religious traditions, meant that by the sixteenth century "*shugenja* perhaps surpassed ordinary Buddhist priests in terms of their presence among the populace."[28] Similarly, the European missionaries were known for their close contact with parishioners. In addition, the solemn rituals of the Catholic sacraments that could only be performed by ordained priests may have resembled the mysterious incantations of the initiates of Shugendō. Symbols were also an important part of both religions, and reports from the Jesuits tell of how eager the converts and lay people were for crosses, rosaries, medals, and even holy water, which they believed would heal them and protect them from harm with powers similar to those of *shugenja* charms.

One of the most important roles of the *shugenja* in the villages was that of healer, and this was another parallel between them and the European missionaries, both in legend and in deed. Though the Jesuits sponsored some hospitals and had two relatively famous physician members, Luis de Almeida and Gregorio de Cespedes, they pulled away from ministering to the sick relatively early on in their time in Japan.[29] The Franciscan friars, however, who arrived in the 1590s, were more active in ministering to the sick, establishing leprosariums wherever they had ministries. But the healing activities of the missionaries were not limited to what we

27. Early Jesuit reports include one about a recent convert praying to Amida Buddha in front of a Christian church, holding a Japanese rosary and wearing the Christian rosary around his waist. When asked by a father why, as a Christian, he was praying to Amida, the man replied that he was afraid his sins might be too great to get into heaven, so he was praying for rebirth in the Pure Land just in case (Higashibaba, *Christianity in Early Modern Japan*, 37–38). While the missionaries were not above taking advantage of the confusion to gain more converts, the portrayal of them in literature as *yamabushi* figures would likely have been greeted with great dismay. Ebisawa points out that they had the greatest contempt for *shugenja* as uneducated conmen who "are direct servants of the devil." For a collection of Jesuit views on *shugenja*, see Ebisawa Arimichi, *Zōtei kirishitanshi no kenkyū* (Tokyo: Shinjinbutsu juraisha, 1971), 85–127. Another source on interaction between the Jesuits and Shugendō in the Kyushu area is Nei Kiyoshi, *Shugendō to Kirishitan* (Tokyo: Tokyodo shuppan, 1988).
28. Higashibaba, *Christianity in Early Modern Japan*, 44.
29. Three different monuments to Almeida and his work with the sick still stand in Kyushu. One is in Nagasaki, while the other two are in Oita city, where Almeida set up the first Jesuit hospital and dispensary.

recognize today as medicine. As mentioned above, countless petitioners sought the healing powers of amulets and holy water, in addition to the herbs and surgical treatments of the doctors, so that it is safe to say that a wide array of missionary activities, both spiritual and medicinal, were viewed as healing practices by the local populace.

In popular literature of the medieval and early modern periods, the *yamabushi* is a somewhat transgressive figure, admired for his obvious devotion to religious practice, but also feared for the powers he acquires through that practice. He is an itinerant priest with no ties to one institution and, as such, no binding social obligations or responsibilities. He was inspired to take on a life of penance, including austerities that allowed him to shed the impurities of worldly life and achieve a state beyond that of normal humanity. Powers gained from those austerities allowed him to heal the sick and prophesy the future. However, as Carmen Blacker points out, "this archetypal traveler, familiar though he may have been for so many centuries, is a figure essentially outside society. He is not only outside the social order; he carries, too, the implication of being not fully human. . . . Like all holy people and things, therefore, the wandering stranger is taboo."[30]

Examples of the popular image of the *yamabushi*, who in many cases is a dishonest opportunist, can be found in medieval tale collections such as *Konjaku monogatarishū* (Tales of Times Now Past) and *Uji shūi monogatari* (Tales from Uji).[31] *Yamabushi*, both good and bad, also are prominent characters in noh and *kyōgen* from the medieval period, where they often transform into *tengu*, the common long-nosed demon of *setsuwa* literature.[32] This association of the *yamabushi* with the *tengu* adds another sinister, taboo element to the figure, though in most narratives he is more of a conman than a demon. Most of the medieval representations of the *yamabushi* share a few common elements. He is a Buddhist priest whose

---

30. Carmen Blacker, "The Religious Traveler in the Edo Period," *Modern Asian Studies* 18.4, Special Issue: Edo Culture and its Modern Legacy (1984): 602.
31. Examples of some of the tales featuring *yamabushi* available in English translation include "How E no Ubasoku Recited Spells and Employed Demonic Deities," in Ury, *Tales*, 82–83, and "The Rice Poop Saint," in Royall Tyler, *Japanese Tales* (New York: Pantheon, 1987), 131–32, both from *Konjaku monogatarishū*, and "How a priest put the magic incantation of the Bodhisattva Zuigu into his forehead" and "How the Middle Counselor Morotoki investigated a priest's penis," both from *Uji shūi monogatari* and in D.E. Mills, *A Collection of Tales From Uji; a Study and Translation of Uji Shūi Monogatari* (Cambridge: Cambridge University Press, 1970), 141–43.
32. Carolyn Morely has produced a monograph on the *yamabushi* figure in *kyōgen*, which also includes a valuable chapter on the figure of the *yamabushi* in popular medieval literature and theater. See Carolyn Morely, *Transformation, Miracles, and Mischief: The Mountain Priest Plays in Kyōgen* (Ithaca, N.Y.: Cornell East Asia Series, 1993).

home is a distant and mysterious mountain, not the centers of civilization where most people live. On that mountain he has acquired certain supernatural powers, which he summons using mantras and dharanis. And with those powers, he is able to transform things, to heal illnesses, and to prophecy the future.

One of the most well-known *yamabushi* figures is that of E no Ubasoku, the legendary founder of Shugendō.[33] In the third story in chapter 11 of the *Konjaku monogatarishū*, we learn that E no Ubasoku lived during the reign of Emperor Monmu (697–707), and that he spent forty years on Mt. Kazuraki living as an ascetic. His daily privations and recitation of the dharani of the Peacock King gave him extraordinary powers with which he could summon demons and ride upon the clouds.[34] "He ran about on the surface of the ocean as though on dry land, and among the mountain peaks he flew just like a bird."[35]

This description of E no Ubasoku is strikingly similar to that of the Kirishitan when they are introduced in *Raichō jikki*. Early in the tale, the Nanban king, Gojimbi, has been advised by his counselor, Lord Gogi, not to attack Japan directly with an army, but rather first to send an adept to convince the people to follow him. The king asks where such a practitioner can be found, and Gogi says that six thousand miles from the capital there is a province called Kirishitan:

> In this land at the top of Tenrin Peak there are large, fragrant sandalwood trees, and on this peak live two men. One of them is called Urugan Bateren, and the other is called Buraten Bateren, and both men practice a magic called *hisōjō*. They are capable of rising into the air and flying, and it is because they can freely breach the boundaries of heaven and ride upon the clouds that they are called "bateren." This is the foundation of the Kirishitan sect. And in this sect the "iruman" is like a disciple at a temple, while the "bateren" is like the chief priest. These two men were both known as "bateren."[36]

---

33. Also known as En no Gyōja, E no Shōkaku, and E no Ozuno, accounts of his life can be found in the *Nihon ryōiki* (Record of Miraculous Events in Japan), *Shoku nihongi* (Chronicles of Japan, Contined), and *En no Gyōja hongi* (History of En no Gyōja), in addition to several entries in the *Konjaku monogatarishū* collection of tales.
34. The Peacock King was one of the Four Guardian Kings of the Dharma. Early ascetics were said to gain their powers from constant repetition of incantations derived from Sanskrit but whose meanings had long been lost. For more on ascetic practices and the history of Shugendō, see Carmen Blacker, *The Catalpa Bow: A Study of Shamanistic Practices in Japan* (London: Allen & Unwin, 1975).
35. Ury, *Tales*, 82–83.
36. Washio, *Nihon shisō tōsō shiryo*, 320.

Bateren was conventionally written as 伴天連, or "followers of heaven," but here it is changed to 破天連, or "companions who rend heaven." In a wonderful play on words, the author changes what was merely a phonetic transcription of the Portuguese word "padre" into a more sinister allusion to the magical powers being attributed to the men. In another manuscript version, they are also capable of summoning the wind and making it rain.[37] It is a striking image of mountain ascetics whose practices have brought them to a level of accomplishment beyond the human, giving them the power to move freely between heaven and earth, and to control nature.

The Kirishitan in the *Raichō jikki* tale also have a dharani and the power to transform things and predict the future. They use a "three-worlds mirror" to show the followers a future in which they have been reborn as animals. When the unfortunates beg the padres to save them from such a fate, they are taught to recite the dharani *Shigo shōten haraisō zensumaro* for seven days, and when they next look in the mirror they see themselves reborn as living buddhas.[38] The most clever of these converts are then taught the secrets of the Kirishitan magic, including how to transform things, how to change the weather, and how to fly.

This resemblance of the Kirishitan to the popular image of the *yamabushi* continues in the representations of the padres as healers in both *Kirishitan monogatari* and *Raichō jikki*. In the former, the padres are described as "healing in one treatment the hare-lipped, lepers, and those afflicted with boils or the Chinese pox."[39] In the *Raichō jikki* tale, the healing role of the Kirishitan is expanded, beginning with the arrival of the second wave of Kirishitan. This group is summoned to Japan by Padre Urugan, who has successfully convinced Nobunaga to allow him to spread his doctrine. The padre then sends a message to his fellow ascetic Padre Buraten, who brings with him two brothers skilled in healing, Kerikori Iruman and Yariisu Iruman. Here we can recognize the names of the two famous Jesuit doctors, Gregorio ("Kerikori") de Cespedes and Luis ("Yariisu") de Almeida. Upon their arrival, the two brothers petition Nobunaga for land to grow medicinal herbs, and they are given a plot on Mt. Ibuki in the province of Ōmi. There, the tale tells us, they plant three thousand varieties of medicinal herbs, including the well-known Ibuki mugwort

---

37. Hiyane Antei, ed., *Nanbanji kōhaiki hoka nihen*, Kirishitan bunkō, vol. 2 (Tokyo: Keiseisha 1926), 86.
38. The dharani is usually rendered in kanji as 死後生天破羅韋曾有善主摩呂 with the *shigo shōten* coming from Japanese for "birth in heaven after death," and the *haraisō zensumaro* coming from the Portuguese and Latin words "paradise Jesus Mary."
39. Washio, *Nihon shisō tōsō shiryo*, 376.

that is so effective in treating a variety of illnesses. With these medicines, they treated the blind and the lame and all manner of other illnesses, until "they gradually cured all of the sick, so that even those who were near death were cured after only one treatment."[40]

Though the reference to Mt. Ibuki appears only once in the text, it acquires a seemingly disproportionate importance in the *Ibuki yomogi* variant of *Raichō jikki*. This variant, of which there are at least ten manuscripts extant, is characterized by a title containing reference to Ibuki mugwort and/or a distinctive preface. In this preface, a man renounces the world upon the death of his wife and child and wanders the country as a Buddhist lay monk, much in the manner of the itinerant *yamabushi* figure. One day he arrives at a temple on Mt. Ibuki, where he is told that the famous mugwort from the region was actually brought by the Kirishitan many years earlier.[41] He asks to hear more, and is told the tale that forms the body of the text.

When the reference to Mt. Ibuki is viewed as an isolated moment, it seems remarkable that it could inspire a preface and the title of an entire work. But the Edo-period reader likely had a stronger chain of associations that justified the focus of the title on this mountain. As we have seen, Mt. Ibuki was associated with the healing powers of mugwort, and in turn healing was associated with the *shugenja* and the European missionaries in the sixteenth and seventeenth centuries.[42] Mt. Ibuki also shows up in the popular medieval tale named after the demon, *Shutendōji*, in which warriors disguise themselves as *yamabushi* in order to penetrate the defenses of the demon's lair on the famous mountain. Not only are the mountain and the *shugenja* present in this tale, the grotesque features of the demon and its threatening presence on the periphery of civilization echo the demonlike appearance of the Nanban people and their shadow lurking just beyond the boundaries of Japan.

In this way, historical events and tropes in popular culture likely combined to inspire the image of the Kirishitan padre as a *yamabushi* figure in *Raichō jikki*. The two padres are able to fly, to conjure spirits, and to alter matter, and the brothers have wondrous powers of healing. Their home base in Nanban is a remote mountaintop, as is the source of their healing powers in Japan. Using a mysterious rosary called a *gondatsu*, they

---

40. Ibid., 335.
41. Mugwort grew in Japan for centuries before the missionaries came. One of the earliest references to the herb can be found in the eighth-century *Man'yōshu* (Collection of Ten Thousand Leaves) collection of poems (18/4116).
42. In the eighteenth century, in particular, the growth in *rangaku*, or studies in Dutch medicine and technology, would strengthen the association of medicine with the West.

chant a magical dharani that alters the cycle of rebirth in their converts.[43] And they perform *disciprinas* that are reminiscent of Buddhist austerities and yet are horrifyingly tainted by the corruption of blood.[44] The image is studded with exotic embellishments and yet is surprisingly familiar.

Whether inspired by actual practice or not, the effect of the literary representation of the Kirishitan as a kind of *yamabushi* is the same as that of the comparisons made of them to animals and demons—to position them within a discourse that marks them as Other but also familiar. In *Raichō jikki*, the representation of the Kirishitan as a *yamabushi* figure conveys the taboo nature of the foreign Other even as it shows that it is a familiar and contained threat. Just as the *yamabushi* in Japan exists outside of society but also is controlled by it, the Kirishitan is a recognizable threat, thrilling in his difference, but ultimately subdued.

The Kirishitan Sect As Buddhist Heresy
At his first audience with Oda Nobunaga, Padre Urugan is asked why he has come to Japan, and he replies that he has come to "spread the teachings of Buddha" (ぶっぽうをひろめる). Though we know that he has been sent to Japan to deceive people, this is not necessarily one of his lies. In fact, much later in the tale when the convert Fabian debates with Hakuo, the lay priest asks the Kirishitan "which buddha" he worships, and Fabian answers that it is the "Buddha Deus." As Nobunaga himself reminds his retainers, all Buddhist sects in Japan were brought to the country from abroad, and this is clearly just one more. While it remains to be seen whether it is a "false" or "true" sect of Buddhism, that it would be anything outside of that religion is never questioned.

During the missionaries' time in Japan, confusion in the translation of Christian concepts into Japanese, as well as the Jesuits' own attempts to be treated as the social equals of Zen priests, likely contributed to an impression that Christianity was actually a form of Buddhism.[45] The perception

---

43. The word *gondatsu* is derived from the Portuguese "*contas*," or rosary.
44. This refers to the missionaries' practice of self-flagellation. See chapter 2 for more on the missionaries' practice and on representations of it in the tales.
45. The danger inherent in translating key Christian terms was recognized early on in the Jesuit mission to Japan. Relying on a translation of "God" provided by his relatively uneducated interpreter, Yajirō, Francis Xavier preached about "Dainichi" (Mahāvairocana) for two full years. Only after discovering that this was a manifestation of Buddha did he revert to the Latin word "Deus." Ten years later, in 1562, the Jesuit Father Luis Almeida would report meeting believers who still insisted that Xavier had taught them to worship Dainichi. See Elison, *Deus Destroyed*, 33 and 401, nn. 9, 11. The question of whether Christian terminology should be translated was the source of a debate between Jesuits in Japan, who from this time on preferred to use Portuguese and Latin terms, and those in China, who relied on translations of Confucian terms. For more on this debate

of the missionaries as *shugenja* was already noted above. In addition, there were a number of scholars from the seventeenth, eighteenth, and nineteenth centuries who argued that followers of Jesus had merely stolen the story of Buddha and packaged it differently, and that Christianity was a misinterpretation of Buddhism. In his 1648 work titled *Taiji jashūron* (On the Extermination of the Evil Religion), Sesshō outlines parallels in a long list of concepts and practices in Buddhism and Christianity to show that they are really one and the same.[46] Other scholars who argued the same included Kumazawa Banzan in the seventeenth century and Arai Hakuseki in the eighteenth century.[47]

While the portrayal of the Kirishitan as a Buddhist sect may have roots in contemporary discourse, it also plays an undeniably important role in the construction of the Kirishitan Other in *Kirishitan monogatari* and *Raichō jikki*. From the references to the "teachings of Buddha" and the Buddha Deus mentioned above, to an entire chapter in *Kirishitan monogatari* titled "Kirishitan buppō," or "The Kirishitan Dharma," throughout the two texts under discussion there is no divergence from the use of Buddhist terminology to refer to the Kirishitan sect. This language effectively

---

see Cooper, *Rodrigues the Interpreter*, 326–29. Though Zen priests were the principal enemies of the Christian missionaries' efforts, Alexandro Valignano recognized the importance of their status in Japanese culture and believed the only way to compete was to claim the same status for the Jesuits. As a result, Valignano stressed the importance of each member clarifying his position in the order by comparing his rank with similar ranks in the "gozan" Zen system. While they did not take on the Japanese designations, they were to make it clear to Japanese believers what their corresponding rank would be. Two important documents outlining Valignano's recommendations for the Jesuit mission in Japan are the *Sumario de las Cosas del Japon* (Summary of Things Japanese) and the *Advertimientos e avisos acerca dos costumes e catangues de Jappão* (Observations and Advice on the Customs and Ceremonies of Japan). An annotated edition of the latter has been published under the title *Il Cerimoniale per i missionari del Giappone: Advertimentos e avisos acerca dos constumes e catangues de Jappão, di Alexandro Valignano* (Etiquette for Missionaries in Japan: Observations and Advice on the Customs and Ceremonies of Japan), Edizione critica, introduzione e note di Giuseppe Fr. Schutte (S.J. Roma, 1946). A comprehensive study of Valignano and his work in English is Josef Schutte, S.J., *Valignano's Mission Principles in Japan*, trans. John J. Coyne, vol. 1 (St. Louis, Mo.: The Institute of Jesuit Sources, 1985).

46. Ebisawa Arimichi et al., eds., *Kirishitansho, haiyasho*, Nihon shisō taikei, vol. 25 (Tokyo: Iwanami shoten, 1970), 462. His observations on this topic are not included in the simplified version of the text called *Jakyō tai'i*.

47. Kumazawa Banzan, *Kumazawa Banzan*, Nihon shisō taikei, vol. 30 (Tokyo: Iwanami shoten, 1971), 233, 445; Matsumura Akira et al., eds., *Seiyō kibun*, Nihon shisō taikei, vol. 35 (Tokyo: Iwanami shoten, 1975), 80–82. There is an interesting parallel here with the twelfth- and thirteenth-century European representations of Islam as a "misguided version of Christianity." "Mohammed is always the imposter (familiar, because he pretends to be the Jesus we know) and always the Oriental (alien, because although he is in some ways 'like' Jesus, he is after all not like him)" (Said, *Orientalism*, 61–71).

establishes the foreign Other within the known framework of Buddhism, just as the early Europeans dealt with Islam from within the familiar tradition of Christianity. And just as the Europeans concluded that Mohammed was an imposter and Islam a misguided version of Christianity, the Kirishitan sect is presented in the tales as a *gedō*, or mistaken path in Buddhism. Clearly this positioning of the Kirishitan within the discourse of Buddhism is essential for any kind of engagement with it. With the language of Buddhism it can be normalized and codified, taming the threat of the foreign and unknowable. But this is also the only way in which it can be argued against. Once it has been placed within the framework of Buddhism, its differences from established sects can be presented clearly as mistakes, and the entire sect itself as heresy. In some cases, the heresy is evident in the appearance and practices of the Kirishitan, and in others it is pointed out in the explanations of the doctrine.

One of the most important qualities of the Kirishitan in the tale that marks them as heretics or at least as straying from the correct path is their wealth and preoccupation with money. While the padres themselves are not greedy for money (as ascetics they refuse to even look at the gifts sent by the Nanban king), they willingly use it in their bid to win Japan's wealth for their king. That king's desire for the riches of Japan is what brings them over, and they are promised the revenue from fifteen provinces in Nanban to buy the loyalty of the Japanese people. Likewise, their converts are all the poorest in Japan who flock to the Nanban temple when they hear of the payments being made. The poor are clothed in beautiful fabrics, housed in the temple, and fed four times a day. And the sick also receive a share of the wealth.

Great sums of money were also spent on the temple and its furnishings in order to dazzle the curious and inflame the desire of the covetous. The Nanban temple was built of stunning stone walls and finished in gold, while the inside was decorated with cotton banners and strands of precious stones. The fragrances of sixty-one kinds of incense wafted through the halls and around the followers, and the padres wore robes of gold. This finery is later flaunted by the same converts who had arrived at the church covered in rags and boils. Fabian's entourage when he visits a noblewoman's home includes twelve servants, while he himself is dressed in multiple layers of silk and velvet.[48] Though with these trappings he "appeared to be of a very high rank," his behavior quickly proves him otherwise, as he sleeps late into the morning, sprawls at the table eating large quantities of food, and presents his backside to the image of Buddha.

48. Washio, *Nihon shisō tōsō shiryo*, 346.

Clearly he is the most common of men, using money to appear better than he is. After returning to the temple, he sends to the woman a gift of aloe wood and five rolls each of damask and silk gauze, all gifts that the woman herself judged "too costly for the occasion."

In addition to the less savory aspects of the medieval *yamabushi* character, a stock character in the popular literature of the seventeenth and eighteenth centuries was a Buddhist priest who engaged in practices considered unbecoming of the clergy, including eating meat, entertaining women, and pursuing profit. The ideal was widely understood to be men or women who had renounced worldly desires to spend their days reading the sutras in solitude. The embodiment of this ideal in the tales is the lay priest Hakuo who debates doctrine with Fabian in both *Kirishitan mongatari* and *Raichō jikki*. The former includes descriptions of him living the life of a hermit, wearing only a paper or hemp robe, and living alone in a hut on the outskirts of Kyoto.[49] The text then goes on to list his numerous scholarly accomplishments and associations with all of the famous temples in the area. In the *Raichō jikki* narrative, he is also described as a learned ascetic who stands in sharp contrast to the lavishly dressed and attended Fabian described above.[50] In *Raichō jikki*, in particular, it is clear that the great differences in appearance and behavior between the two priests are meant to alert the reader to the deceptive practices of the Kirishitan.

The outward appearance of wealth was not the only indication of heresy in the Kirishitan sect. The practice of giving money to the poor also is held up as proof of illegitimacy in both *Kirishitan monogatari* and *Raichō jikki*. In the former, that money is described as nothing more than a bribe to attract converts, and the fact that only the poor (and unlettered) were interested showed that there was no intellectual or spiritual merit upon which the religion could stand. The representation is similar in the *Raichō jikki* narrative, with even more references to the poor and sick flocking to the Nanban temple only for the money they hoped to receive. But the narrative goes even further when Nobunaga describes the practice of giving money as one that goes against the natural order, and thus is proof of the falseness of the sect. In discussing the Kirishitan practices, he remarks that they illustrate the saying, "'From the temple to the supplicant,' which has always meant something that is backward or upside-down."[51] It is only

---

49. Ibid., 381.
50. Yuima is the protagonist of the *Yuima (Vimalakīrti) sutra*, who lived at the same time as Shakyamuni and was known as an exceptional scholar (Ibid., 349).
51. Ibid., 343.

after recognizing this practice as a sign of heresy that Nobunaga begins to explore how he can get rid of a sect he had supported so strongly before.

Another way in which the Kirishitan sect demonstrates its heretical foundation is in its association with the corruptions of blood and disease. Both *Kirishitan monogatari* and *Raichō jikki* contain passages that describe with relish the practice of self-flagellation among the members. *Shugenja* practitioners and other Buddhist sects took part in ascetic practices that caused great physical hardship, but they rarely shed blood because of strong traditions of purity and protection against pollution. However, the tales portray Kirishitan believers with their bare backs shredded and their bloody hands clasped in prayer.[52]

After a similar passage in *Kirishitan monogatari*, the author observes that the bateren wipes the blood from the backs of the penitent and, *without washing his hands*, prays to the Buddha. As the final sentence of the passage in *Raichō jikki* assures the reader, this kind of worship is definitely not Japanese.

The Kirishitan association with the sick and disabled also held implications for its validity as a sect. As was noted earlier, there was no clear distinction in the seventeenth and eighteenth centuries between physical and spiritual illnesses, with most physical ailments thought to be manifestations of bad karma for past misdeeds. People afflicted with disfiguring diseases especially were often rejected by society and required to live in fields and under bridges. The converts in the tales are all examples of these kinds of outcasts, and the narrative makes clear they have earned this misfortune with their actions. Their diseases are not merely the result of bad luck; they are described as punishment for the sins of profligacy and sloth. The Kirishitan association with this group not only links them to outcasts of society, but it also implies that they are no better spiritually.

Once it has been placed within the Buddhist framework, the Kirishitan sect is easily defeated. Money, pollution, and false doctrine all combine to prove its heresy. The ways in which the believers deviate from the path may be exotic—gold and incense, magical mirrors, and the bloodied hands of believers—but the end product is almost pathetically commonplace. Japanese *setsuwa* literature is full of tales of false priests who get their comeuppance, and the Kirishitan in these tales are no different. The great learning of the lay priest Hakuo easily trumps the lies of the Kirishitan Fabian, sending the latter home "with his tale between his legs, muttering to himself incomprehensibly."[53] Only after their doctrine has been

52. Ibid., 338.
53. Ibid., 386.

proven false can the foreign members be sent home and the converts be "convinced" to apostatize.

The overall image of the Kirishitan in the tales is that of a heretical Buddhist sect, of lowly status and corrupted by money, steeped in the taboo practices of magic, and tainted by the disease and disfigurement of the converts and the padres themselves. The sole purpose of the foreign Kirishitan in Japan is to gather converts using money, magic, and medicine, in order to fulfill the ambitions of their king for conquest. But their plot is discovered and foiled by the leader of Japan, who expels the foreign padres and crushes the sect, restoring peace to the land. And just as the foreign Other is subdued in the narrative, it is also controlled in its representation in the tales, with imagery and language that act to domesticate the exotic and alien. In *Kirishitan monogatari* and *Raichō jikki* we see a classic form of Othering in "a strategy of symbolic expulsion, a mundane exorcistic ritual, used to control ambivalence and create boundaries."[54] However, one of the paradoxes of the act of Othering is that even as it attempts to fix an image in place and assert its unchanging "truth," it requires constant repetition to maintain stability.

For the Japanese of the Edo period, "fixing" the image of the Kirishitan into place was particularly problematic because the foreigners and their followers were a constantly moving target. European powers also may have struggled to fix the images of the cultures they were representing, but in most cases that culture's physical location was not in doubt, nor was it expected to move. For Japan, the Kirishitan Other was myriad and shifting, encompassing multiple countries in faraway Europe, their nearby Asian colonies, and mobile fleets that crossed both the Pacific and the Atlantic. Though the Portuguese and Spanish were forbidden to enter the country, traders and missionaries from those countries continued to attempt it until the early part of the eighteenth century. Visits by Russian ships in 1739, 1771, and 1777 preceded a formal request to open trade with Japan and encouraged the British to attempt the same. [55] Events like these contributed to a sense of the Western powers hovering offshore, waiting to gain access, long before opening trade with them became a political debate. And, unaccountably, the Kirishitan threat was still hiding at home, in pockets of believers who continued to be discovered and punished until the ban on Christianity was lifted in 1889. Under these circumstances,

---

54. Michael Pickering, *Stereotyping: the Politics of Representation* (New York: Palgrave, 2001), 47–48.
55. For more on Japanese contact with Western countries in the eighteenth century, see Bob Tadashi Wakabayashi, *Anti-Foreignism and Western Learniing in Early Modern Japan: the New Theses of 1825* (Cambridge, Mass.: Harvard University Press, 1986), 63–68.

the shift in the later *Raichō jikki* narrative to a Kirishitan figure that represents a broader Nanban Other encompassing all foreigners outside of the traditional three realms is understandable.

The need to assert the unchanging truth of the degenerate Kirishitan can be seen in the narrative of his arrival and expulsion that was repeated over and over, starting with *Kirishitan monogatari* and continuing in *Raichō jikki*, for a period of 250 years. But this act of repetition was not confined to the consumption of these tales. It occurred at a more performative level every time the text was copied, passed along, and then copied again. The curious result of the censorship of publications dealing with Kirishitan was that the tales of expulsion could not be printed and had to be written by hand each time. In the case of *Raichō jikki*, in particular, the subjugation of the foreign threat was reproduced countless times as each reader made his own copy by hand, and each copyist took part in an almost ritualistic repetition of the subordination and expulsion of the Kirishitan Other.

THE CENTER HOLDS: IMAGINING JAPAN IN THE WORLD

If the portrayal of the Kirishitan Other in *Kirishitan monogatari* and *Raichō jikki* worked to dominate him at two levels, with the narrative of expulsion and with the representation as a barbaric but familiar Other, it also helped construct a sacred and civilized Japan in opposition to that Other. This sacred identity is asserted in a number of ways in both tales, though with greater insistence in *Raichō jikki*. In *Kirishitan monogatari*, that assertion comes in the final paragraphs that describe the Kirishitan arrival as an assault on the gods and buddhas, who rejoiced when the interlopers were expelled. But in *Raichō jikki*, references to Japan's gods and buddhas, as well as to its long history as a recipient of Buddhist and Confucian traditions, appear throughout the tale in constant affirmation of its position in the sacred three realms and the civilized region of the *ka'i* cosmology. Furthermore, *Raichō jikki* maps Japan and its older Others within the traditional world view and suggests that the home of the Kirishitan/Nanbanjin encompasses all lands outside of that older world.

An awareness of Japan's position in the three realms cosmology can be observed as early as the middle of the Heian period (794–1185).[56] The structure of the cosmology is derived from the history of the transmission of Buddhism, with India as the birthplace of the Buddha at the center and

---

56. Ichikawa Hirofumi, *Nihon chūsei no hikari to kage: "uchinaru sangoku" no shisō* (Tokyo: Perikansha, 1999), 61–62.

China as the first country to receive the law of Buddha not far from it. Because Japan was the "last" to learn the teachings of Buddha, it was considered a small, outlying country on the eastern edge of the region. Medieval maps representing this view of the world show India at the center, with a swirling mandala on Mt. Sumeru, the acknowledged birthplace of Buddhism. China is represented on the same continent as India, and Japan is only a sliver of land in the far eastern regions of the map (see figures 1 and 2). Despite its origins in the history of Buddhism, this image of the three countries' relationship to each other and its built-in hierarchy became the basis for an early "international" awareness of Japan and its place in the known world.[57]

At the end of the Heian and beginning of the medieval periods, this view began to be challenged by some who were reluctant to accept the position of Japan at the fringes of the civilized and the sacred. One of the earliest to do this was Kakuken, priest of Kōfukuji, in a 1173 treatise titled *Sangoku dentōki*, or "Record of the Transmission of the Law in the Three Realms." While he accepts the position of Japan as an "outlying" country because it was the last to receive the transmission, he also argues that it is uniquely sacred among the three lands. He bases this argument on his reading of the *Kegonkyō* (*Avatamsakra sutra*), or the *Flower Sutra*, in which he believes that the sacred mountain Kongōsan, from where the Bodhisattva Hokki was said to have originated, is actually the mountain Katsuragisan in Japan.[58] This would make Japan one of the sources of the Mahayana, rather than just a passive recipient.

The stature of Japan as a sacred land in the three realms cosmology continued to grow during the medieval period with the added influence of the growing *shinkoku* ideology. This view of Japan as the "land of the gods" had been strengthened by the dramatic defeat of the Mongol armies on the two occasions that they attempted to invade Japan in 1274 and 1281. On both occasions, the Mongol fleets were scattered by storms that were seen as "divine winds" sent by the gods in answer to the prayers of countless shrines and temples at the command of the emperor. Although these gods were part of the Shinto pantheon, this did not interfere with the notion of Japan as a sacred Buddhist home. This was because, although a number of rituals and ceremonies were designated as separate Buddhist

---

57. Ibid.
58. The location of the mountain is described in the sutra as being in the oceans to the east, as Japan is in the medieval map in Figures 1 and 2. Ibid., 63. The Japanese mountain is situated on the border of Nara and Osaka Prefectures. Katsuragisan also is said to be the birthplace of En no Gyōja, the founder of Shugendō and the original *yamabushi* figure described earlier in this chapter.

Figure 1. Map of the entire three realms cosmology derived from the history of the transmission of Buddhism. From Ichikawa, *Nihon chūsei no hikari to kage*, 61.

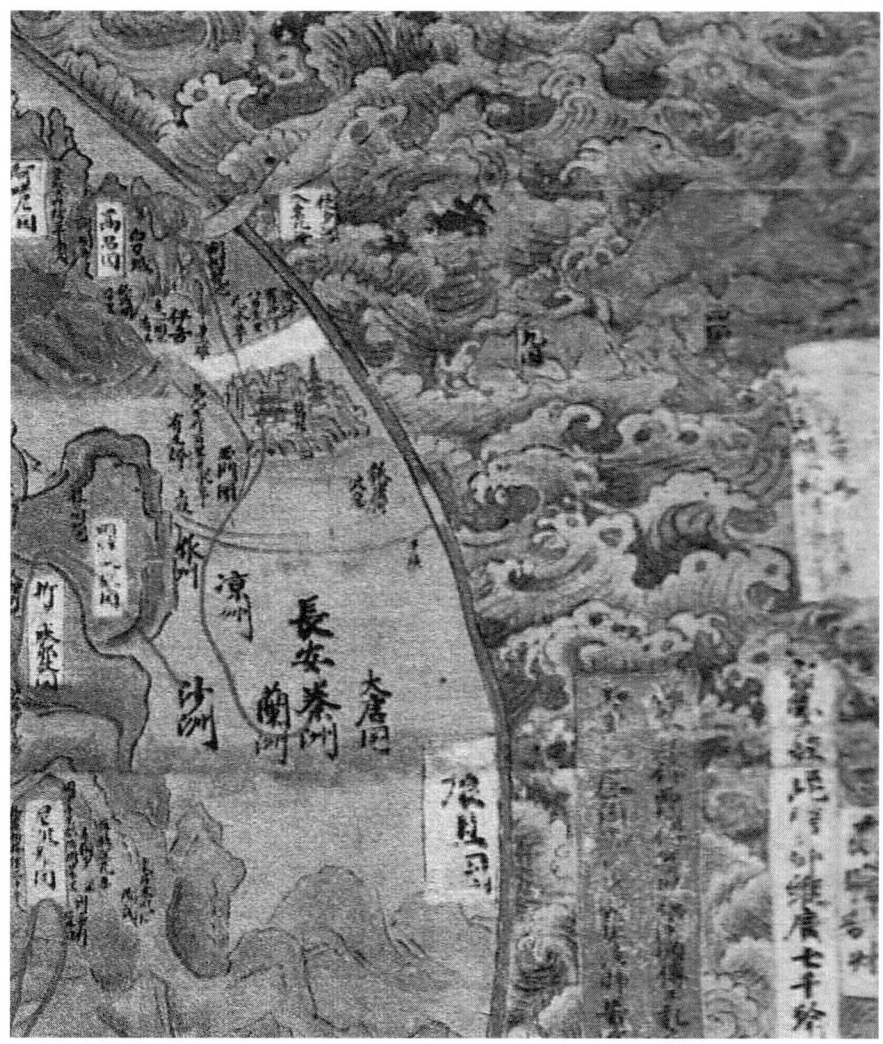

Figure 2. Detail of the three realms cosmology showing the region where Japan (in this case labeled Shikoku and Kyushu) is located. From Ichikawa, *Nihon chūsei no hikari to kage*, 62.

and Shinto rites, mutual influences can be traced in those rituals as far back as the Heian period.[59] In the late Heian and early medieval periods, in particular, doctrinal changes and new religious forms had helped to absorb the relationship of people to the Shinto *kami* (gods) into Buddhism. One of the most common explanations for the coexistence of Shinto and Buddhism was the notion of *honji suijaku*, or the belief that "the *kami* are transformations of the Buddhas manifested in Japan to save all sentient beings."[60] In other words, the buddhas manifest themselves in a form that will be the most effective in bringing people to the "correct path," and in Japan that form can be the *kami*. Not only did the combined efforts of the *kami* and buddhas seem to make Japan a more sacred place in the three realms cosmology, but the emphasis on their cooperation also gave Japanese religion a more cohesive and singular appearance. And the belief was that the strength of those gods had protected Japan for centuries, making it appear inviolable by outside forces. In this way, the religions of Japan were firmly linked to the sovereignty of the realm and its identity as a country.

While the view of Japan as a sacred home of the gods and the buddhas persisted in the fifteenth and sixteenth centuries, we begin to see a change in the role of the gods from protector to protected. In Toyotomi Hideyoshi's first edict of 1587 banishing the Kirishitan, the gods and buddhas are invoked several times as symbols of the realm that must be protected by the lord of the *tenka*.

1. Japan is a country of the Kami [Gods] and for the padres to come hither and preach a devilish law is a most reprehensible and evil thing.
2. For the padres to come to Japan and convert people to their creed, destroying Shinto and Buddhist temples to this end, is a hitherto unseen and unheard-of thing. When the Lord of the Tenka gives fiefs, cities, towns, or income to anybody, it is purely temporarily, and the recipients are obliged to observe inviolably the laws and ordinances of Japan; but to stir up the canaille to commit outrages of this sort is something deserving of severe punishment.
3. If the Lord of the Tenka allowed the padres to propagate their sect, as the Christians wish and intend, this is contrary to the laws of Japan, as previously stated. Since such a thing is intolerable, I am resolved that the padres should not stay on Japanese soil. I therefore order that having settled their

---

59. James C. Dobbins, Kuroda Toshio, Suzanne Gay, "Shinto in the History of Japanese Religions," *Journal of Japanese Studies* 7.1 (1981): 1–9.
60. Ibid., 9.

affairs within twenty days, they must return to their own country. If anyone should harm them within this period, the culprit will be punished.
4. As the Great Ship comes to trade, and this is something quite different, the Portuguese can carry on their commerce unmolested.
5. Henceforward not only merchants, but anyone else coming from India, who does not interfere with the laws of Shinto and Buddhist deities may come freely to Japan, and thus let them take due note of this. On the nineteenth day of the sixth month of the fifteenth year of Tensho [July 25, 1587].[61]

In an inversion of the gods/realm relationship of the Mongol invasion, the gods that had helped Japan protect her sovereignty from military invasion in the thirteenth century now are protected from cultural invasion in the fifteenth and sixteenth centuries by "Japan" in the figure of the shogun. This shift is reflected in the *Baterenki* narrative, in which earlier attempts by the Roman Kirishitan are repulsed by the *kami* in the form of "devil winds" (in the eyes of the invaders). When the Kirishitan are finally successful in penetrating Japan in the sixteenth century, however, it is a regional lord who must find them out and expel them. Because the "law" being taught by the padres threatened the gods and the buddhas, it also threatened the realm. Japan's identity is firmly linked to its religious traditions, and the padres' teachings are foreign not just because they came from outside of Japan's geographic boundaries, but because their teachings came from outside of those traditions.

In the earlier *Kirishitan monogatari*, what those Japanese traditions are and how the Kirishitan ones differ is assumed to be understood by the reader, as is the criminality of the latter. The foreign Kirishitan and their converts are two-dimensional figures whose beliefs are presented as ridiculous, and whose activities are clearly marked as "criminal." After portraying the difference and strangeness in the Kirishitan religious practices, the narrator alludes briefly to a "plot" devised by the brothers, which is discovered by the government and thwarted. The offenders are suitably punished in this and other chapters, and, the pernicious nature of the Kirishitan sect having been discovered for what it is, the foreigners are banished from the land by Tokugawa Ieyasu, and their converts forced

61. Boxer, *The Christian Century in Japan*, 148. For a printed version of the Japanese text, see Ebisawa, *Kirishitanshi no kenkyū*, 146. A picture of the only extant copy of the original edict, held at the Matsuura Shiryō Museum in Hirado, is in Michael Cooper et al., eds., *The Southern Barbarians: the First Europeans in Japan* (Tokyo: Kodansha International Ltd., 1971), 68.

to apostatize.⁶² The final paragraph of the text explains to the reader the danger posed by the foreign sect, but it also emphasizes that the integrity of Japan's sacred realm was never really compromised. The gods and the buddhas who had come to Japan's rescue in the past now rejoice at their own rescue by the wise leader of Japan. Coming out in 1639, not long after the foreign missionaries were expelled, we can hear in it the echo of the expulsion edicts of both Toyotomi Hideyoshi and Tokugawa Ieyasu. We can also see a simple binary asserted as uncomplicated truth: Japan is part of a sacred and civilized realm in opposition to the foreign, which by definition is outside of that realm and therefore heretic and barbaric.

The *Raichō jikki* narrative, in contrast, betrays more ambivalence about the identity of Japan in opposition to the Kirishitan, as we can see in the much greater amount of space devoted to describing the sacred nature of Japan, its membership in the long history of the three realms, and the qualities that distinguish followers of the "correct" path from the Kirishitan. In fact, the difference in the ways that Japan is narrated in the two texts is striking. Whereas the assertion that Japan is the land of the gods comes once in the final paragraph of *Kirishitan monogatari*, the *Raichō jikki* narrative proclaims it several times throughout the tale, even as it attempts to explain how the heresy was permitted to enter and infect the land. Whereas *Kirishitan monogatari* primarily describes the difference of the Kirishitan in opposition to an understood Japanese template, *Raichō jikki* spends more time identifying and explaining that template. And while *Kirishitan monogatari* makes no attempt to locate Nanban or Japan in the world, *Raichō jikki* draws the two onto the map of the three realms, emphasizing Japan's dominance over the other.

The result of that ambivalence and the apparent need to define the Self and Other in *Raichō jikki* is a more clearly articulated Japanese identity grounded in the three traditions of Shinto, Buddhism, and Confucianism, whose long histories in Japan are called upon as proof of their legitimacy. References to the transmission of Buddhism from India and China reinforce Japan's membership in the sacred three realms, and the linking of all three traditions with rituals of respect and civility argue for Japan's greater proximity to the civilized center in the *ka'i* worldview. In a more striking way, a geographic description of the size and location of Nanban places it contiguous to but definitely outside of the three realms, with its

---

62. The text does not mention Tokugawa by name, but when the plot of the Kirishitan king is revealed and the leader of Japan launches measures against the Kirishitan, it takes place at "Suruga," which was where Ieyasu lived after ceding the position of shogun to Hidetada. See Elison, *Deus Destroyed*, 355 and 487 n. 63.

forty-two provinces echoing the popular eighteenth-century view of the world outside of Japan being comprised of forty-two foreign countries.[63] In this way, *Raichō jikki* not only constructs an image of a sacred Japan vis-à-vis the barbarian Kirishitan Other, it also constructs a map of a world dominated by the traditional three realms of India, China, and Japan, with all of the rest of the countries, including its new Western Others, relegated to the barbarian periphery. By the end of the tale, not only have the barbarian Kirishitan been expelled from Japan, but the world on the maps they brought with them has been redrawn to give precedence to Japan and to the traditional three realms.

Clearly, the Kirishitan Other of the anti-Kirishitan narratives came to represent much more than the historical missionaries that were the figure's referent, and became the site of a broader discourse on identity. The development of the Kirishitan figure from *Baterenki* through *Kirishitan monogatari* and finally to *Raichō jikki* reflects changing concerns with the significance of the new Others that figure represented, including the West and a larger world than the three realms; it also reflects a growing interest in what it meant to be Japanese and what Japan represented in the world. The *Raichō jikki* text, in particular, reflects a growing anxiety about those issues. But the narratives do more than reflect changing discourses and anxiety—they contribute to those discourses and in some cases work to allay that anxiety not only by narrating the expulsion but also by rewriting the identities of the Kirishitan, Japan, and even the world. That this project was important is evident in the persistence of the expulsion stories for over two hundred and fifty years despite censorship of works about the Kirishitan. It is also evident in the appearance of the Kirishitan Other outside of those narratives throughout the eighteenth and nineteenth centuries, in the theater and in debates on opening up trade with the West.[64] The need to exclude the Kirishitan is also a key feature of these additional representations, making the Kirishitan expulsion narrative a ubiquitous element of Japan's discourse on identity until the Meiji period, when the Kirishitan finally and irrevocably set foot on Japanese soil.

63. See chapter 3 for more on this.
64. See chapter 4 for more on this.

Chapter Two
Romans and Demons:
Kirishitan Villains in *Baterenki* and *Kirishitan monogatari*

Baterenki, or "Record of the Padres," appears to be the earliest extant chronicle of the arrival and expulsion of the Kirishitan.[1] The text is an odd collection of disjointed vignettes that includes a description of the seven sacraments of the Catholic Church, stories of St. Lucy and the origins of the Catholic Church in Rome, and a longer narrative about

---

1. In *Baterenki* 伴天連記, *Bateren* was the Japanese pronunciation of "padre" and originally referred to the missionary priests. The brothers were called *iruman*, from the Portuguese *irmão*. The *bateren* in the title follows the traditional glossing in Chinese characters as 伴天連, which could be read as "companions of heaven." In later expulsion narratives, where the *bateren* are more villainous, the first character is changed to render it 破天連, making it closer to "band that rends heaven." This change occurs in the *Nanbanji monogatari* variant of the *Raichō jikki* text, in which the narrator explains that the mountain ascetics in the land of "Kirishitan" are called *bateren* (破天連) precisely because they have acquired the ability to fly and ride on the clouds. Ebisawa Arimichi, ed., *Nanbanji kōhaiki, Jakyō tai'i, Myōtei mondō, Ha Daiusu*,Toyo Bunko, vol. 14 (Tokyo: Heibonsha, 1964), 320.

   Though Ebisawa's bibliography on Christian works cites a manuscript of *Baterenki* at Tenri Central Library, it does not appear to be part of the collection anymore. Ebisawa Arimichi, ed,, *Christianity in Japan: a Bibliography of Japanese and Chinese Sources* (Tokyo: International Christian University, 1960), 22.; George Elison, *Deus Destroyed: the Image of Christianity in Early- Modern Japan* (Cambridge: Harvard University Press, 1973), 450. According to the *Kokusho sōmokuroku* (a compendium of Japanese publications), there is only one extant manuscript copy in private hands. See note 1 in the translation of *Baterenki* in this book for more on possible extant manuscripts. Unannotated versions of *Baterenki* have been reproduced in three modern collections: *Zokuzoku gunsho ruijū*, vol. 12 (Tokyo: Kokkusho kankōkai, 1907); Shinmura Izuru, ed., *Kaihyō sōshō*, vol. 1 (Kyoto: Kōseikaku shoten, 1927); and Hiyane Antei, ed., *Kirishitan mono-gatari hoka sanpen*, Kirishitan Bunko, vol. 1 (Tokyo: Keiseisha, 1926).

the church's repeated attempts to conquer Japan. Unlike later Kirishitan texts that paint an exotic picture of a physically grotesque and culturally inferior foreign invader, *Baterenki* confines its criticism of the Kirishitan to their desire to conquer other lands. As a result, there are no physical descriptions or references to magical powers, and only a small part of the text describes their activities in Japan. A much larger portion is given over to fictional accounts of the waves of increasingly larger fleets of soldiers and padres sent by the pope to conquer Japan. These would-be conquerors repeatedly fail to defeat Japan through military means, and the first Kirishitan padre to remain successfully in Japan does so only because he is alone and claims that his ship was driven off course. As the earliest narrative to depict the Kirishitan as a foreign, would-be conqueror that gains access only through deception, *Baterenki* can be seen as the seminal text in the formation of the Edo-period figure of the Kirishitan Other.

Baterenki was probably written in the first or second decade of the seventeenth century and, because commercial printing was only in its infancy in Japan at this time, likely circulated only in manuscript. Both Ebisawa Arimichi and Hiyane Antei point out that it must have been written after 1607, as that is the last dated reference in the text.[2] Several factors, including a lack of references to the expulsion and government persecution of converts beginning in 1614, as well as the inclusion of relatively accurate information on stories and practices of the Catholic Church, indicate it was produced before or just around the expulsion. Similarly, the comparatively large number of accurately glossed Portuguese and Latin words still being used in the context in which they were introduced by the missionaries indicates it was written close to the time when the missionaries were still active, and certainly well before the 1639 printing of *Kirishitan monogatari*.[3] Though the author is anonymous, the relatively accurate description of the sacraments and story of St. Lucy point to either a former convert or someone transcribing the account of one. There is no extant information about how widely the text circulated or how well known it

---

2. Ebisawa Arimichi, *Nihon kirishitanshi* (Tokyo: Hanawa shobō, 1966), 206; idem, *Kirishitanshi no kenkyū* (Tokyo: Unebi shobō, 1942), 208; Hiyane, *Kirishitan monogatari hoka sanpen*, 2.
3. As might be expected, a survey of extant fiction on the Kirishitan shows a diminishing number of foreign Kirishitan terms and a marked distancing from the original meanings of the terms the further the origination date of the text is from the time of the missionaries' expulsion. *Baterenki* has the most Portuguese and Latin terms, followed by *Kirishitan monogatari* (1639). By the time of the *Raichō jikki* narrative of the early eighteenth century, most of the few remaining Portuguese terms form part of a mantra chanted by the Kirishitan converts.

was, but there is reason to believe that Sessho relied on it when he wrote *Taiji jashūron* in 1648.⁴

Baterenki begins rather abruptly with a reference to St. Peter and St. John establishing the seven sacraments of the Catholic Church, which is followed by an explanation of how the sacraments are performed and their significance.⁵ This was not the first time the sacraments were described in Japanese, as the Jesuit publication of the catechism, *Dochiriina kirishitan*, had been printed in Japanese characters in 1591 and 1600, and in Japanese written with Roman characters in 1592 and 1600.⁶ The Jesuit text is set up as a conversation between a teacher and his student, with the student asking about each sacrament and the teacher responding. The explanations of them are full of Portuguese and Latin words transliterated into Japanese, which must have made it difficult reading for anyone without significant training in the church. In *Baterenki*, the description of the sacraments differs from the *Dochiriina kirishitan* in enough ways that it seems unlikely its author relied on the Jesuit text. For example, the passage in *Baterenki* is not written in the form of a dialogue, and it uses many fewer Portuguese and Latin words.⁷ Furthermore, the names of the sacraments are sometimes different, in some cases using Latin, and in others, Portuguese. Finally, the sacraments are listed in a different order, and the descriptions of them, while generally accurate, lack the detail included in the *Dochiriina*.⁸ All of this points to an author either writing from his own memory, as a former convert or brother, or transcribing the account of another with similar experience.

4. Ebisawa Arimichi points out that some portions of Sessho's work include information that was available in *Baterenki*. Ebisawa, *Nanbanji kōhaiki*, 88, n. 10.
5. *Zokuzoku*, 570–72.
6. The text of the *Dochiriina* is in Ebisawa Arimichi et al., eds., *Kirishitansho, haiyasho*, Nihon shisō taikei, vol. 25 (Tokyo: Iwanami Shoten, 1970). For more on the printing history of the *Dochiriina*, see Ikuo Higashibaba, *Christianity in Early Modern Japan:Kirishitan Belief and Practice* (Leiden: Brill, 2001), 50–75.
7. For the most part, however, the Portuguese or Latin words for the sacraments are included, except for Holy Orders, which is rendered in Japanese as *shukke* 出家. Additionally, words such as ひいてす (fides, faith), ぜす きりしと (Jesu Christo), ひすほ (Bispo, bishop), でうす ひいりよ (Deus Filio), and えきれんしや (Igreja, church) appear in the text.
8. The names of the sacraments and their order in the *Dochiriina* are: ばうちずも (Baptism), こんひるまさん (Confirmation or Chrismation), ゑうかりすちや (Eucharist), ぺにてんしや (Penance or Confession), ゑすてれまーうんさん (Extreme Unction), おるでん (Holy Orders), まちりまうにょ (Matrimony). Ebisawa, *Kirishitansho, haiyasho*, 64. *Baterenki* lists them as first, second, third, etc., in the following order: ばうちいすも (Baptism), こんひさん (Confession, or Penance), きりすも (Chrismation), まちりまふにょ (Matrimony), 出家 (Holy Orders), こもかる (likely "convocar," or Eucharist), and うんさん (Extreme Unction, or Anointing the Sick).

Immediately following the description of the seventh sacrament, the author moves on to tell the stories of St. Lucy and the origins of the Catholic Church in Rome. Though little is known of the historical St. Lucy, the most basic information says that she was born in the town of Syracuse in Sicily, and lived in the third century at the time of the anti-Christian Diocletius. Legends about her say that she had pledged her virginity to God but was betrothed by her family to a nonbeliever. She gave her dowry and all of her possessions away to the poor, angering the betrothed so much that he denounced her to the magistrate as a Christian.[9] When the official tried to punish her, her body was for some time indestructible, though eventually she was martyred. Within the Catholic Church, she is among the earliest saints, appearing in the Canon of the Mass of the Roman and Ambrosian rites by Pope Gregory, who served in the late sixth and early seventh centuries.[10] Other legends about St. Lucy that appeared in the Middle Ages say that her eyes were put out, either by her tormenters as part of her punishment, or by her own hand to avoid falling into sin over their purported beauty.[11] As a result of these legends, in later representations she is often depicted holding her eyes on a plate, and within the church she became the patron saint of the blind.

In the *Baterenki* version, Lucy (るしや or 留者, Lucia) is the daughter of a Christian who lives in a place called Saragoza (さらがうざ) in the 430th year after Christ.[12] After her father dies when she is seven, she studies the teachings of Jesus Christ and decides that she wants to share them with others, so she moves away, joins a hermitage, and professes herself a "virgin" (ひるせん). A padre there named Roman falls in love with her at first sight, but because he is a priest, he does not immediately tell her. Instead, he encourages her to come to confession every week, and at one point asks if she suffers from love or desire. When she replies that she is a virgin and therefore has no such desires, he tells her that in order to be a "true" virgin, she should help a man like him, who has accumulated great merit but still suffers from desire. She finally agrees to help him and eventually becomes pregnant. Months later, when the king of the land visits a church and sees Lucy, he also falls in love with her instantly. When she does not answer his letters or accept his proposal, he has her arrested and

---

9. James Bentley, *A Calendar of Saints: the Lives of the Principle Saints of the Christian Year* (London: Macdonald & Co. Ltd, 1988), 239. Another legend says she resisted rape and was punished for it. Richard P. McBrien, *Lives of the Saints: From Mary and St. Francis of Assisi to John XXIII and Mother Theresa* (San Francisco: HarperCollins, 2001), 501–502.
10. McBrien, *Lives of the Saints*, 502.
11. Bentley, *A Calendar of Saints*, 239; McBrien, *Lives of the Saints*, 502.
12. *Zokuzoku*, 572–74. According to church accounts, Lucy died around 304 C.E.

her eyes put out, and she eventually dies in prison.

After telling of her death in prison, the narrator of the *Baterenki* then offers an alternative story for the death of St. Lucy. In this version, she is also a virgin but is pursued by a suitor. When she asks the man what it is he likes about her, he says that her eyes are beautiful. She replies that rather than fall into sin because of them she would take them out herself, knowing that by God's grace she would still be able to see. Then she is pursued by the king and jailed. However, when she is about to die, Saint Paul comes down to her from heaven and takes out his own eyes for her.

An interesting note in the final sentence of the St. Lucy section says that this alternative story originally was told by Tōin Vicente (1540–1609) in Japan. Vicente was a Jesuit brother who, along with his father Paulo, worked as a translator for the Jesuit press. He is known to have written a number of the entries on saints for the press's 1591 *Sanctos no gosagyō* (Lives of the Saints), though that book does not include an entry on St. Lucy.[13] Tōin's work on the Jesuit publication is not made clear in the *Baterenki*, but this reference to him in the context of a saint's life story is another clue that the author had some knowledge about the Jesuits. Furthermore, the similarities between the narrative of St. Lucy told in the Japanese text and the general outlines of the legends and accounts of her in the Catholic Church point to the missionaries as the source of the story.

In contrast, the padre who seduces Lucy, promising that she will accumulate merit by helping one as advanced in his practice as he is, would not have been a part of the original tale, and more resembles a passage from a medieval *setsuwa* than part of a traditional saint's tale from the Catholic Church. In several medieval *setsuwa*, bodhisattva and other female deities show their compassion by agreeing to take the form of women to help holy men deal with the distraction of their carnal desires by satisfying them, as Lucy does for the padre Roman.[14] This very Buddhist view of virginity as a virtue that can be sacrificed for the sake of another's salvation without danger to one's own is the first time that the narrative clearly steps away from the stories that were transmitted by the missionaries. In doing so, it incorporates a more familiar message from the Japanese literary and religious tradition and perhaps makes the merit in Lucy's sacrifice

---

13. Chieko Irie Mulhern, "Cinderella and the Jesuits: An *Otogizoshi* Cycle as Christian Literature," *Monumenta Nipponica* 34, no. 4 (1979): 409–47, 441–42.
14. R. Keller Kimbrough, *Preachers, Poets, Women, and the Way: Izumi Shikibu and the Buddhist Literature of Medieval Japan* (Ann Arbor: Center for Japanese Studies, The University of Michigan, 2008), 222.

more understandable to readers in a culture that had not developed a cult of virginity like that of Europe.

Following the story of St. Lucy, the author tells of a non-Christian (ぜんちよ, or gentile) Roman king living in the year 370 after Christ, who suffers from leprosy but is cured by a padre who is also a skilled doctor.[15] Though the names are all different, the story resembles one associated with the Roman Emperor Constantine (306–37) and Pope Sylvester I (d. 335). Historical records do not show that Silvester had a great impact on the church, but legends that began to circulate as early as the fifth century credit him with curing Constantine of leprosy.[16] This legend was further supported with the appearance in the eighth or ninth century of a purported edict from Constantine to Pope Silvester, also called the Donation of Constantine, which was a forged document that was used for many years by the Catholic Church to justify its rule in Rome and western Italy.[17] According to the document, the Roman emperor Constantine was cured of leprosy and then baptized by Pope Silvester, and in gratitude Constantine handed over Rome and much of western Italy to the pope and his successors in the church. The forged nature of the document was discovered by some scholars as early as the fifteenth century, but it was not fully acknowledged by the church until the early seventeenth century, so it is possible that the story still was being told by the Western missionaries in Japan before the expulsion. While there are some differences in the characters and details, it seems clear that this story formed part of the catechism of the missionaries. However, in the context of *Baterenki*, it is used to explain how the Christians gained control of Rome, and how the practice of taking over other countries goes back to the very origins of Christianity in Europe. In this way, it appears that part of the missionaries' catechism is used in the tale to lay the foundation for the image of the Kirishitan as would-be conquerors.

The remainder of *Baterenki* tells a tale in which the popes make repeated attempts to enter and take over Japan, beginning in "the 624th year after Christ," and continuing through the successful entry of the single padre in the sixteenth century.[18] It begins with the pope (ぱっぱ) in Rome (良魔 or らうま) gathering all of the padres from near and far and telling

---

15. *Zokuzoku*, 574–76.
16. McBrien, *Lives of the Saints*, 527–28.
17. For an English translation of the edict see Mark Edwards, *Constantine and Christendom: the Oration to the Saints, the Greek and Latin Accounts of the Discovery of the Cross, the Edict of Constantine to Pope Silvester* (Liverpool: Liverpool University Press, 2003), 92–115.
18. *Zokuzoku*, 576–89.

them that their teacher Jesus Christ told his followers that they should go forth and make Christians of other kings. It was now time to devise a plan to carry out his wishes. He first sends two different delegations of padres to Siam (しやむらう), but they are captured and punished by the king of that land, who kills one of the leaders and sends the others back with their noses and ears cut. After the failure in Siam, the pope sets his sights on a place he calls Monte Plata, which is rich in silver but also known for its strong warriors. He decides that the best approach this time is through trade, and he equips a ship with many goods to be led by the padre Paulo and eight priests, along with the captain, Don Jacob. Their long voyage takes them to Goa, after which a strong wind blows them back to Portugal, where they wait out the year and then proceed to China.[19] They finally arrive in a place called Satsuma that, after traveling here and there, Paulo concludes is Monte Plata. But the people there are too afraid of the Romans' appearance to approach, so they are unable to trade. Eventually the travelers are forced to sail back to Rome, finally arriving seven years after they had left.

Subsequent missions are turned back by "demon winds" or lost at sea, but all fail to capture the land and wealth of Monte Plata. In one of those attempts, however, the padres learn that the country is actually called "Japon." The successful attempt to enter the country finally comes in the year A.D. 1560, when a single padre comes on a trading ship, claiming that he was on his way to Nova Hispania but was blown off course. He attracts many people with the wares he displays, and he speaks to them of Deus. He manages to baptize one of them and take him back to Rome, where he studies and eventually becomes Brother Lourenço.[20] Returning to Japon several years later with more padres, Lourenço is able to attract converts because he is Japanese, and they build a church.[21] From that point

---

19. This list of cities and countries reflects areas where the Jesuits had major mission presences.
20. This appears to be referring to the first Japanese convert to be admitted to the Society of Jesus as a catechist. Lourenço's Japanese name is unknown, but early Jesuit reports show that he was an invaluable member of the mission as an interpreter and a preacher. He was baptized by Francis Xavier in 1551 and admitted to the order in 1563. He was still serving the mission when he died in 1592. For more on Lourenço see Ebisawa Arimichi, "Irmao Lourenco, the First Japanese Lay-Brother of the Society of Jesus and His Letter," *Monumenta Nipponica* 5, no. 1 (1942): 225–33.
21. Despite the fact that they learn the country is called Nihon (or Japon) earlier in the narrative, it is referred to as Monte Plata until Lourenço returns from Rome, at which time he is described as returning to Nihon (日本). This signals an important change in the point of view of the narrator that is discussed below. *Zokuzoku*, 585.

on, the trade ship continues to come every year, and, according to the narrator, this is the origin of the Kirishitan in Japan.

The narrative goes on to describe the arrival of the trade ships and the different places they docked, finally settling on Nagasaki. It then introduces a character afflicted with leprosy who is told that he can be cured by the padres if he becomes Kirishitan. He listens to the catechism and joins the church, after which his disease is treated and cured. But over the years spent in the church, he learns of the padres' plot to take over the country little by little. The padres know that when they collect believers in various regions, those people will not oppose them for fear of losing salvation, and they plan to make Nagasaki like their home of Rome and their bishop the shogun of Japan. Eventually, a former Japanese brother who left the church after a falling out with the padres tells the daimyo Ōmura, who had also joined with the Kirishitan, all about the history of Rome's attacks on Japan and of the padres' designs on the country. The narrator identifies this former brother as Chijiwa Seizaimon. This is the name of one of four boys from noble families in Kyushu that the Jesuits escorted to Europe between 1582 and 1590 in a kind of diplomatic mission to the Portuguese and Spanish capitals, and to Rome. Though Chijiwa is known to have left the Society around 1603, little more is known of him or his activities, and he is certainly not suspected of working against the Society politically.[22] In this tale, however, he reports on the padres to Ōmura. In the final scene of *Baterenki*, the shocked leader immediately sends all of the Kirishitan in his domain back to Nagasaki, destroys the church in Hakata, and enters the true path of the lotus.[23]

Baterenki is clearly an entertaining and important early anti-Kirishitan text. It can also be seen as a liminal text that is the first to paint a picture of the conquering Kirishitan villain that would be developed further in later popular works, even as it serves as a repository of the language and some of the catechism that was taught by the Jesuits. In this latter role it has largely been ignored by scholars, perhaps because of the more fictional elements in the portrayal of the padres' repeated attempts to enter Japan. There is no doubt that for those interested in how Christianity was understood in a culture steeped in the Shinto, Buddhist, and Confucian

---

22. For the most complete information about the four boys and the mission to Europe, see Michael Cooper, *The Japanese Mission to Europe, 1582-1590* (Kent: Global Oriental, 2005).
23. The final pages of *Baterenki* are a fictionalized account of relations between the Jesuits and Ōmura and of Jesuit control of Nagasaki that sometimes follows the historical record and sometimes does not. For a more detailed discussion of where the story diverges from the historical record, see the notes to the translation of *Baterenki* in this book.

traditions, the works of Fabian Fucan (both *Myōtei mondō* and *Ha Daiusu*), Sesshō, and Christovão Ferreira are richer sources.[24] But while those works take up the fundamental tenets of the different religions and argue for or against their validity, *Baterenki* serves as a resource for how some of the information taught by the missionaries was processed by the converts, presented in a way that is free of argument or controversy about doctrine. In fact, *Baterenki* stands out among all of the Kirishitan-related texts of the seventeenth and eighteenth centuries, both the treatises on the religion and the pseudohistorical narratives, as perhaps the only one that offers no judgment on the Kirishitan teachings. Rather, it transmits some of the lessons that were clearly part of the catechism, in the form of the list of sacraments and the stories of St. Lucy and the origins of the church in

---

24. Fabian Fucan was a Christian convert and Jesuit brother turned apostate who appears as a character in the later two anti-Kirishitan texts as the embodiment of all that is wrong with the Kirishitan. Thought to have been educated at a Zen monastery, the historical Fabian served first as an influential writer and speaker on behalf of Christianity, and later as a devastating critic of the faith. *Myōtei mondō* (The Dialogue of Myoshu and Yutei) is set up as a traditional dialogue between a teacher and students that refutes the teachings of Buddhism, Confucianism, and Shinto and argues for the truth of the Kirishitan teachings. The surviving, partial version of the original text is reproduced in Ebisawa, *Kirishitansho, haiyasho*, 113–81. Several years after leaving the Jesuits (probably in 1608), Fabian wrote the anti-Kirishitan treatise *Ha Daiusu*, in which he reverses many of the arguments he made in *Myōtei mondō*. An extant copy of the original woodblock print of 1620 is in the Kyoto University Library. The text can be found in a number of modern printed collections including *Zokuzoku*; Hiyane, *Kirishitan monogatari hoka sanpen*; Washio Junkei, ed., *Nihon shisō tōsō shiryo*, vol. 10 (Tokyo: Meichō kankyōkai, 1969); and Ebisawa, *Nanbanji kōhaiki*. A complete English translation of the text is in Elison, *Deus Destroyed*, 259–91.

Christovão Ferreira was Vice Provincial of Japan for the Jesuits when he was captured and tortured in 1633. He was one of the most famous Christian apostates not only because of his high position in the Jesuit order, but also because he went on to serve the bakufu as interpreter for the interrogators of other captured Kirishitan. His treatise, *Kengiroku* (顯僞録, translated by George Elison as "Deceit Disclosed"), explains most of the fundamental Christian concepts and then shows them to be completely illogical. The Japanese text is reproduced in Tekkan Yosano et al., eds. *Giya do pekadoru gekan, Myōtei mondō, Ha Daiusu, Kengiroku*, Nihon koten zenshū (Tokyo: Nihon koten zenshu kankokai, 1927). A full English translation is in Elison, *Deus Destroyed*, 293–318.

The Buddhist priest Sesshō wrote *Taiji jashūron* (On Exterminating the Evil Sect) in 1648, as a detailed description and refutation of the Kirishitan teachings. Though the original essay was in *kanbun*, there is also a second, *kana* version (*Jakyō tai'i*) with much of the commentary removed. One manuscript copy of the *kanbun* text is in the Library of Congress. The earliest printed version is an incomplete *kanbun* text in Kiyū Dōnin's *Hekija kannenroku* (On Understanding and Rejecting Heresy) of 1861. The *kanbun* text is also included in Washio, *Nihon shisō tōsō shiryo* and in Ebisawa, *Kirishitansho, haiyasho*. The *kana* version was first printed in Kiyū Dōnin's printed editions of *Nanbanji kōhaiki* of 1868. It is also included in Washio, *Nihon shisō tōsō shiryo* and in Ebisawa, *Nanbanji kōhaiki*.

Rome. It also gives a snapshot of how much of the Kirishitan vocabulary was taught in Portuguese and Latin.[25]

Even as *Baterenki* serves as a partial record of the missionaries' teachings, it also stands at the threshold of the genre of anti-Kirishitan literature, representing the first narrative to construct an image of the padres as part of a conquering force from a foreign land that use religion and deception to try to take over Japan. The idea of the missionaries as the vanguard of Iberian armies was certainly not a new one. But *Baterenki* is the first popular narrative to construct a Kirishitan villain as a wily conqueror, and some elements of the Kirishitan villain in this tale would remain fundamental to the Kirishitan image through its many iterations in Japanese narratives, theatre, and even political rhetoric for nearly three hundred years. One of these elements is a foreign leader with the desire to conquer other countries who cannot succeed by military means, but must use the padres and their religion to turn the Japanese people against their own leaders. Another is the padres themselves, who practice healing and use trade and gifts to attract converts, and only are able to enter Japan initially by disguising their intentions. Finally, in *Baterenki* as in the other popular works about the Kirishitan, the padres' deceit and ulterior motives are ultimately discovered, and they are sent away.

While the elements of the Kirishitan image shared by *Baterenki* and the other popular works on the Kirishitan are fundamental, there are also many ways in which this early text differs from the later ones. Most strikingly, there is no attempt to portray the Kirishitan as barbarians in contrast to the more civilized Japanese culture. Though the Kirishitan are clearly a threat to Japanese sovereignty in *Baterenki*, they are not described as physically grotesque or lacking in cultural refinement, nor are their converts from among the outcasts of Japanese society. In fact, the Kirishitan are not described in physical terms at all, even though the Japanese are. Similarly, the religion is not subjected to criticism or described as magic or a *gedō* (false path). The Kirishitan in the tale are clearly foreign, and that aspect is stressed by several references to problems communicating in unknown languages, but they and the Japanese are portrayed as cultural equals, and their Otherness is situated more in that linguistic difference and in their

---

25. The large number of foreign words used in this text, often without accompanying explanations, raises the question of how prevalent and widely understood these words were and for how long. For the most part, the words are used in a context appropriate to the original meanings in Latin and Portuguese, but one wonders if the author really expected his audience to understand when Paulo responded to the question about what the people of Monte Plata worshipped with the words, "idols (いとろす), like in Jerusalem (ぜるされん)." *Zokuzoku*, 579.

compulsion to conquer other countries than it is in a false religion or a barbaric culture.

The representation of Japan and its people in *Baterenki* also lacks the strident assertions in later texts of Japan's civilized status as a longtime member of the three kingdoms, and as a recipient of the traditions inherited through China and Tenjiku (India). In fact, though India is mentioned in the text, it is mostly referred to not as Tenjiku but as India (いんでや) or Goa (ごあ).[26] Similarly, Japan is called "Monte Plata" for the greater part of the narrative, referring to it as a source of silver and plunder and making it the object of the Roman pope's conquest, rather than the subject of the tale. The pope first learns of Monte Plata by reading Aristotle, and the padres read about the wisdom and strength of the people of Monte Plata in the writings of Santa Maria and "other philosophers," demonstrating that the source of historical knowledge of Japan is firmly situated in the West, not in the three kingdoms or in the traditions of the East.

There are two important factors that could account for most of these differences between the *Baterenki* and later texts. First, and most obviously, is that it was written closer to the time of the missionaries, and likely when they were still in the country, while the later texts were all written decades or even a century after the majority of the Western missionaries had left. With the padres still visible in society, there was little call for descriptions of their appearance and behavior. And most importantly, the Western missionaries and Christianity likely had not yet been outlawed. In fact, for a text that is clearly critical of the Kirishitan, references to the expulsion or to government persecution of Kirishitan are striking in their absence, making it highly likely that the text was produced sometime between 1607 and 1614. This timing would mean that the Kirishitan had not yet been labeled criminals in Japanese society, nor were they yet seen as confirmed enemies of the state, as they were after the expulsion and the Shimabara Rebellion. This difference is significant; in the *Baterenki*, the Kirishitan are still only a *potential* threat, not a known one. Also, the threat in *Baterenki* is still only a regional one that, according to the account, was successfully subdued. As such, the Kirishitan are not yet the national threat they are in the later texts, where they have dealings with Oda Nobunaga and Toyotomi Hideyoshi, nor are they yet a foreign Other against which a Japanese identity is constructed.

---

26. In one reference to many countries that contributed to the fleet sent to Japan by the pope, there is a reference to armies coming from both Goa and India, accurately reflecting the separation at the time between the Portuguese-controlled Goa and the rest of India. *Zokuzoku*, 582.

A second important factor, and one of the more remarkable features of *Baterenki*, is the fact that for the greater part of the text, the narrator's point of view appears to be that of a padre. While the perspective of later texts is primarily that of the Japanese receiving the foreigners, in *Baterenki* it is that of the foreigners traveling to Japan. This perspective helps explain the large number of Portuguese and Latin words in the text, as well as the fact that only the Romans are named, while the Japanese remain anonymous fighters (unless they are baptized and receive a Western name). Likewise, it accounts for the fact that Japan is considered to be "Monte Plata" until a native of the country tells them it is called Nihon (though even then, he is told by the padres that in their language it would be Japon), and it is the Japanese who are foreign and therefore have their physical appearance described to the pope. Even the winds that drive back the invading foreigners, which are clearly serving the same purpose as the protective *kamikaze* (divine winds) of the Mongol invasions, are seen from the perspective of the would-be invaders as evil (悪風) or demon (天狗風) winds. The perspective of the world is decidedly Western, with countries bearing mostly Western names and Japan viewed more as a target of Western conquest than a member of the Sino-centric Asian world.

The effect of this Western perspective in the greater part of the text is to make it look like the writing of a padre—perhaps even a "secret transmission"—which has been discovered and disseminated in order to expose the padres' plot. The history begins with the padres' first conquest of Rome and goes on to chronicle not only their many unsuccessful attempts at Japan, but also their successes in other countries that they target. The narrative shows the padres going to great lengths to hide their secret history and their intentions for the country. The perspective of the text gives it authority as a true account of the padres' treachery, and its dissemination appears to serve as a warning—a factor that would also support the notion that it was written before the expulsion. Under those circumstances, *Baterenki* can be seen almost as a political tool designed to undermine the position of the missionaries in the country. In this way it differs radically from the later texts that set out to chronicle the past activities and downfall of the Kirishitan, even as it lays the groundwork for those later texts with its representation of them as aggressive, would-be conquerors.

The Western point of view continues for about three-quarters of the narrative, until it abruptly shifts to a Japanese perspective when the padres begin to establish themselves in the country. After the padre Cosme successfully enters Japan by claiming to be a trader blown off course, he attracts a convert who agrees to return to Rome with him to study. It is when the pair return to Japan several years later that the text begins to refer regularly to Nihon (日本) rather than Monte Plata or Japon, and this shift is further emphasized at the end of the paragraph when the narrator reports that this event marked the beginning of the Kirishitan presence in "our country" (我が朝).[27] Also from this point, the foreigners are called Nanbanjin (Southern Barbarians) for the first time, and contemporary local officials, like Ōmura, are named. This Japanese point of view occupies the final four pages of the text and differs so markedly from the previous fifteen pages that one cannot help wondering if it was added later by a different author. Regardless of the source, this shift in the final pages to a Japanese point of view that conflates the Kirishitan and Nanbanjin (and obscures their connection to Rome) foreshadows the treatment of the topic in later texts such as *Kirishitan monogatari* and *Raichō jikki*.

As the earliest popular anti-Kirishitan text, *Baterenki* offers a significant first look at the figure of the Kirishitan villain. The failures of the repeated military missions show him to be powerless against the protective forces of Japan when they are aware of him. Only through deception is he able to gain some influence, but when his plan is discovered, his plot is easily foiled. He is clearly an insatiable conqueror, but still a very human one that can be thwarted and controlled. Appearing at a time when the Christian missionaries either were still active in Japan or very recently so, and before the government campaign to eradicate both foreign and Japanese believers, the Kirishitan villain of *Baterenki* is still only a potential threat and not the alarmingly tenacious one that appeared to bewitch tens of thousands of followers into resisting torture and fighting to their deaths in the Shimabara Rebellion. In fact, it is only after the Shimabara Rebellion, when the foreign Kirishitan has disappeared from public view, that both he and the Japanese identity against which he is constructed become more clearly delineated in the anti-Kirishitan popular tales.

The Demon Kirishitan of *Kirishitan monogatari*

The final sentence of *Baterenki* reports that, after Ōmura had destroyed the Kirishitan temples in his domain and sent the padres there back to Nagasaki, the fortunes of the Kirishitan went into decline. In fact, according to

---

27. *Zokuzoku*, 585. When the first flotilla of padres arrives in Japan, the country is referred to as *Nihon akitsushima*, but this happens only once and the padres continue to call it Monte Plata or Japon until the shift at the end. Ibid., 578.

the historical record, in the same year that Ōmura sent the missionaries away from his domain, Tokugawa Ieyasu granted an audience to the Jesuit Bishop, Luis de Cerqueira, and in the following year, he received a visit from the Jesuit Vice-Provincial, Francisco Pasio, and the Dominican mission Superior, Francisco de Morales.[28]

Not long after that, however, relations between the bakufu and the missionaries began to sour, as trade with Portugal was curtailed in favor of agreements with England and Holland. In 1612, Christianity was outlawed by the bakufu, and this was soon followed by an edict expelling all of the missionaries from Japan. Over the next twenty-five years, the missionaries who had stayed in hiding and their converts were hunted down and imprisoned, tortured, or killed in a campaign that by the mid-1630s appeared to have eradicated the Kirishitan or, at least, driven the remainder underground. But the Shimabara Rebellion of 1637–38, carried out by overtaxed peasants carrying banners with Kirishitan slogans, revived fears that the religion had laid indestructible roots in Japanese society. It also captured the imaginations of the burgeoning population of readers, as accounts of the Shimabara Rebellion soon made it into print and continued to be reproduced for centuries.[29]

Kirishitan monogatari is one of the first accounts of the rebellion to appear in print and also one of the major works describing the arrival

---

28. The narrative places the events in 1607, though the grant allowing the expansion of Nagasaki's borders by Ieyasu was made in 1605, and Ōmura's expulsion of the missionaries in 1606. Cerqueira's visit to Ieyasu also took place in 1606. Michael Cooper, *Rodrigues the Interpreter: an Early Jesuit in Japan and China* (New York: Weatherhill, 1974), 207–9.
29. The most well-known of these texts is the *Shimabara-ki* 島原記 (Record of Shimabara), which was printed for the first time around 1642 or 1643, and reprinted at least five more times in 1649, 1673, 1688, 1704, and 1708 (the preface states it was written in 1640, but scholars believe the first printing was not for another two or three years). There are also extant copies with no dates that are thought to be from additional printings. Alternate titles of the same account include *Shimabara kassenki* (Record of the Battles at Shimabara), *Shimabara gun monogatari* (War Tales of Shimabara), and *Amakusa monogatari* (Tale of Amakusa). Two more popular accounts of the battle that are more fictionalized are *Amakusa gunki* (Battle Records of Amakusa) and *Kinka keiransho* (Tales of Storm and Splendor), the latter of which was printed twice in the Meiji period. Both of these also include the *Raichō jikki* narrative as part of the larger account of the rebellion. See below for more on that combination. Edo-period literature on the Shimabara Rebellion is almost a genre by itself and deserves a separate study devoted to it. Except for the versions that include the *Raichō jikki* narrative, the Shimabara battle tales do not feature representations of the Kirishitan Other, and for that reason they are not included in this study. For more information on all of these texts see Wakaki Taiichi, "'Shimabaraki' no seisei to sono tenkai," *Bungaku* 54, no. 12 (1986): 142–51; and Watanabe Kenji, "*Kirishitan to bungaku to nonfikushon bungaku: Shimabara no ran wo chūshin ni*" *16 seiki ikō no nihon to higashi ajia no Kirishitan bungaku no eikyōdo wo meguru sōgōteki hikaku kenkyū*, (Tokyo, 2008).

and expulsion of the Kirishitan.[30] Of the three narratives that helped construct the image of the Kirishitan villain, it is perhaps the most well known because it was printed, even though the later *Raichō jikki* narrative that circulated in manuscript may have reached a larger audience. Though its greater fame among anti-Kirishitan popular works perhaps reflects a more modern privileging of the printed text over the manuscript than was current when it was produced, there is no doubt that *Kirishitan monogatari* occupies an important place not only as an anti-Kirishitan text, but also as an early, commercially printed work at a time when political, social, and economic forces were combining to form a new and broader audience with more shared interests and concerns.[31] Traditionally, *Kirishitan monogatari* has always been classified among the battle tales in the *kanazōshi* genre of the seventeenth century because of its account of the Shimabara Rebellion, but recent scholarship on commercial publishing and the spread of information at this time shows that its timing and subject matter additionally make it a significant representative of a transitional period in the printing industry's understanding not only of literature as both information and entertainment, but also of the potential audience for such works. The text of *Kirishitan monogatari* is dated Kan'ei 16 (1639), and it likely was printed in the same year that it was written. It is also likely to have been printed in Kyoto, where the earliest surge in commercial publishing was based, and where most of the action in the narrative takes place.[32] A second printing with new illustrations in 1665 under the title of *Kirishitan taiji monogatari* is attributed to

---

30. The *Kokusho sōmokuroku* lists six complete and one partial copy of the original woodblock printed text, including a full copy at the Diet library. The *Sōmokuroku* also lists four manuscript copies of the text, and my own research uncovered two more of the *Kirishitan monogatari* narrative copied under different titles. These include a work titled *Kirishitan ranshōki* 切支丹濫觴記 (Sources of the Kirishitan) held at the National Archives, and one titled *Kirishitan yuraiki* 吉利支丹由来記 (Origins of the Kirishitan) in the Tokyo University Library. The latter title is also a common one for the *Raichō jikki* text, and the manuscript should not be confused with that narrative. Modern printed versions of *Kirishitan monogatari* can be found in *Zokuzoku*; Hiyane., *Kirishitan monogatari hoka sanpen*; and Washio, *Nihon shisō tōsō shiryo*. An English translation of *Kirishitan monogatari* is included in Elison, *Deus Destroyed*, 321–74; quotes cited here in English are taken from that translation.
31. Mary Elizabeth Berry, *Japan in Print: Information and Nation in the Early Modern Period* (Berkeley: University of California, 2006), 13–54.
32. Berry notes that Kyoto had over one hundred publishers by the 1640s. Ibid., 31. For a complete history of the book in Japan, see Peter Kornicki, *The Book in Japan: a Cultural History From the Beginnings to the Nineteenth Century* (Honolulu: University of Hawai'i Press, 2001).

Nakano Tarōzaemon of Kyoto.[33]

Though the start of commercial printing in Japan is usually dated to the beginning of the Tokugawa period, production in the first decades of the century was limited to printed versions of traditional Buddhist texts and classical literature, with an increase in the publication of new titles like *Kirishitan monogatari* apparent in the 1640s.[34] Watanabe Kenji has identified a shift during these early decades toward viewing printing as a means of transmitting information on current events to a large audience in a timely manner, rather than primarily as a form of preserving texts. Watanabe has shown how the publication of *Osaka monogatari* (Tale of Osaka) in 1615, during the battle over Osaka Castle, was an early use of printing as a form of "reportage," and also as a tool to sway public opinion of the Tokugawa cause.[35] Though *Kirishitan monogatari* was printed a year after the end of the Shimabara Rebellion, Watanabe points out that it was still an example of relatively quick reporting on a current event. He further argues that, although the work has been analyzed almost exclusively for its anti-Kirishitan message, through its criticism of the Shimabara *han* lord Matsukura's management it also serves as a very timely didactic text aimed at instructing high-ranking samurai and domain lords on the proper way to manage their people in order to avoid similar uprisings.[36]

Kirishitan monogatari also provides an example of a further trend in commercial printing at the time: identifying a more consciously imagined national audience for the books being produced. Mary Berry points out that, "particularly in their new fiction and their accounts of recent wartime history, early modern writers drew on collective experiences of upheaval to appeal to a nascent collectivity of readers, one defined not by station or education or place of residence but by shared crisis."[37] In the

---

33. The *Kokusho sōmokuroku* lists three extant copies of the 1665 printing, including one at Tokyo University Library and another at Kyoto University Library. A facsimile edition in three *kan* of the original woodblock printed text was put out by the *Kisho fukuseikai* in 1928 and 1929. The text is also reproduced in Asakura Haruhiko, ed., *Kirishitan taiji monogatari*, Kanazōshi shūsei, vol. 25 (Tokyo: Tokyodō shuppan, 1999) and Shinmura Izuru, ed., *Kaihyō sōsho*, vol. 2 (Kyoto: Kōseikaku shoten, 1927). Elison points out that the information on the printer is not in the extant copy he examined in the Kyoto University Library, but that the library includes it in the record. Elison, *Deus Destroyed*, 475.
34. On the early years of the book trade, see Kornicki, *The Book in Japan*, 169–221; on the increase in new titles, see Berry, *Japan in Print*, 32.
35. Watanabe Kenji, "Kanazōshi to nonfikushon: Ōsaka no yaku to Shimabara no ran," in *Edo no nonfikushon*, edited by Shiraishi Yoshio, Norizuki Toshihiko, Watanabe Kenji (Tokyo: Tokyo Shoseki, 1993), 30–37.
36. Watanabe, "*Shimabara no ran*," 111.
37. Berry, *Japan in Print*, 22.

case of *Kirishitan monogatari*, the crisis was twofold: the cultural invasion of the Kirishitan, and the subsequent rebellion of their followers and thus the potential threat to the sovereignty of Japan. The scope of this threat to the nation is summed up in the final paragraph of the tale when the narrator claims that barbarians tried to spread their evil doctrine but that the "Kirishitans were exterminated without being allowed to grasp an inch of our soil, to stand on a foot of our land," and then concludes that "the Empire is at peace, the land in tranquility, the reign of longevity."[38] Unlike in *Baterenki*, where the threat is confined to Kyushu and handled by Ōmura, the threat in *Kirishitan monogatari* posed by the Kirishitan and by the Shimabara Rebellion is to the entire realm (天下) and to Nihon (日本). This puts *Kirishitan monogatari* among a significant group of printed works at the time for whom the "great subject became the place variously called Nihon, Dai Nihon, Honchō, and Yamato," and which appealed to a newly forming, national readership.[39]

The importance of *Kirishitan monogatari* as a new kind of commercial text notwithstanding, it is most famous for its portrayal of the Kirishitan, and the significance of that portrayal to the development of the figure of the Kirishitan Other in the Edo period cannot be overstated. Though *Baterenki* is the first to present the Kirishitan villain as a devious would-be conqueror, *Kirishitan monogatari* makes him a more despicable character who pollutes himself by eating meat and lures converts into similar practices or blatantly pays them money to join him. His religion is represented as a laughable mixture of conflicting and illogical beliefs that only attracts the most gullible and the outcasts of society who are promised medical treatment, money, or exotic gifts from abroad. But it is also dangerous precisely because it empowers and mobilizes these uneducated masses. Most importantly, the Kirishitan is no longer the more regional potential threat of the *Baterenki*, but rather a national threat that came close to realizing his goals of conquest before he was found out in time and apparently defeated. *Kirishitan monogatari* relates a sequence of events leading up to this defeat culminating with the Shimabara Rebellion that demonstrates the clearly criminal behavior of the Kirishitan and his threat to the realm. It is a narrative that works to defeat the Kirishitan in two ways—by telling

---

38. Elison, *Deus Destroyed*, 374.
39. Berry, *Japan in Print*, 22. While a threat to Japan is also the topic of *Baterenki*, the predominantly Western perspective of the narrator makes Japan more the object of conquest than the subject of the tale. Another significant difference is that the Kirishitan of the earlier tale never make it to the capital, and their influence is portrayed as being purely at the regional level of Kyushu and not at the national level.

of his punishment and banishment by the authorities, and by portraying him as a cultural and intellectual inferior.

Kirishitan monogatari begins by describing the arrival of the first Kirishitan—a strange and somewhat grotesque foreigner named Padre Urugan—and his audience with Oda Nobunaga, in which he wins the leader's favor by giving him a number of exotic gifts.[40] Subsequent chapters outline the teachings of the "Kirishitan *buppō*," or Kirishitan dharma, tell of Hideyoshi's arrest and punishment of a group of "fratrum," or brothers, and chronicle a debate between a Kirishitan brother and a Japanese lay monk in which the winner is, of course, the Buddhist monk. The narrative also deals with the differences between Buddhist priests and Kirishitan padres and offers advice on how to teach Buddhist doctrine most effectively to those with differing levels of education and understanding. A series of three chapters describes how a disenchanted convert warns Tokugawa Ieyasu of the Kirishitan's plot to take over the country, and that leader's subsequent measures to expel the foreigners and force all believers to apostatize. Then two following chapters relate the events of the Shimabara Rebellion and describe how the poor management of the domain leader in Shimabara (and not, surprisingly, any intrigue on the part of the Kirishitan) led to the uprising. Finally, the narrator offers advice to readers on how to be a wise leader and avoid dissension among subordinates. In a short closing paragraph, the narrator laments the incursions of the Kirishitan but also rejoices that they were "exterminated," and that the gods and Buddhas are safe and the realm at peace.

From the above synopsis of the tale, it is clear that the *Kirishitan monogatari* narrative differs greatly from that of *Baterenki*. The new work primarily narrates events that took place in the region of the capital rather than near Nagasaki, and it also includes a number of events that took place after the time period covered in *Baterenki*. *Kirishitan monogatari* contains a short passage describing the Kirishitan beliefs, but it clearly is not based on the Christian catechism taught by the missionaries, and the explanation is mediated by a heavy use of Buddhist terminology to describe those beliefs. More striking than these structural differences, however, is the disparaging way in which the Kirishitan are portrayed in *Kirishitan monogatari*. In fact, throughout each of the sections outlined above, the narrator criticizes various aspects of the Kirishitan's appearance and behavior, so

---

40. Francis Xavier and his followers were the first missionaries to arrive in Japan, in Kagoshima in 1549. "Urugan" was the Japanese pronunciation of Father Organtino Gnecchi-Soldo, who was the leader of the church in Kyoto for many years, but was not a member of Xavier's original group. See below for more on Organtino.

that by the end of the tale the overall image of the Kirishitan is one of a conniving, uncouth foreigner who uses money, medicine, and false teachings to lure the lowest in society into helping him take over the country.

There are a number of ways in which the Kirishitan of *Kirishitan monogatari* is shown to be an uncultured barbarian, but the most striking has to be his grotesque appearance, which is clearly the physical manifestation of his lowly cultural status. The physical description of the Kirishitan makes an appearance for the first time in *Kirishitan monogatari*, but it is repeated in the later *Raichō jikki* narrative that circulated for over a century, making it an important element in the overall image of the Kirishitan Other. It is particularly memorable in *Kirishitan monogatari* because it also serves as the opening paragraph of the tale:

> In the Kōji era (1555–58), during the reign of Retired Emperor Go-Nara, the 108th sovereign since Emperor Jimmu, he came for the first time on a Southern Barbarian merchant ship.[41] He had the shape of a human being, but also looked like a long-nosed goblin or a *mikoshi nyūdō* and was nothing to which anyone could put a name.[42] He said he was a Padre. His nose was so large, he seemed to have a conch shell (with the warts removed) stuck to his face. His eyes, which were yellow inside, were large and looked like two eyeglasses.[43] His head was small and the nails on his hands and feet long. More than seven feet tall, with black skin and a red nose, he had teeth that were longer than those of a horse. His hair was grey, and where the top of his head was shaved it looked like a white, upside-down saké cup. His words were completely incomprehensible, and his voice sounded like the cry of an owl. People came in droves to see him, and his face was so shocking they were saying that he could be a demon. But was there ever such a demon as that? His name was Padre Urugan.[44]

---

41. Go-Nara reigned from 1526 to 1557, the year he died. For information on the early years of the Jesuit mission, see Cooper, *Rodrigues the Interpreter*, 18.
42. 見越入道, a long-necked, extremely tall goblin in the garb of a novice priest. It is said to hide in the shadows and peer from behind folding screens (*byōbu*).
43. This is a relatively early reference to an item brought to Japan by Western traders. The word for eyeglasses is *megane* written in *hiragana* in the 1639 text, and as a mixture of *kunji* and *hiragana* (日かね) in the 1665 text. According to the *Kokugo daijiten*, the earliest reference to *megane* is in the *Nippo jisho* 日葡辞書, a Portuguese/Japanese dictionary compiled in 1603 by unidentified members of the Jesuit community. *Nippo jisho; Vocabulario da lingoa da Iapam* (Tokyo: Iwanami Shoten, 1960; facsimile of 1604 edition printed by Society of Jesus, Japan).
44. Hiyane, *Kirishitan monogatari hoka sanpen*, 1. *Urugan* was the Japanese pronunciation of the name of Father Organtino Gnecchi-Soldo, an Italian Jesuit priest who arrived in Japan sometime between 1569 and 1576 and served as the leader of the church in the capital of Kyoto for many years. He died in 1609. An extant letter that was written by

As unflattering and grotesque as this description is, we can recognize in it some of the actual physical differences in the Westerners that we know made an impression on Japanese observers. Certainly the large (or "high") nose of the Westerner was often rendered conspicuously in both Nanban art and prints from the Meiji period, and in the description of the padre's head we can recognize the tonsure that was worn by many of the missionaries and is reproduced in contemporary art featuring them.[45] While the skin of the missionaries was probably not black, the Portuguese and Spanish traders often had on their ships Indian or African sailors or servants whose skin color was of great interest not only to ordinary Japanese but also to members of Nobunaga's court.[46] Similarly, the height of the missionaries was generally taller than the average Japanese, but one prominent member in particular, the Visitor Alexandro Valignano, was described by the Jesuit fathers as unusually tall, and he often attracted a crowd when he traveled through towns.[47]

Surprise at the different features of the missionaries might be expected, but this description goes far beyond that when it compares some of the features to those of animals and suggests that the padre may be a form of demon. Gone are the padres of the *Baterenki* who, despite the danger inherent in their religious mandate to conquer other countries, were still portrayed not only as human beings but also as cultural equals. In *Kirishitan monogatari*, the padres are grotesque beings whose features recall those of horses and owls, clearly placing them beneath the status of humans and in the lower level of animals. This association with animals is repeated in a

---

Organtino to some parisioners was signed with the phonetic *kanji* 於留岸 ("Urugan"). Ebisawa Arimichi, "'Kirishitan shūmon raichō jikki' kō," *Shūkyō kenkyū* no. 139, special edition, August 1954, 42. For more information about Organtino, see Cooper, *Rodrigues the Interpreter*.

45. The long noses of the Portuguese and Spaniards are particularly evident in the figures standing in profile. The priests depicted in Nanban art clearly are wearing the tonsure. *Japan Envisions the West: 16th-19th Century Japanese Art From Kobe City Museum* (Seattle: Seattle Art Museum, 2007), 56, 68, 70. In three separate Meiji prints depicting Commodore Matthew Perry and one depicting Henry A. Adams, the noses of the men also are conspicuously large. Ibid., 196, 209.
46. In one incident described by Luis Frois in a letter written in 1579, so many people came to see a black man (*moretto*) staying at the Jesuits' residence that Nobunaga heard of it and ordered the man brought before him. There, he had him strip to the waist because he doubted that the color was natural and believed it had been painted on. *Alcune lettere delle cose del Giappone Scritte da' Reverendi Padri della Compagnia di Iesu Dell' Anno 1579 insino al 1581* (Rome: Francesco Zanette, 1584), 136–37.
47. In another letter written in 1579, the priest Luis Frois describes crowds of people "marveling at the height of the Father [Valignano], and at the blackness of our Moor." Ibid., 133.

later section when the padres are accused of adopting "the manner of wild beasts" because everyday they eat "the flesh of cows, horses, swine, chickens, and meaner yet!"[48] Alternatively, the narrator speculates that they may be a *tengu* or a *mikoshi nyūdō*, both types of demons that have some of the physical characteristics described.[49] In fact, this demon status—still lowly but definitely more sinister than that of animals—is what is highlighted in the illustrations that were included in the second printing of *Kirishitan monogatari* in 1665 (see figures 3 and 4). In these, the face of the Padre is drawn with the classic features of the *tengu*, including the long, hooked nose that is part of the standard depiction of *tengu* but which, in fact, contradicts the text's description of the nose as resembling a conch shell. Overall, the physical description is a striking introduction to the Kirishitan of the tale, and one that sets the tone for a new kind of Kirishitan villain who is still a wily, would-be conqueror, but whose appearance first, and behavior later, mark him as an uncivilized and barbarian Other.

Following this introduction to Padre Urugan, the text describes him meeting Oda Nobunaga at his castle in Azuchi and delivering a variety of exotic gifts. In this scene, again, he is described disparagingly in his clerical habit as looking like "a bat spreading its wings."[50] And in another significant departure from the portrayal of the Kirishitan in *Baterenki*, whose activities were confined to the region of Kyushu and who had no contact with a centralized authority figure, the padre not only meets the leader of

48. Elison, *Deus Destroyed*, 337. In the early years of their mission, the Jesuits raised their own pigs, cows, and chickens around their residences and killed them for food, but the practice was later abolished by the Visitor, Alexandro Valignano. During his initial three-year visit from 1579 to 1582, Valignano composed a number of documents in which he reported on the state of the mission there and gave his recommendations for change. Central to those recommendations was the one that all members of the order should follow the customs of Japan as closely as possible so that their actions did not reflect poorly on the Christian faith. The model he proposed to follow in adapting to the culture was that of the Zen priest. Two of the most important documents Valignano produced on the subject were the *Sumario de las Cosas del Japon* and *Advertimientos e avisos acerca dos costumes e catangues de Jappão*. An annotated edition of the latter has been published under the title *Il Cerimoniale per i missionary del Giappone: Advertimentos e avisos acerca dos constumes e catangues de Jappão, di Alexandro Valignano*, Edizione critica, introduzione e note di Giuseppe Fr. Schutte, S.J. (Rome, 1946). A comprehensive study of Valignano and his work in English is Josef Schutte, S.J., *Valignano's Mission Principles in Japan*, vol. 1, translated by John J. Coyne, (St. Louis: The Institute of Jesuit Sources, 1985).
49. The association with *tengu* also could link the padre to the image of the *yamabushi*, which is a more pronounced characteristic in the description of the foreign padres in the later *Raichō jikki* narrative. Carolyn Morley points out that part of the medieval myth of the mountain priest (*yamabushi*), who was a common character in *kyōgen*, was that he could transform himself into a *tengu*. Carolyn Anne Morley, *Transformation, Miracles, and Mischief: The Mountain Priest Plays in Kyōgen* (Ithaca: Cornell East Asia Series, 1993), 55.
50. Elison, *Deus Destroyed*, 325.

Figure 3. Urugan Bateren arrives in Nagasaki. Illustration from the 1665 *Kirishitan taiji monogatari*.

Figure 4. Urugan Bateren presents his gifts to Oda Nobunaga. Illustration from the 1665 *Kirishitan taiji monogatari*.

Japan, he also presents gifts, almost as if he were an emissary.[51] In actuality, the Jesuits had formal audiences with Nobunaga as early as 1569. The fact that these and other events in the capital are included in *Kirishitan monogatari* and not in *Baterenki* may simply be because the two texts were written in different regions.[52] But as an important element of the image of the Kirishitan Other, meeting a central figure in the capital takes on greater significance, especially when this aspect of the tale is repeated and further developed in the later *Raichō jikki*. In both narratives, this early meeting between the leader of Japan and the Kirishitan enemy establishes the Kirishitan not just as a member of a new religion, but also as the representative of a foreign power on Japanese soil, emphasizing the threat of conquest he embodies.

The grotesque and barbaric nature of the Kirishitan villain in *Kirishitan monogatari* is not only confined to his appearance; it can be seen in his religious practices as well. The first criticism of Kirishitan religious practice comes in a section that in many ways seems to recall the explanation of Kirishitan beliefs in *Baterenki*. Rather ironically titled "On the Kirishitan *buppō* (仏法)," a description of the Kirishitan beliefs includes explanations of the meanings of such concepts as *paraiso* (paradise), *inferno* (hell), *confissão* (confession), and *cruz* (cross). As in *Baterenki*, most of the Portuguese and Latin terms that appear in *Kirishitan monogatari* retain the original meanings that were introduced by the missionaries, though there are considerably fewer in this later text. Only one term, *Quaresma* (くらりずも), which is the Portuguese word for Lent, is erroneously explained as a devotional practice similar to sutra reading in Japan. But another Portuguese term that was not included in *Baterenki* appears in this description of Kirishitan practices and, while accurate in its reference to missionary practices, also serves to build on the barbaric image of the priests. That term is *"penteisha"* (ぺんていしゃ, *penitencia* or penitence); it describes what the missionaries called *disciprinas*, or self-flagellation. It was practiced by the Jesuits and taught to their converts, and there are references in letters written by the early fathers to the zeal with which some

---

51. The later *Raichō jikki* narrative circulated under a variety of titles, the most common of which contain the word *raichō* (来朝). This term can simply refer to the act of coming to Japan, but can also mean "embassy," raising the presence of the Kirishitan/Nanbanjin on Japanese soil to that of a more official visit. See list of titles for *Raichō jikki* in the appendix.
52. References to the audiences with Nobunaga are in Elison, *Deus Destroyed*, 25. Ebisawa Arimichi writes that *Baterenki* is thought to have been written in the Hakata region of Kyushu sometime in the middle of the Keichō era (1596–1615), but after 1607. Ebisawa, *Kirishitanshi no kenkyū*, 208.

of the converts participated.⁵³ In *Kirishitan monogatari*, the believer "flogs his back with an object somewhat like a fly-swatter spiked with copper thorns, besmirching himself with blood."⁵⁴ Later, a padre flogs a penitent believer who is begging forgiveness for his sins and who then, "without washing his hands, offers up prayers to the Buddha. And they call this great indeed!"⁵⁵ Though ascetic practices had long been a part of some Buddhist sects, the Kirishitan practice is clearly objectionable because of the pollution caused by the spilling of blood and then the act of praying while still stained with that blood. To the reader from a culture steeped in the syncretic traditions of Shinto and Buddhism with their strong emphasis on purification before worship, the image of the bloody Kirishitan praying must have been shocking indeed.

The above description is one of several instances in the chapter on the "Kirishitan *buppō*" in which the beliefs and practices of the Kirishitan, which were explained in a rather neutral tone in *Baterenki*, are criticized or ridiculed in *Kirishitan monogatari*. After enumerating several of the Kirishitan practices, including confession, saying the rosary (*contas*), and *penitencia*, the judgment of the narrator is that they represent "all the profundity of a saucer's depths!"⁵⁶ Believers who would be tortured or killed for the sake of salvation (or "Buddhahood," as it is described in the text) are called pitiful. And in the final paragraph of the section, the sect is indicted as not only a false path but one that more closely resembles magic than religion:

> Once a fool has turned a ready ear to something and set his heart on it, nothing will change his mind. To use an analogy: a child of two or three in seeing a reflection in a mirror thinks it an actual figure; a monkey in seeing the moon on the surface of the water tries to grab it with his paws—for such is the simplicity of their minds. All fools are like that. But heretical doctrine must be of deviltry.⁵⁷

53. In a letter written by the priest João Fernandez in 1561, the *disciprinas* merely consisted of pounding the chest (*golpes de pecho*). Manuscripts Jap Sin 4, 209, Jesuit Archives, Rome. But in a letter by Luis Frois in 1582, the priest speaks approvingly of converts during Holy Week being "covered in blood from their disciplines." Manuscripts Jap Sin 9 I, 153, Jesuit Archives, Rome.
54. Elison, *Deus Destroyed*, 329. In the later *Nanbanji monogatari* variant of the *Raichō jikki* narrative, the device is rather comically described as resembling a radish grater (だいこんおろし).
55. Ibid., 331. The "Buddha" here is written as *hotoke* (佛) in the original text, and refers to Deus. This is a good example of how Buddhist terminology is used to describe the Kirishitan beliefs.
56. Ibid., 329.
57. Ibid., 331.

In the final sentence, the words that Elison translates as "heretical doctrine" and "deviltry" are *gedō* (外道) and *mahō* (魔法), respectively. This is the first use among the two early anti-Kirishitan texts of either term in reference to the Kirishitan religion, though it is called *gedō* several more times later in *Kirishitan monogatari*. But the single reference to *mahō* here is of particular interest because of the development of that theme in the later *Raichō jikki* narrative. In the context of the passage above, *mahō* seems to be related to heresy and refer to unorthodox practices. But in *Raichō jikki*, the reference is expanded considerably, and the padres are represented as having magical powers that they teach to their converts. The first use of the word *mahō* here is significant in light of the fact that the association of the Kirishitan with magic is developed and reinforced in eighteenth century narrative and theater, and becomes a significant part of the overall image of the Kirishitan Other.[58]

Another way that the Kirishitan religion and the padres themselves are discredited in *Kirishitan monogatari* is by linking them only to the most gullible members of Japanese society, including the uneducated and the diseased. In the passage quoted above, the narrator stresses that only the foolish (*gujin*), who are no better than children or monkeys, would ever be swayed by the Kirishitan teachings, and in other passages the reader learns that the Kirishitan were able to attract followers only by giving them gifts and money, or by curing them of disease. The money is sent on a yearly basis by the "King of Nanban" and is sufficient to give some to every believer.[59] Converts also join to have the chance to taste the meats that the Kirishitan padres are accused of eating, but which most Japanese people of the time did not. Potential converts from all levels of society are given gifts according to their station, so that beggars are fed a meal, while young men are given trendy, flashy gifts.[60] And "those whom they deemed as great lords they flattered with gifts of baubles and beads, long-seeing spectacles, and similar fare."[61]

---

58. Though *mahō* appears for the first time in print with *Kirishitan monogatari*, accusations about the missionaries and their practice of magic were much older. Ikuo Higashibaba cites a reference to Christianity as *mahō* in the diary of the Shinto Yoshida family as early as 1551. Higashibaba, *Christianity in Early Modern Japan*, 46. In a letter from Juan Fernandez to Francis Xavier, also written in 1551, Fernandez reports that people in the Yamaguchi area were associating the priests with the supernatural, saying that a demon had told them that the missionaries were his disciples. They also reported that the missionaries ate men. Juan G. Ruiz de Medina, ed., *Monumenta Historica Japoniae*, vol. 2 (Rome: Instituto Historico de la Compania de Jesus, 1990), 258.
59. Elison, *Deus Destroyed*, 337.
60. Elison translates *date dōgu* (伊達道具) as "newfangled bric-a-brac." Ibid., 332.
61. Ibid.

This representation of the Kirishitan converts as being motivated only by greed and not by a clear understanding of doctrine is underscored even more by their behavior in a section relating the arrest of a group of Kirishitan converts in Kyoto in 1614. George Elison points out that Western accounts of the historical event describe brutal tortures inflicted on the captives that are far more severe than those described in *Kirishitan monogatari*.[62] But in the tale, the Kirishitan are happy to chant "*zensumaru*" (Jesus Mary) and encourage each other until they begin to grow hungry, at which time many of them quickly apostatize. The remaining "faithful" follow suit after they have been threatened with burning at the stake. Onlookers are scornful that the captives' devotion to the Kirishitan teachings is as shallow as the appetites that presumably attracted them to it in the first place.

Another way that the Kirishitan attract converts in the tale is by healing the sick, and particularly those afflicted with leprosy. Though this may seem laudable, it is clear from the tone of the narrator that it is yet more proof of the Kirishitan's status as barbaric Other. The association of the missionaries with healing is strong in both historical accounts and popular ones, and scenes in which the padres cure patients with leprosy appear in all three major expulsion narratives about the Kirishitan. One of the earliest Jesuits to arrive in Japan, Luis de Almeida, established a hospital in Oita that took in patients suffering from leprosy and syphilis, but it only operated for a few years.[63] Though the Jesuits supported converts' efforts at helping the sick, they avoided directly working with them. In fact, among the many recommendations made in 1583 by the Visitor Alexandro Valignano to better adapt the missions to Japanese society, one was a prohibition against treating lepers and those with venereal disease precisely because they were so despised in Japanese society that any association with them reflected badly on the order.[64] No such prohibition was observed by the Franciscans when they arrived in the early 1590s, and by 1603 they had established a total of six hospitals in Japan, including in the

---

62. Ibid., 216–17. See also note 67 on page 487.
63. Charles F. Boxer, *The Christian Century in Japan 1549-1650* (Berkeley: University of California Press, 1951), 202–4. Despite the short duration of the hospital founded by Almeida, his reputation as a healer in Kyushu is commemorated in three different monuments to him, one in Nagasaki and two in Oita.
64. One exception to this rule was the Santiago Hospital in Nagasaki that had a special ward for leprosy patients, and which was supported by local confraternities organized by the Jesuits. For more on Valignano's views, see Boxer, *The Christian Century*, 204. For more on the hospital see Diego Pacheco, "Diogo De Mesquita, S.J. And the Jesuit Mission Press," *Monumenta Nipponica* 25, no. 4 (1971): 431–43.

cities of Kyoto, Osaka, and Edo, where they treated a number of patients with leprosy and syphilis, among other illnesses.[65]

Rather surprisingly, the distinction between the Jesuit and Franciscan practices is subtly alluded to in the *Kirishitan monogatari* section describing the treatment of the sick. The text notes that during the Bunroku period (1593–96), a number of padres called *furaten* came to Japan. It goes on to say that these padres

> went out on the streets and gathered beggars and the outcasts of society about them. They gave remarkable medical treatment to the harelipped, to lepers, to wretches afflicted with boils and carbuncles, with the Chinese pox and with mange, thus enticing them to join their religion.[66]

The term *furaten* is thought to be the Japanese pronunciation of *fratrum*, so in *Kirishitan monogatari* the association of the padres with the ill and outcasts of society seems to be referring specifically to the practices of the Franciscans and not to all padres.[67] But this distinction is absent in other references to the padres' healing that appear in *Baterenki* and the later *Nanbanji monogatari*, and certainly is not observed in the overall representation of the Kirishitan Other. To varying degrees in all of the tales, the Kirishitan association with the physically deformed and outcastes of society clearly places them at the same social level as those unfortunates, and contributes to their representation as barbarians. This link is further strengthened in *Kirishitan monogatari* and the later *Raichō jikki*, where the grotesque appearance of the padres, in which they resemble animals and demons, seems to be echoed in the disfigured bodies of the outcasts who are their converts.

The criticism described above of the Kirishitan religious beliefs and of the barbaric nature of the padres and their converts is all laid out in the first five sections of *Kirishitan monogatari*. It is in the sixth section, however, in which a Japanese lay monk debates a brother that all of the worst traits of the Kirishitan imagined in the tale are combined and embodied in the despicable character of Fabian. This part of the narrative

---

65. Elison, *Deus Destroyed*, 478–79, n. 17. For more on the healing practices of the missionaries see, Ebisawa Arimichi, *Kirishitan no shakai katsudō oyobi nanban igaku* (Tokyo: Fuzanbō, 1944), 182–231.
66. Elison, *Deus Destroyed*, 332.
67. We see, however, that such a distinction is lost on the author of the later *Raichō jikki* narrative, who uses the same word *furaten* as the name of one of the padre villains in that tale. *Furaten* for *fratrum* is thought to come from the Latin name for the Franciscans, *Ordo Fratrum Minorum*. See ibid., 332–34.

conventionally has been seen as the fictional representation of a historical debate thought to have been held between Hayashi Razan and the Kirishitan convert Fabian Fucan. As one of the few scenes rendered both in *Kirishitan monogatari* and *Raichō jikki*, it plays an important role in the construction of the Kirishitan Other.[68] In the tale, the debate between the learned ascetic Hakuo Koji and the Kirishitan Fabian is arranged in Kyoto after a Kirishitan brother tries to convert the widow of a daimyo and she expresses an interest in hearing the arguments of both the Kirishitan and the more established Buddhist sects. Hakuo is introduced as a selfless ascetic whose life of abstinence has allowed him to master the teachings and mysteries of a number of branches of Buddhism and also to study Shinto. Fabian, on the other hand, is described the following way:

> It appears he had been a Zen monk originally and then turned renegade. The insides of his eyes kept turning round and round, and his mouth also kept revolving, with a flood of words like swift-running water, and never a hitch.[69]

The substance of their debate is clearly meant for an audience with only the most basic understanding of Buddhism, though the logic of the arguments is interesting. It is also notable that Fabian's argument in the tale is similar to one he makes in *Myōtei mondō*. He argues that Deus created the world and existed before that creation, but that the gods and bud-

---

68. Fabian apparently represented the Jesuits in a debate with Hayashi Razan (1583–1657), a former Buddhist priest who became an important Neo-Confucian scholar of the period. Razan wrote an account of the meeting in an essay titled *Haiyaso* ("The Anti-Jesus") that was included in a collection of Razan's essays compiled by his son. Ebisawa, *Kirishitansho, haiyasho*, 490–91 and 413–17. Elison includes an English translation of *Haiyaso* (which he translates as "The Anti-Jesuit") in *Deus Destroyed*, 149–53. Though the Jesuits did not publish their own account of the meeting, there is mention of a debate between a brother who was the most knowledgeable regarding Buddhism (presumably Fabian) and an eminent Buddhist priest in which, not surprisingly, Fabian manages to silence his opponent with his vast understanding; the priest is left bowed and chastened. In a 2006 article on Razan and Fabian, Kiri Paramore argues that the essay by Razan could be a "fabrication" because it more closely resembles Razan's writings of the 1650s, and because the arguments attributed to Fabian bear little resemblance to his writing in *Myōtei mondō*. Paramore speculates that Razan may have written his account of the encounter much later, or that the encounter may never have taken place. While the argument for Razan's essay being written later is thought provoking, the suggestion that they never met contradicts not only Razan's own assertion, but also Jesuit sources that imply such a meeting took place (though they do not name the protagonists). For more on the Jesuit references, see Elison, *Deus Destroyed*, 153–54. Kiri Paramore, "Hayashi Razan's Redeployment of Anti-Christian Discourse: The Fabrication of Haiyaso," *The Japan Forum* 18, no. 2 (2006): 185–206.
69. Elison, *Deus Destroyed*, 343.

dhas of Japan were originally all humans, and therefore *of* that creation and not really gods. In his response, Hakuo questions how Deus could be the one creator of the world but not be known in the Three Kingdoms (India, China and Japan), for if he truly were the creator of all human beings, wouldn't he have also created one religion for all of them so there would be no need to travel thousands of miles to spread the doctrine? He also says that all things in the world have a purpose, but what would the purpose of creating humans have been for Deus? Did he create them to be his playthings, and is that why they nailed him to a cross?

Hakuo's arguments against the Kirishitan beliefs are portrayed as decisive blows to the credibility of the Kirishitan doctrine, and Fabian's behavior in the debate only strengthens the image of the Kirishitan as deceitful barbarians with no education or manners. When he cannot come up with a rebuttal to Hakuo's arguments, he peevishly proposes to prove the primacy of Deus by showing the audience that he can urinate and defecate on the roof of any of the major Japanese shrines without repercussions. Hakuo responds by saying that the gods don't generally punish animals for their transgressions, recalling the associations made earlier in the text of the Kirishitan with animals. This association is taken even further at the end of the debate, after Hakuo has accused Fabian of selling his heresy to "the idiots, the ignorant, the animal-like dolts among your followers."[70] Fabian cannot think of a reply and "merely gulped with his mouth, as though choking on a peach, and finally he let out a wail like a dog's when he turns tail and runs."[71] He flees in defeat, and the Kirishitan never bother the widow again. This performance by the base and clearly uncivilized Fabian is the first time in the tale that the reader has witnessed in detail the behavior of an individual Kirishitan, but it clearly supports the characterization of the sect's members that was drawn in the preceding chapters as barbarians whose behavior marks them as Other. That this particular Kirishitan is also Japanese is of interest as well. By defeating him handily before a Japanese audience in the story and for the readers, Hakuo has shown not only that the Kirishitan beliefs fall outside of the Japanese religious tradition, but also that association with the Kirishitan risks Othering within Japanese society.

In a sermon by Hakuo that follows the debate scene, the status of the Kirishitan as Other in opposition to the Japanese national religious tradition is stressed further. Hakuo firmly states that there is only one Buddhist law, not two, and that "since Japan is the Land of the Gods, [the people]

---

70. Ibid., 348.
71. Ibid.

must first of all believe in the gods and Buddhas and worship them ... and mornings they must pray for peace in the Empire, security in the land, and respect for the ruler."[72] Here, the dual traditions of Shinto and Buddhism are linked to a national identity, and active participation in them is presented as the duty of a good citizen. This serves as a reminder that following the correct path of Buddhism is essential not only for the individual's well-being but also that of the state, and contributes to a discourse on a Japanese identity that is discussed further below.

Up to this point in the tale, the Kirishitan have been described as grotesque, demonlike beings who teach a false religion to which they attract converts by tempting them with gifts, money, and medicines to cure the most intractable diseases. The motives of the converts are to attain the comforts of life in this world, and the fact that the foreign padres cater to those desires clearly marks their religion as a wrong path in the Buddhist context in which it is examined in the tale. But the padres' motive for coming to Japan and seeking out these converts is not clear until the eighth section of the tale, which reports that a monk who was a disgraced Kirishitan brother sought revenge on the sect and told the Tokugawa government of their true intentions. In a scene reminiscent of that at the end of the *Baterenki*, the former Kirishitan tells the authorities that the Kirishitan presence in Japan is all part of a plot by the King of South Barbary to use "his brand of Buddhism" to gain adherents who will then help him to "subjugate Japan."[73] The Kirishitan eventually confess to their plot, and their followers are ordered to leave the sect immediately or face punishment.

The remaining sections of the tale describe the measures taken to root out the ones who continued to practice in hiding, such as registration at Buddhist temples and rewards for turning in padres, brothers, or believers.[74] They also describe ways that the captured Kirishitan are punished,

---

72. Ibid., 352. The Japanese text reads, 先ず日本は神国なるによって、諸神諸佛信じ奉り ... 朝には天下泰平国土安穏主人愛敬と祈る. Hiyane, *Kirishitan mo-nogatari hoka sanpen*, 23.
73. Elison, *Deus Destroyed*, 355. The passage in *Kirishitan monogatari* does not identify the informant by name as *Baterenki* did, and it dates the event much later. *Baterenki* has the informant, Chijiwa Seizaimon, reporting on the Kirishitan to Ōmura around 1607, while the informant of *Kirishitan monogatari* reports to Tokugawa Ieyasu in the Genna Period (1615–24). This later period is also the time when the historical Fabian produced his anti-Kirishitan text, the *Ha Daiusu*, and Elison speculates that the informant in *Kirishitan monogatari* may be modeled after him. Ibid., 486–87, n. 66.
74. The narrative describes notice boards announcing rewards, which were known to have been posted widely and with increasingly large rewards for decades after the expulsion. Higashibaba, *Christianity in Early Modern Japan*, 144–45.

including the roundup of believers in Kyoto mentioned earlier, as well as various methods of torture, such as burning, the water torture, and crucifixion. Additional chapters relating the events of the Shimabara Rebellion and offering advice on how to manage subordinates in order to avoid such rebellions round out the tale. In this latter half of the narrative, descriptions of the Kirishitan appearance and behavior give way to accounts of their persecution and defeat, and a final paragraph exults that "the Kirishitans were exterminated" and that not only the nation, but also the three traditions of Confucianism, Shinto, and Buddhism, are safe and secure. In these final words of a work written shortly after the decisive defeat of the rebels in Shimabara, the reader can discern relief at the escape of Japan from the foreign threat, as well as hope for a lasting victory.

In the thirty years that elapsed between the production of *Baterenki* and *Kirishitan monogatari*, the figure of the Kirishitan clearly evolved significantly.[75] While still characterized as the secret weapon of a foreign king bent on taking over Japan, the Kirishitan padre in the later text is at once more powerful and more despicable. The padres of the *Baterenki* were sent by the pope in Rome, but the padres of the later text are dispatched by the king of the rather indistinct "Nanban," who is rich enough to send "the income of five or ten provinces of his country toward the needs of his Japanese undertaking."[76] *Nanban*, which originally referred to the fact that Iberian missionaries and traders came from the south (*nan*) and from the barbarian reaches outside of the Sino-centric realm of influence (*ban*), in this tale is transformed into the name of a country that seems to be the single origin of all of the undesirable foreigners. And in *Kirishitan monogatari*, those foreigners are not confined to Nagasaki and the Kyushu region as they were in *Baterenki*; they have penetrated the capital and the countryside, and even had audiences with the leader of the country. Their skill at attracting converts has been alarmingly successful, as is evident in the approximately 37,000 souls who marched under Kirishitan banners in the Shimabara Rebellion. Despite, or perhaps because of this power, the foreign Kirishitan in *Kirishitan monogatari* are despised for their uncivilized behavior and false religion, their barbarian status made manifest in their own grotesque appearance and that of their often disfigured converts, who further demonstrate their base nature by joining for the sake of money and gifts. Though the final paragraphs of *Kirishitan monogatari* trumpet the success of the Kirishitan expulsion and the ultimate victory

---

75. The reference to thirty years is approximate, based on the printing of *Kirishitan monogatari* in 1639 and the likely production of *Baterenki* between 1607 and 1614.
76. Elison, *Deus Destroyed*, 355.

of Japan, there remains throughout the work a current of unease at how close the country came to conquest "without even a battle fought with bow and arrow."[77]

The changes in the figure of the Kirishitan obviously were influenced by the fact that the missionaries had disappeared from communities, and their converts had been outlaws for decades by the time *Kirishitan monogatari* was written. Many events that are chronicled in the later text, including the initial expulsion, the roundup of Kirishitan converts in Kyoto, and the Shimabara Rebellion, all represent the Kirishitan as objects of national censure, and all of the Kirishitan, whether foreign or Japanese, are clearly Other within the context of Japanese society. In this later text, the crime of the Kirishitan is not just the plot to subdue Japan that it was in *Baterenki*. It is also their presumed corruption of the most vulnerable in society by catering to their worldly desires for life and wealth, and by luring them away from the traditions that are identified in the tale as part of their Japanese identity.

The strong influences of Confucianism and Buddhism in the more detailed representation of the Kirishitan are actually part of another expanded character in the tale—that of Japan itself. In *Kirishitan monogatari*, Japan is presented as a unified entity with a strong central authority whose identity is rooted in a shared religious tradition within Japan and a broader history of practice and transmission within the three realms.[78] In *Baterenki*, the gods protected Japan from the pope's ships in the form of the "evil winds," but in *Kirishitan monogatari* the central authority, embodied in the figures of Oda Nobunaga, Toyotomi Hideyoshi, and Tokugawa Ieyasu, acts to expel the barbarian and to protect the gods. Echoing the edicts of both Hideyoshi and Tokugawa Ieyasu, the text links that authority to religious tradition by proclaiming that Japan is the land of the gods and buddhas, and is supported by the three traditions of Shinto, Buddhism, and Confucianism.[79] And lest there be any confusion about whether the Kirishitan beliefs are a legitimate form of Buddhism, in his debate with Fabian and the subsequent sermon, the priest Hakuo asserts that there is only one Buddhist Law, and the true path is the one that can be found in the ancient Japanese and Chinese texts.[80] If the Kirishitan version of the

---

77. Ibid., 355.
78. Ibid., 374.
79. Ibid. In fact, Hideyoshi's edict says more simply that Japan is the land of the gods (*kami*), while Ieyasu's edict more explicitly states the roles of the three traditions of Shinto, Buddhism, and Confucianism. See Higashibaba, *Christianity in Early Modern Japan*, 127–40.
80. Elison, *Deus Destroyed*, 345. Hakuō explicitly cites the *Nihongi* (History of Japan) as a source.

Law were true, why is it not present in any of those texts? Hakuo also links good religious practice with the duties of the Japanese subject when he says that the people "must first of all believe in the gods and Buddhas and worship them . . . and mornings they must pray for peace in the Empire, security in the land, and respect for the ruler."[81] In this way, the expanded image of the barbaric Kirishitan Other in *Kirishitan monogatari* is matched by, and constructed in opposition to, an expanded image of Japan as a sacred and unified realm that would remain fundamental in all of the future iterations of the anti-Kirishitan tales.

The fact that *Kirishitan monogatari* was one of a number of early seventeenth-century texts that invoked the subject of Yamato or Dai Nihon was noted earlier. In her work on the influence of print in the early modern period, Mary Elizabeth Berry identified this trend as part of an effort on the part of printers to focus on the shared experiences of a "national" readership. Berry traces the development of a larger audience for the new publishing industry to a confluence of events, including urbanization, the spread of literacy, and disposable wealth, but also to competition among publishers that provoked the need to imagine a new kind of audience with common interests that transcended social status, education, and residence. Works that featured Nihon or Yamato as a subject often dealt with recent battles and wartime activities and appealed to a diverse audience whose common ground was that of the shared crisis of war. Certainly, at the time that *Kirishitan monogatari* was printed in 1639, the more immediate shared crisis was the Shimabara Rebellion, which surprised the bakufu with its persistence and eventually required over one hundred thousand fighters from sixteen different houses before it was put down in 1638.[82] The story of this battle and the victory of the bakufu over foreign and destabilizing influences clearly was one of the more popular battle tales in this period, appearing as it did in two separate printings of *Kirishitan monogatari* and at least five printings of *Shimabaraki* over the course of only about seventy years.[83]

However, tales of war that threatened the stability of Nihon were not the only way to find common ground through crisis. Certainly the decades-long campaign against the Kirishitan, and even the broader encounter with the West, were also destabilizing forces that served as potent catalysts for explorations of identity in texts that imagined Nihon in Asia

---

81. Ibid., 351–52.
82. Ibid., 192.
83. *Kirishitan monogatari* was printed in 1639 and again as *Kirishitan taiji monogatari* in 1665. See earlier for information on the printings of *Shimabaraki*.

and the world. The hunt for Kirishitan believers was a national campaign that was felt at the local level, as thousands were arrested and punished in various towns and cities starting in 1614 and continuing through the years of the Shimabara Rebellion and beyond.[84] Also, by 1635, the temple registration that began in Kyoto to keep track of former Kirishitan was extended to become a practice required by all Japanese people, making every person in the country a participant in the search for members of the outlawed sect.[85] In view of this, the crisis of the Kirishitan was not limited to the Shimabara Rebellion and the destabilizing influence of war; it was felt in the everyday lives of people around the country. *Kirishitan monogatari* clearly responded to a level of anxiety caused by the Kirishitan crisis by explaining its origins and warning readers about the pernicious Kirishitan doctrine and how to distinguish those influenced by it. It also offered advice on what the "true" Buddhist path and, by extension, the true Japanese tradition were, and in doing so it provided a detailed examination not only of the Kirishitan Other, but also of the identity of that Other's opposite, Japan.

That the representation of the Kirishitan in *Kirishitan monogatari* conflates them with all Nanbanjin also indicates that the Kirishitan Other became the repository of a broader anxiety caused by Japan's encounter with the West or, as Ronald Toby calls it, the "Iberian irruption."[86] In his study on representations of Other in Japanese visual media of the seventeenth century, Ronald Toby stresses the importance of Japan's engagement with the early Portuguese and Spanish missionaries and traders in changing "the field on which Japanese dialogues of Self and Other were played out" in the seventeenth century.[87] According to Toby, while Japan had many Others prior to the arrival of the first Westerners in the sixteenth century, in visual media those Others were consistently represented as "Chinese," and they were always "out there." By this he means that in visual representations of these Others, they were rarely shown on Japanese soil, and usually in their imagined places of origin. But with the arrival of the Ibe-

---

84. Though the number of those arrested had fallen off in the years before the rebellion and was also low immediately after it, arrests picked up again in the late 1650s and 1660s. Of those arrests, the majority took place in parts of Kyushu and in the Gokinai region. For details on the arrests and punishments, see Anesaki Masaharu, *Kirishitan shūmon no hakugai to senpuku* (Tokyo: Dōbunkan, 1925).
85. Higashibaba, *Christianity in Early Modern Japan*, 147.
86 Ronald P. Toby, "The 'Indianness' of Iberia and Changing Japanese Iconographies of Other," in *Implicit Understandings: Observing, Reporting, and Reflecting on the Encounters Between Europeans and Other Peoples in the Early Modern Era*, edited by Stuart B. Schwartz (Cambridge: Cambridge University Press, 1994), 323.
87. Ibid., 344–45.

rian traders and missionaries, the first "new" Other in almost a thousand years was suddenly "in here," and art began to depict the Westerners on Japanese soil.[88] This prompted a new exploration of Self and Other, resulting in "the pervasive presence of Other in the performative, literary, and artistic Japanese landscape after 1550—even after the expulsion of the Iberian interloper."[89] But Toby goes on to note that not long after the final expulsion of the Iberians, the Westerners disappeared from representations of the Other "in here" and were replaced by the more traditional Others of China, Korea, and the Ryukyus.

Though the Westerner may have been displaced by Asian Others in visual media after the expulsion, we can see in *Kirishitan monogatari* that the Iberians did not disappear from the written text, and in fact survived in the figure of the Kirishitan/Nanbanjin that was perpetuated in texts like *Kirishitan monogatari*.[90] It is striking that in *Baterenki*, which was produced while the missionaries were still active in Japan, most of the action takes place in Rome or on the ocean, and very little of it in Japan. However, in *Kirishitan monogatari* and later narratives like it that were written after the final expulsion of 1639, the preoccupation is with the Kirishitan in Japan. Despite the chronicle of the various Kirishitan defeats and the claims of final victory at the end of *Kirishitan monogatari*, clearly the Kirishitan—and Nanbanjin—are still "in here."

Historically, it is true that for some time after the first expulsion and even after the Shimabara Rebellion, some foreign missionaries were still in Japan. Between 1614 and 1643, over one hundred missionaries tried to enter Japan secretly to continue proselytizing converts, but most were easily distinguished as foreigners and quickly imprisoned or killed. More alarming, perhaps, were the hidden Japanese converts who continued to be caught and subjected to torture. Unlike the foreign padres, these converts often lived and worked in their communities and showed no outward sign of difference. Observers may have been forgiven for wondering how to distinguish a Kirishitan from a law-abiding citizen. Clearly, "in here" had taken on a whole new meaning as the "foreign" sect now had a Japanese face, and it is perhaps not surprising that the narrator of *Kirishitan monogatari* goes to such lengths to describe not only the actions of the Kirishitan followers, but also the proper behavior of loyal Japanese who followed the "true" path of Buddhism.

88. Ibid., 324.
89. Ibid., 344–45.
90. The Kirishitan also are depicted on Japanese soil in one set of illustrations that were included in the 1665 reprint of *Kirishitan monogatari*. None of the extant *Raichō jikki* manuscripts examined by this author included illustrations.

In 1665, the *Kirishitan monogatari* narrative was reprinted under the title *Kirishitan taiji monogatari*. The new version is nearly identical to the original, except for the addition of illustrations and the deletion of the concluding paragraphs. The absence of those final paragraphs that trumpeted the victory of Japan over the Kirishitan and assured the reader that the foreign sect had not managed to gain a foothold in the country is significant considering the second printing coincided with a wave of arrests of hidden Japanese Kirishitan in Kyushu and in the Mino/Owari region in the early 1660s. Despite the nearly fifteen years of relative calm after the Shimabara Rebellion, the Kirishitan were still being found. The reprint appeared at the same time as two other works on the Kirishitan were printed, and it seemed to be responding to a renewed interest in, or anxiety about, the presence of the foreigners and their followers.[91] However, the production of *Kirishitan taiji monogatari* was stopped by the authorities, presumably for dealing with a topic deemed too sensitive by the bakufu, which had recently begun to take an interest in controlling information in print.[92] From that time on, books on the Kirishitan were avoided by printers, and no text on the subject made it into print until the Meiji period.

In early modern Japan, however, censorship of printed works did not preclude sensitive topics from circulating in manuscript, often through the lending libraries, and the story of the Kirishitan did not end with the aborted second printing of *Kirishitan monogatari* in 1665. Beginning sometime in the early eighteenth century, the basic outlines of the narrative

---

91. Suzuki Shōsan's *Ha Kirishitan* (translated by Elison as "Christians Countered") is thought to have been compiled from the sermons he preached in the Amakusa in an attempt to re-orient residents' views on Buddhism after the rebellion. *Ha Kirishitan* was first printed after Shōsan's death, in 1662, and later was included as the third section of Asai Ryōi's *Kirishitan hakyaku ronden* (Account of the Destruction of the Kirishitan) which appeared sometime between 1660 and 1666 and was primarily an account of the Shimabara Rebellion. In his work, Shōsan claims that the arguments for the existence of Deus make no sense, and that the teachings of the Kirishitan not only create attachment and lead people away from the True Law of Buddhism, but also pervert and oppose the tradition of honoring one's superior as a way of honoring the gods and buddhas. Shōsan links reverence for the gods and buddhas of Japan with the Japanese people's duty to their superiors and their long-held traditions, and states that the goal of the Kirishitan is only to annex Japan to their home of Nanban. The text of *Ha Kirishitan* 破吉理支丹, can be found in Washio, *Nihon shisō tōsō shiryo*, 31–39, or in Ebisawa, *Kirishitanshō, haiyasho*. For more on Suzuki Shōsan and for an English translation of *Ha Kirishitan*, see Elison, *Deus Destroyed*, 223–31 and 375–78. Ryōi's *Kirishitan hakyaku ronden* is reprinted in Shinmura, *Kaihyō sōsho*, vol. 1.
92. There is no evidence of a specific ban on the topic of Christianity in print, but the ban on *Kirishitan taiji monogatari* and one other text dealing with Christianity at the time appears to have led to self-censorship on that topic among printers and booksellers. Kornicki, *The Book in Japan*, 332.

were picked up and expanded with more characters and even more villainous padres, so that the story of the arrival of the Kirishitan, their near conquest of Japan, and their ultimate expulsion continued to circulate into the nineteenth century. This later narrative was not printed until the Meiji period, but an unusually large number of extant manuscripts under a wide range of titles attests to its continued reproduction and dissemination over a long period. Though the campaign against the Kirishitan was over by the eighteenth century, the repeated engagement with and degradation of the Kirishitan Other that played out in the narrative for nearly two hundred more years displays a lasting anxiety not only about the continued effects of the Kirishitan/Nanbanjin intrusion but also about the implications of that event for a knowable Japanese identity.

Chapter 3

Imagining the Kirishitan, Japan, and the World in *Kirishitan shūmon raichō jikki*

Sometime in the Kyōhō era, a new Kirishitan villain appeared in a narrative that promised a record of the Kirishitan arrival and expulsion in Japan. *Kirishitan shūmon raichō jikki*, or "True Account of the Arrival of the Kirishitan sect" (hereafter *Raichō jikki*), is perhaps the most common of the more than sixty-five different titles under which the narrative survives in manuscript copies at libraries throughout Japan. Like the villains of *Kirishitan monogatari*, to which the narrative clearly owes a debt, the *Raichō jikki* padres are grotesque, uncouth, and conniving, but in this text they are also possessed of magical powers that allow them to fly, to transform things, and to divine the future. Yet even as they have become more transgressive, the ways in which they transgress fall into more familiar tropes of Otherness from traditional Japanese literature. Exotic in their difference but also reminiscent of the wicked Buddhist priests of *setsuwa* literature, the padres come to Japan as servants of the Nanban king who has ordered them to use their religion to sway the people into giving up their country to him, and they represent an image of the Kirishitan Other set in opposition to a sacred Japan that would circulate for another hundred and fifty years.

Because it was about a topic that was forbidden in print, the *Raichō jikki* narrative circulated only in manuscript until it was first printed in the Meiji period.[1] Nonetheless, there are more than 150 manuscript copies extant. That number would be remarkable under normal circumstances

---

1. The narrative was printed for the first time as *Nanbanji kōhaiki* in 1868.

even for a popular printed text from the early eighteenth century, but it is extraordinary considering the fact that the text and its topic were both subject to censorship. The numbers suggest a wide diffusion of the text during the eighteenth century and the likelihood that the image of the Kirishitan villain was a broadly familiar one. They also show the continued influence of manuscript culture in Japan, even as commercial printing flourished. An important factor in the dissemination of manuscripts and forbidden texts, including many in the *jitsuroku* genre like the *Raichō jikki* narrative, was the growing popularity of the lending library, which provided cheaper access to reading material and was also less regulated by the self-censorship of the booksellers' and printers' guilds.

MANUSCRIPT CULTURE AND THE "TRUE ACCOUNT" IN THE EDO PERIOD

When the second printing of *Kirishitan monogatari* was banned by authorities in 1665, the print industry and its audience for books already were significantly different from what they had been when the work was first printed in 1639. Samurai were the primary audience for printed works of the early seventeenth century, but by the latter half of the century that audience had grown to include merchants and even some farmers.[2] Contributing to this change were greater access to education for commoners through *terakoya*, or temple schools, and private academies, as well as an increase in leisure time and disposable income, particularly among the merchant class. The printing industry responded quickly to the growth in the audience for books. Production in the first half of the seventeenth century was slow compared to the rest of the Tokugawa period, but even so, the estimated five hundred newly printed works in the period from 1597 to the middle of the seventeenth century were more than all of the books printed in the previous two centuries.[3] Production increased dramatically after that, with one scholar estimating that three thousand titles were published on average each year in the Tokugawa period.[4] Most of these books

---

2. Kornicki points out that the publication of farming guides near the end of the seventeenth century indicates an audience of literate farmers existed for them. Peter Kornicki, *The Book in Japan: a Cultural History From the Beginnings to the Nineteenth Century* (Honolulu: University of Hawai'i Press, 2001), 273. The following information on the book trade and reading audiences primarily comes from Kornicki's book.
3. Ibid., 175.
4. Kornicki cites the work of Raymond G. Nunn, but also speculates that this number could be low because it does not include reprints of Chinese or Buddhist works, which were numerous. Raymond G. Nunn, "On the Number of Books Published in Japan From 1600 to 1868," in *East Asian Occasional Papers (1)*, edited by Harry Jerome Lamley, Asian Studies at Hawaii (Honolulu: University of Hawaii, 1969).; Kornicki, *The Book in Japan*, 140.

were commercially published, and they included contemporary prose literature and classic texts, playbooks, and a host of encyclopedias, guides, manuals, almanacs, directories, and travel accounts that made up what Mary Elizabeth Berry calls the "library of public information."[5]

Some of the more popular prose literature works were accounts of battles and of scandals in various domains, and these were the first works to draw the critical eye of the bakufu. The earliest documented cases of censorship of domestic books were in 1649 and 1659, both for books dealing with Toyotomi Hideyoshi and some of his military campaigns. There was no national edict at that time specifically banning books about Hideyoshi, but one 1657 edict about publishing issued in Kyoto requires those wanting to publish "Japanese military books" to apply first. A later 1673 edict is more specific about prohibiting certain military histories, stories about the Tokugawa or about Hideyoshi, and anything "unusual" (*mezurashiki*) or embarrassing to anyone.[6] There also is no record of a specific edict banning the publication of Japanese works about the Kirishitan, but after *Kirishitan taiji monogatari* was banned around 1665, the topic was generally avoided.[7] As a result, according to Peter Kornicki, "for the remainder of the Tokugawa period Hideyoshi and Christianity were taboo subjects for publishers and were carefully avoided in published works, although manuscripts dealing with such subjects circulated without occasioning any trouble."[8]

An edict promulgated in 1721 and 1722 under the rule of Tokugawa Yoshimune also prohibited books of dubious veracity about certain important families, as well as those containing obscenity or "divergent views." This time, however, the bakufu also required that all printed books include a colophon with the real names of the author and publisher, and that all books be inspected before being sold. As a result of these new measures for reinforcement, the booksellers' guilds began to practice self-censorship and inspection of their members' products in order to avoid attracting the attention of the bakufu and possibly stricter regulation of the

---

5. Mary Elizabeth Berry, *Japan in Print: Information and Nation in the Early Modern Period* (Berkeley: University of California Press, 2006), 13–53.
6. Kornicki, *The Book in Japan*, 332–34.
7. When *Kirishitan monogatari* was first published in 1639, a strict ban on the importation of works about Christianity had been in place since 1630, and even a passing mention of Rome or Christianity could result in an imported book being confiscated. There is no record, however, of action taken against Japanese books about Kirishitan until much later, and *Kirishitan monogatari* was printed without incident, indicating that the earliest censorship gaze was directed outward at books, and Kirishitan, coming from abroad. Kornicki, *The Book in Japan*, 326–31.
8. Ibid., 332.

guilds. Members were warned periodically about which topics and titles they were forbidden to print and sell, and new books had to be approved by a member acting as censor.⁹ In 1771, the Kyoto guild published a *Kinsho mokuroku*, or list of forbidden books and topics for all of its members. On a list of twelve topics that were not to be taken up in books produced by printers or even handled by booksellers, number one on the list is *Kirishitanshū* (the Kirishitan sect), and number seven is *gaikoku no jōkyōtō* (situations in foreign countries). ¹⁰

However, as Kornicki stated above, the ban on printing these texts did not prevent a lively exchange of manuscripts and extensive copying of them. In fact, even as the print industry flourished, manuscript culture in Japan remained strong for a number of reasons.¹¹ One of these was the importance of calligraphy and the aesthetic value attached to certain handwritten texts. Another reason for not printing a text was the desire to limit access to it, especially in the case of certain "secret transmissions" known as *hiden* (秘伝). Additionally, those who wanted to save the expense of buying a printed text would often make their own copies of texts borrowed from friends or from the lending library. Kornicki notes that it was common for a retired man to occupy himself making copies for the family's use.¹²

With the advent of stronger restrictions on the printing industry in the early eighteenth century, producing texts only in manuscript also became a popular way to avoid the censorship gaze of the bakufu. A large number of popular texts on sensitive topics, such as Hideyoshi and the Tokugawa, domain scandals, and even the Kirishitan, all circulated throughout the eighteenth and early nineteenth centuries in manuscript form, until relaxation of the laws allowed them to be printed in the Meiji period. Even some of the more strictly banned Jesuit books from China managed to circulate in manuscript, and Ogyū Sorai was able to make a copy for himself in 1720 of a banned book from China by the Jesuit Matteo Ricci.¹³ Eventually, the bakufu became aware of the practice, and

---

9. Ibid., 337–38.
10. The 1771 *Kinsho mokuroku* (List of Banned Books) is reprinted in Munemasa Isō and Wakabayashi Seiji, eds., *Kinsei Kyōto shuppan shiryō* (Documents on Printing in Early Modern Kyoto) (Tokyo: Nihon Kosho Tsūshinsha, 1965).
11. In addition to information in *The Book in Japan*, Kornicki discusses manuscript culture in Peter Kornicki, "Edo jidai no shahon no kanōsei," *Bungaku gogaku* 186 (2007); and idem, "Manuscript, Not Print: Scribal Culture in the Edo Period," *Journal of Japanese Studies* 32, no. 1 (2006).
12. Kornicki, *The Book in Japan*, 99–111.
13. Ibid., 104.

edicts specifically banning manuscripts (*shahon*) on controversial topics were promulgated. The publishing industry responded by including controversial manuscript titles in its lists of forbidden books. In fact, in the 1771 *Kinsho mokuroku*, the largest section is devoted not to printed works, but to a list of 122 forbidden manuscript titles, which includes two titles of *Raichō jikki* variants.[14] One, *Kirishitan jikki* (True Account of the Kirishitan), was a common title under which there are approximately eighteen manuscripts still extant. The other, *Shimabara jitsuroku* (True Account of Shimabara), is a rare variant that combines entire chapters from *Kirishitan monogatari* and *Raichō jikki*.[15] Titles of controversial manuscript texts were often changed to avoid detection, so that in some cases the same work circulated under a wide variety of titles.

"TRUE ACCOUNTS" AND THE *KASHIHON'YA* SYSTEM

While many manuscript texts circulated privately, the *kashihon'ya*, or lending libraries, of the Edo period also played a large role in their dissemination. The earliest *kashihon'ya* are thought to have operated in conjunction with the sale of books, both in shops and through itinerant salesmen, as early as the Kan'ei period (1624–43).[16] Inventory often came from the same stock that was being sold, though some works were sent out to be copied and then lent in manuscript form (whether the original was manuscript or printed). Some of the later, larger *kashihon'ya* even had permanent staff whose sole job was to make additional copies of texts that were popular or that could only be obtained in manuscript.[17] References in seventeenth-century texts to borrowing books indicate that the itinerant lenders in that period visited towns every one to three months and collected all fees at the end of the year in one bill. Later, however, fees were collected at the time of service, giving the operators more financial freedom to expand.

This expansion was rapid starting in the mid-eighteenth century, and the height of the *kashihon'ya*'s popularity was from the late eighteenth to the early nineteenth centuries. Recent research on the seals used by the *kashihon'ya* to identify their books has shown that during that period the libraries were operating in every prefecture in the country. In fact, the identification of eighty-five seals from different businesses in the Owari/

---

14. Ibid., 105.
15. See the appendix for more on the *Shimabara jitsuroku* variant and for information on extant manuscripts and where they are held.
16. Information on the lending library system can be found in Kornicki, *The Book in Japan*.
17. One of these was the Daiso lending library in the Nagoya area. Nagatomo Chiyoji, *Kinsei kashihon'ya no kenkyū* (Tokyo: Tōōkyodō Shuppan, 1982), 45–61.

Mino province alone has led scholars to speculate that there were approximately 140 to 150 shops operating in that area. Because the seals are not dated, it is impossible to pin down the time periods during which these shops were in business, but it is safe to say that multiple shops were operating in that area at any given time.[18] It was in Edo, however, that the greatest number of *kashihon'ya* operated, and their popularity and influence on the reading public meant that they also exerted considerable power over the publishing industry, which by the late eighteenth century had shifted to the capital. Nakamura Yoshihiko has pointed out that there were as many *kashihon'ya* in Edo by 1808 as there were barbershops and public bathhouses.[19]

In his 1917 work *Saiki kōi*, the author Mori Ōgai recounts his memory of the commercial lending libraries, and of the kinds of books that the vendors offered:

> When I was young, I devoured the books of a lending library man who used to walk around with books stacked on his back in something like a monk's backpack. These books were mainly of three kinds: *yomihon*, *kakihon*, and *ninjōbon*, or popular love stories. The *yomihon* consisted mainly of the works of Kyōden and Bakin, the *ninjōbon* of the works of Shunsui and Kinsui; the *kakihon* were what we now call scenarios for professional storytellers.[20]

The *kakihon* to which Ōgai refers are the predominantly manuscript texts, by anonymous authors, now called *jitsurokutai shōsetsu*, or just *jitsuroku*, which translates as "true-account style novels" or merely "true accounts."[21] Though they have received scant attention from literature scholars and are rarely included in English-language anthologies of Japanese literature, remarks by contemporaries like Ōgai, along with extant records from lending libraries themselves, show that they were hugely

---

18. The Owari/Mino area is in present-day Nagoya. Ibid., 57.
19. Nakamura Yukihiko, "Kinsei no dokusha," *Osaka furitsu toshokan kiyō* 9 (1973), 95.
20. The authors mentioned here are Santō Kyōden (1761–1816), Kyokutei Bakin (1767–1848), Tamenaga Shunsui (1790–1843), and Shōtei Kinsui (1797–1862). Mori Ōgai, *Saiki Kōi and Other Stories* (Honolulu: University Press of Hawai'i, 1977), 143.
21. Information on the *jitsuroku* genre is available in Takahashi Keiichi, *Jitsuroku kenkyū: Suji wo tōsu bungaku* (Osaka: Seibundō, 2002); idem, "Jitsuroku no henyō, 'Nanba Senkimono' wo daizai ni,'" *Bungaku gogaku* 186 (2007); Peter Kornicki, "The Enmeiin Affair of 1803: the Spread of Information in the Tokugawa Period," *Harvard Journal of Asiatic Studies* 41, no. 2 (1981): 461–82; idem, "Edo jidai no shahon no kanōsei,"; Kawatake Shigetoshi, "Jitsuroku no enkaku," in *Kinsei jitsuroku zensho*, vol. 1 (Tokyo: Waseda University, 1929), 1–45; and Mitamura Engyō, "Bungakushi ni habukareta jitsurokutai shōsetsu," in *Mitamura engyō zenshū*, vol. 22 (Tokyo: Chūō Kōronsha, 1975).

popular in the late eighteenth and early nineteenth century. This popularity and the important relationship between them and lending libraries is evident in a bibliography of Japanese works to 1865, first published in 1929, in which the introductory paragraph to the section on "manuscript military stories and *jitsuroku*" describes the works as "all manuscripts that were generally called '*kashihon'yamono*' and which were a favorite of our ancestors."[22]

With their origins in the oral tradition of military tales that were eventually written down by professional storytellers, *jitsuroku* are defined by a number of paradoxes: Though their titles often position them as "true accounts," they are highly fictionalized versions of historical events; though they never benefited from the commercial success of many printed works, they achieved broad distribution through the medium of the commercial lending library; and though they were repeatedly banned and prohibited by the bakufu, they were one of the most popular genre from the mid-eighteenth century to the Meiji period, when many were finally put into print.[23]

Attempts by the authorities to control *jitsuroku* are almost as old as the genre itself and can help to track how early the texts were appearing. Though the earliest attempts to control the publication of particular books in 1649 and 1659 did not specifically target *jitsuroku* by name, they were concerned with texts dealing with ruling families and current events, which were a favorite subject of the genre. Later edicts specifically targeted manuscripts on forbidden topics. The edict of 1722, in particular, was explicit not only about sensitive subject matter but also about the fact that manuscript books had been circulating with this subject matter in an apparent attempt to avoid the restrictions placed on printed books. The edict made it clear that these manuscripts also would now be prohibited. By the

---

22. Yamazaki Fumoto, ed., *Nihon shōsetsu shomoku nenpyō* (Tokyo: Shoshi Kenkyūkai, 1977). This list does not include any of the known titles for the *Raichō jikki* variants; however, it does contain a work titled *Kinka amakusa* 金花天草. This title is not in the *Kokusho sōmokuroku* or in Ebisawa's bibliography of Japanese and Chinese Christian sources, but the reference to the rebellion at Amakusa, as well as the use of "Kinka," which appears in the title of the variant *Kinka keiransho*, all point to the possibility that this is one variant that has since been lost.
23. Scholars trace the origins of the *jitsuroku* to the Edo storytelling tradition, which itself grew out of the practice of the medieval *otogi* and public recitations of battle stories. By the eighteenth century, itinerant storytellers had started to take up residence in Edo and even set up permanent spaces for scheduled readings. It was around this time that scholars believe storytellers began to write down "scripts" for the performances that, like librettos for *kabuki* and *jōruri*, became popular items in lending libraries. This and other information about the storytelling tradition and its relation to *jitsuroku* come from Kawatake, "Jitsuroku no enkaku" and Mitamura, "Bungakushi ni habukareta jitsurokutai shōsetsu."

late eighteenth century, the growing influence of the commercial lending system and its popular item, the *jitsuroku*, was reflected in yet another edict opposing them. This one, issued in the fifth month of 1790, stated, "It is forbidden to make baseless rumours into *shahon* written in *kana* or to lend such books out for a fee."[24] Records show that violators of these edicts, including authors and owners of *kashihon'ya*, were often severely punished with sentences that ranged from house arrest and banishment to death.[25]

It is perhaps because of the danger involved in dealing in *jitsuroku* that so few of the extant copies can be traced to specific *kashihon'ya*. Kornicki points out that during the Tokugawa period most *kashihon'ya* refrained from advertising the *jitsuroku* they carried in the flyers about their stock that they attached to the books they lent to customers, though occasionally wholesalers and suppliers of *kashihon'ya* were bold enough to advertise the manuscript texts in their catalogues.[26] Likewise, it appears the *kashihon'ya* might have chosen not to put their seals in the more controversial items in stock. Kornicki notes that none of the extant copies of a *jitsuroku* on the Enmeiin affair bear the seals of *kashihon'ya*, despite evidence found in records of punishment of many lending libraries buying them. Similarly, of the approximately sixty-five titles of variants of *Raichō jikki* examined, only two bear the seal of the Daisō lending library.[27] Nonetheless, the great number of extant copies testifies to the popularity and diffusion of the tale, which could not have circulated so broadly without the assistance of an extensive network of lending libraries.

A KIRISHITAN *JITSUROKU*

Kirishitan shūmon raichō jikki is one example of a popular *jitsuroku* and of an anti-Kirishitan text that appears to have had the broadest reach over the longest period of time, despite the fact that it was not printed until the Meiji period.[28] Clearly influenced by *Kirishitan monogatari*, it takes a

---

24. *Shahon* here refers to manuscript copies. This is Kornicki's translation of the edict (Kornicki, "The Enmeiin Affair," 507). The original Japanese version is No. 6417 in Takayanagi Shinzō and Ishii Ryōsuki, eds., *Ofuregaki tenpō shūsei* (Tokyo: Iwanami Shoten, 1937), 809–10.
25. Kornicki, "The Enmeiin Affair," 522–23; Konta, *Edo no kinsho*, 21–54.
26. Kornicki, "The Enmeiin Affair," 508–9.
27. These are *Kirishitan shūmonki* (History of the Kirishitan Sect) and *Kirishitan raichōki* (Account of the Arrival of the Kirishitan), both in the Kyoto University Library. It is possible that some texts had seals I did not recognize at the time, or which have not been documented as those of *kashihon'ya*.
28. I make this statement based on the number of extant copies, both manuscript and printed, of this text, *Kirishitan monogatari*, and *Baterenki*.

number of elements that are mentioned only briefly in the earlier tale and develops them to create an epic tale of the padres as a sinister colonial threat that use magic, money, and medicine to lure their converts into almost turning their country over to the Nanban king. In most variants of this text, the Shimabara Rebellion is left out, and the focus is solely on the threat and ultimate defeat of the padres. In a much more cohesive and plot-driven narrative, several characters who were mentioned only once or twice in *Kirishitan monogatari*, including Urugan, the king of Nanban, and even Nobunaga, are fully developed into major actors whose schemes are thoroughly explored through their thoughts and lively exchanges of dialogue that are common in *jitsuroku* texts. Anesaki Masaharu found many of these more dramatic passages and the fanciful additions to the story of the Kirishitan to be evidence of their use by professional storytellers, though there appear to be no records of performances of the tale.[29] Following the information trend of Edo-period publishing and perhaps to bolster the *jitsuroku* claims to truth, the narrative provides many specific details, including names of historical figures for most characters, no matter how minor, as well as specific dates and measurements, including the total area of Nanban and its distance from Japan.

There are only about twenty extant copies of the text bearing the title *Kirishitan shūmon raichō jikki* in libraries around Japan. But as is common with *jitsuroku*, they form part of a total of more than 150 copies of three basic variants of the same narrative under at least sixty-five different titles.[30]

---

29. Anesaki Masaharu, *Kirishitan dendō no kōhai* (Tokyo: Dōbunkan, 1930), 814–20.
30. See the appendix for list of titles examined by the author and the libraries holding them, as well as an explanation of the variants. Initially the search for these texts was based on the list of "Fiction about the Christian Missions" in Ebisawa Arimichi's bibliography of Christian sources and on a search of the titles in the *Kokusho sōmokuroku*, both of which are somewhat outdated. Several texts turned out to be in collections that were lost to fire, and others had been sold to other institutions. In the end, over one hundred texts from Ebisawa's list were examined, of which approximately sixty-five turned out to be the same narrative. *Christianity in Japan: a Bibliography of Japanese and Chinese Sources* (Tokyo: Committee on Asian Cultural Studies, International Christian University, 1960), 38–42. A copy of the *Kirishitan shūmon raichō jikki* variant is reproduced in Hiyane Antei, ed., *Kirishitan monogatari hoka sanpen*, Kirishitan Bunkō, vol. 1 (Tokyo: Keiseisha, 1926), 83–131. An early, anonymous English translation of the text that was first printed in the Japan Herald in 1864 is included in M. Paske-Smith, ed., *Japanese Traditions of Christianity, Being Some Old Translations From the Japanese, With British Consular Reports of the Persecutions of 1868-1872* (Kobe: J.L. Thompson & Co, 1930), 6–48. Other variants of the tale include *Nanbanji monogatari*, reprinted in Washio Junkei, ed., *Nihon shisō tōsō shiryo*, vol. 10 (Tokyo: Meichō Kankyōkai, 1969), 1–52 (see English translation in this volume), and *Nanbanji kōhaiki*, which is available both in Hiyane Antei, ed., *Nanbanji kōhaiki hoka nihen*, Kirishitan Bunkō, vol. 2 (Tokyo: Keiseisha, 1926), and in Ebisawa Arimichi, ed., *Nanbanji kōhaiki, Jakyō tai'i, Myōtei mondō, Ha Daiusu*, Toyo Bunko, vol. 14 (Tokyo: Heibonsha, 1964).

Some of these titles are very similar, such as *Kirishitan jikki* (True Account of the Kirishitan) or *Kirishitan yuraiki* (Origins of the Kirishitan), while others avoid the word Kirishitan altogether, such as *Nanbanji monogatari* (Tale of the Southern Barbarian Temple) or *Ibukiyama mogusaki* (Account of the Mugwort of Mt. Ibuki). For many titles, there is only one copy extant, while others, such as *Kirishitan shūmon raichō jikki*, survive in groups of up to twenty. In addition to the manuscripts of only the *Raichō jikki* narrative, there also exist a number of longer manuscripts that incorporate the same narrative in the first portion of the text, and then go on to tell the story of the Shimabara Rebellion.[31] Available copy dates on the extant *Raichō jikki* manuscripts range from 1743 to 1859, with a larger number from the late eighteenth and early nineteenth centuries, and the first printed text coming out in 1868.[32] Though there is no extant manuscript with a copy date earlier than 1743, the *Raichō jikki* text appears to have evolved from a combination of *Kirishitan monogatari* and *Shimabaraki*, with the basic narrative emerging around the Kyōhō era (1716–35).[33]

THE MAGICIAN PADRE OF *KIRISHITAN SHŪMON RAICHŌ JIKKI*

The *Raichō jikki* narrative is a very new kind of text, though the influence of *Kirishitan monogatari* on it is undeniable. The main characters are the

---

31. These include manuscripts with the titles *Amakusa sōdō* (天草騒動, The Amakusa Uprising), *Kinka keiransho* (金花傾嵐抄), *Kirishitan amakusa gunki* (切支丹天草軍記, Battle Record of the Amakusa Kirishitan), and *Amakusa seibatsuki* (天草征伐記, Record of the Subjugation of Amakusa). A copy of *Amakusa sōdō* is at the Kyushu University Library, and copies of the other three are in the Ebisawa Bunko at Rikkyō University. Though the *Kokusho sōmokuroku* states that *Kinka keiranshō* dates to 1669, there is no text extant from that period, and there appears to be no further confirmation of that date. In addition to the manuscripts, a version of this text was printed under the title *Sankō amakusa gunki* in 1883 and again in 1885. Copies of these printed versions are also held by the Ebisawa Bunko at Rikkyō University. This text should not be confused with the *Shimabara jitsuroku* text discussed in the appendix, which combines passages from *Kirishitan monogatari* and *Raichō jikki*. In addition to these texts that include the *Raichō jikki* narrative along with the story of the Shimabara rebellion, there are a large number of texts that primarily narrate the rebellion and only make passing mention of the Kirishitan. The number and variety of texts about the rebellion are impressive, and they merit separate research. Because this study is primarily interested in representations of the Kirishitan, however, it does not include them in its scope.
32. The 1743 manuscript is in the Nagoya Tsurumi Central Library and bears the title *Kirishitan shūmon wachō ni wataru kongenki* (切支丹宗門渡和朝根元記, Record of the Origins of the Crossing of the Kirishitan Sect). The title of the first printed version of the narrative is *Nanbanji kōhaiki* (南蛮寺興廃記). See the appendix for a range of available copy dates on all manuscripts examined.
33. Watanabe Kenji, "*Kirishitan to bungaku to nonfikushon bungaku: Shimabara no ran wo chūshin ni*," paper presented at the *16 seiki ikō no nihon to higashi ajia no Kirishitan bungaku no eikyōdo wo meguru sōgōteki hikaku kenkyū*, Tokyo, 2008.

same, and the religious debate in *Kirishitan monogatari* between the Buddhist lay priest and Fabian remains almost intact in *Raichō jikki*, but the later narrative has built onto the brief passages about the arrival of the priests and their proselytizing and developed them into a tale three times the size of the earlier *monogatari*. The chapter explaining the "Kirishitan dharma" is gone, as are the accounts of the crackdown in Kyoto and other contemporary events. A small group of variants tells the Shimabara Rebellion story in the second half of the text (also much more developed than in *Kirishitan monogatari*), but the majority only mention it briefly at the end. And perhaps most strikingly, the disjointed "reportage" of the earlier *monogatari* has been replaced with a chronological and much more coherent narrative that purports to tell the story of the Kirishitan from before they landed to the day they were expelled. However, along with a smoother narrative comes a greater distance from historical events and a more exotic tale of padres steeped in magic whose plans to take over the country are aided by the avarice and ignorance of Oda Nobunaga.

While *Kirishitan monogatari* begins with the arrival of Padre Urugan on the shores of Nagasaki, *Raichō jikki* opens long before that in the land of Nanban, where we see the king and his counselors discussing how they can make the wealth of Japan their own. This opening scene is reminiscent of *Baterenki*'s portrayal of the pope and his plotting in Rome, though the evidence of some knowledge of the Catholic Church in that text is nowhere visible in the description of the mythical Nanban. The wise minister, Lord Gogi, warns the king that Japan is protected by the gods and history has shown it cannot be taken by force. Rather, he suggests, they should follow the strategy that was successful in other countries and employ men skilled in magic to dupe the populace into following them. Then, when they finally invade the country, the followers will guide them to victory. When asked where they could find such practitioners of magic, Lord Gogi explains that in the province of Kirishitan, 3000 *li* away, there are two adepts who live on a mountain and practice *hisōjō*.[34] They are so accomplished in the occult arts that they are free of the limitations of normal human beings and can even rise above the clouds. For this reason they are called *bateren*

---

34. "Filosofia," according to Elisonas. I have not found any other reference to the meaning of *hisōjō* (written as ひそうじよう or as 非相定), and it is quite different from a contemporary transcription of "filosofia" as ひろそひや in Inoue Masashige's *Kirisutoki* 契利斯督記 (a mid-seventeenth-century handbook on Christianity and how to detect adherents). George Elison, *Deus Destroyed: the Image of Christianity in Early Modern Japan* (Cambridge, Mass.: Harvard University Press, 1973), 214. Also, see Ebisawa, *Nanbanji kōhaiki*, 114.

(padres).³⁵ Gogi suggests that the king send them to Japan to gather followers and prepare the way for the armies.

After several attempts, they finally convince one of the adepts, Padre Urugan, to go to Japan, where he meets Nobunaga and tells him he wants to preach Buddhism (*buppō*). Over the objections of his advisors, Nobunaga gives the padre land to build a temple, called the Nanbanji, and encourages him to bring more people from Nanban to help him. As a result, Urugan is eventually joined by Padre Furaten and two *iruman* (brothers) skilled in medicine, Kerikori and Yariisu.³⁶ They promptly set about healing the sick and handing out money and clothing to the poor, which attracts crowds from all levels of society to their temple. Patients who have been cured are shown a magical "three worlds mirror" that can show the past, present, and future. In it, the patients all see their future incarnations as animals and are terrified, begging the padres to help them avoid this dreaded rebirth. Pleased at the ease with which they've duped their followers, the padres teach them how to chant the rosary saying *Shigo shōten haraiso zensumaro* ("After death, life in paradise, Jesus Mary") for seven days straight. When the followers next look into the mirror, they see themselves as living buddhas in cloth of purple and gold.³⁷ Then the padres unveil a statue of a woman holding a child and an object called a "*cruz*," which has a long handle and nails set into a paddle. The *cruz* is dragged across the backs of the converts until the blood flows freely, and the padres teach them to smear their hands with that blood and pray to the image.³⁸ Those converts chosen to become brothers are also initiated into the magical arts of the padres and learn "how to turn a towel into a

---

35. As mentioned earlier, the word *bateren* came from the Portuguese word "padre" for father, or priest. It was usually written phonetically as 伴天連. In *Raichō jikki* and all of its variants, however, the first character was replaced with 破, and in the story the narrator puns on that by saying the 破天連 are capable of breaking (破る) the boundaries of heaven (天).
36. Notice how the Franciscan *furaten (fratrum)* of *Kirishitan monogatari* have become a single padre named Furaten. *Iruman* comes from the Portuguese *irmão*, or brother. Kerikori is thought to be modeled after Brother Gregorio de Cespedes, who was skilled in medicine, and Yariis is thought to refer to either Luis de Almeida, also a doctor, or Luis Frois, a famous priest who served for decades in the Kyoto mission.
37. The chant remains the same among the different variants and is usually written with the kanji 死後生天破羅韋僧有善須摩呂. *Haraiso* is the word for paradise in *Kirishitan monogatari*, and the last part, *zensumaro* (Jesus Mary), was the chant in that tale.
38. In *Kirishitan monogatari*, the *cruz* was described as an amulet of the utmost importance to the Kirishitan, but here the word is used to describe the instrument of self-flagellation that was called a *penitencia* in the earlier tale. Though the use of *cruz* here appears to show a departure from the original meaning of the word used by the missionaries, it is not inconceivable that the instrument of penance was referred to by the missionaries as a "cross," in the sense that it was the penitent's cross to bear for his sins.

horse, how to sprinkle powder and turn a dead tree into a flower, how to turn earth into a jewel, how to float in the air and sink into the earth, and how to summon black clouds and make it rain and snow."[39]

The narrative goes on to describe more conversion activities, as well as events surrounding the death of Nobunaga and the rise to power of Toyotomi Hideyoshi. It is at the home of one of Hideyoshi's retainers that the religious debate seen in *Kirishitan monogatari* takes place. The decisive victory of the Buddhist lay priest in this debate makes it clear to Hideyoshi and his court that the Kirishitan sect is a false one, and the leader finally has the foreigners expelled from the land. However, the converted Japanese brothers escape punishment. Years later, Hideyoshi hears of two doctors in Sakai who are very skilled at sleight of hand, and they are invited to his castle to give a performance. They conjure up great wonders, even making Mt. Fuji appear in the rear garden. But when they bring back the ghost of a former mistress that Hideyoshi had ordered killed, he becomes suspicious of them and suddenly realizes they are the fugitive Kirishitan brothers. They are promptly captured and sentenced to death. In the final part of the narrative, there are descriptions of various forms of punishment to which captured Kirishitan are subjected (though not the same ones as in *Kirishitan monogatari*), and then, after a brief mention of the Shimabara Rebellion, the narrative ends.

The *Raichō jikki* narrative includes many elements from *Kirishitan monogatari* and even an echo from *Baterenki*, while also reflecting the influences of the time in which it was written. Much of the debate between Fabian and Hakuo is repeated in the later text, as is the physical description of the foreign padre that opened *Kirishitan monogatari*. In addition, the opening scene of *Raichō jikki* in which the king of Nanban plans his attacks on Japan is reminiscent of similar scenes of the pope in *Baterenki*, and the advisor's warning that "men from all forty-two provinces have tried to enter Japan countless times" without succeeding recalls the many failed attempts at conquering Japan that make up a large part of that earliest text. But the *Raichō jikki* text is also a very different narrative written in the more dramatic, storytelling style of the *jitsuroku*. The early seventeenth-century emphasis on reporting current events is missing from the later work, as are the reports on the Shimabara Rebellion and other measures taken against the Kirishitan during the first decades of the century. In *Kirishitan monogatari*, the narrator's voice supplemented the reports on events, often offering commentary that disparaged the Kirishitan. In the *Raichō jikki* narrative, however, the narrator's voice rarely intrudes. Rather, the reader

---

39. Washio, *Nihon shisō tōsō shiryō*, 340–41.

follows an omniscient narrator, listening in on the scheming of the king of Nanban or of the Kirishitan padres. Tension is heightened in the tale by the inclusion of Oda Nobunaga as a villain who, oblivious to the countless signs that the Kirishitan are not who they seem to be, nearly sells out his own country to the Nanban king. Though the word "true" in the title suggests a dry but accurate account of historical events, this later narrative actually abandons the didactic reporting style of *Kirishitan monogatari* for a fast-paced style driven by dialogue that is clearly designed to entertain.

With about one hundred years separating the *Raichō jikki* narrative from the time of the expulsion, it is perhaps understandable that there is little recognizably Christian about the Kirishitan in the tale. Though *Kirishitan monogatari* already was conflating the Kirishitan with a Buddhist sect by referring to the Kirishitan *"buppō,"* it still contained a chapter describing their beliefs that used a number of Portuguese and Latin terms in their original context and laid out some of the basics of the missionaries' teachings. There is no chapter on the Kirishitan beliefs in *Raichō jikki*, leaving only Fabian's brief description during his debate with Hakuo near the end of the tale. The representation of the Kirishitan as a heretical Buddhist sect is more pronounced, with the Kirishitan asking Nobunaga for permission to spread the teachings of Buddha, and promising their followers that Deus will help them be reborn as "living buddhas." In *Raichō jikki*, a *contas* is still a rosary, but the word *cruz* describes the instrument of self-flagellation, and the only other remnants of the Christian terms the missionaries taught are a few words that form a "dharani" taught by the Kirishitan to their followers. Though the Kirishitan are not recognizably Christian to Western readers familiar with the religion, that probably was not apparent to contemporary Japanese readers, for whom they are still sufficiently foreign and exotic. In the later tale, that exoticism resides less in the use of Portuguese and Latin words or the daily religious practice of the foreigners, and more in their use of magic and in the increased focus on their relationship with the Nanban king.

All of this contributes to significant changes in the overall image of the Kirishitan Other that is further developed in the later tale. He is still a fraud who uses money, medicine, and his false religious teachings in a plot to take over the country. But with the addition of scenes at the Nanban king's court, the Kirishitan is portrayed more clearly as the agent of a powerful foreign king, and his religion is a more transparent tool for conquest. Money is a key part of that religion, not only as a means of luring new converts but also as evidence of the prosperity of Nanban, which the padres assure their followers will also come to them if they convert. As such, in *Raichō jikki* money is a mark of the Kirishitan's power, even as his preoccupation with wealth stands out as proof of his barbarism and heresy. The addition of magical powers makes the Kirishitan exotic and fearsome, while also explaining his ability to attract so many to his church. With more money than ever, new magical powers, and the resources of the forty-two provinces of Nanban behind him, the Kirishitan of *Raichō jikki* is a much greater and less predictable threat than he was in the two earlier tales.

As in *Kirishitan monogatari*, the portrayal of the Kirishitan as a barbaric Other in opposition to the civilized, sacred realm of Japan is central to the *Raichō jikki* narrative, and the barbaric nature of the Kirishitan is still evident in his and his converts' grotesque appearances, as well as in his unconventional behavior and religious practices. The physical description of Padre Urugan that opens *Kirishitan monogatari* is reproduced in the *Raichō jikki* narrative, though it is not the opening passage and appears later, when Nobunaga first meets the foreigner. With the addition of Padre Buraten (or Furaten), who joins Padre Urugan later in the tale, we get a second physical description that is even more bizarre than Urugan's. While Urugan is nine feet tall with a red face and yellow eyes, Buraten is more than eleven feet tall with a green face and yellow hair. The grotesque nature of the Kirishitan is further expanded with descriptions of the disfigurement of their converts. Though *Kirishitan monogatari* merely mentioned the diseases of converts who were treated by the padres, *Raichō jikki* includes descriptions of the symptoms of three who are admitted to the order. Two are afflicted with scabs from syphilis, and the famous Fabian is "covered in blood and pus" from a severe case of leprosy. In all three cases, the converts' illnesses are attributed to karma from bad behavior in this life that already represents them as Other within Japanese society.

The new features of the Kirishitan religion that appear in the *Raichō jikki* narrative also mark the followers more transparently as Other. Unlike the explanation of the Kirishitan religion in *Kirishitan monogatari*, which required some interpretation to show its heresy, the magical powers attributed to the Kirishitan in *Raichō jikki* are an exotic but unambiguous sign of his place outside of the mainstream Buddhist sects. This relationship between the Kirishitan and magic is introduced in the opening scene of the narrative, when the Nanban king asks his advisors where he can find adepts skilled in magic to carry out his plans in Japan, and they tell him that such men live in the "land of Kirishitan," a province of his realm. Like the iconic *yamabushi* of medieval Japanese literature, the Kirishitan padres can fly, change the weather, and do conjuring tricks. They also use a "three-worlds mirror," whose image they can control in order to frighten or reassure converts about their prospects for rebirth. Converts who are invited to join the order are taught to conjure as well. And in an interesting twist, it is precisely because they continue to practice this magic that the converts who go into hiding are eventually discovered. This association of Kirishitan and magic is an additional mark of Otherness in the *Raichō jikki* narrative, and one that seems to have traveled beyond this text and endured in theatrical works featuring the Kirishitan and in the public imagination throughout the Edo period.

The Kirishitan relationship with money was already a mark of his barbarism in *Kirishitan monogatari*, but in *Raichō jikki* money plays an even greater role both as a tool for recruitment and as "proof" of the power and beneficence of the Kirishitan god. When Urugan first meets with the Nanban king to plan his "attack," he warns that the Japanese gods are too strong to be overcome by his magic alone, and he will need lavish gifts with which to buy the favor of the Japanese king. These gifts are well received by Oda Nobunaga, who gives Urugan land to build a church and also urges him to bring more padres to Japan. This allows the Nanban king to send Padre Buraten to Japan, who also brings gifts. But before leaving Nanban, Buraten counsels the king that the best way to sway the minds of the Japanese people is to relieve their suffering by providing medicine for the sick and gold and silver for the poor. The king's advisor agrees and suggests they use "the yearly income from the fifteen eastern provinces for this purpose." When Urugan and Buraten finally set up their church in Kyoto, it is decorated with precious stones and cotton banners and permeated with the fragrance of many kinds of incense. Any sick person who comes to the church is first cured and then clothed in fine cotton and fed three times a day with fish and chicken. The poor are given money, and eventually every family member of every convert is given money and measures of rice. Though the narrator does not say so explicitly, the detailed descriptions of the money and how it is distributed clearly demonstrate not only an attachment to wealth that goes against Buddhist teaching but also a merchant's preoccupation with money that was conventionally frowned upon in Edo-period society. Ironically, it is only after hearing of the Kirishitan generosity to their followers that Nobunaga finally perceives their religion to be heresy. Because the practice of giving to their adherents rather than receiving donations from them is the opposite of traditional Buddhist practice, he realizes he may have been wrong about them all along.

For the Kirishitan in *Raichō jikki*, money is not just a recruiting tool, it is a symbol of the power of Deus as well as the benevolence of the king of Nanban, and as such a powerful tool of conquest and yet another sign of the heresy of the sect. The padres tell their followers that Japan is poor and its people are sick because they do not worship Deus. But in the padres' own land, many times larger than Japan, there is no disease and no poverty because they are Kirishitan *and* because the king is good to all of his people. "Our king is merciful and compassionate, and all people down to the lowest commoner have experienced his benevolence. And this is not limited to Nanban alone, but is spread to all of the lands that we govern. In his mercy, our king wishes to save all of the poor and sick of the world. Those lands that do not worship Deus have many poor and sick."[40] In this way, the relationship of the padres to the king of Nanban is more overt in *Raichō jikki*, and the savior of the believers is not only Deus but also the Nanban king. And the money that is the source of their salvation on earth is a sign both of the heresy of Deus and Nanban and of their power.

In the *Raichō jikki* narrative, the Kirishitan is still exotic and Other, but his Otherness is situated less in the more subtle differences of Buddhist doctrine and practice and more in his practice of magic and his service to a threatening foreign power. These more obvious markers of Otherness likely appealed to a broader audience than the religious comparisons in *Kirishitan monogatari*, and they made the narrative more understandable to an audience that was one hundred years removed from the time of the missionaries and had never been exposed to the Christianity those missionaries taught. The greater emphasis on the "country" of Nanban as the power behind the Kirishitan in *Raichō jikki* also focused the tale less on the internal battle with the Kirishitan and more on Japan's battle for sovereignty against forces from the outside world. As they were in *Kirishitan monogatari*, those forces are identified as barbaric because they do not conform to the traditions of Japan. But in *Raichō jikki*, the Japanese traditions are also identified with those of the Three Realms and the more civilized center of the Confucian *ka'i* (civilized/barbarian) cosmology. In fact, *Raichō jikki* goes even further than *Kirishitan monogatari* in reasserting this Three Realms and *ka'i* mapping of the world and explicitly places Nanban outside of that sacred space. And the fact that the location and boundaries of Nanban were indistinct in the minds of most readers of the time meant the threat of the Kirishitan was everywhere outside of that sacred space, and nowhere in particular—as unpredictable and ominous as the magic they practiced.

A SACRED JAPAN IN THE THREE REALMS

In the opening scene of *Raichō jikki*, King Gojimbi of the land of Nanban announces to his lords that he wants to conquer Japan for the wealth it

---

40. Ibid., 336.

holds, and one of his top generals volunteers to lead an army in the campaign. But the wise counselor, Lord Gogi, who clearly knows his history, cautions that many Nanbanjin have already tried invading Japan without success. "The Mongol fleet tried to invade the country seven times and failed because Japan is the land of the gods and their gods protect them well. It will not be taken with these simple efforts."[41] Instead, Gogi suggests, they should try to use money and magic to convince the poor to follow a practitioner of the way, who will then rally those followers when they are ready to send the army. The message is clear, however, that the use of force alone would be useless against the protective power of Japan's gods. This is the first of many references throughout the *Raichō jikki* narrative to Japan's status not only as a sacred land but also as one that is impervious to barbarian attack. Reference to Japan's gods and buddhas is also made in *Kirishitan monogatari*, but in *Raichō jikki* almost as much space is devoted to constructing Japan as a sacred land as is given over to the abjection of the Kirishitan as barbarians. This is done through references throughout the tale of the Shinto gods as protectors, and of Japan as a recipient both of the Buddhist dharma within the traditional Three Realms cosmology and of Confucian edification that marks it as civilized in the Chinese *ka'i* worldview.

The practitioners that Gogi proposes to send to Japan are Padre Urugan and Padre Buraten, who live on a remote mountain peak in the land of the Kirishitan. Presumably, the same powers that enable them to fly and perform magic also give them insights into the world of the gods and spirits, for they too are aware of the gods in Japan. When King Gojimbi's messenger tries to convince Urugan to go to Japan, he first refuses because he has chosen reclusion and does not preach in the world. However, when the messenger leaves, he visits Buraten to confer with him on the king's request, and the latter observes, "I think that the king is avaricious and means to use us to test the hearts of the Japanese people. But the forces in the northeast are strong and too difficult to overcome. I believe we should refuse the king's request."[42] Here, the "forces in the northeast" refer to natural forces that are protecting Japan from outside penetration.[43] Though there is no specific mention of the Shinto gods, their intimate connection to the natural world of Japan points to them by implication. Eventually,

41. Ibid., 320.
42. Ibid., 321–22.
43. Because Nanban was described as lying southwest of Japan, "northeast" here refers to the direction of Japan. The word translated as "forces" here is *unki* (運気), which could mean destiny or fate, but also refers to the natural forces of the world that control men's lives.

when Urugan is forced to agree to the king's request (or be banished from his mountain top), he tells the king, "Though [Japan] is small, it follows the way of the gods, and thus it will be very difficult to conquer. In case I encounter difficulties when I arrive, perhaps I should bring gifts for the king of Japan."[44] As a result, in addition to the money and medicine taken to bribe potential followers, Urugan is also provided with seven special gifts for the "king" of Japan. Clearly, the power of the gods is vulnerable to the corruption of man.

Oda Nobunaga accepts the gifts and becomes complicit with the foreign king by allowing the Kirishitan "heresy" to infect the land in his own quest for power. However, we learn that though the gods have turned their backs on him, they have not completely forsaken Japan, and soon after Urugan arrives in the country, they send a warning to the realm. In the *Raichō jikki* text, we hear of this warning in what is almost an aside to the main narrative. After a long passage on the political machinations of Oda Nobunaga as he tries to bring the foreigner to his own castle, the narrative breaks to give the following account.

> On the twenty-fourth day of the eighth month of the eleventh year of Eiroku (1569), there was an earthquake that felled sixty-six pine trees at Sumiyoshi Shrine. This appeared to be an omen of bad things to come, and it was later understood that this strange event was a sign that Padre Urugan had come to carry out the king's plot to take over Japan. The attendants at the shrine were surprised, and Priest Kunitoyo of the Third Rank, Governor of Settsu, informed Retired Emperor Ōgimachi of the event. The emperor was also amazed. Certainly, if one or two hundred pines had been felled, it would have been a shocking event, but the number was even more alarming because sixty-six was also the number of provinces in Japan. In response to this event, an order came down from the emperor that the priests in all of the temples and shrines in the Gokinai area were to say prayers for the country. These pine trees fell on the twenty-fourth day of the eighth month, and it was only ten days later, on the third day of the ninth month, that Urugan Bateren arrived at the gates of Tōji,[45] the Eastern Temple.[46]

With the number of pines corresponding to the number of provinces in Japan, the passage clearly shows that the arrival of the padre is an

---

44. Ibid., 323.
45. The full name of the temple is Kyōōgokuji (教王護国寺), and it is in Minami Ku in Kyoto. It was founded in 794 along with a Western Temple (Saiji, was destroyed soon after it was built) to protect the newly established capital of Heian.
46. Ibid., 325–26.

attack on the integrity of the realm. That integrity is symbolized by the two religious guardians of Tōji and the Sumiyoshi Shrine, both of which were "penetrated" by the arrival of the foreigner. Historically, Tōji was the surviving one of two Buddhist temples built in Kyoto during the eighth century to pacify the country and preserve it from harm. Nonetheless, Padre Urugan is met at the temple by Nobunaga's retainers and escorted past it to his castle. Thus, it is with the help of the leader that the foreign threat is allowed to pass through the Buddhist symbol of protection, despite the earnest prayers of the emperor and all of the priests of the region.

The other guardian of the country is the deity of Sumiyoshi Shrine where the sixty-six pines were toppled in warning. The Sumiyoshi deity is traditionally understood to be the god of Japanese native poetry and of seafarers. In accounts of the earlier Mongol invasion, to which parallels are drawn here when it is mentioned at the opening of the *Raichō jikki* narrative, the deity is among the many who help protect the country from the barbarians, including the god of war Hachiman and, as we see later in the tale, the god of the Ise Shrine. However, the Sumiyoshi deity has also appeared in other major works as a protector of the realm, most prominently in the noh drama titled *Hakurakuten*, the Japanese name for the Chinese poet Bo Juyi, who is the protagonist.[47] In the play, Bo Juyi (772–847) is sent to Japan by the Tang emperor to test the waters for a Chinese invasion. However, the god Sumiyoshi, disguised as a fisherman, meets him off the coast and challenges him on the subject of poetry. Naturally, the god wins the challenge, Bo Juyi is sent back to China in disgrace, and Japan is saved from the predations of the Tang emperor.

In the preface to his translation, Arthur Waley describes the encounter as an allegory for the "literary peril" Japan was experiencing during the medieval period as it once again came under the strong Chinese influences that threatened the near extinction of "traditional" Japanese forms.[48] Whether this interprets the situation at that time accurately or not, the plot definitely alludes to the threat of a cultural invasion, and one that is in some ways similar to the one the Kirishitan posed. Most importantly, it is not an invasion of armies, but one in which the cultural superiority of the Japanese is being tested. Just as the Kirishitan padres are sent by their

---

47. The play was written by Zeami in the late fourteenth century. The Japanese text can be found in *Yōkyokushū*, Nihon koten bungaku taikei, vol. 41 (Tokyo: Iwanami shoten,, 1960); an English translation is in Arthur Waley, *The Nō Plays of Japan* (Rutland, Vt.: Charles E. Tuttle Co, 1976), 207–15.
48. Waley, *The Nō Plays of Japan*, 207.

king to "test the hearts" of the Japanese people and prepare them for an invasion, so Bo Juyi claims he has been sent by his prince to "make proof of the wisdom of its people."[49] And in fact, despite the long tradition in Japan of respect paid to China and to Bo Juyi in particular, in this play he is portrayed as an almost uncouth foreigner, who speaks in rough language that contrasts sharply with the highly polite language of the supposedly uneducated "fisherman" who challenges him. In like manner the Kirishitan are shown to be grotesque beings lacking an understanding of the most fundamental social graces. In both cases, the god Sumiyoshi presides over the nonmilitary incursions of these cultural Others. In the first, the deity meets the foreigner personally and successfully turns him back. But in the *Raichō jikki* narrative, he can only sound the alarm. Despite the prayers ordered by the emperor (which were believed successful in summoning divine assistance during the medieval Mongol invasions), the job of meeting the foreigner falls on the secular leader, whose heart is being tested. Only this time the leader is corrupt and ignorant of tradition and precedent, and he fails miserably.

Nobunaga is guilty of ignoring the warning of the Sumiyoshi deity and allowing the Kirishitan menace into the country, but Toyotomi Hideyoshi is the hero of the *Raichō jikki* narrative as the leader who recognizes the heresy and promptly expels them from the land. Though the action itself clearly defines him as a wise ruler, he is also able to show his superior judgment and understanding of Japan's history as a sacred country when he discusses with his advisors what to do with the foreign padres.[50] The discussion becomes the occasion for another reference to the Mongol invasion as a precedent for the Kirishitan one, in which Hideyoshi recalls the lessons learned by the Japanese leaders of the time. In a rather long passage, he recounts both battles against the Mongol forces, though his version is rather different from the traditional account. Hideyoshi claims that the Western daimyo prevailed in the first invasion, but that their decision to execute the captured enemy commander led the Mongol armies to seek revenge with the second attack. In that second attack, the Japanese forces fought hard but would have lost without the help of the divine winds that came in answer to the emperor's prayers to the gods.[51]

---

49. The Japanese in the *Nanbanji monogatari* variant of *Raichō jikki* is 日本人の心を謀り見させん and in *Hakurakuten* it is 日本の知恵を測る.
50. It is worth noting here that the positive representation of Hideyoshi in the *Raichō jikki* narrative also may have been an important factor in keeping it from print. While the Kirishitan topic was clearly a forbidden one, this kind of treatment of Hideyoshi as hero and savior of Japan also would have been objectionable to the Tokugawa bakufu.
51. Washio, *Nihon shisō tōsō shiryō*, 361–62.

This is an element that is missing from conventional historical accounts of the Mongol invasion, which do not see revenge as the motive for the second invasion.[52] While most accounts have the Mongols coming again simply because they failed the first time, Hideyoshi blames the second attack on the decision made by the Hōjō leader to execute the Mongol prisoner. In this passage, Hideyoshi points to the importance of the decisions made by leaders at these times of barbarian invasion, and, once again, we are shown the dangerous consequences of poor leadership decisions. In contrast, Hideyoshi, by displaying his knowledge of history and precedent, shows that he has the wisdom to get rid of the foreign heresy without inviting retaliation.

Beyond its importance in showing the better judgment of Hideyoshi in contrast to Oda Nobunaga, the passage is another opportunity to reiterate Japan's sacred status as not only the land of the gods, but also the one that has repeatedly repelled barbarian incursions before. Here, Hideyoshi paints a picture of a sacred and strong Japan that expelled the barbarians successfully once and will do it again this time. He also equates the legendary Mongolian "barbarians" with those of Nanban, emphasizing not only their lack of civilization but also their inevitable subjection to the will of Japan. In doing so, he shows that Japan has both military strength and the strength of a long history of religious and cultural superiority against which the barbarians can ultimately have no success.

The passage above demonstrates Hideyoshi's knowledge of Japan's sacred nature in contrast to Oda Nobunaga's ignorance and neglect in the face of the warning at Sumiyoshi Shrine. But this ignorance of Nobunaga's is not confined to the history of the gods and Japan; it also extends to the history and cultural significance of Japan's links to India and China and their role in the transmission of Buddhism to Japan. This is demonstrated in a scene in which Nobunaga asks his advisors if he should allow the padres to preach in Japan. Coming soon after the sixty-six pines fall at Sumiyoshi Shrine, the scene depicts a pivotal moment when Nobunaga could have listened to his wise advisors and sent the foreigners away. It also provides those advisors with the opportunity to elaborate on the cultural superiority of Japan's religious traditions, and how to tell the difference between the foreign heresy and the "Japanese" way.

The passage begins after Nobunaga has received Urugan in audience. He gathers together all of his advisors and asks them whether he should

52. The accounts referred to here are those of George Sansom, *A History of Japan to 1334* (Stanford, Calif.: Stanford University Press, 1958); and Thomas Conlan, *In Little Need of Divine Intervention: Takezaki Suenaga's Scrolls of the Mongol Invasions of Japan* (Ithaca, N.Y.: Cornell East Asia Series, 2001), 254–75.

allow the padre from Nanban to "spread the teachings of Buddha." Though most members of the gathering hang back in silence, the scholar and priest Bunkyōin Hokkyō steps forward to object to the foreigner. He proceeds to explain how the three major modes of thought in Japan (i.e., Shinto, Buddhism and Confucianism) are linked by common rituals of respect and reverence, of which this foreigner has shown no understanding.

> The ways of Shinto, Confucious, and Buddha are well established.[53] While these are grounded in rituals of respect, I see none of that respect in this man. Many of the Shinto gods have manifested themselves as buddhas or bodhisatvas, for if it is true that disguising one's glory to walk among sentient beings is the beginning of the bond, and the eight stages of Buddhahood are the culmination of the benefit to all living things, then the god's intent in becoming a bodhisatva and mixing with the beings of this earth is to form a bond with them and bring them to Buddhism.[54] They say that when we bow to the Shinto gods, we are also bowing to the buddhas and bodhisatvas. And when we bow to Buddha, we are also bowing to the Three Jewels, which are the Buddha, the Law, and the Priests. So in effect we are bowing three times. In Confucianism, understanding and gratitude are expressed by bowing low. These are the ways of men. But this Padre Urugan stretches his legs out before him and does not lower his head. Raising one's head does not show reverence; it is the way of animals. His appearance is vulgar, like the people of Ebisu or Mongolia.[55] It seems unlikely he would know any Buddhist teachings that we would want."[56]

In the first part of his speech, Bunkyōin manages to unite the three "religious" traditions in Japan under one common principle. First, he links Shinto and Buddhism by citing the *honji suijaku* argument explained

---

53. しんじゅ仏にはさだまれるほうあり. Here the author uses one phrase to refer to Shinto, Confucionism, and Buddhism.
54. This is an allusion to the *wakō dōjin* doctrine, according to which it is believed that the buddhas and bodhisattvas appear on earth as humans in order to help lead other human beings to salvation through Buddhism. In Japan it was also believed that Shinto gods could appear as bodhisattvas. In *Deus Destroyed*, Elison includes a translation of the passage on this topic from the *Taishō shinshū daizōkyō* 大正新修大蔵経, the Tripitaka in Chinese, edited by Takakusu Junjirō, vol. 46, no. 1911, 80: "In subdued brilliance sharing/this world of dust/is the beginning of the tie/[between Buddha and man]; the Eight Stages/[of the Buddha's earthly life]/and the establishment of the Way/are termed its completion." See Elison, *Deus Destroyed*, 465–66, n. 15.
55. The words used here are *mōko* and *ebisu*. *Mōko* refers to Mongolia, but *ebisu* could be either Ezo, which referred to present-day Hokkaido, or Mongolia. Later in the text, Ezo clearly refers to Mongolia.
56. Washio, *Nihon shisō tōsō shiryō*, 328.

above, in which it was understood that the Shinto gods returned to the earth in the form of bodhisattvas in order to help lead living beings to the true path. But then he also finds a way to link Shinto and Buddhist traditions with Confucianism. Specifically, he points out that all three "ways" incorporate the ritual of bowing, and that this particular practice is a common marker of the "established," or orthodox, ways. But this foreigner is incapable of even this simple mark of civilization. Indeed, Urugan was described as greeting the leader Nobunaga with his leg(s) stretched out before him, his arms crossed on his chest, and his head raised.[57] This lack of civility marks him in the scholar's eyes as no better than the more well-known barbarian Others of Mongolia and Ezo.

But Bunkyōin takes his argument one step further by saying that people lacking in civility must also be lacking in any worthwhile religious teachings, thereby equating the transmission of Buddhism with a kind of "ritual edification" that formed part of the Chinese-centered view of the civilized and the barbarian.[58] Unlike the Three Realms worldview described above, which was based on the transmission of the Law of Buddha, the traditional *ka'i* (華夷) worldview was based on Chinese social hierarchy and presumed a more civilized existence closer to the center of the empire, and a descent into barbarism the greater the distance from that center. That civilized existence consisted of an education in the Chinese classics, as well as a knowledge of the "rites, rituals, and the rules of proper behavior."[59] While a complete understanding of all of these things marked the most civilized people, some of the rituals and behavior could be taught by a ruler to a less civilized people, who then participated in these rituals as a sign of respect. "In short, ritual edification was designed to produce submissive adherence to the existing social hierarchy. In like manner, edified aliens signified their proper subservience to Middle Kingdom Civilization by submitting themselves to rituals such as the kowtow."[60] By the seventeenth century in Japan, scholars were arguing that it was the behavior of people and adherence to these rules rather than geography

---

57. The image conveyed here is strikingly similar to a surviving painting of Francis Xavier that was painted in the European style by an unknown Japanese artist. Though the subject is standing, his arms are crossed over his chest as he gazes up and to his left at a vision in the sky of Jesus on the cross. The painting is held at the Kobe Museum of Nanban Art. A picture is in Michael Cooper et al., eds., *The Southern Barbarians: the First Europeans in Japan* (Tokyo: Kodansha International Ltd., 1971), 26.
58. Bob Tadashi Wakabayashi, *Anti-Foreignism and Western Learning in Early-Modern Japan: the New Theses of 1825* (Cambridge, Mass.: Harvard University Asia Center, 1986), 17–30.
59. Ibid., 18.
60. Ibid., 19.

that dictated where the civilized "center" was, with some claiming the center for Japan. And in Bunkyōin's speech we see him arguing that the foreigner's ignorance of the proper ritual of bowing places him and his country outside of the civilized realm and, by inference, outside of the sacred influence of the three "ways" that govern Japan. By drawing this parallel between civilization and religion, he draws a map in which the *ka'i* worldview overlaps that of the Three Realms.

Though Bunkyōin has pointed out that the strange ways of the padres place them outside the *civilized* world, Nobunaga chooses to hear Bunkyōin's argument as one opposing the padres simply because they come from outside of Japan. And, as the narrative tells us, he was determined to allow the foreigner to preach, so he told the gathering that they should not despise the man because he came from abroad.

> Remember how Buddhism was transmitted to us. One thousand years after the death of Shakamuni, Mato loaded the scrolls containing the Buddhist canon onto a white horse and carried them to China. There, he gave them to Genso Komei Kotei, second emperor of the Han Dynasty, who honored him. Of the nine halls in the emperor's palace, the innermost guest hall was called Kōroji, and because he had traveled from such a great distance, Mato was entertained by the emperor in this hall. Eventually, the teachings of Buddha spread to more than four hundred lands. It was Emperor Kinmei, 30th emperor of Japan, who brought the canon from Korea to Japan. That is how we learned the way of Buddha. So, you see, all of the teachings were brought from another country. That is the only reason why we learned of the Buddha and why his teachings remain with us today. You could even say that only the Buddhism that comes from abroad is really Buddhism. Urugan may have something worthwhile to teach us. And he is not so objectionable. Therefore, I have decided to let him preach.[61]

Where Bunkyōin clearly distinguishes between civilized countries with knowledge of the "true path" and uncivilized ones without it, Nobunaga implies that all "other countries" are equal, and since the Buddhism of Japan came from "other" countries in the past, there is every reason to believe the Buddhism brought by the padres could also be useful.[62] He fails

---

61. Washio, *Nihon shisō tōsō shiryō*, 328–29.
62. The term used here by Nobunaga is *ikoku* 異国, which refers to difference without specifying the level of civilization. Toby points out that this term was used in the seventeenth century to refer to China and India, but was also used as a category in the 1713 Terajima Ryōan encyclopedia of foreign peoples to refer to eleven different Northeast Asian countries, including the traditionally barbarian peoples of Ezo. Terajima's opposing

to make a distinction between the historically respected lands of India and China and all other countries, just as he fails to perceive the importance of ritual and social hierarchy. But the reader has come to expect this of the leader who, when he hears of the arrival of the strange foreigner in Nagasaki, forges a letter from the Ashikaga shogun to trick the officials holding Urugan into sending him to Nobunaga's castle. Clearly, Nobunaga's understanding of propriety and the rules of behavior for a man of his status is deficient. As the narrative goes on to show, the tragic consequences of Nobunaga's ignorance are the deaths of tens of thousands of converts, and we learn that his error was not in permitting someone from outside the boundaries of Japan to preach; rather, it was in not recognizing in the strange behavior and features of the padres the outward signs of heresy. In fact, he has a moment of regret later in the tale, when he finally realizes that the Kirishitan are a heretical sect (based on strange practices that recall the earlier bow of Urugan), and he laments to those around him his own error in not listening to Bunkyōin.

Nobunaga is eventually killed before he can rectify the situation, but his successor, Toyotomi Hideyoshi, manages to banish the foreign missionaries and order the apostasy of all of their Japanese followers. This action is prompted by news of the victory of the lay priest Hakuo in a religious debate with the Kirishitan convert Fabian, and it is in the context of this debate that the reader is again reminded of the historic relationship among India, China, and Japan that was formed through the transmission of Buddhism.

In the *Nanbanji monogatari* and *Ibuki yomogi* variants of the *Raichō jikki* narrative, in particular, it comes in the form of the sermon given by the lay priest Hakuo after his defeat of Fabian in the debate.[63] Most of the debate is taken up by Fabian expounding on the superiority of the Kirishitan sect, and at one point in the text the members of the audience wonder nervously why Hakuo is silent and whether he is going to concede. However, when Fabian finally finishes talking, Hakuo throws out a few swift

---

category of *gai'i jinbutsu* ("outer barbarian peoples") included European countries as well as Cambodia, Champa (Annan), and Siam. Clearly the term was used to refer to a shifting group of countries, making it difficult to ascribe a value judgment to its use here. See Ronald P. Toby, "Three Realms/Myriad Countries: an 'Ethnography' of Other and the ReBounding of Japan, 1550-1750," in *Constructing Nationhood in Modern East Asia*, edited by Kai-wing Chow, Kevin Doak, and Poshek Fu (Ann Arbor: The University of Michigan Press, 2001), 34, 38n.12.

63. Only one or two of the *Ibuki yomogi* variants do not contain this sermon. Of the extant manuscripts of this text, approximately one-third have the sermon in them. See chart of extant manuscripts in the appendix for specific texts.

and (apparently) devastating rebuttals, reducing Fabian to mumbling incoherence, after which the Kirishitan scuttles out the door in disgrace.[64] Though he has said very little to this point about what exactly the true path is, Hakuo assures the audience that they have just witnessed an evil sect being defeated by the true one, and he asks them to remain and listen to more about the Buddha's teachings and "the things of this world." He then proceeds to tell them stories about the origins of Buddhism in India, and its transmission to China. The first two stories tell of how the first monastery was built in India and how a disciple of the Buddha managed to defeat the leader of a heretical sect in a battle of wits and superhuman powers. The third story is about the transmission of Buddhism from India to China and the construction of the first Buddhist temple there. The stories were well known and are variations of ones that appear in the sections of Indian and Chinese tales of the medieval collection *Konjaku monogatarishū*, or "Tales of Times Now Past."[65]

The sermon takes up several pages of the text and serves as rebuttal to the now debunked Kirishitan sect described by Fabian. And it is significant that the choice of lesson for the audience is not Buddhist doctrine or even appropriate ritual practices for the audience to emulate. Rather, it is the importance of locating the origins of Buddhism in the lands of India and China, and tracing the cultural links between Japan and those countries. This contrasts sharply with the sermon by Hakuo as it appears in the earlier *Kirishitan monogatari*. In both works, Hakuo faces off with Fabian and, of course, defeats him handily. However, the sermon Hakuo delivers in the earlier tale includes a rebuttal of the creation story told by the Kirishitan Fabian, as well as a lesson on the three styles of instruction in the way of Buddha and the appropriateness of each to the petitioner's level of education.[66] Packed with more references to Buddhist doctrine,

---

64. I say "apparently" because Hakuo only has to accuse Fabian of lying and the latter falls apart. The debate in this narrative was obviously intended for a popular audience with a shallow understanding of Buddhist doctrine.
65. Specifically, the first resembles tale 1:31 in the Indian tales section, with the English title "How the Wealthy Shudatsu Built the Temple in Gionshōja." The second resembles tale 1:9 in the Indian tales section, titled "How Sharihotsu Pitted his Skills against the Heretics"; and the third resembles tale 6:2 in the Chinese tales section, titled "How the Buddhist Law Was Transmitted at the Time of Emperor Ming of the Later Han Period." The Japanese tales can be found in Kazuo Mabuchi et al., *Konjaku monogatarishū*, Nihon koten bungaku zenshū, vols. 21–24 (Tokyo: Shogakukan, 1971). English translations of all of the tales can be found in Yoshiko Kurata Dykstra, ed., *The Konjaku Tales* (Osaka: Intercultural Research Institute, 1986).
66. The presence of this kind of sermon supports Watanabe Kenji's view that *Kirishitan monogatari*, though often represented as primarily an anti-Kirishitan text, was also a didactic work aimed at instructing high-ranking samurai and domain lords on how to manage

it is relatively inaccessible to the average reader of popular tales, which may explain the shift in the later text to simple Buddhist tales that would have been well known to a wide audience. Regardless of the reason for the change, the effect in the later text is to focus this lesson about the "correct" and the "false" paths less on doctrinal differences and more on the traditional cultural distinctions between the "civilized" countries of India, China, and Japan and the barbarian Others.

The shift of the focus in this section mirrors a broader trend in the *Raichō jikki* narrative toward explaining Japan and its place in the world through a religious identity that is rooted in cultural and religious traditions linked to its historically familiar others of India and China. These traditions are represented in opposition to the Kirishitan more as cultural differences than as doctrinal ones. Bunkyōin demonstrates that Japanese tradition combines three distinct "ways," which are all unified by a common cultural experience rooted in the understanding of social hierarchy and ritual practices drawn from the Chinese tradition but practiced successfully in the equally civilized center of Japan. Similarly, the authenticity of Japanese Buddhism (as opposed to the "Buddhist" teachings of the Kirishitan) is identified by its origin in India and transmission through China. In this way, "Japan" is represented in the tales as an independent country with a unique unity of the three "ways," but also as an entity participating in a historically sacred region—one that was diminished in the modern maps of the seventeenth century.

The Three Realms in the World

> Christianity is an evil sect that came from Nanban in the time of the 107th emperor, Retired Emperor Ōgimachi, in the eleventh year of Eiroku (1568). More than ninety thousand miles southwest of Japan by sea, Nanban is comprised of forty-two provinces within an area of 244,000 square miles.[67] It is surrounded by India and China to the west, Ume to the south, Shoku to the

---

people and avoid rebellion. In this context, the sermon serves to teach the reader how best to get people with very different educational backgrounds to follow the correct path of Buddhism. (Watanabe Kenji, "Kanazōshi to nonfikushon: Ōsaka no yaku to Shimabara no ran," in *Edo no Nonfikushon*, edited by Shiraishi Yoshio, Norizuki Toshihiko, and Watanabe Kenji (Tokyo: Tōkyō shoseki, 1993).

67. The original text puts the distance from Japan as 海上三万七千余里 and the area of Nanban as 寛さ十万里四方. The calculations in miles are approximate using an equivalent of 3,927 meters or 2.44 miles per *li*, which was the standard measure of the *li* during the Tokugawa period.

north, and by many great oceans to the east.⁶⁸ The lord of the land is called King Gojimbi.⁶⁹

The barbarian status made clear by the Othering of the Kirishitan character is also represented geographically by the description of Nanban, which opens the *Raichō jikki* narrative. In one part of that description, Japan, India, and China are the point of reference for the location of Nanban, which is on the periphery reserved for the barbarian. However, that periphery is not in Europe, as one might expect, but in the region of present-day Vietnam. In another part of the description, Nanban is said to be ninety thousand miles from Japan—a distance so exaggerated that anyone who followed it would have found himself circumnavigating the globe nearly three times before arriving back where he began.

These discrepancies were troubling to more than one educated reader in the late eighteenth and early nineteenth centuries who knew the origins of the word *nanbanjin* and who had access to relatively accurate maps of the world. As a result, in some later adaptations of the *Raichō jikki* narrative, this portion of the story is changed. In Miura Baien's 1784 *Samidareshō* (Musings During the Early Summer Rain), for example, the entire section about the country of Nanban is omitted, and in a later section of his work he gives descriptions of the Western countries based on Nishikawa Joken's 1708 *Zōhō ka'i tsūshōkō* (Revised Treatise on Relations with Chinese and Barbarian Countries). He also complains that the author of the *Raichō jikki* variant he used (*Ibuki mogusa*) was ignorant of these matters and should not be believed.⁷⁰ Similarly, in the first printed version of the narrative that came out in 1868 and was titled *Nanbanji kōhaiki*, the section on the

---

68. India and China is a translation of *Tenjiku shinadakoku*. Tenjiku originally meant India and later came to mean any place foreign ships came from, or just a foreign country. In his *Historia de Japam*, Luis Frois describes a child pointing at the fathers and calling them *tenjikujin*, which Frois interpreted as meaning "men of Siam." See Luis Frois, S.J., *Historia de Japam*, vol. I., edited by Joseph Wicki (Lisbon: Biblioteca Nacional de Lisboa, 1976), 138. The word used for Szechuan here is *Shoku*. *Ume* (usually written 宇め) in this text is written as *Uba* (usually written 烏馬) in the *Kirishitan shūmon raichō jikki* variant, while a few other variants refer to *Roba* (驢馬) or "Luzon," in the Philippines. In the work of Chau Ju-Kua on twelfth- and thirteenth-century Chinese and Arab trade, he cites a place called Wu Ma Pa (烏馬抜) that was a dependency of Annam/Champa (in present-day Vietnam), and this fits with the physical description of the location. I am grateful to Peter Shapinsky for making me aware of this reference in Chau Ju-Kua, *Chau Ju-Kua, His Work on the Chinese and Arab Trade in the Twelfth and Thirteenth Centuries, Entitled Chu-Fan-Chi/ Translated From the Chinese and Annotated By Friedrich Hirth and W.W. Rockhill* (St. Petersburg: Imperial Academy of Sciences, 1911).
69. Washio, *Nihon shisō tōsō shiryō*, 319.
70. Miura Baien, *Samidareshō*, Baien zenshū, vol. 1 (Tokyo: Butsudōkan, 1912). In English, Miura Baien, "Samidare-Shō (Musings During the Early Summer Rain)," *Monumenta Nipponica* 9, no. 1/2 (1953): 343.

location of Nanban is omitted. This omission is explained in an appendix written by the publication's editor, Kiyu Dōnin, where he summarizes the omitted portion and then also cites the work of Nishikawa Joken to show why it was inaccurate and therefore removed from the final text. Still, these alterations to the original text are only seen in a few cases, and the vast majority of manuscripts copied in the eighteenth and nineteenth centuries retained the original description of the land of Nanban.

Of course, a country called "Nanban" did not exist and was derived from the term *nanbanjin*, which was applied to the Iberians who had come to Japan from outside of the traditional Sino-centric realm of civilization, and whose ships sailed to Japan from Macao and Manila in the south. The location of these Portuguese and Spanish colonies in Asia likely contributed to some confusion about the location of the Iberians' home. Though *Baterenki* (ca. 1610) locates their home in "Roma," beginning with *Kirishitan monogatari* in 1639 and continuing with the *Raichō jikki* narrative, the Kirishitan come from the land of Nanban, which is ruled by its own king. However, *Raichō jikki* is the first of the two later tales to attempt to map Nanban in relation to Japan. While the placement of Nanban in the world appears contradictory and odd even to Baien and Kiyū Dōjin, the location and description of the barbarian country appear to have been drawn from a number of representations of both Japan and Nanban available in the media of the times. More importantly, they complement the Othering of the Kirishitan character by locating his home on the barbarian periphery of a three-worlds realm. And just as the threat of the Kirishitan Other is tamed by portraying him as a more familiar, knowable Other, the land of Nanban is controlled by being mapped on the barbarian fringes of the traditional, *known* world of the Three Realms.

In the *Raichō jikki* description, the country of Nanban is bounded by India and China, as well as many great oceans to the east, but it is also clearly outside of those sacred places. Though this land cannot be found in most Western-inspired maps of the period, it does fit a rather unusual map of Tenjiku (or India) that appeared in an encyclopedia printed in 1642.[71]

---

71. One Western-inspired map that does feature Nanban is on a late eighteenth-century pair of screens known as *Sekai yondaishū zu/Yonjūhachi-ka-koku jinbutsu zu* (Regional Maps with Pictures of Forty-eight Peoples). In this map, under the larger name of Portugal (保留土) at the appropriate place on the map is the name in smaller print of Nanban (南蠻). In addition, among the various people of the world featured in the surrounding cartouches, the people of Nanban (the man in breeches, a hat and a cape, the woman in a mantilla) are included, but those of Portugal are not. Though the details of the illustrations are hard to make out in photographs of the screens, they can be found in *Japan Envisions the West: 16th-19th Century Japanese Art From Kobe City Museum* (Seattle, Wash.: Seattle Art Museum, 2007), 44–45.

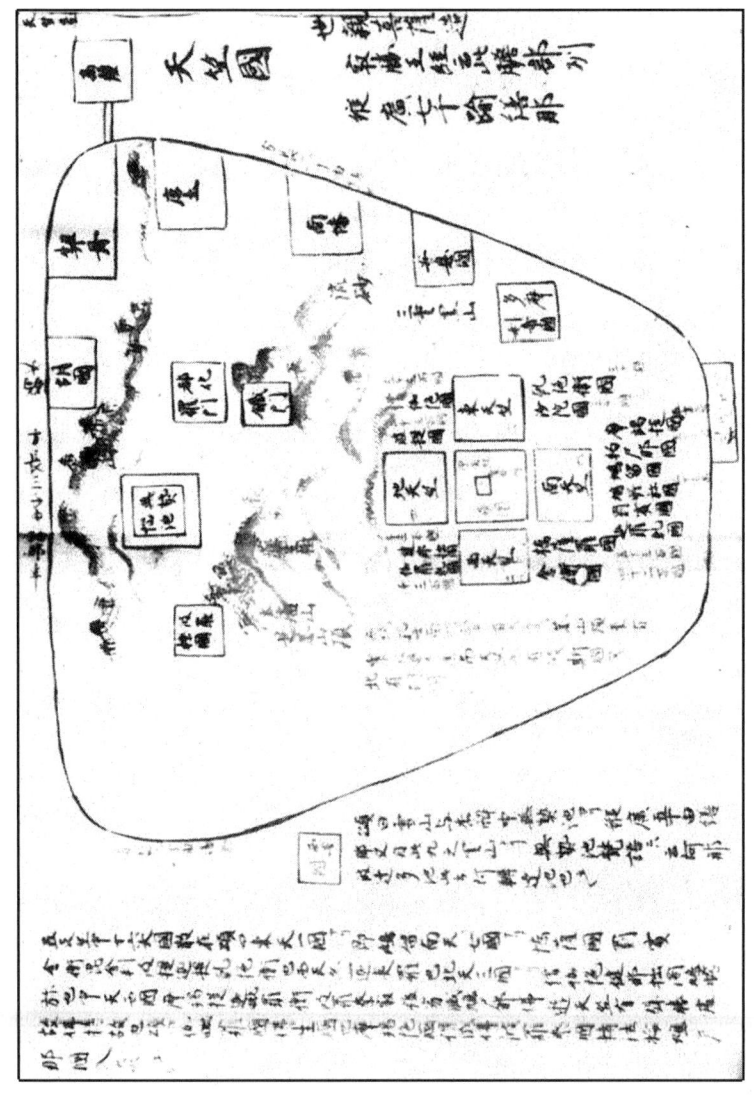

Figure 5. Map of India from manuscript copy of *Shūgaihō* (in Ueno National Library, Tokyo). Source: Muroga Nobuo and Unno Kazutaka, "The Buddhist World Map in Japan and Its Contact With European Maps," *Imago Mundi* 16 (1962): 53.

The book was compiled in the fourteenth century and added to over the years, but Unno Kazutaka and Muroga Nobuo estimate that the map of Tenjiku was a late addition that was inserted no earlier than the beginning of the seventeenth century.[72] The map (see facing page, figure 5) is a rather crude rendition of the Buddhist map of the world (*Jambu-dvīpa*) with Tenjiku at the center and China to the right.[73] In this particular version, Nanban is located just below China and to the right of India, with the ocean to the east. This mirrors the description of the location of Nanban that appears in the *Raichō jikki* narrative.

Buddhist maps of the world were produced in Japan starting in the medieval period, and the earliest extant example of one is the 1364 *Gotenjiku zu*, or Map of the Five Indies, in the collection of Hōryūji temple in Nara.[74] As Muroga and Unno point out in their article, the new geographic information brought to Japan by the Western missionaries and traders did not inhibit the continued production of these maps or change the basic shape of them, although as in the case described above, some "new" countries were added to the outer edges of that world. In the 1710 *Nansenbushū bankoku shōka no zu* (Buddhist Map of the World) produced by the scholar-priest Hōtan, the Japanese archipelago is mapped in detail to the east of Tenjiku, with all of its provinces labeled (see figure 6).[75] In addition, a seemingly random collection of islands in the northwest corner are marked with the names of some of the European countries. In this newer version of the traditional Buddhist map of the world, Japan is a significant presence alongside India and China, while the foreign countries that occupy so much space in the newer western maps are relegated to obscurity in the corner. These kinds of Buddhist maps were printed into the nineteenth century, demonstrating what Onno and Muroga call "a dogmatic insistence on the authenticity of the Buddhist world-conception."[76] The description of the location of Nanban in the *Raichō jikki* narrative taps into

---

72. Muroga Nobuo and Unno Kazutaka, "The Buddhist World Map in Japan and Its Contact With European Maps," *Imago Mundi* 16 (1962): 49—69.
73. Muroga and Unno note that the origins of the Buddhist maps of the world were in a map drawn to depict the lands traveled in the pilgrimage to India of the seventh-century Chinese priest Hsüan-tsang. Over time, a map that was meant to depict the "holy land" of India came to symbolize the entire world. See Ibid., 51.
74. In this map, the Japanese islands of Shikoku and Kyushu float in the waves near the right margin. Nanba Matsutaro, Muroga Nobuo, and Unno Kazutaka, *Nihon no kochizu* (Tokyo: Sōgensha, 1969), 1.
75. Ibid., 13. An original 1710 print of this map is in the map room at the University of Michigan library.
76. Muroga and Unno, "The Buddhist World Map," 63.

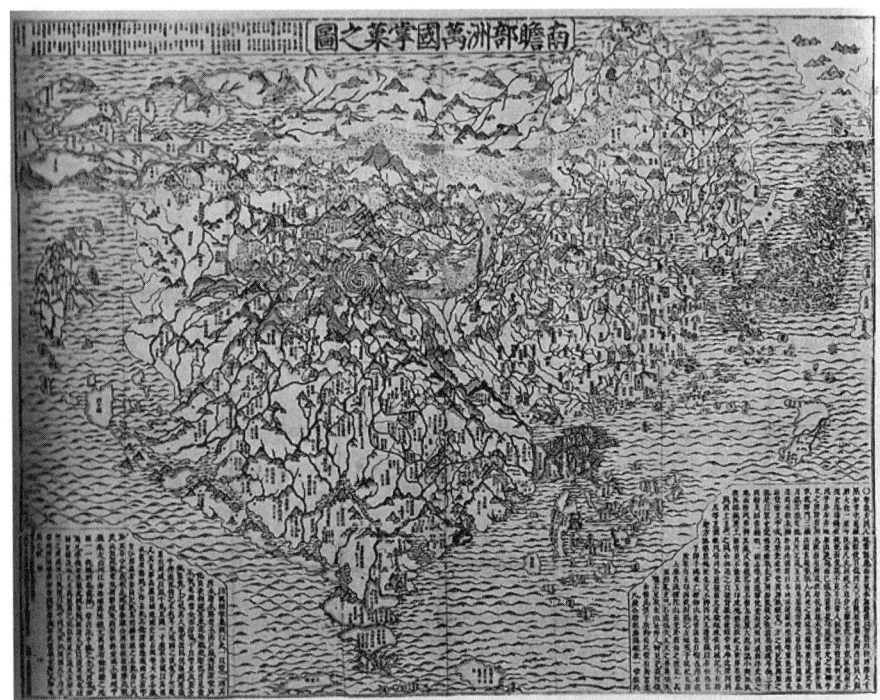

Figure 6. 1710 *Nansenbushū bankoku shōka no zu* (Buddhist World Map), by Hōtan. Source: Nanba Matsutaro, Muroga Nobuo, and Unno Kazutaka, *Nihon no kochizu* (Tokyo: Sōgensha, 1969), 13.

and perpetuates this insistence on the Buddhist worldview.

Nonetheless, a comparison of the description of the country with a variety of seventeenth and eighteenth century popular representations of the world and foreign peoples shows that the Buddhist worldview was also influenced by newer maps of the world. Many of the maps printed and sold in the seventeenth and eighteenth centuries represented the world as it appeared on the maps brought by Western missionaries, though they also sometimes included mythical countries from Chinese sources.[77] These maps were often accompanied by cartouches depicting the peoples of the world, and though the peoples named and the iconography used to depict them varied among the different maps, the number of peoples depicted (i.e., the number of peoples of the world) remained relatively steady at forty-two in the earliest imperial *bankoku* screen, and forty in the *Shōho bankokuzu* of 1647 (see figure 7).[78]

This number continues to be used in subsequent encyclopedias of foreign peoples, which began to come out in the early eighteenth century. The most influential of these was the 1720 *Shijūnikoku jinbutsu zusetsu* (The Peoples of the Forty-two Countries) by Nishikawa Joken. This and other works by Joken were consistently quoted by scholars who were writing about the countries of the world until as late as the mid-nineteenth century, and as we saw above, his works were cited by Miura Baien and Kiyu Dojin to show that the location and very existence of Nanban as it is described in the *Raichō jikki* narrative must have been wrong. But an interesting feature of Joken's work is that he returned to the original number of forty-two for the total number of countries in the world. Ronald Toby notes, "The encyclopedist Nishikawa Joken began to reorganize anthropological knowledge from a myriad countries that number forty to a specified number of countries—he returned to the forty-two of the imperial Bankoku screen—that would become canonical in later iterations, well into the nineteenth century."[79] In fact, a text titled *Ka'i jinbutsu zu* (A Map of the Peoples of Barbarian and Civilized Countries) and published by Sugiya Yukinao as late as 1827 copies Joken's world of forty-two countries exactly.[80] However, an important difference between Joken's world and that of the earlier maps with forty and forty-two countries, is that Joken's forty-two are all foreign and do not include Japan. As a result, after the

---

77. See chapter 1, n. 13 for more details on the maps and encyclopedias described here.
78. Toby, "Three Realms/Myriad Countries," 25–26.
79. Ibid, 31.
80. Ibid, 44n.53. An original copy of the map is held in the Spencer Collection of the New York Public Library.

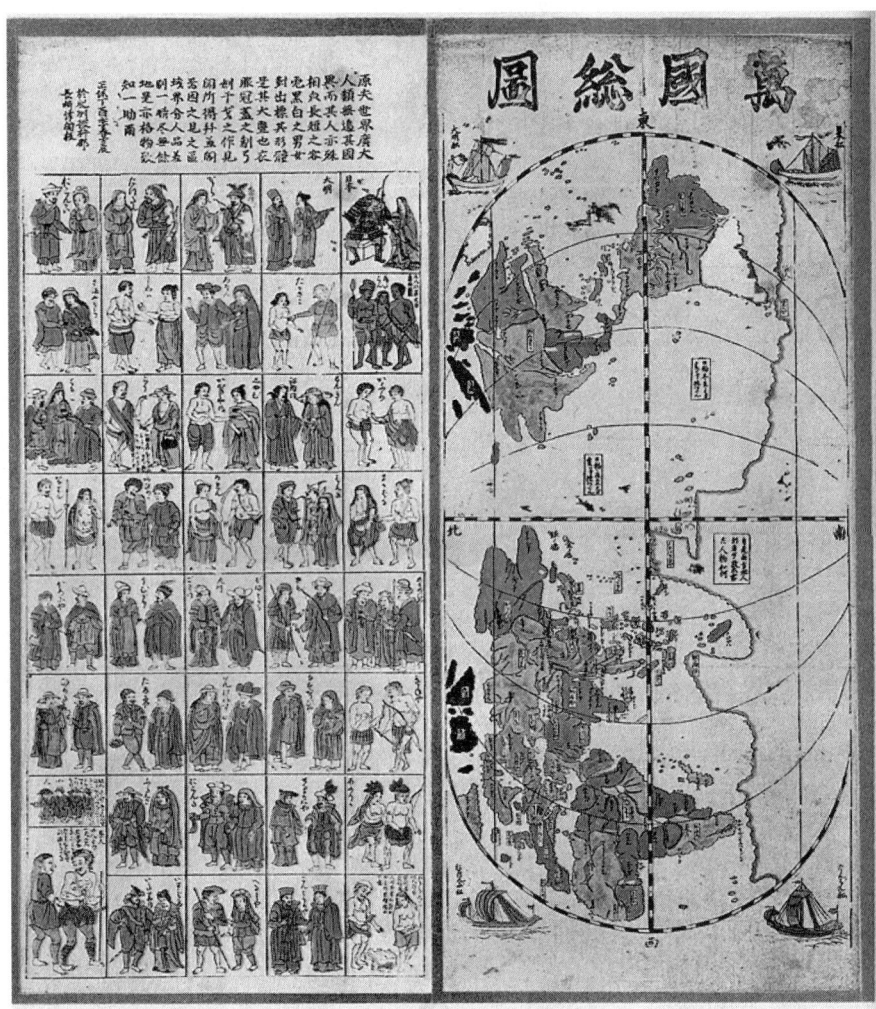

Figure 7. 1645 *Bankoku sōzu* (World Map), in the Kobe City Museum of Nanban Art. Source: Nanba Matsutaro, Muroga Nobuo, and Unno Kazutaka, *Nihon no kochizu* (Tokyo: Sōgensha, 1969), 12.

1720 printing of the text, what Toby calls the "canonical" representation of the world's countries saw all forty-two as foreign to Japan.

If we return to the description of Nanban that opens *Raichō jikki* with this knowledge about the popular representation of foreign countries, a previously unremarkable part of the description fairly leaps off the page: Nanban is comprised of forty-two provinces. Later, we learn that among those forty-two is the province of the Kirishitan, though the nature of the remaining forty-one is unclear. Of course, the word translated here as provinces is *kuni* 國, which is the same word used to refer to the larger country of Nanban. This is common usage for that word, but the usage becomes more significant in the context of this description of Nanban, in which we see the forty-two provinces being synonymous with the popular idea of the forty-two foreign countries outside of Japan. From this perspective, the origins of the word Nanban used by the first traders coming from the southwest and the fact that there was no actual country of that name become usefully vague, supporting the image of Nanban as a repository for all things foreign. Of course, the forty-two countries of the world in Joken's and other's encyclopedias naturally included Kara (China) and Tenjiku (India), which are clearly not meant to be part of Nanban in this narrative. But as Miura Baien and Kiyu Dōjin observed, the author of the text occasionally sacrificed accuracy to the cause of effect. Whether used consciously or not, the representation of Nanban as having forty-two provinces helped conjure the image of an entire barbarian world of the "not Japanese" bent on the conquest of Japan.

Significantly, the number of the provinces not only is mentioned in the opening description of the country but is repeated several times throughout the *Raichō jikki* narrative. When Lord Gogi speaks to the Nanban king and argues against sending an army to conquer Japan, he says specifically that "men from all forty-two provinces have tried to enter Japan countless times and not one has succeeded."[81] And later, when the brothers are convincing their new followers to join the sect, they assure them: "Our country has forty-two provinces and is one hundred times larger than Japan. Because we worship Deus, no one in our land is poor, and there is no disease."[82] But the most striking reference to the forty-two provinces is in connection with the rosaries used by the Kirishitan and distributed to their converts. The text points out that the "Japanese" rosary has 108 beads to signify the 108 worldly desires, but that the Kirishitan rosary has forty-two beads to represent the forty-two provinces of Nanban. As a first

---

81. Washio, *Nihon shisō tōsō shiryō*, 320.
82. Ibid., 335–36.

step in the conversion of the new followers, the brothers give them each one of these rosaries and teach them a special chant. They are told that the only way they can achieve a good rebirth is by saying this chant with the rosary, *bead by bead*. The resulting, remarkable image is of the Japanese converts chanting for their own salvation with beads representing the realm of the foreign Other, with the implication that they will not only become Kirishitan through that salvation but also Nanbanjin. In this representation, not only are the Kirishitan Other "in here," so is their world. And just as the first stage of the conquest was signaled by the fall of the sixty-six pines symbolizing the provinces of Japan, the second is represented by the "physical" presence of the foreign countries in the hands of the believers.

This representation of Nanban and its forty-two provinces, added to the consistently invoked image of a sacred Japan in the three realms, helps construct a "map" of the world in the *Raichō jikki* narrative that resembles the 1710 Buddhist map of the world (figure 6). In this one, India, China and Japan are all prominent at the center, while other Asian countries and Europe are represented peripherally. Though we never learn the identities of the other forty-one provinces of Nanban, their names are irrelevant. In fact, their lack of specific identity makes them all the more identifiable as a kind of universal barbarian Other—the nonmembers of the civilized three realms. This map rejects the diminished place of Japan in the world shown in Western geography and reasserts its central position in the three realms, and in so doing represents yet another way in which the foreign is dominated and othered in the *Raichō jikki* narrative.

Chapter Four

Conjurers and Conquerors:
The Kirishitan Figure in Other Late Edo Discourses

The popular figure of the Kirishitan villain that originated in *Baterenki* and *Kirishitan monogatari* and saw its fullest development in *Kirishitan shūmon raichō jikki* was not confined to these popular narratives; it appears in various incarnations in other discourses of the Edo period. These discourses range from the sensational plots of *jōruri* puppet plays and *kabuki* to the more scholarly writings of participants in the debates over opening trade with the West. The Kirishitan of the former includes a quick-change artist who can use his magical powers to change into a giant toad and back again, while that of the latter roams the waves in ships from Russia, England, and America in a constant search for lands to conquer. On the surface, these two figures are not so similar, but the Kirishitan of the Tenjiku Tokubei plays and that of Aizawa Seishisai's *Shinron* (New Theses) maintain many common characteristics, while also showing the influence of the expulsion narratives. In fact, in both we can still recognize the wily and charismatic figure of the *Raichō jikki* narrative who uses his Kirishitan religion to gather followers in an attempt to take over Japan. In this chapter, a sample of various texts from the eighteenth and nineteenth centuries that represent the Kirishitan demonstrates not only the different uses to which the Kirishitan figure was put but also the pervasive presence of the Kirishitan Other in Edo-period discourse.

"DEI DEI PARAISO"—THE KIRISHITAN VILLAIN ON STAGE

Beginning as early as 1719 and continuing into the Meiji period, a villain who is Kirishitan and possesses magical powers appears in nearly a dozen *jōruri* and *kabuki* plays, including two by the famous playwrights Chikamatsu Monzaemon and Tsuruya Nanboku. Though the identity of the villains in the plays varies considerably, the villains have a number of characteristics in common: they are invariably not who they seem, often presenting themselves as upstanding Japanese citizens, only to be exposed as the sons of disgraced samurai or as foreigners in disguise; they are constantly plotting to topple the government or take over the country; and they all have special powers and use incantations that are reminiscent of the Kirishitan chants in *Kirishitan monogatari* and *Kirishitan shūmon raichō jikki*.

Though only one of the plays actually mentions the word "Kirishitan," the villains are recognizable as such in a number of ways.[1] Four of the plays use an alternative word for Christianity and describe the religion of the villain as *yaso shūmon* (the Jesus Sect), or as *tenshukyō* (teachings of the Lord of Heaven), using the Chinese renditions of Jesus and Deus, respectively.[2] Several of the plays also indicate that the main deity of the villain's false teachings is Deus, *tenshu*, or *tentai*, all of which were words used by the missionaries to indicate God, while others mention *zensumaru* (Jesus Mary), *sandamaru* (Saint Mary), or simply refer to the main deity of *yaso shūmon*. Perhaps most recognizable of all are the incantations mentioned above, which appear in all of the plays and contain various combinations of the phrases *shigo shōten paraiso* (after death, life in paradise), *dei dei paraiso* (Deus, Deus, paradise), and *zensumaro, sandamaro, paraiso* (Jesus Mary, Saint Mary, paradise).

---

1. In one play the word is part of the villain's name, "Kirishitanzō." The play is *Keisei takasago ura* in Tsuchida Mamoru and Matsuzaki Hitoshi, eds., *Keisei takasago ura* 傾城高砂浦, Kabuki daichō shūsei, vol. 18 (Tokyo: Benseisha, 1989). It was first performed in Kyoto in 1765. This and other information about the Kirishitan themes in plays of the eighteenth and nineteenth centuries was first presented in a talk by Katō Atsuko at a conference in 2007. Katō Atsuko, "*Nihon kinsei engeki ni miru 'Kirishitan' no imēji no henyō*" ("The Changing Image of the 'Kirishitan' Seen in Early Modern Japanese Theater"), panel presentation, *Kirishitan bunka to nichiō kōryrū* (Symposium on Christianity and Japanese/European Relations), Strasbourg, France, March 27, 2007.
2. In *yaso shūmon* 耶蘇宗門, *yaso* is the Chinese word for Jesus, and *tenshu* 天主 or *tentei* 天帝 were the Chinese words for Deus. The latter two words were included in the *Nippo jisho* (Japanese-Portuguese Dictionary), the dictionary published by the Jesuits, as the words for God. *Yaso* was probably transmitted to Japan through Chinese books on Christianity that entered the country before the ban on such imports. *Yaso shūmon* was commonly used by Confucian scholars to describe Christianity. The three plays that describe *yaso shūmon* are: *Keisei sato no kawazu* (The Frog in the Pleasure District), Kabuki daichō shūsei, vol. 10 (1986); *Kanazōshi kokusenya jitsuroku*, Kabuki daichō shūsei, vol. 13 (1987); and *Keisei takasago ura*, Kabuki daichō shūsei, vol.18 (1989). The play that mentions *tenshukyō* is *Keisei to kakugedai no hajimari* (Courtesans and the Origins of Heresy), Kabuki daichō shūsei, vol. 38 (1999).

The origins of the villains and their true identities vary from play to play, but the two most commonly used characters of Nanagusa Shirō and Tenjiku Tokubei are in another way recognizable as the Kirishitan/foreign Other. Nanagusa Shirō is a rather thinly disguised reference to Amakusa Shirō, the name by which the purported leader of the Shimabara Rebellion is most commonly known. Though we know that his real name was Masuda Tokisada, not much else is known of the Amakusa Shirō character of legend.[3] In the plays featuring Nanagusa Shirō, the name is used as a cover in one case for a member of a disgraced Fujiwara branch, and in other cases for high-ranking retainers and spies for the Ming Dynasty and the king of the Ryukyus. Similarly, Tenjiku Tokubei was the name of a historical figure of the seventeenth century who wrote memoirs of his travels to India (*Tenjiku*) and countries in Southeast Asia, but in the plays it is a cover for the sons of disgraced families or for disgruntled Koreans seeking revenge for Hideyoshi's invasion.[4] While the Nanagusa Shirō name creates a historical association with the Kirishitan, the use of Tenjiku Tokubei places greater emphasis on the foreign aspect of the villain. However, the Tenjiku Tokubei plays also feature the most spectacular demonstrations of magic, and since the image of the Kirishitan as magician was firmly in place by the middle of the eighteenth century, that provided another strong association with the Kirishitan.[5]

An interesting feature of many of these plays is the fact that the villain often represents a number of Japan's Others in one character. For example, one of the Tenjiku Tokubei characters is really the son of a retainer of the Korean king bent on revenge for Hideyoshi's invasion. However, he practices "toad magic" that includes an incantation with Kirishitan words, carries an image of Deus, and dresses in a costume that has Ainu and seventeenth-century Dutch characteristics.[6] This kind of all-purpose foreigner, or *tōjin*, was visible in a number of popular plays and visual media

---

3. In popular works about the Shimabara Rebellion, such as *Shimabaraki*, Amakusa Shirō is a villainous and somewhat mystical figure, though he does not much resemble the Kirishitan villain of the popular anti-Kirishitan tales. However, Ivan Morris, in a chapter on Amakusa Shirō in his book *The Nobility of Failure*, shows how Amakusa Shirō has been portrayed as an anti-establishment hero in a number of books and movies in the twentieth century. See Ivan Morris, *The Nobility of Failure: Tragic Heroes in the History of Japan* (New York: Meridian, 1975), 143–79.
4. The memoirs of the historical figure are called *Tenjiku tokai monogatari* (Tales of a Crossing to Tenjiku).
5. See the anecdote below about the police investigation of performances of *Tenjiku Tokubei ikoku banashi* (The Tale of Tokubei from India).
6. This is the character in *Tenjiku Tokubei ikoku banashi*. See a description of Tenjiku Tokubei plays below. For more on toad magic, see the section on *Shimabara kaeru kassen* below.

of the Edo period.⁷ Ronald Toby has identified a conflation of the Nanban Other with the *tōjin* in visual representations as early as 1635, and, as these plays show, the Kirishitan appears to have become an important part of that "omnium gatherum for foreigners" in written texts by the early eighteenth century.⁸

Plays featuring a villain with Kirishitan powers who often was foreign were introduced regularly throughout the eighteenth and early nineteenth century, and there is evidence that most were staged more than once, making the Kirishitan Other a rather ubiquitous one on stage. But access to these representations of the Kirishitan was not confined to attendance at performances, since librettos for *kabuki* and *jōruri* were as popular at lending libraries as other kinds of texts.⁹ With the availability of a variety of scripts featuring the Kirishitan Other, along with the continued circulation of manuscripts of *Kirishitan monogatari* and of the many variants of *Raichō jikki* for over a century, it is clear that the Kirishitan villain was a familiar Other in the discourse of Edo-period Japan. Table 1 shows a list of some of the plays and the Kirishitan/foreign characteristics they share, and detailed descriptions of three of the plays below illustrate some distinctive ways that the Kirishitan/foreign Other appeared on stage between 1719 and 1804.¹⁰

---

7. Ronald Toby and Keiko Suzuki have both written about the *tōjin* figure in prints and paintings of the Edo period. See Ronald P. Toby, "The 'Indianness' of Iberia and Changing Japanese Iconographies of Other," in *Implicit Understandings: Observing, Reporting, and Reflecting on the Encounters Between Europeans and Other Peoples in the Early Modern Era*, edited byedited by Stuart B Schwartz (Cambridge: Cambridge University Press, 1994), 323—51;and Keiko Suzuki, "The Making of Tōjin Construction of the Other in Early Modern Japan," *Asian Folklore Studies* 66, no. 1/2 (2007): 83–105.
8. Toby, "Changing Japanese Iconographies," 335–36.
9. The catalogue of the Daisō lending library that was dismantled and sold in 1898 shows an extensive collection of *kabuki* and *jōruri* scripts. See Shibata Mitsuhiko, ed., *Daisō zōsho mokuroku to kenkyū*, 2 vols. (Tokyo: Seishōdō shoten, 1983).
10. There is a *kojōruri* called *Amakusa monogatari* (Tale of Amakusa) that dates to 1666. I do not include it in this group because it is fundamentally a summary of the first chapters of the *Shimabaraki* text and therefore does not represent the same kind of Kirishitan villain. It is also considered to have been a text that was read more than it was performed. It is unclear whether it was ever performed as a puppet play, though scholars seem to think it might have been performed informally for gatherings of higher-ranking samurai or daimyo. See Yokoyama Shigeru, ed, *Amakusa monogatari*, Kojōruri shohonshu, vol. 3 (Tokyo: Kadokawa shoten, 1964). Some information on the staging of the individual plays is available in the explanatory remarks included with each play reproduced in the *Kabuki daichō shusei*. In many cases there are separate *nenpyō* listing all of the stagings of particular plays. For example, a *nenpyō* recording presentations of *Tenjiku tokubei ikoku banashi* lists performances from 1804 to the 1980s. See Kokuritsu Gekijō Geinō Chōsashitsu, ed., *Tenjiku Tokubei ikoku banashi*, Kokuritsu gekijō jōen shiryōshu, vol. 248 (Tokyo: 1986), 4–41.

Table 1. *Kabuki* and *jōruri* plays featuring a Kirishitan villain.*

Title/date of first performance	Main villain	Special powers	Incantation	Other
Keisei shimabara kaeru kassen 傾城島原蛙合戦／ Takemotoza, 1719	Nanagusa Shirō/ really Fujiwara Takahira (of Ainu origins)	Toad magic**	None	Magic mirror, *fumie*
Keisei sato no kawazu けいせい花街蛙／ Kyoto, 1756	Son of Ōuchi Yoshitaka	*Yaso shūmon*/ Christianity	"*Araikitsu* **shigo shoden** *sandamaru, zensumaru, paraiso, paraiso*"	Images of "*sandamaro*," "*zensumaro*"
Tenjiku tokubei kikigaki ourai 天竺徳兵衛聞書往／ Osaka, 1757	Tenjiku Tokubei/ really retainer of Korean king	Toad magic	"*Dei, dei, deikō, deisubaru*"	Image of *yaso* (Jesus)
Kanazōshi kokusenya jitsuroku 仮名草紙国性爺実録／ Osaka, 1759	Nanagusa Shirō/ really retainer of Ming dynasty	*Yaso shūmon*/ Christianity	"*Araikitsu* **shigo shoten** *dei, dei, deikō, deisumaru, sandamaru, paraiso, paraiso*"	Retainers Bateren Dorozō and Iruman Tochizō; *fumie*
Tenjiku tokubei sato no sugatami 天竺徳兵衛郷鏡／ Takemotoza, 1763	Tenjiku Tokubei/ really son of retainer of Korean king	Toad magic	"*Dei, dei, paraiso, paraiso*"	*Fumie*
Keisei takasago ura 傾城高砂浦／ Kyoto, 1765	Yaso Tokiya	*Yaso shūmon*/ Christianity and toad magic	"*Ōikitsu,* **shigo shoten,** *santamaru, zensumaru, paraiso, paraiso*"	Retainer named Kirishitanzō
Keisei sato no odamaki けいせい廓苧環／ Osaka, 1769	Enron/really a retainer of the Ogata family	Toad magic	None	Image of *Deus tentei*
Keisei kane no naruto 傾城鐘鳴渡／ Kyoto, 1775	Yoshino Saburō/ really son of king of Ryukyus; Nanagusa Shirō/really retainer of prince of Ryukyus	*Jashūmon* (evil religion)	"*Shigo shoten paraizo*"	*Fumie*; image of Deus; image of *tentei*
Keisei to kakugedai no hajimari 傾城と書外始／ Kyoto, 1779	Amine Shirō Katsuhisa	*Tenshūkyō*/ Christianity	"*Aoikitsu,* **shigo shoten** *zensumaru ya sandamaru, haraiso, haraiso*"	Image from *Tenshūkyō*
Tenjiku Tokubei ikoku banashi 天竺徳兵衛韓噺／ Edo, 1804	Tenjiku Tokubei/ really son of Korean retainer	Toad magic	"*Namu sashitaru magundaria,* **shugo shoden** *paraiso, paraiso*"	Image of Deus
Tenjiku Tokubei keshō no sugatami 天竺徳兵衛化粧鏡 Edo, 1809	Tenjiku Tokubei/ really son of Akamatsu Mitsusuke	False religion and toad magic	"*Namu tatsutaruma bundarigya, ensumaru, sandamaru,* **shigo shoden** *araiso, araiso*"	None

*This list is by no means exhaustive and is a revised version of a similar one presented by Katō Atsuko in 2007 (Katō, "*Nihon kinsei engeki ni miru 'Kirishitan' no imēji no henyō*").
**See the discussion of toad magic in the section below on *Shimabara kaeru kassen*.

111

Keisei Shimabara kaeru kassen

On the sixth day of the eleventh month of Kyōhō 4 (1719), a new play by Chikamatsu Monzaemon was staged at the Takemotoza theater in Osaka. Titled *Keisei Shimabara kaeru kassen* (傾城島原蛙合戦) or "Frog Battle of the Shimabara Beauties," it seemed to promise a mysterious mix of fighting frogs and courtesans from the famous Kyoto pleasure quarters. But as his audiences knew well, Chikamatsu's plays often dealt with more recent and controversial events disguised as ancient history in order to avoid the gaze of the censors. As a result, most patrons probably saw the double meanings in the title, referring to the Shimabara Rebellion and the siege of Hara Castle that took place eighty years earlier. In fact, the Kyoto pleasure quarter had been established shortly after the uprising and was said to have taken its name from it. And the word *keisei* also alluded to both the pleasure quarters and the siege. Meaning a beautiful courtesan, it referred to a woman whose beauty could bring men to ruin, with characters that literally meant to "topple cities."

The play is set early in the Kamakura period during the reign of Emperor Go-Toba, shortly after the victory of the Minamoto clan over the Heike in the latter half of the twelfth century. In the opening scene, we learn that the emperor has had an ominous dream in which "there was a stranger (異人) who was neither priest nor layman. He rode on a cloud, standing with one foot on the sun and the other on the moon. From his mouth came a five-colored rainbow, and gold flowers bloomed on the land below."[11] Concerned that this might augur unrest in the land, the emperor asks his diviner to interpret it. The latter's conclusion is that the sun in the dream signifies the sun (日) in Japanese Shinto (日本神道), while the moon (月) signifies the early Indian Buddhists (月支仏道).[12] These two paths of Buddhism and Shinto form the two wings of the law of the kingdom. In addition, among the ying-yang masters there are some who possess a frog that can exhale and produce a rainbow. This frog is the product of the wizardry of the Gama sennin, or Toad Hermit, which is considered

---

11. *Keisei Shimabara kaeru kassen*, Chikamatsu zenshu, vol. 11 (Tokyo: Iwanami shoten, 1989), 240.
12. The *gesshi* (月支 or 月氏) was a nomadic tribe that made its home in the border areas between China and India. Early accounts of the transmission of Buddhism such as the 1173 *Sangoku dentōki* (History of the Three Realms) by Kakuken say that the Ming emperor of the Gokan period (A.D. 28–75) dreamt of a golden figure and was told the person in his dream was the Buddha. He sent a message to the land of the *gesshi* in the west asking about this person, and he was sent in return an image of the Buddha and forty-two sutra scrolls. According to this story, that was how Buddhism came to China. For more on Kakukan and the *Sangoku dentōki*, see Hirofumi Ichikawa, *Nihon chūsei no hikari to kage: 'Uchinaru sangoku' no shisō* (Tokyo: Perikansha, 1999), 46–79.

heresy among Confucians and Buddhists.[13] According to the diviner, this dream could only mean that a stranger had come to spread heresy and gather adherents in order to stamp out the empire and its underpinnings, the laws of Buddha and Shinto.[14]

The villain who eventually proves the diviner correct turns out to be Fujiwara Takahira, the fourth son of a family of Ainu descent that were loyal to the defeated Heike. He goes by the name of Nanagusa Shirō (七草四郎). A practitioner of "toad magic," he has escaped capture numerous times as he travels the country, gathering adherents in an attempt to become the sole ruler of the realm. Kasai is a samurai who has failed in his mission to capture Shirō and commits *seppuku* to take responsibility. The greater part of the story follows the efforts of his son and daughter to find Shirō and avenge their father's death. At one point Shirō hides himself in the Shimabara pleasure quarters, where he befriends a young courtesan named Sarashina. But she soon turns against him and joins the children of Kasai in trying to destroy the "number one enemy of the realm." The final scene recalls the siege of Hara Castle, with Shirō and his followers starving inside his castle after being surrounded by the enemy for months. Finally, Sarashina and Kasai's daughter manage to sneak into the castle, where they use a special rope from the shrine of Benzaiten of E no Shima to neutralize Shirō's magical powers and defeat him. In a nod to the *keisei* of the title, it is the women who manage to bring down the villain, in a symbolic "toppling" of the walls.

By using the name Nanagusa Shirō and the plot of a subversive figure and his army of converts who are cornered in a castle and eventually defeated, Chikamatsu copied the more politically safe story of the Amakusa Rebellion that had been printed without interference or censorship. The three-volume work *Shimabaraki* tells the story of Amakusa Shirō and the rebellion and was printed four times in the seventeenth century and again in 1704 and 1708.[15] The lack of censorship of the work was likely due to the fact that it dealt primarily with the rebellion and contains little about the foreign missionaries or their religion, except to say that Shirō and his followers were Kirishitan. However, while he avoids any mention of the

---

13. *Gama sennin* 蝦墓仙人 (Toad Hermit) is a famous mountain hermit of the Three Kingdoms period in China. See below for literary origins.
14. *Shimabara kaeru kassen*, 241–42.
15. The earlier dates are 1642 or 1643, 1649, 1673, and 1688. For more information on this text, see Wakaki Taiichi, "'*Shimabaraki*' no seisei to sono tenkai," *Bungaku* 54, no. 12 (1986): 142–51; and Watanabe Kenji, "Kirishitan to bungaku to nonfikushon bungaku," in *Shimabara no ran wo chūshin ni 16 seiki ikō no nihon to higashi ajia no Kirishitan bungaku no eikyōdo wo meguru sōgōteki hikaku kenkyū* (Tokyo: Rikkyo University, 2008).

Kirishitan by necessity, it is clear that Chikamatsu's main character is a combination of the padres in *Raichō jikki* and the figure of the "Toad Hermit" from Chinese folklore.

In a chapter tracing the "frog motif" in Edo-period literature, Takagi Gen points out that the frog had appeared in Japanese folk tales for centuries, but that the image of the toad hermit (*gama sennin*) and toad magic that became popular in the Edo period first appeared in this Chikamatsu play.[16] The figure of Gama sennin is based on the story of the ruler Ryū Kai Sen (劉海蟾) of the Three Kingdoms period in tenth-century China. The third character in his name means toad. Kai Sen purportedly went into the mountains, where he acquired magical powers and eventually emerged as a wild-haired, unwashed ascetic, with a three-legged toad as a companion. In Chikamatsu's play, Nanagusa Shirō is said to be a disciple of *Gama Tekkai Kaizon Sennin*, which appears to be an amalgamation of the *gama sennin* figure and *tekkai*, one of the Eight Sages of Chinese folklore. The story of Kai Sen appears in the *Sangokushi* (Romance of the Three Kingdoms), a Ming dynasty historical tale that became popular in Japan after it was translated and published as *Tsūzoku sangokushi*. This version first appeared in 1692, and it is possible that Chikamatsu drew the figure of the Toad Hermit and the idea for toad magic from that work. The image was used in many subsequent Edo-period works and is associated with the Kirishitan villain in seven of the eleven plays listed above.

As a practitioner of toad magic, Chikamatsu's Shirō is not directly labeled a Kirishitan, but as a sinister magician bent on gathering converts and taking over the country, he closely resembles the padres of the *Raichō jikki* narrative. In fact, the Chinese origins of the toad magic motif lend him the air of an exotic foreigner who is clearly outside the boundaries of normal society. This is reinforced by the fact that he is said to come from *okushū* (奥州), far from the civilization of the capital. An allusion to this distance comes with an omen that occurs in the garden of the emperor's palace. The frogs in the pond take sides and, to a chorus of deafening cries, attack each other, turning the pond red with blood. A fortuneteller for the emperor says that similar battles took place in China before an attack of the northern barbarians, and also in Japan in ancient times before an attack of the Ezo from the north. The event is seen as a sign that Shirō is just

---

16. Takagi Gen, *Edo yomihon no kenkyū—19-seiki Edo shōsetsu yōshiki kō* (Tokyo: Perikansha, 1995), 326–49. Chikamatsu's play is thought to be based on the early *kojōruri* play *Amakusa monogatari* of 1666, but that play does not include the figure of the *gama sennin*. In her presentation, Katō Atsuko pointed out that the toad magic motif in Chikamatsu's play is so well developed that it is likely there is an earlier play with the same theme that is no longer extant. Katō, "'Kirishitan' no imēji no henyō."

as dangerous, but also it clearly equates him with "barbarian" peoples. Further references to him as having no civility (不礼) and being like an animal (畜類に同じき) recall the image of the Kirishitan in *Raichō jikki*.

Shirō's magical powers are variously described as *senjutsu* (仙術), *mahō* (魔法), and *jahō* (邪法). The latter two words were also used to describe the powers of the padres, and the first alludes to the powers of the *yamabushi*, a figure with which they were associated. Shirō is said to be able to ride upon the clouds, and he also possesses a magical mirror, which he uses to show his converts how they have been duped by conventional Buddhism. In a scene that clearly echoes several in *Raichō jikki*, he has them look at their reflection in the mirror, and they see themselves as cows, horses, and cats. Shirō tells them this is proof that Buddhism has been no help to them and that they are destined to be reborn as animals, but that he can save them from such a fate. If they follow his sect, he says, they will never get sick again, and they will always have plenty of money and rice. When the followers promise to convert, they are each given ten coins and a bolt of cloth.[17]

Shirō is also a clear threat to the state. In the Kirishitan tales, the Japanese state and its stability are equated with Buddhism and Shinto, and the Kirishitan threat to those religions is also a threat to the state. Similarly in Chikamatsu's play, we are told that Shinto and Buddhism are the two wings that support the laws of the emperor's land, and Shiro is trying to destroy them and take over the country for himself. In the scene with his followers, he burns Buddhist images in a fire, and he later tries to convince a convert to step on an image of the Buddha, in a clear reference to the practice of *fumie* during the government searches for hidden Kirishitan. Throughout the play, he is described as the "worst criminal" (大罪人) and an "enemy of the realm" (天下の朝敵), and he is known to be intent on "tricking the populace and stealing the kingdom."[18] Like the Kirishitan, he has come from outside the bounds of civilization and uses magic, money, and medicine to lure converts to his heretical sect in order to take over the country.

Though direct references to Kirishitan probably had to be removed for public consumption, the resemblance to parts of the *Raichō jikki* narrative is unmistakable. Because both texts originated in the Kyōhō period and the author and exact production date for *Raichō jikki* are unknown, it is impossible to say which appeared first. It seems clear, however, that by the time they were produced, the association of the Kirishitan with magic

---

17. *Shimabara kaeru kassen*, 270
18. 万民をなびけ王法を奪い. Ibid., 285.

was firm, and audiences for Chikamatsu's play probably had no difficulty recognizing the Kirishitan references. Though the play had a very limited run, the text was likely widely available in lending libraries. This particular play was also revised and presented again in 1747 under the title *Keisei makura gundan* (Pillow War Tales).[19] A copy of the libretto for the latter play and two copies of Chikamatsu's *Keisei shimabara kaeru kassen* were in the collection of the Daisō lending library when it was dismantled in Meiji 31 (1898), showing that the story continued to be read long after the performances ended.[20]

Kanazōshi kokusenya jitsuroku

Not long after the revised version of Chikamatsu's play was staged, a new *kyōgen* debuted in Osaka featuring a Nanagusa Shirō figure with perhaps the most obvious Kirishitan features of all. *Kanazōshi kokusenya jitsuroku* (仮名草紙国性爺実録, True Account of Kokusenya) was first performed in 1759 and features Oda Nobutada as shogun and Mashida Hisayoshi as his deputy. Hisayoshi has recently led a campaign in China and conquered the castles and lands of the Ming Dynasty retainer, Kokusenya.[21] The latter is a follower of Christianity (*yaso shūmon*) and therefore a practitioner of magic, but Hisayoshi carried the sacred sword of Japan, given to him by the emperor for this campaign, which neutralized the powers of Kokusenya and brought victory to the Japanese. When the play opens the audience learns of Hisayoshi's success, and soon after that ships arrive from abroad (*kara*), supposedly bearing emissaries from Hisayoshi and a bride for Nobutada. The emissaries include Kaibei and his retainers, Padre Dorozō (Bateren Dorozō) and Brother Tsuchizō (Iruman Tsuchizō). Once in Japan, Kaibei changes his name to Nanagusa Shirō and, along with his retainers, sets out trying to gather recruits to his religion and his plan for a rebellion. Eventually, we learn that he is actually Kokusenya, who has come to take over Japan and avenge his defeat. He subsequently joins forces with a Korean ship captain, who also has designs on Japan and who managed to steal the sacred sword from Hisayoshi while he was on his way back to Japan. The captain hid the sword at the bottom of the bay in Shimabara, but a bright light that shines on the horizon at night shows where it rests. The authorities' search for the sword and for a way to stop

---

19. 傾城枕軍談. Fujimura Tsukuru, ed., *Nihon bungaku daijiten* (Tokyo: Shinchyosha, 1963), 371–72.
20. Shibata, *Daisō zōsho mokuroku to kenkyū*, 570 and 589.
21. This name has been translated as Coxinga by Donald Keene in his translation of Chikamatsu's *Battles of Coxinga,* from which this play seems to be borrowing part of the villain's identity.

Kokusenya and his allies occupies the rest of the play, which takes many twists and turns featuring hidden identities and the discovery of long-lost siblings and children. Kokusenya discovers that his own son, whom he had abandoned in Japan twenty years earlier, had been raised by one of the Japanese nobles that he killed soon after arriving, and now that same son is trying to kill Kokusenya in revenge. Nobutada and Hisayoshi eventually learn that if the blood of Kokusenya or his descendants is shed, his Kirishitan powers will be neutralized. That blood is spilled when purported Korean spies allied with Kokusenya, who are really secret allies of Hisayoshi trying to defeat Kokusenya, wound the son in a sword fight. In the end, Kokusenya's plans for a rebellion are thwarted, and he is captured and sent back to China.

While the authors of this play also avoid any use of the word "Kirishitan," the association of Kokusenya with Christianity is much more clearly drawn in *Kanazōshi kokusenya jitsuroku* than in the earlier Chikamatsu play, whose Nanagusa Shirō character they also borrow. By using the term *yaso shūmon* the authors avoided the censorship directed at the word Kirishitan while still clearly referencing Christianity, and the addition of the two characters with "Padre" and "Brother" in their names recalls the missionaries and the characters of the popular anti-Kirishitan tales. In the play, Kokusenya's religion is described as an evil one, or *jahō*, as the Kirishitan religion commonly was in official and popular texts. Similarly, the resulting powers were described as magic (*yōjutsu*) from a barbarian country (*bankoku*), recalling the magic (*mahō*) of the Nanbanjin in the *Raichō jikki* narrative. Additionally, the incantation Kokusenya uses to call up his followers contains parts of the dharani from *Raichō jikki* as well as some of the chant used in *Kirishitan monogatari*: "Araikitsu, shigo shōten dei, dei, deikō, deisumaru, sandamaru, paraiso, paraiso." In this incantation we can recognize variations on the words Deus, Saint Mary, and paradise. These words are used in varying combinations and with surprising consistency in the chants of almost all of the Kirishitan villains in the plays listed above over the course of nearly sixty years. Though it is unlikely the words were understandable to audiences, it does appear they were in some way recognizable as Kirishitan.[22]

Like Nanagusa Shirō of Chikamatsu's play and the Kirishitan of the popular tales, Kokusenya is also a threat to the realm from outside. While

22. If they were not recognizable to the audiences, one wonders why the same words were consistently preserved and not simply replaced with other, exotic-sounding phrases. Though some unidentifiable words were added over the years, and other words evolved away from the original Portuguese and Latin ones, there is surprising consistency in the use of the words Deus, *paraiso, zensumaro, santamaro,* and *shigo shōten.*

Chikamatsu's Nanagusa was marked as Other by his uncouth behavior and his origins in *okushū*, or the remote provinces far from the capital, Kokusenya is decidedly foreign, as are his co-conspirators. Also, as in the Chikamatsu play, that threat is to a realm supported by the religious traditions of Japan. Though those traditions included Buddhism and Shinto in Chikamatsu's play, it is the power of the Shinto goddess Benzaiten that defeats the Nanagusa Shirō of that play, and the power of the sacred sword given by the emperor at one point neutralizes Kokusenya's powers in *Kanazōshi kokusenya jitsuroku*. Building on the traditional representation of the Shinto gods as protectors of the realm, in these plays we see the gods not only protecting Japan against military attack, but also protecting it against the mysterious and threatening powers of the Kirishitan magic that seems to be the dominant threat to the country's sovereignty.

The villain of *Kanazōshi kokusenya jitsuroku* in some ways resembles the Kirishitan villain of the popular narratives but also introduces some new features that tend to be repeated often in similar plays of the period. In this and other plays, the words of the incantations closely resemble the *dharani* of the *Raichō jikki* narrative and the chants of *Kirishitan monogatari*, consistently invoking Deus, *paraiso*, and Mary. The authors of *Kanazōshi* even managed to incorporate the words for padre and brother into the names of some of the villains. The Kirishitan characters are foreign and not who they pretend to be, and they are plotting to take over the country by gathering adherents not only to their religion, as in *Raichō jikki* and *Kirishitan monogatari*, but also to their rebellion (*ikki*). As was the case in the Chikamatsu play, this shows the influence of the Nanagusa Shirō character of narratives on the Shimabara Rebellion combining with that of the Kirishitan villain of popular anti-Kirishitan tales. However, *Kanazoshi* does not include scenes that echo those of the *Raichō jikki* narrative. Also, perhaps because of its dramatic potential, the element of magic is emphasized in the Kirishitan character of *Kanazōshi* and later plays, while the use of money and medicine to lure converts is no longer a feature of the villain. Finally, the villain in all of these plays is not from Nanban, but from Japan's more traditional Others in Asia. In fact, as we can see in the case of the Tenjiku Tokubei characters outlined below, the villain's identity is often composite, and the Kirishitan powers become a tool for any foreign or domestic Other with the goal of conquest in Japan.

Tenjiku Tokubei

The Tenjiku Tokubei character was a popular one in *jōruri* and *kabuki* plays beginning in 1757, but his greatest fame came with the production written by Tsuruya Nanboku and staged in 1804. Borrowing elements of the padres in the *Raichō jikki* narrative, and of Shirō in Chikamatsu's *jōruri*, the Tenjiku Tokubei character is a decidedly foreign practitioner of toad magic who plans to use his powers to take over Japan. In his earliest incarnations he is associated with the historical Amakusa Shirō character, but in the early nineteenth century that device is no longer used. All of the Tenjiku Tokubei characters practice a form of toad magic that includes the now typical Kirishitan incantations, and most also carry an image or picture of Deus or *yaso* (Jesus).

The first play about Tenjiku Tokubei was *Tenjiku Tokubei kikigaki ōrai* (天竺徳兵衛聞書往来, The Legend of Tenjiku Tokubei) by Namiki Shōzō, which was staged in Osaka in 1758.[23] Set in the Muromachi period during the rule of Ashikaga Yoshiteru, it tells the story of the ship's captain, Tenjiku Tokubei, who is a survivor of the Amakusa rebellion and has allied himself with Korea to plot a new attack on the bakufu. Possessed of special powers, he is able to transform himself into a frog and perform other feats of magic. He takes the name Nanagusa Shichirō and vows to take control of the realm himself, but is eventually defeated by a disguised Yoshiteru. While we can see the resemblance to Chikamatsu's play in the Amakusa Shirō figure and the toad magic he practices, in this later play that toad magic is more clearly associated with the Kirishitan religion. In this play the character carries an image of *yaso*, and his magical incantation calls on Deus (*Dei, dei, deikō, deisubaru*).

The Namiki play was successful and inspired a number of adaptations and copies, including a *jōruri* written by Chikamatsu Hanji and Takemoto Saburobee that was first staged in 1764 at the Takemotoza in Osaka. Titled *Tenjiku Tokubei sato no sugatami* (天竺徳兵衛郷鏡, Tenjiku Tokubei and the Mirror of Protection), it was set in the slightly later period of Toyotomi Hidetsugu. In this story, Tenjiku Tokubei is the son of a Korean official defeated in the offensive launched by Hidetsugu's uncle, Hideyoshi, and he has come to Japan for revenge. This Tokubei also practices toad magic and chants "*Dei, dei paraiso, paraiso*," and a scene that features *fumie*, or stepping on the image of a deity, reinforces his association with the Kirishitan.

In 1804, a new *kabuki* version of the Tenjiku Tokubei story was staged by Tsuruya Nanboku. Popular for its many special effects, including a quick change in which a large toad "turns into" Tokubei, the show ran

---

23. Information on this and other Tenjiku Tokubei plays in this section comes from Fujimura Tsukuru, ed., *Nihon bungaku daijiten*, vol. 5 (Tokyo: Shinchōsha, 1963), 170–73; and Gunji Masakatsu, ed., *Tsuruya Nanboku zenshu*, vol. 1 (Tokyo: San'ichi Shobō, 1971), 463–72.

for three months and helped establish Nanboku as a playwright.[24] In this version, Tokubei arrives in Japan after being blown off course to India five years earlier. He is brought to the authorities of the town where he lands and is asked to tell tales of his adventures. The lord of the house, Sōkan, recognizes him as a long-lost son, but says nothing. While Tokubei is still there, two samurai come to demand the return of a famous sword with which Sōkan was entrusted and which he apparently lost. Sōkan pretends to have it and tells his wife to bring the sword, but instead she understands his intentions and brings the implements necessary for ritual suicide. Sōkan takes responsibility for losing the sword by taking his own life. With his last breath he tells the visitors that he was born Korean, and came to Japan to start a rebellion against its leader in retaliation for Hideyoshi's invasion. He pulls the blade across his stomach and then presses a magical pouch to the wound. After making a mysterious gesture, he throws the pouch behind a screen, and immediately a large toad appears, crashing through the screen. Sōkan vows to pass his magic on to his son so that he may accomplish the task of rebellion and revenge, and with a final tug of the sword, he dies.

In the next scene, Tokubei is on his ship, where the ghost of Sōkan visits him. He learns that he is Sōkan's son, who was sent away as a child to keep his father's identity a secret. Sōkan gives him the famous sword he was accused of losing, along with a magical mirror which he says can make Tokubei invisible or change form in order to avoid being captured. Then Sōkan teaches Tokubei the incantations of toad magic that will help him lead the rebellion against Japan's leadership. Tokubei masters the chant "*Namu satsu daruma gundaria shigo shoden haraiso*" and exults in his new powers, saying he will "ride on the clouds and move through the waves" and "crush Japan."[25]

In common with the earlier incarnations of Tokubei, Nanboku's character is a foreigner possessed of the powers of toad magic who is intent on conquering Japan. His costumes emphasize his foreignness,

---

24. James Brandon and Samuel Leiter, eds., *The Tale of Tokubei From India*, Kabuki Plays on Stage, vol. 3: Darkness and Desire, 1804-1864 (Honolulu: University of Hawai'i Press, 2002), 34. This translation of *Tenjiku Tokubei ikoku banashi* is limited to the second act. The full text of the play in Japanese under the title *Tenjiku Tokubei banri no irifune* 天竺徳兵衛万里入船 (Tenjiku Tokubei and the Ship from Far Away) is in Gunji, *Tsuruya Nanboku zenshu*, vol. 1. The different title reflects the use of a manuscript from the later nineteenth century, after the title had been changed. Earlier manuscripts are not extant. On the history of the production of Nanboku's play and the various name changes, see the introduction of *Tenjiku Tokubei banri no irifune* in Gunji, *Tsuruya Nanboku zenshu*, vol. 1, 463-72.

25. Gunji, *Tsuruya Nanboku zenshu*, vol. 1, 35.

with stage directions specifying an Ainu-style coat in one scene, and a Dutch ship captain's uniform in another. But this incarnation of Tenjiku Tokubei recalls the villain of *Kanazōshi kokusenya jitsuroku*, with much more pronounced Kirishitan elements. In the chant above, the last three words are almost identical to the first three words of the chant *"Shigo shōten haraisō zensumaro,"* which is present in all of the *Raichō jikki* variants, and another chant of Tokubei's, *"Dei, dei haraiso,"* which calls on Deus. Deus also appears near the end of the play when Tenjiku Tokubei's enemies are supposed to deliver the banner of office for Kyushu after he has conquered it, but substitute for it a picture of "Deus."

An interesting anecdote told about the play shows that the Kirishitan association in plays was still a somewhat perilous one. The story was that "a magistrate investigated a rumor, probably spread by Nanboku or Matsusuke I, that Christian sorcery was being used in the plays."[26] After the magistrate was taken backstage and shown how all of the apparent instances of magic were performed, he was satisfied. In the end, no one was charged, and the play was staged again several times. In fact, it has continued to be popular, with one scholar estimating that from the late nineteenth century to the present it has been staged an additional seventy times.[27] As with all of the other plays, its popularity can also be measured by the fact that a copy of it was held in the Daisō lending library, along with seven other volumes of *jōruri* and narratives about Tenjiku Tokubei.

In all of the plays featuring villains with Kirishitan powers the threat is diffused and the evil character is either killed or sent back to his country. In this way, just as the plays' villains share some of the characteristics of the padres in the popular tales, their plots echo the cycle of penetration and expulsion of a foreign Other whose threat to Japan is disguised by his false identity. The dramatic potential of the theme of deception that the popular tales presented in the form of padres posing as Buddhist priests, and in the magic they practiced, is taken full advantage of in the plays, in which physical transformations often take place and the names of characters are constantly changing as each layer of identity is revealed. But in each play it is clear that if the Kirishitan villain's magical powers are neutralized, the threat he poses will also disappear. In many cases, the magic powers are dissolved with the help of some sacred object connected to the emperor or a Shinto shrine, showing the superior power of the Japanese gods over the foreign one and proving the latter to be a false path. In the

---

26. Onoe Matsusuke I was the actor who starred as Tokubei. Brandon and Leiter, *The Tale of Tokubei From India,*, 35.
27. Takagi, *Edo yomihon no kenkyū*, 331.

end, the villain is exposed and helpless, with no suggestion that he is supported by outside forces, as the padres in *Raichō jikki* were by the Nanban king. The resulting impression of the Kirishitan in the plays is that he is less sinister than the one of the popular tales.

In a similar way, the more simplified representation of the Kirishitan in the plays results in a caricature that is less threatening than the more full-blown characters of the popular narratives. Though there are several features in the characters of the plays that recall the Kirishitan of the popular narratives, they have been reduced to a kind of Kirishitan code: Nanagusa Shirō, Tenjiku Tokubei, Deus, *yaso*, *paraiso*. And these code words signify a tool for conquest more than the conqueror himself, who in these plays has a hybrid identity combining several of Japan's traditional Others. As a result, the Kirishitan of the plays, with his spectacular feats of magic, is more bizarre than sinister, more entertaining than fearful. In fact, despite the greater emphasis on the uncanny in the plays, it is likely that audiences of the late eighteenth and early nineteenth centuries found the marauding barbarian Kirishitan of the anti-Western writings more fearsome than the Kirishitan sorcerers of the *kabuki* stage.

THE KIRISHITAN IN ANTI-WESTERN DISCOURSE

In 1771, a Russian captain delivered messages to the Satsuma domain in Kyushu to be transmitted to the Dutch at Nagasaki. The messages threatened an attack on Matsumae on the southern tip of Hokkaido. The threat was meant to be to Dutch trade interests, but the message was "leaked to the Japanese in garbled form, and caused in the last quarter of the century great consternation over a possible Russian threat from the north."[28] The tension inspired by this and other visits by Russian ships in the late eighteenth century only increased after several other incidents with foreign ships in the early nineteenth century, and prominent scholars and government officials fiercely debated what lay behind those countries' requests for trade, and whether or not to respond to them. Many of those opposed to dealing with the Westerners clearly tapped into the available anti-Kirishitan discourse, including the popular narratives, for information to support their views. Miura Baien (1723–89) and Aizawa Seishisai (1782–1863) were two contributors to this debate, and each wrote treatises opposing any interaction with the foreigners because they were all

---

28. Bob Tadashi Wakabayashi, *Anti-Foreignism and Western Learning in Early-Modern Japan: the New Theses of 1825* (Cambridge, Mass.: Council on East Asian Studies, Harvard University, 1986), 65.

Kirishitan and would inevitably try to conquer Japan. Basing much of their arguments on their reading of past documents regarding interactions with the Iberian traders and missionaries, the two authors paint an interesting and familiar picture of a Western Barbarian/Kirishitan Other with designs on Japan.

In many ways, these scholarly essays contrast sharply with the popular narratives and plays. Both works were written in *kanbun* and were aimed at educated audiences. In addition, the writers appear to have had access to a wide variety of sources to help them understand the foreigners and their possible intentions. Certainly, due to censorship and restrictions on the importation of books, those sources were mostly limited to Japanese and Chinese books on relations with Western traders and missionaries in the sixteenth and seventeenth centuries, as well as some more recent reports on the visits of ships to Japanese shores. But it is clear that both Baien and Seishisai were up-to-date on whatever knowledge of the West was available. Among the books cited by Miura Baien in his work, *Samidare-shō* (Musings dDuring the Early Summer Rains), are some by Arai Hakuseki and Nishikawa Jōken on the countries of the world, as well as several about the Shimabara Rebellion and government reactions to the missionaries, including Suzuki Shōsan's *Hakirishitan*.[29] Seishisai also relies heavily on Arai Hakuseki's writing, and. though he does not directly cite them, as a member of the Mito school it is likely that he had access to all of the familiar anti-Kirishitan works of the seventeenth and eighteenth centuries, including those of Shōsan, Fabian Fucan, and others.[30]

Despite the different backgrounds of the work of these scholars and the popular narratives, the image of the Kirishitan in Baien's *Samidareshō* and Seishisai's *Shinron* is similar to that in the stories and clearly shows the influence of them. In the case of Baien, that influence is most obvious in the inclusion of a variant of the *Raichō jikki* narrative that he uses as a source and summarizes in *Samidareshō*.[31] In Seishisai's *Shinron* the

---

29. Arai Hakuseki wrote about his interviews with Father Giovanni Battista Sidotti. The Jesuit priest was the last in a line of European missionaries who tried to sneak into Japan to minister to the Christian converts. He arrived in Japan in 1708 and was captured soon after. Hakuseki conducted his interviews over a few months between 1709 and 1710, and five years later compiled his notes from the interviews into the work titled *Seiyō kibun* (Tidings of the West). This work and others he produced contain information on European countries that was difficult to obtain elsewhere in Japan at the time. It circulated only in manuscript until 1882, when it was printed for the first time. Nishikawa Jōken wrote encyclopedias about the countries of the world. See chapter 3 for more on those works.
30. See below for more on the Mito school.
31. The variant is *Ibuki mogusa*. See below for more on the text.

influence is more subtle, but he clearly shows concern for the uncanny power of the Christian religion and also briefly quotes the *Raichō jikki* narrative. Both appear to read the narratives critically and do not pass on information about the grotesque appearance of the Kirishitan or about the mythical Nanban and its King Gojimbi. The two authors identify the relevant European countries, Russia and America, and describe their different cultures and histories, but they also contend that all Westerners equally share an insatiable appetite for conquest and a common religion, and as such can be expected to use their Kirishitan religion to beguile people into following them and eventually surrendering the country to them. And in the view of Seishisai, that religion brings with it uncanny powers that recall the magic wielded by the padres of *Raichō jikki* and by Tenjiku Tokubei. As a result, the enemy described in the two treatises is a Western Kirishitan who uses trade, charitable works, and a false religion to attract the hearts of the uneducated in order to conquer other countries. It is a familiar image whose presence in the more scholarly debates about opening trade with the West underscores the important place that the Kirishitan Other of the popular works occupied at all levels of Edo-period discourse.

Musings on the Kirishitan Threat
The Confucian scholar Miura Baien composed *Samidare-shō* in 1784, apparently inspired by the current of alarm running through society at the time over reports of Russian threats to the northern territories in Japan.[32] In the preface to *Samidare-shō*, Baien reports that when he visited Nagasaki he was told that "the Occidentals had recently succeeded in taking Northern Ezo by these very means, and that the nation should be vitally concerned for its northern areas."[33] The means to which he refers are the indirect ones of helping the weak with money and medicines first, and then luring them into following the Kirishitan doctrine. Once the Westerners have converted enough people to that doctrine, they invade the country and easily take control. This process is described by Baien in the first page of his preface to the work:

> I have heard that when Occidentals plan to seize another country they consider direct military action an inferior method.

---

32. Miura Baien, *Samidareshō*, Baien zenshū, vol. 1 (Tokyo: Butsudōkan, 1912). An English translation to the text is Miura Baien and Leon Hurvitz, "*Samidare-shō* (Musings During the Early Summer Rain)," *Monumenta Nipponica* 8, no. 1/2 (1952): 289–326 (part 1); and Miura Baien and Leon Hurvitz. "*Samidare-shō* (Musings During the Early Summer Rain)." *Monumenta Nipponica* 9, no. 1/2 (1953): 330–56 (part 2).
33. Miura and Hurvitz, *Samidare-shō*, part 1, 293–94.

Consequently, in planning to conquer a country they first help the weak and restore the poor to prosperity with gifts of gold, silver, grain, and cloth; then heal the sick with medicine and beguile men's eyes and ears with their wiles; finally bedevil their hearts with the doctrine of the Lord of Heaven and the three worlds and make them think that these are infinitely more precious than parents and rulers; and, when they see that their preaching has had its effect, they follow it up with invasion, thereby achieving their foul aim with one stroke.[34]

Though in the preface Baien generally refers to Westerners and Western doctrines, it soon becomes clear that he views these as synonymous with Kirishitan. This is indicated early on the first page when Baien concedes there is some danger in the topic he is engaging (he quotes his child asking, "Is this not the very thing we are forbidden to discuss?"), but he argues that the only way to avoid making the mistakes of the past is to remember and learn from them.[35] Thus, he sets out to review the records of past contact with the West, most of which are records about the ban on Kirishitan and the Shimabara Rebellion, in order to remind his readers of the danger they pose to the country. Baien is careful to cite most of his sources, and the majority are compilations of historical records or the military deeds of various prominent daimyo who participated in the Kirishitan persecutions. Some of these works include records of "confessions" made by captured priests who admitted under torture that they were sent to subvert the government of Japan.[36] He also cites two works by Arai Hakuseki, the Confucian scholar and advisor to the bakufu, who wrote a number of books on Western countries based on his interviews with Father Giovanni Battista Sidotti.

Another source that Baien uses extensively is the *Ibuki mogusa* variant of the *Raichō jikki* narrative.[37] In fact, while he cites short segments of other

34. Ibid., 292–93.
35. Ibid.
36. Miura sites the *Hitō senki* 肥島戦記 (Military History of the Islands of Hizen) in his text, but these confessions appeared in other "records" of the time as well. A manuscript titled *Yaso seibatsuki* (The Subjugation of the Jesus Sect), of which there are approximately fourteen extant copies, also contains reference to this confession. This text contains a number of elements that appear to come from the *Raichō jikki* narrative, but it is mostly about the Shimabara Rebellion and events after it. I consulted copies of this manuscript at the National Archives, Tokyo University, and Rikkyo University, all in Tokyo.
37. The *Ibuki mogusa* variant is usually the more complete of the *Raichō jikki* narratives, which contains the sermon by Hakuo after he defeats Fabian. It is also distinguished by a preface that tells of a pilgrim who stays at a temple on Mt. Ibuki and learns of the origins of the famous *mogusa* herb of the region, used in moxa treatments. The story he hears is that of the Kirishitan, who are credited (falsely) with bringing *mogusa* to Japan in this text.

texts, in the case of *Ibuki mogusa* Baien gives a condensed but very accurate rendition that takes up a full eight pages of the Japanese text of the treatise. Significantly, however, he leaves out the first section of the tale about the location of the country of Nanban and about its King Gojimbi. He also skips the portions that describe the grotesque appearance of the foreigners. Though Baien does not comment on these omissions at this point in the text, much later in the second part he dismisses the author of the *Ibuki mogusa* as someone ignorant of foreign countries: "The section in the *Ibuki mogusa* dealing with the designs of foreign countries on our country is made up of stray rumors from foolish people, thanks to the author's ignorance of the subject. It is unreliable."[38] Since Baien himself has already accused the Western countries of plotting to lure the gullible into their religion in order to take over other countries, one can only imagine he is objecting to the portrayal of the fictional King Gojimbi as an inaccurate description of a monarch who does not exist. He clearly has no objection to suspecting the Western powers of hoping to conquer Japan.

The rest of the *Ibuki mogusa/Raichō jikki* narrative remains intact, though in a condensed form. As a result, we still see the foreigners telling Nobunaga that they want to preach Buddhism, and being given land for a church. They give money and medicines to the poor, and then take advantage of the gratitude of those unfortunates to preach their religion. They dupe the gullible with reflections in the "Three Worlds Mirror" and show them how to drag the dreaded *cruz* across their backs and smear their hands with blood. Fabian loses his debate with the Buddhist lay monk Hakuo. And there is even mention of the fugitive brothers performing wonders for Hideyoshi. But in this version they only conjure the ghost of Hideyoshi's former mistress. Baien's rendition of the tale leaves out the ghoulish description of the padres and any mention of the more spectacular feats of magic. Still, it is easy to see the influence of the popular narrative on Baien's own views of the foreigners that he lays out in his preface.

Over the course of the treatise, Baien explains that hundreds of thousands have died in Japan because of the "false doctrine" of the foreigners, and he claims that this should serve as a lesson. He points out that there are still countless rumors of people performing feats of magic and that everyone should refute such superstitious speculation and expose those who try to profit from it. He also attacks the tenets of the Kirishitan religion and shows its weaknesses in comparison with Confucianism. While many earlier Kirishitan texts equated Buddhism with Japan in opposition to the foreignness of the Kirishitan, Baien follows the lead of Arai Hakuseki in

---

38. Miura and Hurvitz, *Samidare-shō*, part 2, 343.

arguing that Confucian principles are the foundation of Japanese stability, and that the emphasis on the individual in the Kirishitan faith inevitably subverts the proper order of any society.

Baien's use of the *Ibuki mogusa* text along with other historical records of the period implies that he considered the narrative to be a somewhat accurate record of its time and not necessarily the purely fictional work it was seen to be by later scholars. Though he was critical of some parts of it, he rendered almost all of it into *kanbun* for a scholarly treatise, joining in the re-production of the tale of penetration and expulsion that had already been circulating for over one hundred years, and putting that discourse to use in a new debate about an outside Other.[39] Though that Other was originally identified as Russian, English, and even American, in the debate on relations with the West, those all seem to have come together under the umbrella of a Western/Kirishitan Other that borrowed many of the characteristics of the subject of seventeenth century anti-Kirishitan treatises as well as the expulsion narratives like *Raichō jikki*. He is still a threatening foreigner who uses money and "tricks" to lure the ignorant into a false religion in order to take over the country. And while Baien flatly rejects any notion of the Kirishitan as magicians and conjurors, others like Aizawa Seishisai incorporate that aspect of the popular Kirishitan image into their representation of the Western enemies of Japan.

Aizawa Seishisai's Shinron

One group that was strongly opposed to contact with the Western countries was the Mito school of scholars. Originally set up in 1657 by Tokugawa Mitsukuni as a center for scholarship on Japan, the school's most famous project was a comprehensive history of Japan that was not completed until 1908. In the early nineteenth century, however, and in the face of incursions by ships from Western countries, several scholars from the school became very vocal opponents of relations with those countries. Among the Mito scholars who were fiercely opposed to contact with Western countries was Aizawa Seishisai, who wrote several anti-Western treatises and *memoria* to the bakufu urging the leadership to reject any advances by the Western countries and giving advice on how to strengthen the country against attack. The most famous and influential of these *memoria*

---

39. It should be noted that he was not the only one to render the story in *kanbun*. One version called *Nanbanshi* (History of Nanban), a manuscript held at the Seikadō Bunko, is also in *kanbun*. In fact, one of the more interesting features of the various manuscripts is the wide range of scripts used, ranging from all Chinese characters to almost all *hiragana*, and several combinations in between.

was *Shinron*, written in 1825.⁴⁰ The work is divided into five treatises that explain the crisis that Japan is facing at the time and that lay out proposals to deal with immediate problems and the long-term issues of building a stronger national unity. One reason for the crisis is the threat of the Western nations, and in the section on "The Nature of the Barbarian," Seishisai describes the foreigners and why they are so dangerous.

He asserts that they are a low form of being, a "wily foreign cur" who, "unmindful of their base position as the lower extremities of the world, have been scurrying impudently across the Four Seas, trampling other nations underfoot."⁴¹ But in doing this they never attack those countries openly, but offer them the profit from trade, or give trinkets and money to the most gullible of their citizens in order to lure them into belief in a false doctrine. This false doctrine is the "evil" Christian religion and the source of their great success in conquering other countries.⁴²

> They win a reputation for benevolence by performing small acts of kindness temporarily to peoples they seek to conquer. After they capture a people's hearts and minds, they propagate their doctrines. Their gross falsehoods and misrepresentations deceive many, particularly those who yearn for things foreign. ... Once beguiled by Christianity, they cannot be brought back to their senses. Herein lies the secret of the barbarians' success.⁴³

Along with other anti-Western writers, such as Ōhara Sakingo and his fellow Mito scholar, Fujita Yūkoku, Seishisai believed that the source of the Westerners' success at conquest and their most dangerous asset was the Christian religion.⁴⁴ Though he expresses great contempt for the Christian teachings, it is clear that he respects their ability to sway the minds of the masses and their usefulness as a tool for governing. Throughout *Shinron*, he warns over and over again of the dangers of letting the Westerners first trade and then introduce their religion, attributing to both an almost uncanny power to lead people astray. In fact, in addition to referring to Christianity as the more familiar *jakyō* 邪教 (evil religion) and *yasokyō* 耶

---

40. *Shinron* in Imai Usaburō et al., eds., *Mitogaku*, Nihon shisō taikei, vol. 53 (Tokyo: Iwanami shoten, 1973). A full English translation appears in Wakabayashi, *Anti-Foreignism and Western Learning*, 149–277.
41. Wakabayashi, *Anti-Foreignism and Western Learning*, 170 and 149.
42. Following the Chinese tradition, Seishisai uses the term *kirisutokyō* (基督教) when specifying Christianity, although most of the time he refers to it as the "evil religion" or *jakyō* (邪教).
43. Wakabayashi, *Anti-Foreignism and Western Learning*, 200.
44. Ibid., 68–76.

蘇教 (teachings of Jesus), Seishisai also uses the terms *ikyō* 夷教 (barbarian teachings), *yōkyō* 妖教 (occult teachings), and *kijutsu* 詭術 (trickery). This collection of terms describing the Kirishitan teachings make it resemble more the magic of the Kirishitan in *Raichō jikki* and the plays than simply a false religion.

Though there were some reports of crew members leaving Christian bibles or symbols behind, and others of Russians teaching Christianity to the residents of some of the northern islands they visited, it seems likely that the great emphasis on Christianity as a means of conquest in the anti-Western writings was influenced by the anti-Kirishitan discourse that had been circulating in a variety of texts since the expulsion.[45] In 1844, the Mito school issued a kind of anti-Kirishitan anthology called *Sokkyohen* (Anthology of Heretical Texts), which included most of the well-known works of the seventeenth century, such as Fabian's *Ha Daiusu*, Suzuki Shōsan's *Hakirishitan*, and Sesshu's *Taiji jashūron*.[46] It also included *Kirishitan monogatari* and Miura Baien's *Samidareshō*, which in turn included an adaptation of the *Raichō jikki* narrative. There can be no doubt that all of these texts were in the Mito school library and available to Seishisai and other scholars there, and likely important sources for their opinions on Western countries.

Evidence that Seishisai read a version of the *Raichō jikki* narrative also appears in one part of *Shinron*. While he is describing the history of the missionaries in Japan during the rule of Oda Nobunaga, Seishisai says that the leader built a church for the missionaries in Kyoto and invited more priests to come and preach there. This is an assertion made in *Raichō jikki* that is contradicted by records of the time. Then Seishisai discusses Nobunaga's regret of his decision to allow the padres to preach, and he includes this "quote" of the leader:

> When Nobunaga first decided to build the church, his trusted retainer, Gyōbu Masanori, tried to dissuade him, but to no avail. Nobunaga probably planned to use Christianity to subvert his enemies as he once subverted Araki Murashige. But he soon realized his mistake and lamented, "Gyōbu was right about those Christians. I have heard of believers in Buddha giving alms to clerics, but never have I heard of almsgiving from clerics to believers. Yet that is exactly what the barbarian clerics do. When they first came, they said they wanted to trade, but they do not seek profits. Quite the contrary, they engage in charitable works. They must be out to subvert our land."[47]

---

45. Ibid., 82–83, 310n.74.
46. A manuscript copy of *Sokkyohen* dating from 1855 is in the National Archives in Tokyo.
47. Ibid., 202–3.

While the passage is not identical in its wording, it closely resembles a passage in *Raichō jikki* that also quotes Nobunaga saying that his advisor was right about the padres, and that he has never heard of priests giving money to believers. The style of a direct quote, in particular, seems to point to a narrative format like the *jikki* as his source. The resemblance between the two texts was also noted by the editors of *Shinron* in *Nihon shisō taikei*, who identified a similar quote from the *Raichō jikki* variant *Nanbanji kōhaiki* in a note to the text.[48]

Like Miura Baien, Seishisai retells the now familiar tale of Kirishitan conquest and puts it to the service of a new discourse—the debate over Japan's relations with the West. The works of the Mito school and particularly of Aizawa Seishisai were significant ideological contributions in late Edo-period discourse, and it is important to recognize the influence of long-standing anti-Kirishitan discourse on them. In Seishisai's characterization of the Western barbarian it is possible to see the common image of the Kirishitan Other as would-be conquerors using trade, gifts of money, medicinal cures, and their religion to deceive the uneducated into giving up their countries to them. Some of the features of that Other are recognizable in what modern readers consider the more scholarly works of Fabian Fucan, Suzuki Shosan, and Arai Hakuseki. But others developed over time in expulsion narratives like *Kirishitan monogatari* and the *Raichō jikki* narrative. Based on the inclusion of the latter works in the Mito school's *Sokkyohen* and in the writing of Baien and Seishisai, it seems likely that eighteenth- and nineteenth-century readers did not distinguish between "fictional" and "scholarly" accounts, and that all contributed to the construction of a Kirishitan Other that circulated widely and was applied to a new Western enemy when concerns arose over incursions by Western ships.

Even as Tenjiku Tokubei and Nanagusa Shirō thrilled audiences with their magical exploits, scholars and the political elite responded to recent contact with Western ships by warning of a common Kirishitan threat posed by all Western nations. At the same time, the *Raichō jikki* narrative continued to circulate widely; of the surviving *Raichō jikki* manuscripts with copy dates, the vast majority range from the 1770s through the Meiji period, showing that the narrative was quite popular with readers of the late Edo period.[49] Over two hundred years after the last missionaries' departure, the Kirishitan was still the protagonist in the familiar narrative of penetra-

---

48. Imai, *Mitogaku*, 96.
49. See the appendix for a list of manuscripts and their copy dates.

tion and expulsion, still the repository of a generalized anxiety about the world outside of Japan's borders that was not eased by the abjection and expulsion that had been replayed for centuries. How that anxiety was processed, however, differs in the plays and the anti-Western discourse. In the plays, the Kirishitan Other was domesticated by a simplified representation and by his absorption into the *tōjin* figure of hybrid foreignness representing all of Japan's Others, as well as in the narrative act of expulsion. The coded marks of his Otherness had become so familiar that he could be recognized as Kirishitan without even using that word. And though he still represented a threat to Japan, his domestication also made him a less sinister one that was easily defeated by the native gods. In the anti-Western discourse of Baien and Seishisai, the goal is not to domesticate the Kirishitan or allay the anxiety associated with him. Rather, the anxiety inherent in the Kirishitan figure is tapped in support of their political positions. In fact, the Kirishitan was a ready-made Other that became a unifying factor for disparate incidents with ships from different Western countries and a compelling argument for many of the reforms and policies they advocated.

Epilogue

A nineteenth-century manuscript collection of reports on temples and shrines contains the following account of Kirishitan sorcery:

> Two men and a woman once crossed the border from Mino to Bishū in order to deliver the woman as a bride. Three years later, the woman traveled back to her home to visit her parents. One day, the mother decided to cook an egg for their meal and brought one home from the market. However, the daughter told her it would be impossible to eat it because that egg was the Buddha's body. Her mother scoffed at this, asking to see this body, even as she put the egg in a pot to cook. But when the mother went to remove the egg, there was a one-inch figure of the Buddha between her chopsticks. Surprised, she called in the father, who was shocked and accused his daughter of using "strange arts" (奇妙の術). When the superior heard about the event, he remarked that similar arts were practiced by the Kirishitan sect, and the girl confessed that her new husband and his family were all Kirishitan who practiced magic (魔法). The news reached the official in charge of investigating Kirishitan activities, and when he questioned the young couple, they revealed that there were many more like them in Mino and Bishū. The official remarked that there must be a way to recognize them, and the couple said that believers wear their hair and tie their sashes in a distinctive manner, and they were easily recognizable at any market in the area. So, officials were dispatched to area markets and discovered two hundred believers, who were all eventually sentenced to death.

The entry explains the fate of a group of Kirishitan executed in Owari in 1664, and is included in the *Shisō zasshiki* 祠曹雑識, a manuscript in the National Archives in Tokyo. The miscellany is thought to have been compiled around 1835 by an official in the bakufu Bureau of Temples and

Shrines who had gathered random items of interest from records there and planned to copy them into his own collection of musings. Under the heading *Bishū Kirishitan shimatsu* (Account of the Bishū Kirishitan), the author writes that the bakufu received a report in the year Kanbun 3 (1664) on the execution of 207 people in the province of Owari (also called Bishū). When more details were requested, an official sent the above account. The year of the reported incident and the number of dead coincide with historical records on the persecutions in Owari, though other records do not refer to the accused practicing magic.[1]

Whether the entry is historically accurate or not, it represents another contribution to the already considerable discourse on the Kirishitan and magic that circulated in the nineteenth century. The Kirishitan missionaries and their converts had not been seen in daily life for well over two hundred years, but the Kirishitan Other continued to be held up as a very real threat in a number of different media and were well known at all levels of society. From the vehement anti-Western discourse of Aizawa Seishisai and the Mito school to the many stage productions featuring a conquering, Kirishitan villain, the Kirishitan had become a ubiquitous target in Edo culture of a generalized anxiety about the world coming to Japan. Records show that the *Raichō jikki* narrative also continued to circulate at this time, with sixteen of the thirty-two dated manuscripts coming from the nineteenth century. All of this helped perpetuate the association of Kirishitan with magic to the extent that missionaries arriving in Japan after the ban on Christianity was lifted in the 1880s reported meeting resistance to the religion from people who were convinced that Christians were practitioners of magic.

Though distrust of the Kirishitan and Christianity persisted well into the Meiji period, the exposure to Western cultures brought by trade and by the government's concerted efforts to learn about them rather quickly shifted attention away from the idea and the stories of a ubiquitous Kirishitan menace. The *Raichō jikki* narrative was finally put into print in 1868, with the title *Nanbanji kōhaiki*. Though that work appears to have been popular, its production seems to mark the beginning of the end of circulation of the narrative. Several printings came out in the 1880s, but few of those books survive today, and there is no sign that the narrative continued to be copied in manuscript beyond that period. While a number of factors likely contributed to that decline, including lower attendance at storytelling performances and a decline in the influence of the commercial

---

1. Ebisawa Arimichi, ed., *Nanbanji kōhaiki, Jakyō tai'i, Myōtei mondō, Ha Daiusu*, Toyo Bunko, vol. 14 (Tokyo: Heibonsha, 1964), 6.

lending libraries, certainly the most important factor was the actual arrival of the dreaded Kirishitan himself, in the form of Western traders and diplomats. The expelled barbarian was "in here" again, and the focus shifted from chronicling his former expulsion to examining his newest incarnation. While the subsequent surge of publications about Westerners and their countries included some representations of them that resembled the demon padres of seventeenth-century illustrations, the issues and concerns were no longer the same. The perpetually deferred return of the Kirishitan Other that was so feared in the anti-Kirishitan tales had finally come to pass, but instead of medicines, money, and magic, he brought guns and demands for trade, and Christianity was not, in fact, the new foreigners' most powerful weapon, nor his most defining characteristic. Though the West would continue to be an important Other (perhaps *the* most important Other) in Japan's discourse on identity, by the late nineteenth century, Kirishitan was no longer synonymous with the West, and the very real presence of new Western Others had finally brought an end to the "exorcistic ritual" of the expulsion tales.

TRANSLATIONS

Baterenki

"History of the Padres"[1]

St. Peter established the seven sacraments after he secretly conferred with St. John.[2] The first sacrament is the anointing of water, called Baptism, which is performed when one becomes a Kirishitan.[3] A white cloth is placed on the forehead to show that the soul that has been stained is cleaned by the water of baptism and becomes as white as the cloth. A

---

1. *Baterenki* 伴天連記 was written by an anonymous author sometime after 1607 but likely before *Kirishitan monogatari* in 1639. See chapter 2 for more on publication history. The text used for this translation is in *Zokuzoku gunsho ruijū*, vol. 12 (Tokyo: Kokkusho Kankōkai, 1907) because it appears to most faithfully reproduce the original manuscript, particularly by maintaining the foreign words as well as many Japanese words in the original *hiragana*. Other versions that transcribe the foreign words into *katakana* and *kanji* are reproduced in Hiyane Antei, ed., *Kirishitan monogatari hoka sanpen*, Kirishitan Bunkō vol. 1 (Tokyo: Keiseisha, 1926), and Shinmura Izuru, ed., *Kaihyō sōshō*, vol. 1 (Kyoto: Kōseikaku shoten, 1927). These versions were also consulted. None of the printed versions are annotated. In the introduction to the *Kaihyō sōshō* version, Shinmura identifies the manuscript used in the reproduction as one recently acquired by H. Iijima from the Shikata Shōundō booksellers in Osaka, and he adds that the manuscript had originally come from the family library of the Japanese scholars Kurokawa Mayori and his son, Kurokawa Mamichi. Shinmura also points out that neither the *Zokuzoku gunsho ruijū* editor nor Hiyane Antei identifies the source for his text, but he deems it likely that the *Zokuzoku gunsho ruijū* version was made either directly or indirectly from the same manuscript he used. According to the current *Kokusho sōmokuroku*, the only extant manuscript of *Baterenki* is still owned by the Iijima family. See Shinmura, *Kaihyō sōshō*, 9–10.
2. The names are written in Japanese as さん平とろ and 三壽庵. "Sacrament" is written as さからめんと, *Zokuzoku*, 570.
3. "Baptism" is written as ばうちいすも. Ibid.

candle is lit and held by the participant to represent his movement out of darkness and into the light. Salt is placed in the mouth to remind the believer that he should uphold the Kirishitan teachings in all things, just as salt retains its flavor and purity even when hidden in trash. The participant lowers his head to receive the baptismal waters to demonstrate that everyone, no matter his circumstances in life, must bow to receive the mark of Jesus Christ's grace and mercy, which is the water of baptism representing the blood Jesus Christ shed on the cross.[4] Two godparents are chosen to serve as witnesses and to provide guidance and education to the young Kirishitan at a time when his faith may still be weak. They further symbolize the spiritual parents of the newly baptized child of God, with one representing God the Father, and the other the soul's mother, the Holy Ghost.[5] Of the seven sacraments, the sacrament of baptism is number one.

The second sacrament is Confession.[6] Each Kirishitan is called before a priest to confess his sins to him face-to-face, in order that his true heart may be known. In time, the Kirishitan comes to the understanding that he must give both his body and his life to the service of Jesus Christ, showing his strong faith and becoming an outstanding servant of the church.[7] Confession is like *zange* (懺悔). We show faith when we make a blood oath not to change even when everyone in the world is changing.

The third sacrament of Chrismation takes place after becoming a Kirishitan.[8] In the ceremony, the bishop, who is the head of the padres, draws a cross on the forehead, anoints the head with oil, and then gives a slap to the right side of the face.[9] The cross is drawn on the forehead to inscribe on the face something akin to the family crest of Jesus Christ. The bishop draws the shape of the cross on which Jesus Christ was hung to show that we are followers of Christ, ready to take arms against the

---

4. In this sentence ぜすきりしと is used for "Jesus Christ," and くるす for "cross." Ibid.
5. The word for "soul" here is *anima* (あにま), for "son," *Deus filio* (でうすひいりよ), for "God the Father," *Deus bateren* (でうす伴天連), and for "Holy Ghost," *Spiritu Santo* (すいりつさんと). Ibid.
6. The word used here is こひさん from the Portuguese *confissão*. Ibid.
7. Here the word *fides* (ひいです) refers to faith. The word used for "church" is *igreja* (えきれんしや). Ibid.
8. Here the word is きりすも, or Chrismo. Also known as the sacrament of Confirmation. The word "Chrisma" refers specifically to the oil used in anointing the believer. Ibid.
9. The word for "bishop" here is ひすほ, from the Portuguese word *bispo*. Ibid. The slap was eliminated from the Catholic ritual after the Second Vatican Council that ended in 1965, partly because its significance was not widely understood, though the most common interpretation was that it reminded the confirmed that they needed to be "soldiers" for Christ and willing to suffer for him.

gentiles.[10] The believer is anointed with oil to follow the example of Jesus, who was anointed with oil soon after his birth. On the thirteenth day after Jesus' birth, three kings from distant lands came bringing myrrh, with which they anointed his head to help protect him from illness. The believer becomes like the Christ child at birth and therefore is also anointed with oil at the time of chrismation. The slap on the right cheek recalls the fact that in his thirty-third year, at the end of his life, Jesus Christ suffered many blows to the face at the hands of Jewish soldiers.[11] The bishop gives a slap to the confirmed as a way of putting the seal of God on the believer's face, so that he should never forget. Also, chrismation means that when you serve God, you come with armor and swords, ready to head into battle for him.

The fourth sacrament is Matrimony.[12] This sacrament requires that when a man and woman become a couple, they must go before a padre to make a written pledge. In it, the man promises that he will not leave the woman during his lifetime, and the woman promises that she will join with the man for the rest of her life, and they both pledge that this will never change. The reason for this sacrament is that women are deeply jealous beings, and, if a man has many wives, they will come to hate him. Naturally, it would be unfortunate if a Kirishitan were denounced as a bad person.[13]

The fifth sacrament is the Priesthood.[14] In this sacrament, of course, one enters a temple and devotes oneself to study.

The sixth sacrament is Communion.[15] The scriptures tell us that on the day before Jesus Christ was raised on the cross he went to the home of Lazarus.[16] There, as he prepared to say good-bye, Jesus Christ took the

---

10. *Gentio*, or "gentile," was the word used by the Jesuits to denote non-Christians. Here it is written せんちよ. Ibid., 571.
11. I have translated the word しゆていし as "Jewish soldiers." Hiyane Antei and Shinmura presumably did not recognize it as a foreign word and therefore left it in *hiragana*. But in the *Dochiriina kirishitan* and Sesshō's *Taiji jashūron* the word じゆでよ is used to mean "Jewish person." With the final し representing 士, "Jewish soldiers" makes sense in the context. See the glossary of loanwords in the back of *Kirishitansho, Haiyasho*, Nihon shisō taikei, vol. 25 (Tokyo: Iwanami shoten, 1970). *Zokuzoku*, 571.
12. Here written as まちりもふにょ, for the Portuguese *matrimonio*. *Zokuzoku*, 571.
13. The text is garbled here and difficult to decipher.
14. This is the only sacrament not to be named with a Portuguese or Latin term. The term used is *shukke* (出家).
15. The word here is こもかる, for the Portuguese *convocar*, or communion. Ibid.
16. The word here is べたにやあの, or *betaniano*. The Portuguese word for "Bethany" would have been "Betania," with *betaniano* meaning "someone from Betania." A feast was prepared for Jesus at the home of Lazarus in Bethany before the Last Supper, and Lazarus is described as a *betaniano*, so the author likely confused the two suppers. Shinmura's version in *Kaihyō sōsho* glosses it as ベタニャア野, implying the fields of Bethany, but it seems more likely the word refers to Lazarus of Bethany.

food from the table and raised it saying, "My disciples, after I die if you want to honor me, think of this food as my body and eat it in remembrance of me. When you do so, my spirit will come and enter the food, thereby entering the bodies of those who eat it and forming a deep and precious bond." Kirishitan with strong faith go before a padre and, after confessing, place in their mouths the food of communion. This food has been prepared from wheat flour and is smaller than a *sen* coin and as thin as paper. After that, the padre puts water in a cup and has them drink it following the words of Jesus Christ: "After I die, draw the flowing water and drink it, knowing that it is my blood." Communion is a ritual that teaches reverence. In the vernacular, it would be the same as *shinsei* (申請).

The seventh sacrament is Unction.[17] Unction takes place at the end of life, when the afflicted takes communion. In this ritual, though the believer is dying, it is more of a farewell to this life, because if he eats the host before dying he will be returned to Deus. Deus is the origin of all understanding.[18]

* * * * *

Saint John the Evangelist lived in the capital of Greece, and after he died his disciples scattered to many lands to spread the Kirishitan faith.[19] Then, in about the year A.D. 430, there was a man named Estevão, who was originally from Rome but was assigned to a post in a province called Saragoza.[20] He had one daughter named Lucia.[21] When she was only seven years old, Lucia's father died, leaving her mother to raise her alone. Lucia surpassed all others in beauty of both body and spirit. In her tenth year she began to study the word of Jesus Christ, and she decided that, even though she was a woman, she wanted to spread Christ's teachings and

---

17. The word here is うんさん, referring to Extreme Unction, which is also known as Anointing the Sick.
18. Though the *Zokuzoku* and Hiyane texts have the words かんねつのこんぼん, I follow Shinmura's text in *Kaihyō sōshō* that transcribes it as かんねんのこんぼん, which makes more sense. *Kaihyō sōsho*, 5; *Zokuzoku*, 571; *Kirishitan monogatari*, 46.
19. The name of St. John is written as 三壽庵ゑわんせりすた, or San João Evangelista, and Greece is written as げれしょの國. *Zokuzoku*, 572.
20. The name is written as ゑして庵, closely resembling the Portuguese name for Steven, or Estevão. Also, the word for province is ほろひんしよ, likely from the Portuguese *provincio* (or *provincia*). The Jesuits divided the areas of their missions into "provinces," over which a leader was assigned as Provincial or Vice Provincial, so it is not surprising that this word became part of what was predominantly a Christian lexicon of borrowed Portuguese and Latin words. Zaragosa is written as さらがうざ. Ibid.
21. Lucia's name is written as 留しや in some places, and as るしや in others.

secure her place in heaven. She first preached in the area where she lived, but then went to a place called Cataseina, where she entered a hermitage and pronounced herself a virgin.[22]

At that hermitage there lived a padre named Roman who fell in love with Lucia at first sight, but because he was a priest he could not speak to her of it. Occasionally he would say to Lucia, "Your heart is truly virtuous. But if you call yourself a virgin, then I suggest that instead of confessing once a month, you do it every Sunday." His design in suggesting this was to use the occasion of meeting her in confession to steal her heart. At that time Lucia was sixteen years old and even more beautiful than ever. One day, Lucia went to the church as usual and, in the deserted building, confessed her sins. After the confession, the padre said to her, "Now, Lucia, you are a young person. Don't you ever suffer from the desires of love and lust?" But Lucia laughed and said, "As a virgin, I have no such desires." Hearing this, the padre said, "Truly, you are a woman of virtue. But now I must teach you the true meaning of the word virgin. With laymen it is the custom for you to hold fast to your pledge. But a priest like myself who is deeply devoted to religious practice and who has acquired power through meritorious practice still has not lost the sexual desire that is so much a part of human behavior. And if you should grant such a person his wish it would be a completely appropriate way of forming a bond with heaven.[23] If you go against your secular pledge and have an affair with a priest, you will gain meritorious power that will allow you to experience the pleasures of heaven—only then you will truly be a virgin. My body is old, but we cannot achieve our goals if we do not form this bond." From that day they secretly became a couple.

Some time passed and Lucia became pregnant. Roman was very pleased and said, "Lucia, when this child is born, you must tell no one it is mine. When it is young you must tell everyone that it is a fatherless child, even if it is laughed at by others. Later, the child will learn of me, and when it grows up, whether it is a boy or a girl, I will pass on Christ's teachings. By the will of God the child will be made king of the land, and there is no doubt good things will come in our grandchildren's generation."

One day around the third month, the king of the province was on pilgrimage at a temple, where he saw Lucia and fell in love at first sight. He

22. Cataseina is a phonetic transcription of the Japanese かたせいな. It is unclear whether it refers to an actual place or not. The word "virgin" is written here as ひるせん, following the Portuguese pronunciation of the word *virgem*. The traditional story of St. Lucy says that she lived in Syracuse, Sicily.
23. I have translated 結縁の道理 as "way of forming a bond with heaven." In Buddhism, 結縁 refers to participating in certain Buddhist practices that form a link with the Buddha.

had countless letters written to her, but because she was pledged to the priest she sent no reply. After he had sent numerous imperial commands but still failed to win her heart, the king became very angry. "I don't know what they do in China or India, but in my country no one refuses an imperial order. Investigate immediately." Lucia was arrested and brought to the palace. The king looked at her and asked many times why she would not give her heart to him, but she closed her eyes, sealed her mouth, and gave no answer. Then the monarch said, "Take her outside the gates and put out her eyes, then put her in prison." So Lucia was taken outside the gates, and both her eyes were put out, and then she was placed in prison. At dawn on the thirty-seventh day the priest came and gave gifts to the guards so he could say his final goodbye. Lucia died soon thereafter. According to the Kirishitan, after that she was called Santa Lucia because she was a virgin of great virtue.

In Japon, Vicente Tōin of Kamigata tells this version of the story. A soldier fell in love with Lucia, and when she asked him what he loved about her, he said it was her eyes. Lucia believed that her eyes could easily cause her to fall into sin, but she knew that if they were taken from her, through God's grace she would get them back again. She decided then to take vows, and told the soldier so. After that, when the king fell in love with her and she did not return his love, she was made a prisoner. On the thirty-seventh day in prison, the beloved padre came to visit and lo, Saint Paul came down to her from heaven and took out his own eyes for her.

The above happened in the year A.D. 430. Sometime before that, after St. James fought and lost in battle, a gentile was the emperor of Rome.[24] The Christians had been mercilessly suppressed for 370 years, and they fearfully hid themselves high on mountains and deep in valleys, where they secretly preached the gospel. The emperor's suppression was so widespread that it was said that over the past 370 years, 1,362,004 people had been seized. Nonetheless, in the year 370, there was one man who became a padre. The few remaining Kirishitan lamented the fact that there was only one padre and that the Kirishitan faith would surely disappear, and they prayed fervently that they would be able to find disciples who could eventually take over for the priest. Because images of Santa Maria and others could not be placed outside, they were forced to hide them in the deepest recesses of their bedchambers and pray to them there.

---

24. The reference to St. James (さんちやあこ, Santiago) in battle here is unclear. The legend of St. James is that he preached in Spain but returned to Jerusalem, where he was beheaded. His reputation as a warrior comes later, when he is said to have appeared before the Spaniards and led them into battle against the Moors in the ninth century.

The Roman emperor, whose name was Don Justo, had contracted leprosy, which had severely disfigured his body.[25] Meanwhile, the Kirishitan priest lived on the side of a tall mountain in the region of Hordencio to escape the persecution. There, he lived in a hole in the floor at the home of a wet nurse named Sabina, coming out of the hole only in the evenings, and hiding there again during the daylight hours.[26] His name was Bernanto, and he was also a very skilled doctor.[27]

One day, the priest approached the wet nurse and said, "I have heard that the emperor of this land is afflicted with leprosy. You should go to the gate of the palace and repeat in a very loud voice, 'Last night I saw a strange and wonderful dream. In it, a spirit came to me and said there is a priest called Bernanto, and if Your Majesty the Emperor should meet with the priest and grant his wish, he will surely cure you.'" The wet nurse was happy to comply and went to the gate of the palace, where she did as she was told and shouted with a voice that reverberated loudly. The people gathered inside the palace heard her words and repeated them to the emperor, who immediately had the wet nurse brought before him and asked her to tell him her dream, just as she had seen it. "Last night I saw a strange and mysterious dream," she said. "It was at the hour of the ox, and the dream came as I slept with my pillow facing east.[28] According to the dream, in that direction there is a high mountain where a priest called Bernanto lives. If you were to grant this priest his wish, he would immediately cure you of your illness. My lord, I saw this dream repeated

---

25. The basic outline of this story follows the legend, based on a forged document called the *Donation of Constantine*, that the Roman emperor Constantine I granted to Pope Sylvester I and his successors Italy, Greece, Asia, Africa, and the city of Rome. The document said that the donation was made to thank Sylvester for baptizing him, teaching him about Christianity, and curing him from leprosy. Mark Edwards, *Constantine and Christendom: the Oration to the Saints, the Greek and Latin Accounts of the Discovery of the Cross, the Edict of Constantine to Pope Silvester* (Liverpool: Liverpool University Press, 2003), 92–115. The names here are different, but it is of interest that the name chosen for the emperor should be the same by which the Jesuits called one of their most important converts, Takayama Ukon. In Jesuit texts, Takayama is often referred to as Don Justo, or Justo Ukondono. For more on Takayama Ukon, see George Elison, *Deus Destroyed: The Image of Christianity in Early Modern Japan* (Cambridge, Mass.: Harvard University Press, 1973), and Johannes Laures, S.J., "Takayama Ukon: A Critical Essay," *Monumenta Nipponica* 5, no. 1 (1942): 86–112. Though the latter is perhaps not as objective as he could be, he has clearly done extensive research in the Jesuit archives and other sources for information on Ukon.
26. The name of the town is written as ほるでんしょ, but it is unclear if it refers to a historical place. The name of the wet nurse is written as さびいな.
27. The name of the priest is written as べるなんと and was perhaps meant to be Fernando or Bernardo.
28. The hour of the ox is between 1 and 3 A.M.

three times." The emperor was struck by her story. He ordered her to find the priest and bring him to the palace, and he sent Sabina home bearing many gifts.

Due east from her bedroom there was a mountain called Saramonte, so Sabina had the padre climb it and hide himself in a grove of cedars. Then the emperor chose his closest retainer, Tosano, and after giving him more than six hundred men, dispatched them to the wet nurse's house. Then Tosano asked Sabina, "Where is this tall mountain in the east that you spoke of to the emperor?" Sabina replied, "That towering mountain over there is called Saramonte. It is east of here, so that must be the one." Tosano told Sabina to find the priest, and he had Sabina go before them as they climbed Saramonte. Because she had hidden Bernanto there herself, she led them directly to the cedar grove. The padre looked terrified and trembled in fear. Seeing that, Tosano said, "Do not be surprised. I come by orders of the emperor to take you to him."

Bernanto eventually arrived at the palace. When the emperor saw him, he said, "The nurse's dream was correct. Are you the priest called Bernanto?" When Bernanto replied that he was, the emperor said, "What must you do to cure my illness?" Bernanto measured his words carefully and said, "With all due respect, it can be done quite easily. If only Your Majesty would receive the baptismal waters and become a Kirishitan, you would soon be cured." The emperor considered this for a moment. "Because I was born a prince, I have followed tradition and worshipped the heavenly deities," he replied.[29] "But if there is no other way for me to be cured of this illness, I will follow your teachings."

Then Bernanto, who had come prepared for this, made a potion by dissolving some myrrh into water, the liver of a person who had two spectacles in his eyes, and the brain of an albino.[30] He baptized the emperor and then covered his whole body from head to toe in the potion. After he was treated for seven days, the emperor was completely cured. Then he asked, "What is the padre's wish?" Bernanto replied, "I have no other wish than that you make everyone in each and every province a Kirishitan." So the emperor made every last person become a Kirishitan. In addition, he built a tremendous church only ten blocks from the palace, and he had Bernanto installed there. The church was given the name of Hospitali, and it became the healing center for all

---

29. The term used here is 神明. This term is rather vague and could mean a single deity or plural deities, and it could also refer to Buddhist or Shinto gods.
30. The word translated here as spectacles is 物見, which is a nonspecific item that helps to see things. It is unclear to what the author is referring.

of the provinces.³¹ Furthermore, the wet nurse Sabina was made the landlord of Hordencio, and she shaved her head and became the first nun in Rome.

After these events, the padre Bernanto petitioned several times for the pope, who was the descendant of Saint Peter and was in hiding in a place called Egypt, to be made the king of Rome.³² He said to the emperor, "In return for curing you, I would like you to retire to the land of Castile and make the pope emperor of Rome. If you or I do not earn grace in this life for the next, then according to the teachings of Christ we could be excommunicated, and we would sink into the flames of burning hell not only in this life but in the next as well.³³ So, what is Your Majesty's will?" When the emperor heard all of this, he was consumed with worry, and though he wanted to live out his life in his own country more than anything, it was no use. He retired to Castile at a young age. It is said that from that day on Rome was ruled by the pope. This method of drawing people into the religion—warning them about life after death, and then taking over the country—was an ingenious one that has been used from ancient times.

* * * * *

Now, in the spring of the year A.D. 620, there was a gathering in Rome of the pope and padres from many regions. After some discussion, the group came to a decision. "Our master Jesus Christ told us that after he died those descendants of his disciples who believed his teachings should convert all of the kings of the world to them. We should discuss a plan to send out missionaries throughout the world." They discussed the issue further and decided to consult the writing of the ancestor Moses, and then they pulled out several scrolls.³⁴ Looking at all of the countries of the world,

---

31. Though naming the church a "hospital" may seem odd, the early Jesuits in Japan, and other orders that came later in the sixteenth century, were very involved in healing. They often took in people with leprosy who were outcasts in Japanese society. The Visitor Alexandro Valignano soon ended the practice among the Jesuits, realizing that such contact with the outcasts of Japanese society damaged how the Jesuits and their teachings were received. But the Dominicans/Franciscans continued the practice until the expulsion of 1614.
32. "Egypt" is written as えじつと, and the "pope" is written as ぱっぱ, for "*papa*."
33. There is a lacuna in the text that makes this passage difficult to decipher. Here I translate ゑすくもがあと in the *Zokuzoku* text as "excommunicated" (*excomungato*). Both Shinmura and Hiyane edited the word to read エスクモが跡, but this does not seem to have any meaning that would fit the context.
34. The Japanese name is もんてす, which could be a copy error for Moses (*Moises* in Portuguese).

they saw that there were countries that worshipped Buddha or the heavenly deities, others that revered the elements or animals such as sheep, and some where people crossed into other worlds at birth. Under these circumstances, it was probably not possible to make all of the countries Kirishitan through force of arms. So, the most clever of the padres, who was named Reseina, was appointed general and given sixteen padres and thirty brothers to accompany him.[35] He was also given several thousand *kanme* of silver and a large number of ships. The pope said, "You must go to Siam and teach the law of Jesus. If, however, you cannot do that, you must buy the scriptures of their gods and bring them back here."[36] The general replied that he would do as the pope asked. They launched the ships and let the favorable wind guide them, and they soon arrived in Siam.

The Romans tried to preach about their law, but they were unable to translate it into the proper language, and so were unsuccessful. Then they asked around and were able to buy some sermons and commentaries on Buddhism. But when they tried to set sail for home, the king of Siam told them that they would not be permitted to take the teachings of his religion to another country, and each and every one of the forty-six priests was punished. At the end of the following spring, everyone in Rome was waiting for the padres. When no word came, they sent another group with thirty priests led by Padre Simon.[37] When they arrived in Siam, all of them were also punished. Simon and eight priests had their noses and ears slashed and were then sent home. Several years later, in Siam, Padre Reseina was martyred. His portrait was painted as proof of his martyrdom, and many later generations revered him.

The pope said to everyone, "North of here there is an island called Monte Plata.[38] Aristotle said that north of here there is an island of silver born from the deepest reaches of the earth.[39] It has been called Kōreizan, but is also known as Monte Plata. Our Lord Jesus Christ said that the

---

35. Here the word for "brothers" is ゆるまん (instead of the usual いるまん), based on the Portuguese word *irmão*.
36. The term for "Siam" here is しやむろう.
37. The word here for "Simon" is 四もん.
38. The name is written as もんてふらた.
39. In this sentence, the word I have translated as "Aristotle" is すたうてす, and I follow Shinmura's interpretation of this as Aristotle. The term referring to the "deepest reaches of the earth" is 金輪際. The three different versions of the text all read one character differently, and I have compromised by using the rather vague word "from" in the translation. The three different readings are 金輪際よりすゑ出たる in Shinmura, *Kaihyō sōsho*, 16; 金輪際よりおゑ出たる in *Zokuzoku*, 577; and 金輪際より生出たる in Hiyane, *Kirishitan monogatari*, 57.

countries that are the wisest were meant to belong to Santa Maria.[40] Send people there to check on their defenses and learn about their gods, and they will submit, either to the teachings of Jesus Christ or to the sword." From among many priests, he chose a padre named Paulo, who was the cleverest and had the most eloquent tongue.

Now, according to Santa Maria, when we read the books of the philosophers, the island of Monte Plata is a country that rules the world with an iron whip. The spirit of its people is braver and more steadfast than even a lion's. They surpass all in the world in the military arts. Bearing in mind the teachings of Santa Maria, the padres decided to use trade as a pretence and then to make a study of the island's defenses. They prepared a large ship and many different kinds of goods to trade. Eight priests joined Paulo, and the captain of the ship was named Don Jacob.

They sailed from Rome and arrived in a place called Goa, where they stayed through year's end. In the following spring they caught a fair wind heading north, but just when they thought they were getting close to Monte Plata, a wind fierce enough to bend trees blew them back almost to where they had started. So they landed in Portugal and waited out the year.[41] When the south wind began to blow in the fifth month of the following year, they set sail again, and in the middle of the eighth month they arrived in a place called China.[42] They tried to disembark, but the people there found their appearance so strange that they were not allowed to leave the ship. So, without setting foot on land, they set sail again. Another year came to an end as the ship was tossed about in the rough seas of regions unknown. In the fourth month of the following year, they finally caught a fair wind again, and before the end of the sixth month they had arrived in Satsuma in Japan.[43]

The padres disembarked and tried to sell the goods they had brought, but their appearance was so fearsome that no one would approach them. So, Paulo and the other padres traveled the country, from province to province, looking at everything and measuring the length and breadth

---

40. I follow the Shinmura text here, which transcribes the phrase as ちへ第一の國サンタマリヤ御私所のために作りたまふ. Both Hiyane and the editor of the *Zokuzoku* version transcribe it as サンタマリヤ御船所, which makes less sense in the context. Shinmura, *Kaihyō sōsho*, 16.
41. The word for "Portugal" is written ふるとがると.
42. The term for "China" here is 大唐, which could mean China or, more specifically, Tang Dynasty China.
43. "Japan" is referred to here as 日本あきつしま, which combines the names of 日本 with another name for Japan 豊秋津洲 used in the *Kojiki* in the section about the creation of the islands.

of islands, the height of mountains, and the flow of rivers. Judging from what they saw, they knew this must be Monte Plata. Since they had no place to lodge, they spent the days sleeping in fields and on mountains, and eventually they returned to the original port and joined the other priests, without having preached about their law. Every time they tried to approach someone to speak of it, they were regarded with fear. When they asked the captain about his success in trading, Jacob said, "In order to convince people to come near us I had to use the goods as gifts, so no one actually bought anything."

Thus, without accomplishing the tasks they had been set by the pope, they set sail for home in the second month of the following year, arriving back in Rome a full seven years from the time they had left. When the ship from Monte Plata came back to Rome, everyone there was overjoyed. In celebration of the ship's return, guns and cannons roared, and there was a tremendous commotion. But Padre Paulo and Captain Jacob looked dejected as they descended from the ship and came before the pope. "Eventually we arrived in Monte Plata, but it was all to no avail. I had Jacob set about trading goods and sent the eight priests in eight directions to learn more about the country. After examining the height of the mountains and the flow of the rivers, we were certain it was Monte Plata. But we could not preach to anyone because people would not approach us. The people there are about the same coloring as those of Goa, Portugal, and Rome, but they are shorter and their eyes are smaller. Their stride is as graceful as a bird on the wing, and they are clearly the best in the military arts. If they were to oppose our teachings, there would be little we could do about it." Such was the report of Padre Paulo.

Then the lords and officials of Rome gathered to discuss their course of action. Some said that the country was far away and for that reason would be difficult to defeat and conquer. Others said that it should be conquered by means of the Kirishitan law, while still others thought that military means would work best. At that moment, the pope's subject named Chōbito stepped forward and asked, "What gods do they worship in Monte Plata?"[44] And Padre Paulo replied, "Idols, as in Jerusalem."[45] When Chōbito heard this, he said, "If that is the case, clearly their learning is outdated, and their teachings full of errors. We should try to take them by force first, but if that it not successful, then we should convert them to our religion." With this suggestion, the gathering was quieted and

---

44. The name of the subject here is not recognizable as any Western name. It is written as ちやうびいと.
45. Here the interesting reply by Paulo is ぜるされんのごとく、いとろす成.

the pope also was relieved. This time, the pope made Chōbito a general along with his brother, Acabita, and gave them eight hundred thousand mounted soldiers and countless foot soldiers. They boarded one hundred sixty thousand ships flying red flags, and they left the port of Rome, feeling that being on the water was like floating in paradise.

The Romans sailed joyfully until they eventually reached the port of Goa. Because Goa and Portugal were vassal states of Rome, the Romans could wait out the end of the year in those ports. When spring came and the supplies of food and ammunition were low, tribute paid by Goa and Portugal to Rome was loaded onto the ships. Then the captains of all of the ships said, "Now that we have plenty of supplies, we only need to decide on an auspicious date of departure." General Chōbito said, "Since we left Rome in the third month last year, we should leave this time on the twenty-eighth day of the third month." But because this day fell on a Friday, they said, "This is the day when our lord Jesus Christ was hung on the cross, so it is an inauspicious day for Kirishitan. As long as the first day of the fourth month is a Sunday, we should set sail on that day."[46] They agreed to do this, and the ships left port on the first day of the fourth month. The one hundred sixty thousand ships all advanced quickly and managed to arrive at a small island near the port of Monte Plata by the beginning of the ninth month of that year. When the ninth month had passed, and they had just entered the tenth month, they left that island and made for Monte Plata.

The residents must have known the Romans were coming, as they had armed themselves with a variety of weapons and fought fiercely to defend themselves. The roar of the canon and guns shot from the ships was deafening. The men of Monte Plata fought only with long swords and bows, and they could not prevail against the guns. After they had withdrawn, the soldiers left the ships and searched the area, but they found all the houses empty. One soldier, serving General Acabito, managed to capture a young man of about twenty-four or twenty-five. The two generals realized they could use this person to learn the country's language, and they both gave thanks to Santa Maria. One hundred sixty-four padres were also on this voyage, and they were thrilled by the conquest and performed rituals of celebration.

Later, when the heads of the dead of Monte Plata were counted, there were 103. The Roman soldiers counted one hundred of their own wounded

---

46. The word that I am translating as "Friday" is ぜすた, which corresponds with the Portuguese *sexta-feira* for Friday. In Portuguese, Good Friday, which is observed as the day Jesus died on the cross, would be *Sexta-Feira Santa*.

and eighty-four dead. When the two generals heard this, they said, "If that is the case, then this country is truly strong in the military arts. If our country of Rome had been attacked by one hundred sixty thousand ships from another country, there is no doubt it would have been crushed. They fight very well! Still, even though their weapons are strong, there will be no problem. We must be very careful with that prisoner."

After teaching the prisoner a few things and gradually training him in the language, they asked him some questions. "What is the name of this island?" The prisoner answered loudly, "This country is called Nihon." The generals heard this and said, "In our language it would be called Japon. You shall be our guide to Japon. If you teach us about this country, you shall be made a lord." They asked him the name of their current location, and he replied that they were in Satsuma, in Kyushu. "How far is the capital from here?" they asked him, and he told them that it was a distance of 380 *li*.[47] The generals decided that waging battle on the country from one end to the other would not benefit them, and that first they should go to the capital.

Then they asked the prisoner if they could get to the capital from there by ship. He replied, "Last year we traveled with my lord, so I know the way. If I were your guide, I would have you sail to Nanba Bay in Settsu Province. From there it is just over 10 *li* to the capital, but no more than 20 *li* on foot. But I should warn you of my country's prowess in the military arts. We do not train for sea battles, but on land our warriors scatter armies like flower petals, so you should be extremely careful." When he had finished speaking, they looked back and saw millions of fluttering red and white flags break through the Roman forces and surge forward, cutting down rows of horses. Without hesitating a moment, everyone ran for the ships. General Chōbito managed to make it to the ships, but his bow arm was wounded and he died soon after boarding. They placed the prisoner on General Acabito's ship to make sure he did not escape.

When the remaining horses were all in place on board and they were ready to bring the ships about, they looked to the east and saw about one hundred halos of light all come together to form two or three, and then a strange, evil wind began to blow. The east wind and the south wind met and blew with crushing force, and winds from all directions came together and battled against each other, making it difficult for the ships to avoid colliding with each other. Just as the order was given to moor them again, a north wind strong enough to topple trees began to blow water into the sky and sand from the beach into the air. People remarked that

47. One *li* 里 was equal to approximately 3.9 kilometers.

this was no ordinary wind of this world. In year one in the time of David, when Castile was attacked, the winds all came together and brought a devil wind, and they said that this must be the same. Lightning came down from the sky over the ships, striking many of the soldiers and setting many ships on fire. The remaining ships were scattered about by the great winds and destroyed when they were dashed upon the cliffs and shoals. General Acabito's ship was the only one that survived. For a long time it was tossed on the waves and carried here and there by the winds until finally, in the fourth year, it arrived back in the port of Rome.

A downcast Acabito descended from the ship and went before the pope. "I bring a report of our battles in Japon, which took place in the tenth month. In the first battle, fortune appeared to be with us, and we were winning. But in the next day's battles our forces were scattered, General Chōbito was struck down, and the armies were decimated. Eventually we boarded the ships, but a demon was summoned from somewhere in Japan and suddenly an evil wind rose, scattering the ships and destroying them. Then lightning fell from the sky and burned more of them. Of the one hundred sixty thousand ships, only mine was spared and returned here." The pope said, "Why has heaven brought us to this fate?" and there was none around him who did not weep. In the beginning, when Rome was established, all of the strongest soldiers in Italy were recruited. Now all had been lost in Japon, and not even a lowly arrow bearer remained. The pope said they now would have to think of strategies for protecting their own country from attack, and from that day he devoted himself only to the administration of Rome.

Sixteen years later, there was a Roman subject by the name of Francisco, who one day gathered all of the members of his clan to discuss a plan. The group said, "Many years ago missions were sent to Monte Plata a number of times, but it was too difficult to enter. Now, Francisco has proposed that we go to Japon and try again." They recruited soldiers from all of the lands around and gathered a force that exceeded two hundred thousand. But knowing that their plans would not succeed with a small army, they also recruited from such countries as Goa, Portugal, Castile, India, Greece, Egypt, Alicante, Abarão and the provinces, until it was said that the total number of mounted soldiers reached one million one hundred sixty thousand.[48] There were forty-four ships for the Roman soldiers, and many more smaller boats for the other armies, so that the surface of the sea looked like it was covered with scattered leaves.

48. Though most of the countries are recognizable, the last one, Abaran, is not. The countries are written as ごあ、ふるとがる、かすていら、いんでや、けれしよ、ゑじつと、ありしあんて、あはらん、ほろびんしよ (provincia).

The Japanese man who had been brought back sixteen years ago had been made a Kirishitan and was now named João, and he was chosen to be the guide for this trip. The pope also made João the general over one hundred thousand horsemen. Francisco chose the eighth day of the fourth month as the date of departure from Rome. That day was a Wednesday.[49] Francisco explained his choice, saying, "Many years ago, when Chōbito left Goa and Portugal, he chose a Sunday to depart, but that is a bad day to begin an enterprise. This time we will merely depart on a Wednesday. Let us pray to Santa Maria." Then he brought more than seven hundred priests on board, so that throughout the ships all that could be heard was the sound of their prayers.

That year the boat arrived first in Portugal, where it stayed until year's end. At the beginning of the second month, it set sail from there and, catching a strong wind, made great speed towards its goal. The second year ended while they were still at sea, and they finally drew close to Monte Plata in the third year. This time as well, they saw a host of white flags above the clouds. It was a bad omen. They wondered if these were storm clouds, and before they even had the chance to say the words, a north wind strong enough to topple trees came and scattered all of the ships that had been lined up in a row. The ships were blown to China, to Takasago, and to countries and provinces everywhere, so that of the more than forty ships that started the voyage, only the two ships carrying General Francisco and João managed to land on a tiny island together.

When they got off of the ships and looked around, the two realized that this island was also part of Monte Plata. Just then, some ten million small boats from Monte Plata landed there, and a hail of arrows fell on them like the rains of the fifth month. Francisco and João both boarded the ships and defended themselves with gun and cannon fire, but when the ammunition was about to run out, they went back onto the island and hid behind a small hill, taking with them a small force of soldiers. On the two ships there were less than two hundred people left, most of them foot soldiers and commoners. Because there was no more ammunition, they all drew their swords and ran into the enemy forces. But the enemy was a huge force, and the Romans were no force at all, and soon there was not a single soldier left.

Only General Francisco managed to escape and hide himself in a cave. When the large army had retreated, he came out of the cave and down to the shore to look for food. For two years he stayed on that island, at the

---

49. The term used here for "Wednesday" is くわるた. The Portuguese word for "Wednesday" is *quarta-feira*. "Sunday" in the next sentence is どみんこ, or the Portuguese *domingo*.

mercy of the rain and the dew. One day, when a ship from China stopped to take on fresh water, he said, "I was abandoned on this island a long time ago and have led a wretched life here. Now this ship has come in answer to my prayers. Please take me aboard." So he was taken aboard and carried to China, where he stayed for three years in a place called Etsu.[50] After that he boarded a Siamese ship, gradually making his way back, spending seven years in Siam and then traveling to India, until he finally returned to Rome. All of the people of that age heard the story told by Francisco of the strategies in the battles of Monte Plata, and it was clear to them that military means were not effective, and that only by means of the law of Jesus would they be able to take over the country. But many years passed with no further attempts.

Some time later, two padres named Siman and Pietro and twenty brothers decided to use trade as a pretext for conquering Monte Plata, so they loaded a ship with thousands of treasures and set off for the country. The captain's name was Don Massimo. After they had left Rome, people waited for six years but heard no word of them, so a padre named Simon, along with eight other padres and seventeen brothers, set sail for Monte Plata on a ship under the command of Captain Don João. But this ship also never returned. Now that two ships had been lost, it was clear that they were simply not meant to go to that island, and some time passed with no more attempts. Eventually they decided to try to conquer only nearby countries, and they successfully took over many countries, including France, Eborio, and Omobicio.[51] But it could hardly be said that Rome was flourishing.

Then, in the year A.D. 1560, a padre named Cosme decided to try to conquer Monte Plata using only religion.[52] He boarded a ship under the command of Captain Don Groigo.[53] They sailed for Monte Plata, and in

---

50. The name of this place in China is written in *hiragana* (and glossed in *katakana* by Shinmura and Hiyane). It probably refers to an area that was once part of southern China and later part of Vietnam (粵 or 越).
51. The actual names of the last two "countries" are unclear, though "Eborio" might refer to *Evora* in Portugal. The names in Japanese are written as ゑはうりよ and おもびしよ國.
52. A Jesuit from Valencia by the name of Cosme de Torres was one of the earliest Jesuits in Japan. He was a companion of Francis Xavier upon his arrival in Japan in 1549 and was put in charge of the mission when Xavier left in 1551. Torres was the mission superior until 1570, and he died in Japan that same year.
53. The name is given as どくろいご, but since all previous captain's names began with "Don," it appears a copy error has omitted the ん. Though the name is not recognizable in a Western language, it is possible it was an attempt at Gregorio, which was the name of a famous Jesuit and one that appears in the other two major fiction pieces on the Kirishitan, *Kirishitan monogatari* and *Nanbanji monogatari*.

the third year after leaving Rome, they arrived in the town of Bōnotsu in Satsuma. When he disembarked, Cosme said to the people there, "We have come from Rome to trade with a country to the east of here called Nova Hispania, but the winds carried us here."[54] Because he did not know the language well, he brought out many goods to trade, and he was able to sell some. People did not hesitate to approach him, and gradually he learned the language.

Eventually, Cosme asked those around him, "What do you worship in this country?" They responded by pointing to shrines and pagodas. Cosme thought that this moment was a perfect time to talk about religion, so he said, "In our country, the things you are pointing to are called 'idols,' and there is no reason for them to be built. The only deity we worship is Deus, who resides in heaven. He is the creator of all things." In the large group of people there was a one-eyed man of about twenty-four or twenty-five years who had come to hear about the religion. The padre asked him his name and where he was from. He replied, "I am from a place called Yamato near the capital, and my name is Ryōsai." Cosme said that it was an unusual name, but he urged Ryōsai to join his religion. Ryōsai replied, "After carefully listening to your sermons, I know that these teachings are superior, and I would like to become a disciple." After that he was baptized and worked with Cosme in trade for the rest of the year.

The following year, when the ship prepared to return to Rome, the padre suggested to Ryōsai that he return with them and join the order. Ryōsei replied, "I am an orphan with no ties to this country, so I will accompany you," and he boarded the ship. After that, Ryōsei was known as Lourenço.[55] In three years he arrived in Rome, and there he studied the Kirishitan teachings in depth. After staying for six years in Rome, he was sent to work in Japon.

On the return trip there were three priests, including Lourenço, a brother, and a padre named Francisco Gaspar; the captain this time was

---

54. Nova Hispania (のうびすばんや) refers to Mexico.
55. Brother Lourenço was one of the first Japanese converts to join the order. There is no record of his Japanese name in the Jesuit archives, but the records do say that he was born in Hizen (not Yamato) and was baptized by Francis Xavier in Yamaguchi in 1551. In 1563 he was received into the order as a brother by Cosme de Torres, and for many years he served in Kyoto under Father Gaspar Vilela. Jesuit records confirm that he was almost completely blind, having lost one eye and most of the sight in the other. There is no reason to believe that he traveled to Europe. For more on Lourenço, see Ebisawa Arimichi, "Irmao Lourenco, the First Japanese Lay-Brother of the Society of Jesus and His Letter," *Monumenta Nipponica* 5, no. 1 (1942): 225–33.

named Jacob.⁵⁶ They landed at Bungo in Japan.⁵⁷ Because Lourenço was Japanese, they left the speaking to him and had him give the sermons, and that year about one hundred people joined the religion. The following year, Padre Gaspar returned to Rome, and, because he was Lourenço's master, the Japanese man traveled as well. While they were staying in Portugal, they devised a plan to break up the very long round trip to Japan by stopping to buy goods in Macao in China, and by building churches while they were there. In the fourth year, then, the padre and his student returned to Japan, but this time the ship landed on the island of Hirado in the Matsuura domain of Higo Province. It is said that ever since then the ship has made the trip to Macao each year from Hirado because it is the closest port. This was the beginning of the Kirishitan presence in our country.

After that, the ship docked at Hirado again. One day, a Japanese man and a foreign lord were having a small argument, and Itō Jinzaburō happened by and asked what was the matter.⁵⁸ The Japanese man, who understood the language, answered that it was just about a little trade, and Jinzaburō replied, "Well, if it is only about sales, there is no need to argue." But the foreign lord, who did not understand the language, thought that Jinzaburō was starting a fight, so he drew his sword and wounded Jinzaburō's right hand. The wounded man then immediately struck down the foreign lord. With that, foreign foot soldiers and commoners began to shout that there was a fight with the Japanese, and all of the Southern Barbarians poured out of the ship onto land and surrounded Jinzaburō. Then the samurai and townsmen of Hirado came running and surrounded the Southern Barbarians, and they fell to fighting until all were in a daze.⁵⁹ The fight began at a place called Miyanomae, and the foreigners were pursued

56. There were two well-known Jesuits with the first name of Gaspar, the most famous of these being Gaspar Coelho, who served as vice-provincial in Japan from 1580 until his death in 1590. Another was Gaspar Vilela, who arrived in Japan in 1556 and founded the mission in Kyoto with the assistance of Brother Lourenço, among others.
57. This is the first time in the text that the narrator refers to Japan as 日本 and not Japon or Monte Plata (other than in the dialogue of the Japanese captive earlier). The perspective clearly shifts in this paragraph from that of Rome as it tries to breach Japan's defenses, to that of Japan as it receives the Kirishitan. This shift is highlighted in the last sentence of the paragraph, which refers to Japan as *wagachō* 我が朝.
58. Here the word for "foreign lord" is しによろ, likely for the Portuguese *senhor*.
59. This is the first time that the foreigners are called Nanbanjin 南蛮人, or Southern Barbarians, again marking the difference in perspective from that of Rome looking toward Japan, to Japan and its interaction with foreigners. The earlier reference to Macao may have inspired this change, as most early traders who came from Macao or the Philippines were called Nanbanjin (as barbarians, from outside of the Sino-centric sphere of civility, who sailed up from the south).

to a place called Iyanosaki. Many of the foreign lords, foot soldiers, and other commoners were killed, so that only one third of them managed to escape to their ship.

The governor of Hirado sent a messenger who said, "It is shameful to act this way with ships that have come asking for permission to land, and what we have heard of the foreigners' behavior is no better. The fighting must stop, and from now on all people who come must have their names registered." As a result, the Japanese fighters withdrew, and what was left of the Southern Barbarians gathered their dead and wounded and returned to the ship. For the rest of that year they continued to trade without incident, and then the foreigners returned to Macao.

The following year, the ship docked in Yokoseura, which was in the domain of Lord Ōmura. The foreigners introduced themselves to that lord and told him that if they were able to preach their religion, all would certainly join, and that it would be an act of compassion and a means of accumulating merit for him to allow people to learn about their law. Eventually, the lord also joined the religion. After that, certain circumstances led to the ship landing at a place called Fukuda, and later it began to land in Nagasaki, as it still does now. Gradually, the foreigners began to prosper and thrive.

After that, a dreadful truth came to light. It all began in the middle of the second month of 1605. There was a church in Hakata, in the province of Chikuzen, and the priest there was named Herloman. The brother there was named Nicolao, and the *dōjuku* was named Ignacio.[60] At that time in Hakata, the Kirishitan were flourishing. The name of the governor of that area was Lord Kuroda of Kai Province.

Also at that time, there was a man named Lião in Hakata. He was born in Hirado but had lived in the capital since childhood. Now he had left the capital, but for various reasons he did not return to Hirado and was living in Hakata. Lião had developed lesions on his leg, and he soon began to fear for his life. Then someone said to him, "It is well-known that there is a doctor at the church. If you were a Kirishitan, you would probably soon be cured." When Lião heard this he thought that if all they asked of him in return for a cure was to become a Kirishitan, then that was an easy thing to do. He went to the church and listened to the sermons for seven days.[61]

---

60. *Dōjuku* were laymen who served in and supported the Jesuit mission, sometimes as a precursor to admission as brothers.
61. The Jesuits' basic catechism before a convert could be baptized was delivered over a seven-day period. In a letter written to Rome by Luis Frois, he explains that this was established because it was a familiar practice already instituted in Buddhist temples. *Cartas de Iapão que escreverão os padres & irmãos da companhia de Iesus* (Evora, 1598), facsimile edition, vol. 2 (Tokyo: Tenri Central Library, 1972), F. 179.

Though the teachings were not convincing, he received baptism in order to get treatment, and he was given the name Lião. Then he said to the head priest at the church, "With your help I have become a Kirishitan. But my opportunities are limited now because if I tell people I am a Kirishitan, many of them will hate me. So I ask that you allow me to work as a *dōjuku* in the temple." The priest agreed to do that. Eventually Lião was taken to the doctor and had his lesions treated, and he soon was cured. He then began to study the Kirishitan teachings. The padres were overjoyed that, despite knowing some of the Buddhist law, he was turning away from it, and they initiated him into the innermost teachings.

Lião had been at the church for three years when, on the twenty-first day of the third month of 1607, a great number of padres and brothers all came from Nagasaki. Lião was suspicious and asked some of them why they had come, but no one would explain. When he privately asked the head priest about it, the priest answered that it was a secret that he would derive no benefit from knowing. To this Lião replied, "For three years I have lived at this temple and faithfully studied the innermost teachings. It is unfortunate that now you feel the need to conceal this from me, but if that is the case, then I shall leave the temple."

When the head priest heard this he realized that it would be harmful if this man left the temple, so he explained the situation to him. "You must not tell anyone this. We must all be as one in this. Right now, Nagasaki is flourishing, and while it is a small domain, the domains of Ōmura and Arima are also Kirishitan. In other domains as well there are many Kirishitan, but at this point we probably cannot achieve our ultimate goal. For that reason, the priests have all gathered to discuss a plan. There are too many acquaintances in Nagasaki who might see them, so the visitors have come in secret to this church for the meeting. One of those visitors is Kuroda Sōemon of Kai Province, who has been a Kirishitan from early on. Starting with him, if we could convince ten or more of the greater and lesser domain lords around Japan to join our faith, they would represent the seeds of battle. So we have gathered the priests and will send them to all of the provinces to preach and spread the teachings and gather converts. After that, when we have taken the realm without even firing a single arrow, if there are any who refuse to submit, we will simply threaten them with excommunication and frighten them by describing the horrors of the afterlife. Then there will be no one who fails to join the padres, and we will become the leaders of the realm, with the bishop made shogun of Japan. The priests have assembled to discuss how to carry out this plan."

The conference began on the twenty-second day of the third month, and everyone attended. It continued for seven days until the twenty-eighth. Internal meetings continued beyond that, with ten padres closeting themselves for three days and nights at a place called San Yoshia, where no others were allowed to enter. As a result, they decided that Brother Fabian would be sent to preach in Chikuzen to urge the people there to join the religion as Kai Province had.[62] Brother Canbō would be sent to recruit daimyo in Satsuma to join the faith. Brother Decōrius and Tsuji Takaaki would be sent to Buzen, and Takaura Julian would be sent to Higo.[63] The padres also brought up another matter. They pointed out that Nagasaki in Japan is the equivalent of Rome in their own country, and that when the church does not have its own estates, it cannot support the necessary workers. They suggested that the church petition the government for use of the bakufu region of Urakami as a church domain. Then two padres named Meian and Francisco stepped forward and said, "As all of you know well, Urakami is some distance from Nagasaki. Right now, Nagasaki is administered by Lord Ōmura, but we should ask the authorities to exchange it for Urakami and declare Nagasaki bakufu land. Then, the church may remain where it is, and we can eventually make the town our own. This should be our plan." Hearing this, the head priest Herloman said, "If we want to take over the country, why would we want to rule such an insignificant town as Nagasaki?" But the other padres responded, "Even in heaven, moving from one sphere to the next is a gradual process. We should begin with Nagasaki." They decided on this course of action, and all returned to Nagasaki.

62. The name of Fabian is written as はいあん. This is most likely a reference to Fabian Fucan, the famous Japanese convert and then apostate who wrote tracts both for and against Christianity. He is a central Kirishitan character in all of the eighteenth-century *Raichō jikki* variants, some of which write his name as it is here.
63. Takaura Julian was the name of one of the young boys who formed the Japanese mission to Europe led by the Jesuit Visitor, Alexandro Valignano. All four boys came from prominent samurai families that had converted to Christianity. The trip lasted eight years and took them to Portugal, Spain, and Rome, where they had an audience with the pope (though Julian did not attend due to illness). After their return, Julian joined the order and was eventually ordained. He ministered to the Kirishitan in Japan long after the general expulsion, until he was captured in 1632. He was tortured with a group of captives that included the famous apostate, Christovão Ferreira, who apostatized after five hours of torture. Julian held out for four days and died on October 21, 1633. For more on the Japanese mission to Europe and Julian, see Michael Cooper, *The Japanese Mission to Europe, 1582-1590* (Kent: Global Oriental, 2005). Father Tsuji, whose Christian name was Thomas, was canonized by the Catholic Church after being arrested and killed by Japanese authorities in 1627. I have not been able to find confirmation of the reading of his first name as Takaaki, as most sources list him with his Christian first name.

Then Padre Tçuzzu was sent as a messenger to the authorities.[64] He was asked to tell them, "Urakami is bakufu land, while Nagasaki is administered by Lord Ōmura. But Urakami is rural while Nagasaki is a port of call for ships from China, Tenjiku, and South Barbary and is an extremely busy place.[65] May we suggest that the two be exchanged?" The three magistrates agreed to this, and eventually the sealed approval was delivered to the padres.[66] As a result, the domain of Urakami was divided: one part was assigned to Ōmura, while the remainder along with Nagasaki became a new bakufu domain. Then the padres felt secure living there. And when Tōan eventually became magistrate of Nagasaki, it was another part of their plan.[67] This was because Tōan's son, Francisco, was a padre and served the bishop.[68] So Tōan was made magistrate of Nagasaki with the hope that, once he had helped the padres carry out their plans, it would be easy to convince those in surrounding domains to follow them.

At that time, in the Ōmura domain, there was a samurai named

---

64. I follow Shinmura's interpretation of the Japanese つふつ here for the padre's name as a reference to João Rodrigues, a priest who often served as official interpreter for the Jesuits, and who was often called Rodrigues Tçuzzu to distinguish him from another priest of the same name. The word *tçuzzu* was the Portuguese rendition of the Japanese word for interpreter (*tsūji*), so we have a remarkable example here of a Japanese *kana* rendition of the Portuguese pronunciation of a Japanese word. Rodrigues arrived in Japan as a teenager and quickly absorbed the language and customs. He was usually the interpreter for the Jesuits when they met with Japan's leaders, including Oda Nobunaga, Toyotomi Hideyoshi, and Tokugawa Ieyasu, and he wrote one of the first grammars of Japanese. For more on Rodrigues, see Michael Cooper, *Rodrigues the Interpreter: An Early Jesuit in Japan and China* (New York: Weatherhill, 1974). For Shinmura's discussion of the word つふつ in *Baterenki*, see *Kaihyō sōsho*, 15–16.
65. Here, "India" is referred to as 天竺, Tenjiku, rather than the いんでや used earlier in reference to the different countries that helped Rome with its attacks. Similarly, 南蛮, or "South Barbary," replaces references to Rome, Goa, and Portugal.
66. The reference to three magistrates here is 三奉行. These were the three representatives of the bakufu in day-to-day administration of a region, and they included a city magistrate, a superintendent of temples and shrines, and a superintendent of finance.
67. "Tōan" here refers to Murayama Tōan, also known as Antonio. He was a trader in Nagasaki who converted to Christianity and whose son, Francisco, became a Jesuit priest. Some reports say that Tōan was appointed magistrate at the suggestion of João Rodrigues Tçuzzu, but a later falling out with the Jesuits led to his association with the Dominicans. Tōan eventually was denounced for his support of the Kirishitan and executed by the bakufu. His son, Francisco, was with Toyotomi Hideyori and died when Osaka Castle fell to bakufu forces in 1615. For more on the career of Murayama Tōan, see Elison, *Deus Destroyed*, 159–63.
68. The name of Francisco is written as ししこ but clearly refers to the historical figure of Francisco Tōan.

Chijiwa Seizaimon.[69] He had once been a padre long ago and had traveled to Rome, where he studied for ten years. After returning to Japan, he became a brother in the Society, but he grew to resent the padres and eventually left the church. He served Lord Ōmura, and because he knew well that the Kirishitan had a long history of taking over countries, he told his lord in detail about the plot of Jesus Christ, the battles of St. James, and the many times that forces had been sent against Japan. In response, Lord Ōmura said, "This is shocking. I regret that I did not believe this group could be involved in such evil deeds." He immediately ordered all of the padres and brothers in his house back to Nagasaki, and he had a great number of churches destroyed. Then he asked a learned priest from Higo who preached the Lotus Sutra to visit him, and he entered the correct path. From then on, the conspiracy of the heretic Kirishitan was all for naught, and gradually they dwindled away.[70]

---

69. This is the name of another of the four boys who formed the Japanese mission to Europe. His Christian name was Michael, and his role in the mission was to represent both his uncle, the daimyo Ōmura Sumitada, and his second cousin, the daimyo of Arima. He entered the novitiate when he returned from Europe, but for reasons that are unclear, he appears to have left the Society sometime around 1603. Some reports say that he also left the church, while others say he remained a Christian until his death, which recently discovered evidence puts in 1633. For more on Chijiwa, see Cooper, *The Japanese Mission*.

70. Though the events and the role of Ōmura narrated here do not accurately reflect historical events, they do allude to several events that occurred around 1606. In his book on Rodrigues, Michael Cooper relates the events surrounding the exchange of Urakami for Nagasaki. Nagasaki had been ceded to the Jesuits by the Christian convert Ōmura Sumitada in 1580, but it had expanded to meet the borders of Ōmura land and needed more room. Though Sumitada's successor, Ōmura Yoshiaki, permitted expansion onto his land, confusion over jurisdictions prompted the visiting governor, Ogasawara Ichian, to propose to Tokugawa Ieyasu in 1605 that the Ōmura land surrounding Nagasaki be added to the city and that the daimyo be compensated accordingly. Ieyasu agreed to this, but when Ōmura learned of the change he accused the Jesuits of orchestrating it. As a result, he ordered all missionaries off of his land in 1606 and, one year later, joined the Nichiren sect (which teaches devotion to the Lotus Sutra). See Cooper, *Rodrigues the Interpreter*, 207–9. For more on the original transfer of Nagasaki to the Jesuits, see Elison, *Deus Destroyed*, 92–96.

Nanbanji monogatari[1]

"Tale of the Southern Barbarian Temple"

Christianity is an evil sect that came from South Barbary in the time of the 107th emperor, Retired Emperor Ōgimachi, in the eleventh year of Eiroku.[2] More than seventy-eight thousand miles southwest of Japan by sea, South Barbary is comprised of forty-two provinces within an area of two hundred ten thousand square miles. It is surrounded by India and China to the west, Ume to the south, Szechuan to the north, and by many great oceans to the east.[3] The lord of the land is called King Gōjinbi.

---

1. The source text for this translation was taken from Washio Junkei, ed., *Nihon shisō tōsō shiryo*, vol. 10 (Tokyo: Meicho kankōkai, 1969), 319–70. The original is a manuscript held in the Diet Library that was copied in 1771. The name of the copyist is unknown. *Nanbanji monogatari* is the title of one manuscript in a group that makes up one of the two most common variants of the *Raichō jikki* text. This variant was chosen for translation because it is the most complete and contains the sermon by Hakuo after his debate with Fabian.
2. This would be 1569, twenty years after the first Jesuit set foot in Japan, but the correct year for the establishment of the Jesuit mission in Kyoto, of which Father Organtino was the superior for twenty-five years. *Kirishitan monogatari* puts the time of arrival two emperors back, in the time of Go-Nara, actually closer to the date that the first Jesuit, Francis Xavier, arrived. For a historical account of the arrival of the missionaries see Michael Cooper, *Rodrigues the Interpreter: An Early Jesuit in Japan and China* (New York: Weatherhill, 1974). For the text of *Kirishitan monogatari* see Hiyane Antei, ed., *Kirishitan monogatari hoka sanpen*, Kirishitan bunko, vol. 1 (Tokyo: Keiseisha, 1926), 1–39. An English translation of the story is in George Elison, *Deus Destroyed: The Image of Christianity in Early Modern Japan* (Cambridge, Mass.: Harvard University Press, 1973).
3. India and China is a translation of *Tenjiku shinadakoku*. Tenjiku originally meant India and later came to mean any place foreign ships came from, or just a foreign country. In his *Historia de Japam*, Luis Frois describes a child pointing at the fathers and calling them *tenjikujin*, which Frois interpreted as meaning "men of Siam." See Luis J. Frois, *Historia*

One day, the king assembled the lords and retainers of his land and said to them, "There is a country northeast of here called Japan. Though it is small, ships from Northern China, India, Holland, and other countries have gone there to trade, and they sold everything they brought. Clearly this land is rich in gold and silver. If we made it part of my own, I could live in splendor and do anything I chose, and our entire country would be prosperous."

When the king asked for the lords' opinions, the great General Shotenriki stepped forward. Over nine feet tall, with black skin and red hair, he spoke with a voice that could shatter china and splinter bamboo trees. "I will do as my lord desires. Only give me enough men and I will go to Japan immediately and subdue it for my king." The king was pleased and said, "These are my orders. Go and conquer Japan for me."

Then Lord Gogi, a man of deep wisdom, came forward and faced General Shotenriki with a stern look in his eyes. "It would be no use," he said. "You will recall that men from all forty-two provinces have tried to enter Japan countless times, and not one has succeeded. The Mongol fleet tried to invade the country seven times, and it failed because Japan is the land of the gods and their gods protect them well. It will not be taken with these simple efforts. We should do as we did in the land of Romé and send to Japan an accomplished practitioner of the way who will use magic and money to convert the poor among them.[4] Once he has

---

de Japam, vol. 1, edited by Joseph Wikki S.J., ed. (Lisbon: Biblioteca Nacional de Lisboa, 1976–1984), 138. The word used for Szechuan here is *Shoku*. "Ume" (usually written 宇め) in this text is written as "Uba" (usually written 鳥馬) in the *Kirishitan shūmon raichō jikki* variant, while a few other variants refer to "Roba" (驢馬) or "Luzon," in the Philippines. Though it is tempting to consider Roba and the later Romé as a copyist's mistake for "Roma," none of the manuscript copies used "Roma," and it does not work in the context. In the work of Chao Ju-Kua on twelfth and thirteenth-century Chinese and Arab trade, he cites a place called Wu Ma Pa (鳥馬拔) that was a dependency of Annam/Champa (in present-day Vietnam). Since a later reference in the text to "Rome" can be traced to Annam/Champa, which was invaded by Spanish forces from Manila in 1596, it seems likely that this is the place being referred to. See n. 4 below. This puts the country of Nanban somewhere around present-day Vietnam. See Chau Ju-Kua, *Chau Ju-Kua: His Work on the Chinese and Arab Trade in the Twelfth and Thirteenth centuries, entitled Chu-fan-chi*, translated and annotated by Friedrich Hirth (St. Petersburg: Imperial Academy of Sciences, 1911).

4. This is written ろめ国 in the text. It is unclear what "Rome" referred to, but in two other versions that tell an almost identical story but are written primarily in *kanji*, the name of this country is different each time. In a version titled *Nanbanji kōhaiki*,, the same passage refers to 呂宋国, with the accompanying *furigana* ルソン. This refers to the Philippine island of Luzon where Manila was located, and which Spain controlled starting in 1571. Since the first character in 呂宋 can be read ろ, it is possible that ろめ国 was a misreading of the name in the earlier text. It should also be noted that in the *Kirishitan*

persuaded one third of the people to join him, we can send in our armies. If we are guided by the converts, we could take Japan easily, but it will not happen overnight."

The king saw the wisdom in Lord Gogi's words and agreed. They discussed how to follow the strategy they used in Romé and where they could find a person who excelled in magic. Then Lord Gogi said that there was a province six thousand miles to the west called the land of the Kirishitan.[5] In this land at the top of Tenrin Peak there are large, fragrant sandalwood trees, and on this peak live two men. One of them is called Padre Urugan, and the other is called Padre Buraten, and both men practice a magic called *hisōjō*.[6] They are capable of rising into the air and flying, and it is because they can freely breach the boundaries of heaven and ride upon the clouds that they are called "padres."[7] This is the foundation of the Kirishitan sect. In this sect the "brother" is like a disciple at a temple, while the "padre" is like the chief priest.[8] These two men are both padres. Then Lord Gogi said, "You could ask these men to go to Japan and convert the people there, and they could carry out your plan." The king was

---

  shūmon raicho jikki version, the name of the country is 占国 (*sengoku*), also known as the kingdom of Champa or Tshiampa, or sometimes Champan (Annam), in what is now Vietnam. A 1596 military expedition sent by the Spaniards from Manila to help the kingdom of Cambodia conquer Champan is an event that would have been known to the Japanese, since trading junks traveled often between Japan and Champan. Thus, in both variants of this story, the countries conquered by the Southern Barbarians are areas that were controlled at one time by the Spanish.

5. Text refers to it as 切死丹という国. Note the *kanji* for death in this version of "Kirishitan."
6. One of the more well-known Jesuits who spent many years as the superior of the Kyoto mission was Father Gnecchi Soldo Organtino. He appears in several Kirishitan texts as Padre Urugan. Furaten does not seem to correspond to the name of any historical Jesuits and mostly likely is taken from the term ふらてん used to describe the Franciscan missionaries, who were remembered for their work with the poor and sick. The Japanese word is thought to be derived from the Latin name of the order, *Ordo Fratrum Minorum*. George Elison describes this part of the story in *Deus Destroyed* and translates *hisōjō* (ひそうじょう) as *filosofia*. Though it is possible the transcription eroded over time, as it did with a number of other Latin-based words written in *hiragana*, the word *filosofia* is written as ひろそひや in Inoue Masashige's *Kirisutoki* 契利斯督記 (a mid-seventeenth century handbook on Christianity and how to detect adherents). Because the words seem a little too far apart, I have chosen to just transcribe *hisōjō* as is. Elison, *Deus Destroyed*, 214; Hiyane Antei, ed,, *Nanbanji kōhaiki hoka nihen*, Kirishitan bunko, vol. 2 (Tokyo: Keiseisha, 1926), 114.
7. The Japanese rendition of "padre" was *bateren*. Conventionally, the characters for "padre" were 伴天連, which could be read as "followers of heaven," but the characters used for *bateren* here are 破天連, or "companions who can rend heaven." The word "padre" was derived from the Portuguese *padre*, or "father."
8. *Iruman* was the term used to describe brothers in the Society of Jesus. It is derived from the Portuguese *irmão*.

pleased to hear this, and when he asked whom he should send to Tenrin Peak, Lord Gogi suggested his own son, Lord Goga.

So, Lord Goga was sent off to the mountain peak, where he searched everywhere for the padre. When he found Padre Urugan he said to him, "I have come for no reason of my own, but on a mission from the king, who requests that you come to the capital where he has something to ask of you." Then Padre Urugan said, "What could the king possibly want with a mountain hermit?" And Lord Goga answered, "We have heard that you excel in the magical arts, and we would like you and your friend to go to Japan and convert the people of the country with your teachings." But Padre Urugan said, "I cannot do such a thing. I am not a wise man who goes to distant countries and spreads the word of the law. Please say as much to the king," and he disappeared. Lord Goga was very surprised. He looked for the padre everywhere, but black clouds had rolled in and he could not see where he was going, and, growing tired, he finally returned to the capital. When he reported what had happened, his father Lord Gogi remarked, "Padre Urugan sounds like a wise man. Judging from this reception he must have thought we were playing him for a fool. Next time if we take him bolts of cloth, gold, and silver, he will surely not refuse to come." So Lord Goga took many treasures and returned to Tenrin Peak.

After Lord Goga had left him the first time, Padre Urugan went to the cave of his friend, Padre Buraten, and told him what the messenger had said. Buraten said, "I think that the king is avaricious and means to use us to test the hearts of the Japanese people. But the forces in the northeast are strong and too difficult to overcome. I believe we should refuse the king's request."[9] Padre Urugan was of the same opinion, and after agreeing to decline if they were asked again, they parted ways.

Lord Goga returned to their former meeting place carrying many gifts. He placed the gifts before the mountain man and again asked Padre Urugan to accompany him to the capital. But the priest replied, "I am an ascetic. I may not look at such things," and he vanished immediately. For the second time, the messenger was nonplussed and returned to the capital. Both the king and Lord Gogi were now certain that Padre Urugan was a wise man, and because of this they came up with a plan that they knew would be successful. Lord Gogi would accompany his son to the mountain this time. He would tell Padre Urugan that by refusing to come when he was summoned by the king, he was being disobedient to his sovereign. The king was the lord of all of the land under heaven, and if he should disobey the lord's orders, Padre Urugan would not be allowed to

---

9. Here the forces in the northeast are the gods that protect Japan.

live on his mountain anymore. They were sure that after hearing this, he would come to the capital. So the father and son set off for the mountain peak, and they delivered their message to Padre Urugan. He replied, "If that is the case, I will do as you ask. But I have a friend with whom I must speak. Please wait here until I return," and he disappeared before their eyes. Father and son feared they had been deceived, but because he had told them he would return, they decided to wait.

Padre Urugan told Padre Buraten that he had been unable to refuse the two imperial messengers, and he had no choice but to go to the capital. He would go to Japan and deceive the people as had been done in the land of Romé. And if things went well in Japan, he would send for Padre Buraten, so they could join forces there. Then leaving his friend, he appeared suddenly before the father and son and told them he would do as the king asked and return with them. They were overjoyed, and the three traveled together over six thousand miles, eventually arriving safely in the capital.

The king was very pleased to see them, and he told Padre Urugan: "You shall go to Japan and take measure of the people's wit, and using your magic you shall spread the teachings of South Barbary.[10] If the people of Japan follow you, then you shall lead a great army and take the country. Now, go swiftly." Then Padre Urugan answered, "I will do your bidding and go to Japan. But though the country is small, it follows the way of the gods, and thus it will be very difficult to conquer. In case I encounter difficulties once I arrive, perhaps I should bring gifts for the king of Japan." The king saw the wisdom in Urugan's words. "Then you shall take seven different treasures, and with these gifts you shall deceive them. Inform us by letter immediately if you are successful," the king said, and Padre Urugan replied, "I shall."

The seven treasures he took with him were a telescope that, when held to one eye, would make things one hundred fifty miles away appear close; a magnifying glass that could make a mustard seed appear as large as an egg; fifteen tiger skins; muskets of great accuracy; one hundred pounds of aloes wood; one mosquito net large enough to cover a space of twelve square feet but, when folded, could fit into a two-inch square box; and finally, a rosary called a *gondatsu*, made of bronze with forty-two beads signifying the forty-two provinces of South Barbary.[11]

---

10. Note they are the teachings of South Barbary, not the land of the Kirishitan. Though a distinction between the two is made in the beginning of the tale, from now on they are generally conflated.
11. *Contas* is the Portuguese word for "rosary." It appears in many of the stories on the foreign missionaries, usually written as こんたつ or, as it is here, ごんだつ.

Urugan boarded a South Barbary ship and, weighing anchor, he let the wind take him along the shipping lanes for countless days, heading for Chikuzen.[12] Finally, after almost a year, he landed in Nagasaki in the province of Hizen.[13] Making sure he was noticed, he walked freely far and wide, through the towns and villages in Nagasaki, and to the temples and the shrines. Men and women of all ages flocked to see him so that the throngs were impenetrable. News of this traveled to Kyoto, where some said that a demon had come to Nagasaki, and others said it was not a demon but a strange kind of foreigner.

In those days Lord Nobunaga was very pleased that he had been designated shogun by Lord Ashikaga Yoshiteru, the fifteenth in line in the ruling house.[14] He had also been accorded the privilege of attending court by Retired Emperor Ōgimachi, so that his power was as great as that of the dragons above the clouds. The entire Gokinai region bowed down to him like the grasses in the fields before a strong wind, and there was no official who could brook his authority.

One day, when he was staying at Azuchi Castle in Kōshū, he gathered his retainers about him and asked them to tell him stories they had heard from around the land. There was among those retainers a young page that had been to Kyoto, and he told Nobunaga of the strange story he had heard. First, the story was that a devil had appeared in Nagasaki, but then they said it was not a devil but a different kind of foreigner. His head looked like a watermelon but also appeared very small on his body. After listening to many such stories, the leader called his chief steward, Sugenoya Kyūemon, to his side, and said that he wanted to see this strange person. The steward replied, "Very well, sir, but we do not yet have any allied families in the Western provinces. Nagasaki is in the province belonging to Ryūzōji Takashige, who is not one of our retainers. If he should not agree to send the man, we would need to think of another plan."

Nobunaga agreed and said, "From what I hear this foreigner is very unusual, and I must see him. Let us send a forged letter from Lord Ashikaga Yoshiteru to Takashige using a messenger from the house of Yoshiteru." After summoning one of the servants of the Ashikaga, they told him their plan, and the servant immediately went back to his master and told him he was resigning from service because he was ill. The man's name was Gennai. Then he went to the house of Takashige in Nagasaki and told

---

12. A domain that was in the northwest part of present-day Fukuoka.
13. A domain that occupied what are now parts of Nagasaki Prefecture and Saga Prefecture.
14. The text says he was designated shogun by Ashikaga Yoshiteru, though later in the text the term "shogun" refers to Yoshiteru.

him he had a message from the Shogun Yoshiteru. After reading the fake letter, Takashige agreed to fulfill the request, and he gave orders to send the Southern Barbarian to Kyoto. To meet with Yoshiteru he chose as his representatives his steward Nakanishi Kenmotsu and a samurai from his own house, Sasahara Yazaemon. Then they loaded the Southern Barbarian into a palanquin and sent him and an interpreter up to Kyoto.

Nobunaga was pleased to hear of this, but he was worried that Yoshiteru would hear of the forgery once the group reached Kyoto. So, he sent a man to meet them at the Tōji Yotsuzuka and Tobanawate area and had them brought directly to Azuchi. When Takashige heard this, he realized he had been tricked by Nobunaga, and he ground his teeth in rage.

On the twenty-fourth day of the eighth month of the eleventh year of Eiroku (1569), there was an earthquake that felled sixty-six pine trees at the Sumiyoshi Shrine. This appeared to be an omen of bad things to come, and it was later understood that this strange event was a sign that Padre Urugan had come to carry out the king's plot to take over Japan. The attendants at the shrine were surprised, and Priest Kunitoyo of the Third Rank, governor of Settsu, informed Retired Emperor Ōgimachi of the event. The emperor was also amazed. Certainly if one or two hundred pines had been felled, it would be a shocking event, but this number was even more alarming because sixty-six was also the number of provinces in Japan. In response to this event, an order came down from the emperor that the priests in all of the temples and shrines in the Gokinai area were to say prayers for the country. These pine trees fell on the twenty-fourth day of the eighth month, and it was only ten days later, on the third day of the ninth month, that Padre Urugan arrived at the gates of Tōji, the Eastern Temple.[15]

When Nobunaga was informed of the arrival of what the people of Nagasaki were calling an oddity, he ordered that the man should first be given a rest, so Padre Urugan was lodged for three days at the Nichiren temple named Myohōji.[16] After that, on the sixth day of the ninth month, he was brought before the leader. Even though Nobunaga was a powerful

---

15. The full name of the temple is Kyōōgokuji 教王護国寺, and it is in Minami-ku in Kyoto. It was founded in 794 along with a Western Temple (Saiji, destroyed soon after it was built) to protect the newly established capital of Heian. It is obviously significant that Urugan as would-be conqueror of Japan should make his first stop in the capital at the temple built to protect the city.
16. The word used here is *kijin* きじん, and the use of *hiragana* perhaps allows for multiple meanings. Most likely it refers to 奇人, which is a "character" or an eccentric. But the same word written with different *kanji* (鬼神) is a Buddhist term for a demon deity with supernatural powers, which the reader has been told Urugan possesses.

man, he was meeting a man from a country he knew little about. He felt that this would be no ordinary audience, so he dressed with great care and took his seat at the head of the room. To his left were seated his family members, and to his right were ranged his loyal followers, including Hashiba, governor of Chikuzen,[17] Niwa Goroemon,[18] the steward Sugenoya Kyūemon, and many others. In the presence of this splendid group, Hasegawa Chikuan led in the padre. The seven treasures the stranger had brought were arrayed on a red-painted stand and presented to Nobunaga. A wonderful fragrance of such quality that it seemed to have come from paradise itself rose from the gifts and wafted over the gathering.

Padre Urugan sat at the foot of the steps leading to the lords' seats. But from where he sat Nobunaga could not see him well and he ordered him to approach. When the padre had moved forward, everyone could see that he stood over nine feet tall with a small head, a red face, and round yellow eyes. His nose was big and his ears so long that they brushed his shoulders. His mouth was wide, stretching all the way to his ears, and his teeth were as long as a horse's and as white as snow. His nails looked like a bear's claws. His hair and beard were mouse-colored, and he appeared to be about fifty years old. His speech was incomprehensible and sounded like the "coo, coo" of a dove. He wore a garment called an *aito* that appeared to be made from a rug.[19] It had a short hem and long sleeves, and it was narrow and wrapped in front with the left side over the right. The clothing was very strange and not very impressive, and he looked like a bat spreading its wings to fly away. Altogether, he was extremely ugly.

The padre was enveloped in the same extraordinary fragrance, and it wafted from him to the place where Nobunaga sat. As the leader stared at the strange thing before him, Urugan bowed to him by stretching both legs out in front, crossing his hands over his chest and turning his face up. Speaking through the page Inoko Hyōsuke, Nobunaga asked the stranger when and for what reason he had come to Japan from South Barbary. Through the interpreter the latter replied that his name was Padre Urugan and he had come to spread the teachings of Buddha.[20] To this Nobunaga

---

17. At that time, this was the name held by Toyotomi Hideyoshi (1537–98), who became leader of Japan after Nobunaga.
18. Also known as Niwa Nagahide (1535–85), who later also served Toyotomi Hideyoshi.
19. Later also called *abito*, which refers to the "habito" or habit worn by the missionary fathers.
20. The phrase here is 仏ぽうひろむるため. It is worth noting here that there was considerable confusion among early Japanese Christians and many lay people about the Buddhist sect to which Christianity belonged. For the first two years of his tenure in Japan, Francis Xavier preached about *dainichi*, believing that this was the best translation for the one, supreme God, and not realizing that the term referred to an incarnation of Buddha. Even after the missionaries began using the term "Deus" for God, there seem to

answered, "Only I can grant you permission to spread the law of Buddha. For now, you will stay where you are and be entertained by the priest Nakaizumi Fujisaemon."

Then Nobunaga summoned to his castle at Azuchi the members of his family, his loyal retainers, priests, scholars, and doctors. When they were all gathered he said, "Recently a foreigner named Padre Urugan has come to our country and says he wants to spread the word of Buddha. I have asked you all here for one purpose only. Tell me, should or should I not allow him to do as he proposes?" When asked this, all who were present closed their mouths and remained silent, except for the venerable priest Bunkyōin Hokkyo. The priest said, "The ways of Shinto, Confucius, and Buddha are well established.[21] While these are grounded in rituals of respect, I see none of that respect in this man. Many of the Shinto gods have manifested themselves as buddhas or bodhisattvas, for if it is true that disguising one's glory to walk among sentient beings is the beginning of the bond, and the eight stages of Buddhahood are the culmination of the benefit to all living things, then the god's intent in being a bodhisattva and mixing with the beings of this earth is to form a bond with them and bring them to Buddhism.[22] They say that when we bow to the Shinto gods, we are also bowing to the buddhas and boddhisatvas. And when we bow to Buddha, we are also bowing to the Three Jewels, which are the Buddha, the Law, and the Priests. So, in effect, we are bowing three times. In Confucianism, understanding and gratitude are expressed by bowing low. These are the ways of men. But this Padre Urugan stretches his legs out before him and does not lower his head. Raising one's head does not show reverence; it is the way of animals. His appearance is vulgar, like

---

have been many who thought that Christianity was a branch of Buddhism. In *Kirishitan monogatari*, a chapter describing the sect is titled *Kirishitan buppō* 吉利支丹仏法, or "The Christian Dharma." Throughout the remainder of this text, *Kirishitan* is used to describe a heretical Buddhist sect, and the padres themselves talk about spreading the teachings of Buddha. For more on Xavier and Dainichi see Elison, *Deus Destroyed*, 177–79.

21. Here the author uses one phrase to refer to Shinto, Confucianism, and Buddhism: しんじゅ仏にはさだまれるほうあり.

22. This is an allusion to the *wakō dōjin* doctrine, according to which it is believed that the buddhas and boddhisatvas appear on earth as humans in order to help lead other human beings to salvation through Buddhism. In Japan it was also believed that Shinto gods could appear as boddhisatvas. In *Deus Destroyed*, Elison includes a translation of the passage on this topic from the *Taishō shinshū daizōkyō* 大正新修大蔵経 (The Tripitaka in Chinese), edited by Takakusu Junjirō, vol. 46, no. 1911, 80: "In subdued brilliance sharing/this world of dust/is the beginning of the tie/[between Buddha and man]; the Eight Stages/[of the Buddha's earthly life]/and the establishment of the Way/are termed its completion." See *Deus Destroyed*, 465–66, n. 15.

the people of Ebisu or Mongolia.²³ It seems unlikely he would know any Buddhist teachings that we would want. Please consider this carefully."

When Bunkyōin had finished speaking, those gathered in the room agreed with him. But in his heart Nobunaga wanted to allow Padre Urugan to preach, so he replied, "I agree that what you say is true, but there is no reason to despise him. Remember how Buddhism was transmitted to us. One thousand years after the death of Shakyamuni, Mato loaded the scrolls containing the Buddhist canon onto a white horse and carried them to China. There, he gave them to Genso Komei Kotei, second emperor of the Han Dynasty, who honored him. Of the nine halls in the emperor's palace, the innermost guest hall was called Kōroji, and because he had traveled from such a great distance, Mato was entertained by the emperor in this hall. Eventually, the teachings of Buddha spread to more than four hundred lands. It was Emperor Kinmei, thirtieth emperor of Japan, who brought the canon from Korea to Japan. That is how we learned the way of Buddha. So, you see, all of the teachings were brought from another country. That is the only reason why we learned of the Buddha and why his teachings remain with us today. You could even say that only the Buddhism that comes from abroad is really Buddhism. Padre Urugan may have something worthwhile to teach us, and he is not so objectionable. Therefore, I have decided to let him preach."

Then Nobunaga ordered Sugenoya Kyūemon to give the padre a plot of land with a perimeter of four hundred meters at Shijō Bōmon in the capital.²⁴ Great stones were brought from Kitayama, and a temple was built sparing no expense. It had a monastery with seven halls built with spectacular stonewalls, and it was named Eirokuji, after the emperor's reign in which it was founded. The temple was finished in gold and sparkled so in the light that it seemed it must surpass even the palace of Amida Buddha.

Until that time in the history of Japan only one temple had been named after an emperor's reign, and that was the great Enryakuji on Mt. Hiei. Now, when the priests of that temple heard of the new temple's name, they became angry and complained to the head priest, Bishop Myōen.

---

23. The words used here are *mōko* and *ebisu*. *Mōko* refers to Mongolia, but *ebisu* could be either Ezo, which referred to present-day Hokkaido, or Mongolia. Later in the text, *ebisu* clearly refers to Mongolia.
24. The term here is Shijō Bōmon 四条坊門, and it refers to the neighborhood in the capital where the Jesuits built their first church in 1568. In a fan painting by Kanō Motohide, the church is depicted as a three-story Japanese style building. It was named Our Lady of the Assumption but was known by local residents as Nanbanji. It was destroyed in 1588 shortly after the first expulsion edict issued by Hideyoshi. For more on the church see Cooper, *Rodrigues the Interpreter*, 42–44.

But the priest responded, "There is precedent for your claims, but in these latter days of the Law the position and power of the emperor and of the Dharma are weak, and therefore the power of Buddhism is also weak.[25] Nobunaga's military position is strong, and if we criticize his choice of Eirokuji as the temple's name, he would fight us, and Mt. Hiei would surely be destroyed." But the priests refused to accept Myōen's warning, since his reasoning was useless for them. Instead, they climbed to the top of the bell tower and rang the bell until it seemed it would crack. Then all of the priests on the mountain and many from the valley gathered in the garden of the main hall, trading their opinions about the affair.

Master Kyōgaku of the Senjō Hall at Yokawa temple on Mt. Hiei was a great militant priest. At that moment he stepped forward and said, "This mountain temple was built by Emperor Kanmu, the fiftieth emperor of Japan, in order to guard his palace from the northeast.[26] Because it was established in his reign-era of Enryaku, this temple was given the name Enryakuji. There is no other temple named for the reign in which it was built. The fifty-first emperor Heizei of the Daidō reign-era built a temple on Mt. Kataoka in the province of Yamato that he tried to name Daidōji, but the sign bearing the name of the temple was destroyed by the priests of Mt. Hiei. Thus, the precedent has been set. Just because it was Nobunaga who named the temple is no reason why it should be allowed to stand."

All who heard him agreed, and the priests decided to take their complaint to the emperor. A group of one hundred thirty put on armor under their robes and marched to the imperial palace to deliver a petition expressing their outrage and asking that the new temple's name be changed. Those who remained on Mt. Hiei decorated the portable shrines of the mountain temples, and, clad in armor and carrying swords, they descended the mountain and tried to carry the shrines into the imperial palace. The emperor and his counselors were greatly alarmed and gathered to discuss the disturbing events. As a result, the Kazan'in Middle Counselor Hiromasa was sent to deliver the following message from the emperor to Nobunaga: "I understand that recently you built a temple in Kyoto, and I am pleased that you are showing favor to Buddhism. However, Enryakuji has always been the only temple to be named after a reign, and I have received a petition of protest from Mt. Hiei. Whatever we may think, there

---

25. The latter days of the Law are in the third of the three major periods in which the history of Buddhism was said to be divided. In this final period ten thousand years after the life of Buddha, it was thought that the strength of the Law of Buddha was in decline. In Japan, this final period was believed to have begun in the year 1052.
26. Here, the northeast corner is the 鬼門, or the direction from which evil came.

is a precedent for their petition, and I hereby order you to change the name of your temple." The order angered Nobunaga, but he had no choice but to obey, and he renamed the temple Nanbanji, or Southern Barbarian Temple.

Then Nobunaga told Padre Urugan that one priest was not enough to spread the teachings of the sect, and he suggested that the padre call more priests from South Barbary. At the same time, Nobunaga donated to Nanbanji land in Kōga County in the province of Gōshu with a yield of five hundred *kan* in revenue.[27] Padre Urugan replied that he would do as Nobunaga requested and summon his friend Padre Buraten. Then he sent one letter to the king of South Barbary to report that things were going well and that a man named Nobunaga had asked him to spread the teachings of his sect. A second letter he sent to Padre Buraten, asking him to come immediately and join forces with him.

When the king heard the news, he summoned Padre Buraten. The latter was pleased by Urugan's success, and, keeping the promise he had made earlier, he answered the summons of King Gōjinbi. The king was also pleased and ordered Padre Buraten to travel to Japan and join forces with Urugan to take over the country. Padre Buraten replied that he would do as the king asked, but that convincing the Japanese people would be no easy task. "If you know of a way to do so, please tell us," the king said. Then Padre Buraten said, "Many people are poor and sick. If we bring great quantities of money and medicines, we can give silver and gold to the poor and medicines to the sick, and in this way relieve their suffering. In addition, we can use magic to tell them about the three worlds of the past, present, and future, so that without even asking, the poor and the sick will gladly follow us. I possess a mirror that can show the three worlds to me. It can be used to divert people from other faiths and encourage them to follow only ours. This I will take with me to Japan." Lord Gogi stepped forward and said, "This is an excellent plan, and, because it is so important, we must ensure that the money flows like water. We can use the yearly income from the fifteen eastern provinces for this purpose."[28] Then Padre Buraten continued, "In a place called Bibito to the south there are two doctors who received their training in Tenjiku.[29] They are both

---

27. Kōgagōri 甲賀郡 is in the former province of Ōmi, now Shiga Prefecture.
28. Though this text says "fifty eastern provinces," the *Kirishitan shūmon raichō jikki* says fifteen provinces. Since Southern Barbary only has forty-two provinces, it seems likely the fifty here was miscopied.
29. The text is みなみにびびとうというところに. In the *Kirishitan shūmon raichō jikki* it is written as 南ビコドウ, but neither seems to correspond to any known place at the time. Tenjiku, as mentioned above, refers to either India or any foreign country in that direction.

Brothers. The first is Brother Kerikori, and the second is Brother Yariisu.[30] These two should both be made to accompany me." So the king had all of the required items gathered and sent them off with the three men to Japan. This time six different kinds of gifts were prepared. After setting sail over the ocean, the group finally neared Japan.

Though the ship was bound for Nagasaki in the province of Hizen, Padre Buraten consulted the stars and said, "If this ship enters the port of Nagasaki, it will meet with misfortune. We should head northeast of Nagasaki instead." So they turned away from Nagasaki toward Tsushima and eventually reached an area near the capital of the province of Iki.[31] When the lord of Iki heard of their arrival, he feared trouble and sent out a sea patrol to stop the ship. But their interpreter sent the message that they were here at the request of Lord Nobunaga, and that they had come to Japan from South Barbary and should not be turned back. Then the Lord of Iki, fearing the power of Nobunaga, called back his patrol, and the ship was allowed to land in the capital. The visitors gathered a group of smaller boats and left the provincial capital to sail up the Obama River to the province of Wakasa, in the direction of the Nanbanji. Following the Obama, Buraten reached a lake and finally arrived at Ōtsu, from where he traveled on to the Nanbanji. After Buraten, Yariisu, and Gerikori finally reached the church, they first met with Urugan, and then they rested for four or five days. During that time, they sent word of their arrival to Nobunaga, who was at his castle in Azuchi.

Nobunaga ordered that Buraten be brought to Myohōji Temple to pay his respects, just as Urugan had before him. So Hasegawa Chikuan went to get the three newcomers, and they were brought before Nobunaga, where they bowed to the leader the same way that Urugan had. The six gifts that they had brought included a rod of lapis lazuli, a large quantity of incense, ten dog skins, a low stand made of agate, ten tiger skins, and fifty pieces of five-colored wool cloth. Buraten was a full two feet five inches taller than Urugan, with a green face and yellow hair, and he wore an *abito* in the same style as the other. As a result, he looked exceptionally ugly. Nobunaga, marveling to himself at what foul beings had come over, told the men they would be working for him to spread the teachings of

---

30. Kerikori, later written as "Gerikori," is likely a reference to the Jesuit Gregorio de Cespedes, who worked primarily in the Kyushu area for over twenty years. Yariisu likely comes from "Luis" and probably refers to Brother Luis de Almeida, who was famous for his work as a doctor. Three different monuments to Almeida and his work with the sick still stand in Kyushu. One is in Nagasaki, while the other two are in Oita city, where Almeida set up the first hospital and dispensary.
31. The former province of Iki is now in Nagasaki Prefecture.

their sect. Then, after gazing at them for a long time, he gave them leave to go, and they returned to the Nanbanji.

From that time, they began to teach people about their sect. First, the four men sat in the Nanbanji and discussed their strategy. They talked of how King Gōjimbi wanted to rule Japan and take its silver and gold, and how Shōtenriki had offered to take an army and take over the country for his lord. But Lord Gogi had said that Japan was protected by the gods and could not be easily won, but if one third of the people were convinced to follow the Buddhist path, then an army would be able to enter and take control.[32] Therefore, their task was to spread the teachings of the Buddha. But there are many paths in Buddhism, and if they didn't teach the right one, it might not be accepted. So, the four decided that the best way to start was by helping the poor and the sick.

In order to give medicine to the sick, they needed to grow medicinal plants. So the two doctors received permission from Nobunaga to look for land in Yamashiro and Ōmi. They climbed Mt. Ibuki in Gōshū and found a five thousand square meter plot, where they planted seeds and sprouts of more than three thousand varieties of medicinal plants.[33] Now, two hundred years later, many of those seeds remain, and we can still find Chinese lovage, mulberry, and mugwort—Mt. Ibuki mugwort is especially useful.[34] The Southern Barbarian style of treatment became very popular, and mugwort in particular was recognized as a superior medicine.

In the splendid temple built by Nobunaga there was no central image, and it was decorated with strands of the seven precious stones and cotton banners. The fragrance of sixty-one kinds of incense wafted through the gates to the passersby outside so that the place seemed to be paradise itself. All who saw it marveled that there could be such a place on the face of the earth. Certainly there could be no fault in the people who lived

---

32. This short section appears to be a review of the earlier part of the tale, which would be necessary if this were the script of a storyteller performing it over two or more consecutive days.
33. Gōshū is another name for Ōmi. The plot was fifty square 丁 (町), with one *chō* equaling approximately one hundred nine meters.
34. *Ibukiyama mogusa* is a form of mugwort that was burned in moxa treatments. The Latin name of Chinese lovage is *Ligusticum chuanxiong*. The dispensing of medicines to the sick on the part of Jesuits seems to have captured the imagination of the Japanese at the time, as several of the *Kirishitan* texts have *Ibukiyama* or *yomogi* in the titles. While the Jesuit letters and reports contain ample references to hospitals and a medicine dispensary set up in Funai, I have yet to find any reference in them to the use of *yomogi* or to growing medicinal herbs on Ibukiyama. They did, however, have a mission and a school in Ōmi, near the court of Nobunaga. Though the passage implies that the missionaries were the first to bring mugwort to Japan, its mention in poetry as far back as the eighth century shows it was in use long before their arrival.

in such a palace. Word of the Nanbanji spread quickly, and people from Gokinai, Kingoku, Tōzai, and all directions came to Kyoto to see it, so that the temple was crowded with sightseers.[35] Because it was a sect that had come from abroad, it was naturally difficult for people to pray to a new god right away, but there were many who came to look. Court nobles and samurai and even the lowest of the low came from all over the country.

In addition, the poor and the sick flocked to Nanbanji to ask for help. There were beggars dressed in straw who had been living under bridges, and the diseased and crippled who slept in mountain fields. All were ill in some way and had been abandoned by the world. Scores of these people were bathed and clothed at the Nanbanji, and the poor were given money. A new and wondrous kind of cloth was given to all, so that those who had gone naked covered their shame with the finest cotton, and a rare fragrance surrounded them. Yesterday's straw was today's cotton, and where once they had huddled beneath a bridge, now they slept under a splendid roof. Three and four times a day they were given meals of fish and chicken, so that former beggars found themselves too full to eat more. Gerikori and Yariisu excelled in the medical arts, gradually curing all of the sick, and even those who were near death were cured after only one treatment. The blind, the lame, and the crippled were all given treatment and cured, and their joy was boundless.

To their patients the two Brothers said, "We have come from far away as special messengers of the great King of South Barbary. Our country has forty-two provinces and is one hundred times larger than Japan. Because we worship Deus, no one in our land is poor, and there is no disease.[36] Our king is merciful and compassionate, and all people down to the lowest commoner have experienced his benevolence. And compassion is not limited to South Barbary alone, but is spread to all of the lands that we govern. In his mercy, our King wishes to save all of the poor and sick of the world. Those lands that do not worship Deus have many poor and sick. Because they are steeped in earthly desires, these people break into

---

35. "Gokinai" was a term referring to the five provinces closest to the capital, which were Settsu, Izumi, Kawachi, Yamashiro, and Yamato. "Kingoku" specifically referred to seventeen more provinces in the vicinity of the capital, including Iga, Ise, Shima, Owari, Mikawa, Tanba, Bizen, Awa, Kii, Mino, Awaji, Ōmi, Inaba, Wakasa, Tajima, Harima, and Sanuki. "Tōzai" meant the regions east and west of the capital.
36. The term used in this section is variously *Tentaishaku*, *Tentai*, or *Tentei*. *Tentaishaku* can refer to a specific incarnation of Buddha but can also simply mean a god that is in heaven. In the *Kirishitan shūmon raichō jikki*, the phrase used is *Tentai Deusu*, or the Deus (Latin for God) that is in heaven. Because Deus is used often in later passages, I use it here for consistency.

storehouses at night and steal their contents, and they cannot prevent the sins born of this evil, or escape the wheel of karma. Japan is poor because it does not worship Deus. Because the people are poor, they stray from the correct path and in their hearts they grow angry. This then causes grave illness and suffering. Though with our treatments we may be able to bring relief to the ills in this life, there is no escaping future sickness and poverty. This life is only one part of our existence, but you also want to avoid sin in the future. We can show you that future."

Then the Brothers pulled out the Three Worlds Mirror and held it up. The people who were getting better expected to see that reflected in the mirror, but to their surprise they saw instead the reflections of animals, with some seeing the head of a cow or a horse, and others different kinds of birds. The patients were shocked to learn this meant that they would be reborn as animals in their next lives, and where they had once been joyful at being cured at the Nanbanji, now they were filled with sadness. Their cries of despair filled the temple, and they prostrated themselves and begged, "Please have mercy and help us escape rebirth as animals." Now the two Brothers were secretly pleased that their patients had been deceived so easily, but they were careful not to show their feelings. Rather, they taught the people how to worship Deus and gave them each a rosary with forty-two beads called a *gondatsu*. The Japanese rosary has one hundred eight beads in order to eliminate the one hundred eight worldly desires, but the forty-two beads on this rosary represent the forty-two provinces of South Barbary. The dharani the Brothers taught them was *Goshōten haraisō zensumaru*.[37] The Brothers said that this dharani would protect them from evil thoughts and that they should say it with the rosary, bead by bead, until they reached the end. Then, after they had said it day and night for seven days, they would go before the head priests of the Nanbanji and say it for them. After meeting with the two padres and receiving their teachings, they would be shown how to achieve a better rebirth.[38]

---

37. *Goshōten* refers to life in heaven after death (i.e., 後生天). *Haraisō* means paradise and comes from the Portuguese *paraiso*, and *zensumaru* appears in *Kirishitan monogatari* and is a Japanese transcription of "Jesu Maria."

38. The seven-day period of indoctrination also appears in *Kirishitan monogatari* and seems to be based on the actual practice of the Jesuits in Japan. In a letter to the Jesuits in Rome, Luis Frois describes a seven-step process by which converts were brought into the church, including lessons on God as Creator, the immortality of the soul, and a refutation of the Japanese sects. In this letter Frois says that the seven-step process was adopted specifically because it was familiar to Japanese converts since Buddhist priests used the same number of lessons to teach Buddhist doctrine. *Cartas de Iapão que escreverão os padres & irmãos de companhia de Iesus*, Evora, 1598, facsimile edition, vol. 2 (Tokyo: Tenri Central Library, 1972), F. 179.

After hearing this, many said they would worship Deus. For seven days they closeted themselves and did as the Brother had told them, and at the end of that period they met with Gerikori and Yariisu, who took them to see the two padres. When they entered the priests' quarters, they saw that the rooms sparkled with light, and the visitors gazed in awe, wondering if such a place could truly exist in this world of men. In these quarters, both padres wore robes of gold and moved about in solemn silence, so that they appeared to be living incarnations of boddhisatva. The two Brothers presented the supplicants saying, "These people have suffered greatly until now, but slowly their illnesses are healing. Now they ask that you teach them how to achieve a good rebirth." Then the Brothers turned to the converts and said, "We will now look for proof of how well you have applied yourselves," and they brought out the Three Worlds Mirror once more. Afraid that they would again see the ugly images of before, the supplicants peered into the mirror fearfully, but they did not see reflections of animals. Rather, they saw themselves as buddhas, resplendent in purple and gold, and they were filled with joy and gratitude beyond words.

The two padres said, "That you have been able to see such a wonderful rebirth after only seven days of practice is due to the grace of God and the work of the dharani. Those who devote themselves completely to the worship of God may be assured of their next life, even though in this life they may suffer the tortures of water or fire, or they may be drawn and quartered, burned at the stake, or crucified. Whatever your lot in life, you need not envy others. You should have no doubt that you will live in heaven after death, and nothing in this life can change that."

Then the padres said, "Let us pray," and they pulled out an instrument called a *cruz*.[39] This *cruz* was made of gold and was two and a half inches square at one end, with a handle that was two feet long. Nails were imbedded in rows along the end, and it looked very much like a radish grater.[40] The supplicants bared their right shoulders and the padres dragged the cruz across their backs, tearing their flesh and causing them great pain. Then the padres smeared the hands of the supplicants with the blood from their own backs and told them to join their hands and pray to the image of Deus.[41] In

---

39. *Cruz* is くるす in the text, which is the Portuguese and Spanish word for "cross," though the subsequent description is not that of a cross. The Jesuits did have instruments for self-flagellation, but it is unclear if they called any of those instruments a *cruz*.
40. "Radish grater" is *wasabi oroshi* わさびおろし in the text.
41. In more than one letter by Luis Frois there is mention of *disciprinas*, or "self-flagellation." Though sometimes *disciprinas* merely consisted of pounding the chest (*golpes de pechos*), in one letter Frois speaks approvingly of Christians during Holy Week being "covered in blood from their self-flagellation." Jap Sin 4, 209; Jap Sin 9 I, 153.

Japan, people worship very differently, but this is a sect in which people are happy to die a painful death. The padres told them, "Your next life will be good thanks to the grace of the dharani, and whatever may happen to you, you need not worry as long as you recite it."

Then the padres raised a curtain behind the small shrine, and the converts could see a gilded image of a woman. She was dressed in rich clothing and wearing a jeweled crown, and in her arms she held the figure of a small child who suckled at her breast. The two padres said to the group, "Just as this mother holds the child to her heart and gives him milk, so will Deus bestow his love on you simple souls." Then they began to worship earnestly, pressing their bloody hands together in prayer.

Among the sick who flocked to the Nanbanji, there were thirty who came for treatment of skin diseases and disabilities. Once they were cured, they looked into the Three Worlds Mirror and were overjoyed to see themselves as boddhisatvas in the next life, and all of them became adherents of the new sect. Now in that group there were three very clever men. One of them was the Zen priest Ejun from the province of Kaga whom the Kirishitan called Babian.[42] Unable to escape the karma he had built up in the past, he was afflicted with such a severe case of leprosy that he was covered in blood and pus, so that no one wanted to come near him. Eventually, he left his home and became a beggar, letting his feet carry him where they would until he came to Makuzugawara in the capital. One day he went to the Nanbanji, where he was treated and cured completely. After that, he retained his priestly appearance and, taking the name Babian, became a novice in the new sect.

Of the other two, one was a cloth seller named Yasuuemon from Izumi Province. Even though he was a merchant of some renown, he neglected his business and spent all of his time with entertainers and artists, so that his reputation was ruined and he eventually was reduced to begging. Be-

---

42. This refers to the convert turned apostate, Fabian Fucan. Fabian entered the Society of Jesus in 1586 as a brother, and there is evidence that he was a Buddhist monk before entering. He was responsible for the Jesuit publication of the romanized *Heike monogatari* and was a valuable member who could use his training in Buddhism to argue skillfully against it. He also wrote the *Myōtei mondō* of 1606, which argues the merits of Christianity through a discussion between two ladies about the pros and cons of different religions. Fabian left the Society a few years after writing this text and soon after became a vociferous critic of Christianity, eventually publishing the *Ha Daiusu* (Deus Destroyed), the title of which plays on the similarity in pronunciation between Deus and *dai uso*, or "big lie." In this work, he again uses his training in Buddhism, but this time to argue against Christianity instead of for it. Fucan appears as Fabian or Babian in almost all of the variant *monogatari* on the Kirishitan and is invariably portrayed as an evil, cunning character that is defeated in a debate with the Buddhist monk Hakuo.

cause he developed scabs from syphilis, he also left his home and took to the road, but everywhere he went people were dismayed by his appearance. When he arrived in Kyoto, there was no place that would take him in, so he ended up sleeping under the porch of the cloister at Tōji, where he received the leftovers from the priests' table and eked out a hand-to-mouth existence.

The third man was a farmer named Zengoro from the town of Kurodo in Izumi province. At one time he had many fertile fields, but he wasted his money on the good life, and eventually he fell into poverty and became a beggar like the other two. Since he also suffered from scabs, he could not find any work, so he wrapped himself in a straw mat and made his way to the capital, where he ended up under the same porch at Tōji with Yasuuemon. At first they were ashamed of their own appearances and did not speak to each other, but eventually they began to speak of their home in Izumi and of their shared sorrows.

One day, Zengoro and Yasuuemon went to the Nanbanji, where they were bathed and clothed in rich robes, and their diseases were cured. After that, Yasuuemon was given the name Cosmo, and Zengoro was given the name Simon. Then one night these two and Fabian were taken to the inner rooms of the Nanbanji, where the two padres taught them the dharani and magic. Using this magic they learned how to turn a towel into a horse, how to sprinkle powder and turn a dead tree into a flower, how to turn earth into a jewel, how to float in the air and sink into the earth, and how to summon black clouds and make it rain and snow.

Of the thirty people who had come to the Nanbanji to be cured, it was these three who began to work in the church. The remaining people who were not as clever were dressed as merchants and sent out to spread the word about the church in and around the capital. To everyone they met they said, "Nobunaga has built a temple, where two priests named Urugan and Buraten serve, along with the two doctors whom Nobunaga has invited, Gerikori and Yariisu. We are truly fortunate to be alive in these times, for these doctors are very good, and for no fee whatsoever they treat serious illnesses using strange and wonderful medicines." Those who heard this wondered if it could possibly be true, and they went to Nanbanji to see for themselves. Some complained of this disease, others of that one, but all who went were cured. Then these people told more people, and great numbers came. To others they said, "I had this disease, but when I went there they gave me beautiful clothes, and they even visited my home and gave money to all of my family. They also taught me a spell that would make me a living buddha, and now I worship Deus and I know I will be reborn in a good place. Rather than wasting money on

Buddhist studies, or wasting time chanting the *nenbutsu*, if you become an adherent of the Nanbanji your disease will be cured and your entire family will benefit. If you are sick, you should do as we did." With this encouragement, sick people came to the Nanbanji in droves, so that the throngs appeared to encircle the temple like a cloud.

At the Nanbanji the four men decided that it was difficult for families to survive while the wage-earner was being treated at the temple, so naturally money should be paid to the families. As a result, each family member down to the babe born yesterday received one coin for every day that the sick person was in treatment. Those who had arrived at the temple unaware of this policy were overcome with joy when they received the money, and others who heard about it and were not sick arrived complaining of ailments in order to receive their coins. For this reason people flocked to the temple. Later, those who officially joined the church were given one measure of rice and eight coins per person. Because all of this was given to even the newest born child, it took eight people to direct the crowds, another eight to distribute the alms, and four secretaries to keep track of the books, all working morning to night to meet the demand. With twenty people employed in giving alms continually, the number of adherents increased daily, and those who came to learn about becoming a living buddha even began to include court nobles and military officials.

On the eleventh day of the fifth month in the twelfth year of Eiroku, Nobunaga left the capital, arriving in Gifu on the thirteenth day. At that time, when his steward was in attendance on him he said, "I have been hearing many things about the temple I built while I was in Kyoto. Last year, when I summoned the padre from Nagasaki and asked my advisors if I should support them or not, Bunkyōin advised me not to do so and said they were no better than people from Ebisu or Mongolia. But I did not listen to him, and now they have become a problem. That was a mistake on my part. When I sent a spy to the Nanbanji to see if they were breaking the law, he said that they are giving alms to each of their adherents. In Buddhism, adherents give half a penny or a penny to ensure their rebirth in the next life. But I hear that at the Nanbanji it is the opposite of all other sects, and instead of taking donations from the adherents, the temple is giving out money. It is just like the saying 'From the temple to the supplicant,' which has always meant something that is backward or upside-down. If this turns out to be a heretic sect, what shall I do? How could I drive out the padres and destroy the Nanbanji when I am the one who built the church and named it?"

Maeda Gen'i Tokuzenin Hōin was in attendance on Nobunaga at that time, and now he stepped forward to speak.[43] "It is too late to try to destroy the Nanbanji now. It would be like trying to stop a flood with one hand. I don't know about the retainers in this room, but there are many daimyo and small landowners, including those who have sworn loyalty to you, who have already joined this sect. If you move to destroy the temple, you will set your own people against each other, and it may encourage some of those loyal to you to change their allegiance. It is better not to discuss this too openly right now." Nobunaga saw the wisdom in what Maeda said, and replied, "Lately I have not made very good decisions. If any of you come up with a good plan for doing away with the Nanbanji, please let me know." Then there was much discussion among those present about whether the padres should be killed or driven out of the country.

Even as Nobunaga puzzled over what to do, an urgent message arrived announcing that Araki Murashige, governor of Settsu, was mounting an army against Nobunaga. As a result, the discussion of how to destroy the Nanbanji was put aside. From that time on there were uprisings here and there, and slowly Nobunaga's hold on the country began to weaken. When, in the eleventh month of the sixth year of Tenshō, Takayama Ukon rose in opposition against him, Nobunaga in his wisdom knew it was because of the Kirishitan sect.[44] He summoned Padre Urugan from the Nanbanji and delivered the following message through Sugenoya Kyūemon: "Even though it was new, I heard that the sect of the Nanbanji was honest, so I allowed you to proselytize. Takayama Ukon also heard of the integrity of the Nanbanji sect and joined the temple. But now Araki Murashige, governor of Settsu, who was an important retainer of mine, has turned against me and become my enemy. A sect that would admit such a traitor as Murashige cannot be called honest. If you want to establish the integrity of your sect, you can start by convincing Takayama Ukon to swear his allegiance to me. If he does not do so, your sect will be eliminated. But if he does, you will be permitted to proselytize without hindrance for a long time." Urugan feared the end of his sect, so he agreed and spoke to Takayama Ukon. Takayama was devoted to the sect and gladly swore allegiance to Nobunaga for its sake.

43. Maeda Gen'i (1539–1602) served as governor of Kyoto and as Minister of Temples and Shrines under Toyotomi Hideyoshi.
44. This was in 1579. Takayama Ukon was perhaps the most famous of the Christian daimyo who was known for zealously requiring all of his retainers and farmers to become Christian, and for destroying many Buddhist temples in his domain. He was forced into exile after Tokugawa Ieyasu's expulsion edict of 1614, and Takayama later died in Manila.

Now, as the Nanbanji continued to hand out money, it attracted adherents from among the best in the land, and since Nobunaga valued the allegiance of Takayama Ukon, he allowed the two padres to teach the Kirishitan doctrine as much as they wanted. Then on the second day of the sixth month in the tenth year of Tenshō, Nobunaga was killed at Honnōji Temple in Kyoto by Akechi Mitsuhide, governor of Hyūga. But even in the wake of this event, day after day the sect flourished. Then Hashiba Hideyoshi, governor of Chikuzen, killed Mitsuhide of Hyūga and seized power for himself, becoming the leader of the realm as shogun.[45] The Nanbanji had flourished from the eleventh year of Eiroku until the thirteenth year of Tenshō, or a total of eighteen years. But it was in the eighteenth year that Hideyoshi finally destroyed this sect.

After Nobunaga and Mitsuhide were killed and the country had been brought under his rule, Hideyoshi stayed at Yodo Castle in Yamashiro. In this castle town there lived a very talented carpenter named Nakai Hanbei. Hearing of the carpenter's fame, Hideyoshi summoned him and found his work to be very pleasing. Thereafter, he kept him by his side at all times and gave him the title of Shuri, or Master Carpenter, so that his rank was above that of all the carpenters in the realm.[46] In addition, Hideyoshi gave the Shuri a house, though because he kept the carpenter at his side, it remained empty. So, the Shuri brought his mother to live in the house and take care of it.

At the Nanbanji, Babian was trying to think of how to further the plot of the king of South Barbary by increasing the number of converts to the sect. Then he thought that if this Shuri became a member of the sect, his reputation with all of the carpenters in the land would lead them to join as well, and the numbers could be increased by one hundred fold. Unfortunately, the Shuri was at the castle every day and inaccessible to him, but then Babian heard about the carpenter's mother. Surely, if the mother were convinced to join, then the Shuri would as well. So, in his cunning way, Babian set about planning a way to meet the Shuri's mother.

One day he put on beautiful robes and got into a splendid palanquin, and on his way from Yamazaki to Hirakata, he purposefully arrived in Yodo at dusk.[47] Stopping the palanquin before the gate of the Shuri's home, he sent a young servant to deliver this message: "I am a priest from the main temple in Kyoto, returning from a trip to the province of Senshu.

---

45. This was in 1582. Hashiba was the name used by Hideyoshi before he changed it to Toyotomi.
46. The title is しゅり, which is short for 修理太夫, an official position of the fifth rank.
47. Yodo is an area on the outskirts of Kyoto.

Though we are close to Kyoto, dusk has fallen, and in these uncertain times there may be robbers or other criminals on the road. I know Kyoto is only five miles from here, but I am afraid of the dark roads and ask to be given a night's lodging here." When the Shuri's mother heard this, she believed he truly was a priest from the capital. Since her son had been treated so well there, she replied that there was a guest house, and though it might be crowded if he had many retainers with him, he was welcome to stay there. Then she had the servants bring his palanquin to the guest house, and she went out to greet him as if she were lodging a boddhisattva himself.

Babian's group comprised twelve people who needed to be accommodated overnight, including two outrunners, an umbrella bearer, a trunk bearer, a sandal holder, two young servants, and four palanquin bearers. The Kirishitan appeared to be of a very high rank, dressed in a double-layer outer kimono, with a white robe beneath it and an under-robe of scarlet silk, all topped with a velvet collar. When the Shuri's mother saw this, she felt pleased to be helping a person of such obvious consequence, and she entertained Fabian with great quantities of food and drink. Then she got him settled for the night and went to sleep in her own quarters.

The next morning the Shuri's mother got up earlier than usual to light the lamps, set up the offerings, and burn incense at the Buddhist altar, thinking the priest would want to say morning prayers there. When he did not appear, she thought he must have stayed up praying the night before and for that reason was sleeping late. But when Babian finally did make his appearance, he did not bow to the altar or even look at it. Rather, he sprawled in the middle of the reception room with his backside to the image of Buddha and ate the countless delicacies brought to him with even more gusto than he had the night before. After finishing, he quickly thanked the woman and left. The Shuri's mother was shocked and couldn't help thinking that Babian's behavior was unacceptable. Even a priest from a different sect should at least read the sutras. Not bowing to the image of Buddha was unthinkable, and surely it would not be condoned even at such a place as the Nanbanji.

Four or five days later, a samurai appeared at the house with a servant bearing a trunk. He said, "I am an assistant at the Nanbanji, and I have been sent here by Babian. Recently you gave him lodging, delicious food, and a good night's rest, for which he was very grateful. Please take these as an expression of his gratitude." Then the samurai opened the trunk and began to pull out gifts, which included a pound of aloes wood, five bolts of damask, and another five of silk gauze. The woman thought the gifts too costly for the occasion, and she did not want to accept them. But the samurai insisted that she keep them, so she finally relented. After that Babian sent many more gifts of cloth and other beautiful objects, forging a strong relationship with the Shuri's mother.

Sometime later in the fall, Babian purposely left Kyoto late on a rainy night and stopped at the home of the Shuri's mother. Once again, he said he was on the way home from a trip to Sakai and asked for a night's lodging. By now they were close friends, and the mother came out to greet Babian and bring him to the guest house, where she thanked him warmly for all of the gifts he had sent. Babian in return thanked her for her hospitality and remarked on the elegance of the rooms in which he was staying.

That evening the two spoke of many things. At one point Babian said, "I am not sure to what sect you belong, but while it is very difficult to achieve Buddhahood in other sects, in ours there is abundant proof that believers bear the mark of living Buddhas." Worried that the Shuri's mother had no great understanding of these matters, Babian used every argument he could think of to convince her to convert. Wanting to be polite, she remained noncommittal and told him, "I am sure what you say is not wrong." Then Babian urged her even more strongly to convert. After thinking over her response very carefully she said, "I thank you for your concern, but I have been a practitioner of the *nenbutsu* since I was a young girl, and now that I am over sixty I can even say it in my sleep. You must forgive me, but trying to remember a new chant at my age would be much too difficult. And if you asked my son the Master Carpenter, I think he would say the same. However, that is not to say I would never change sects. If you were willing to debate the merits of the two sects with someone who knows the teachings of the *nenbutsu* more thoroughly, I would make up my mind based on the results of that debate." Babian said he would be happy to participate in such a debate. Then he said, "Women are such pitiful creatures. They think that because gold and brass are the same color, a sect as pure as gold and one the color of brass are one and the same. If you know a practitioner of the *nenbutsu*, we will come some day soon to talk with him, and our logic will be so persuasive that you will have no choice but to abandon the *nenbutsu*." With this final boast, he left and returned to the capital.

After hearing him say that, the mother of the Shuri was very eager to see this debate. Among the adherents of the Tendai, Shingon, Zen, Jōdo, Nichiren, Ikkōshu, and Jishu sects there were certainly many monks who could win this debate against Babian.[48] But, she thought, there is no tell-

---

48. Ikkōshū (一向宗) is another name for the Jōdo sect, and Jishū (時宗) is one branch of the Jōdo sect.

ing what cunning things Babian might say, and if a monk were to lose, it would bring shame to the Japanese sects. However, if a scholar specializing in the *Shu Ching* were brought to a private house for the debate, even if he lost it would not reflect on the monks or on Buddhist law.[49] So she asked many people in and around the capital, and learned of a layman called Hakuo who lived in Yanaginobaba on Shijō Avenue. He was formerly a resident of the Southern Temple on Mt. Hiei, but he suffered from severe headaches that got worse every time his head was shaved, so that he grew dizzy and was unable to stand. As a result, he left the temple and let his hair grow out and, following the example of the Disciple Yuima, lived in a nine-by-nine foot hut, burning incense and praying for purity of spirit.[50]

Hakuo came to Yodo to visit the Shuri's mother, and she asked him if he would be willing to debate Babian. The scholar was eager for this opportunity, believing that the teachings of this popular new sect were not the true teachings of the Buddha. Though he had long thought it an evil and heretical sect, he had done nothing until now because it was supported by Nobunaga. But to hear the religion of Shakyamuni compared to brass while the evil sect was described as pure gold was just too much to bear, and he told the Shuri's mother that he would be happy to debate Babian as soon as possible. The lady was pleased to hear that and sent a message to Babian, who rushed over.

Thus, on the twelfth day of the ninth month in the thirteenth year of Tenshō, the group gathered at the home of the Master Carpenter.[51] Babian arrived in the evening, accompanied by a bearer shading him with a parasol. He wore an under-robe of white silk, with a Korean fabric over that and a grey outer-robe. On his head he wore a light blue wool cap. Word had spread in the neighborhood that Babian and Hakuo were having a

---

49. The *Shu ching* is the book of documents in the Chinese Classics.
50. Yuima is the protagonist of the *Yuima* (*Vimalakīrti*) *sutra*; he was a layman who lived at the same time as Shakyamuni and was known for his exceptional wisdom.
51. This would be 1586. The debate between Fabian and Hakuo appears in *Kirishitan monogatari* as well as all versions of the *Raichō jikki* narrative. Scholars believe this account is based on an actual encounter between Fabian and the Confucian scholar Hayashi Razan that took place on July 19, 1906. Razan's own account of the debate, *Hai yaso* 排耶蘇 (Anti-Jesus), can be found in Ebisawa Arimichi et al., eds., *Kirishitansho, haiyasho*, Nihon shisō taikei 25 (Tokyo: Iwanami shoten, 1970), 490–91. Elison provides a full English translation in *Deus Destroyed*, 149–53, and notes that, though there is no full account of the debate from the Jesuit side, there is reference to what appears to be the same encounter in the annual letter of the Jesuits for 1606. More recently, Kiri Paramore has questioned whether Razan ever had such a debate. See Kiri Paramore, "Hayashi Razan's Redeployment of Anti-Christian Discourse: The Fabrication of Haiyaso," *The Japan Forum* 18, no. 2 (2006): 185–206.

debate, and many had gathered to listen. The throng grew quiet, and everyone held his breath, waiting to see who would win.

Babian and Hakuo were escorted to a reception room, where the Shuri's mother introduced them and they exchanged greetings. Sweets and sake were served, and the participants relaxed while they enjoyed the refreshments. During this time, Babian called a servant and had him bring in a carrying case. Inside there were many boxes made of lacquer and precious metals, and from among these he pulled out one lacquer box embossed with gold and silver, and placed it to his right.

When the sake was gone, everyone grew quiet, and the room buzzed with anticipation. Hakuo began by asking, "Which Buddha is the central deity in your sect?" Babian lifted the lid of the box next to him and removed the eight scrolls of the *Lotus sutra*. He placed these scrolls on the lid of the box, knelt in a formal position, and answered, "That is a very good question. The principle deity of this sect is one who appeared before the Bodhisattva Kannon, when nothing else existed between heaven and earth. He is the Buddha Deus, and in all the world there was no other being before him.[52] It was this Buddha who created the sun and the moon, human beings, birds and animals, and trees and grass. In the beginning, the hearts of men were pure and in harmony with the heart of Deus, and without even asking they received the fruit of heaven. But as time passed, the hearts of men grew covetous and avaricious, and they were cut off from the bounty of heaven. Then Deus was saddened to see the people's suffering, and he suffered as well, so he decided to help anyone who chanted '*Goshōten haraisō zensumaru*.' In Japan you have Buddhism and Shinto, and the two Buddhas in Japan are Amida and Shaka, correct?" Then Hakuo answered, "Yes, the Buddhas who share a bond with people are Shaka and Amida."

Babian continued, "First, Amida was the Priest Hōzō, and therefore a human being.[53] Shaka was the prince Shitta, and therefore also a human being.[54] Tenshodaijin was the child of gods, Hachiman was Emperor Ujin, and Tenjin was the court noble Michizane. So your gods were all human beings.[55] It is hard to believe that human beings could be the saviors of

---

52. In this passage, the Christian god is described with the Buddhist terminology でいうす如来という仏.
53. The name of Amida Buddha during his lifetime was ほうぞうびく (法蔵比丘).
54. The Buddha Shaka was born a prince, and his full name was Siddhartha Shakyamuni. "Shitta" here is an abbreviation of his first name.
55. Tenshodaijin (天照大神) refers to the sun god Amaterasu, and though the text says "Ujin," it was the fifth-century emperor Ōjin (応神天皇) who is deified as the god Hachiman. The ninth-century statesman Sugawara no Michizane is enshrined as Tenjin. These are all Shinto deities.

other human beings. When Shaka was nineteen years old he was scolded by his parents and left to roam the Tandoku Mountains, wearing only rags and living off of anything he could find.[56] And these days priests who live their lives in cast-off robes and beg for food are only copying Shaka, are they not? They deceive people who barely have any food of their own by saying if they give enough they will go to heaven, but if they do not give any alms they will descend into hell and be tormented by demons. In this way they collect money and rice, all following the way of the merchant priest Shaka. If you look at the gathering of the sixteen disciples, they were all petty officials, and the same with the gathering of the five hundred disciples. It was just a meeting of petty officials. Because the law of Deus is not observed in Japan, you have countless beggars and poor people, the sick and the diseased. In the forty-two provinces of South Barbary, because Deus is worshipped, there are no poor and no sick. Because there are no poor and sick, there are no unsatisfied desires, and when there are no desires, there is no sin. Because there is no sin, there is no bad karma, and when there is no bad karma, people receive the fruits of heaven and become living Buddhas. If Shaka and Amida were truly Buddhas, you would certainly see me struck down for this. Look here!" Saying this, he picked up the three sutras of the Jodo sect and the eight scrolls of the *Lotus Sutra* and tore them to pieces. Then he blew his nose into the pieces, threw them into the garden and urinated on them. Finally, he returned to his seat. "Do you all understand now? Do you still believe that other religion is real? Better to follow a law that will make you a living Buddha, so you may receive the fruits of heaven."

At the beginning of Fabian's speech Hakuo had tried to comment once or twice, but after that he didn't say a word and only bowed his head in silence. Seeing this, the Shuri's mother and the rest of the audience wondered if this was the end and Hakuo had been defeated. They held their breath and stared at the layman nervously, wondering if he had been swayed by Babian's argument and would now change religions. Hakuo allowed Babian to say his piece and then quietly asked him, "Is that all?" Babian replied that there was a great deal more, but that he had explained the most important points.

Then Hakuo said, "To beg for charity is the role of the Buddha. I cannot believe you, Babian. What you said earlier—that Deus is a Buddha that is older than Kannon; that before anything existed in the world he created the sun and moon, human beings, the birds and the animals, the plants and the trees; and that later on he promised to help people who

---

56. In Sanskrit, the Dandaka Mountains.

chanted something as incomprehensible as *'Goshōten haraisō zensumaru'*—all of that is a lie, isn't it?" Babian answered that it was not at all a lie, and then Hakuo felt his blood begin to boil, and he said, "It seems to me this Deus did a very stupid thing. There is nothing in this world that does not have its use. Even a simple container has its purpose, and there is nothing that is ever completely useless. But for what purpose did he create these men—who in these latter days of the law can only suffer unspeakably—only to then try to save them by accepting their penance? Certainly he would have done better not to have made them at all!" At this point Hakuo rose up on his knees and faced Babian, but the latter had no answer and only hung his head. Approached by Hakuo, Babian for the first time felt cornered in the argument and said, "You are a fool, and talking to you is like talking to a stone. 'Those who will not believe, cannot be saved.'" Then he got up to leave, but Hakuo grabbed the hem of his robe saying, "'Those who will not believe, cannot be saved'—that is part of the Buddha's own teaching. How dare you use his wise words as a parting shot!" and he began to beat Babian over the head. But Babian wrenched his robe from the layman, and, mumbling incomprehensibly under his breath, he made his escape.

Then the Shuri's mother and the rest of the audience were amazed at Hakuo's achievement and said, "When you didn't answer at first we were worried. But that heretic was silenced quickly and ran away with his tail between his legs. This is great news indeed!" And Hakuo replied, "If you want to speak using the Buddha's teachings you should also answer with the Buddha's teachings. Since we have spoken of the things of this world, let us now say more on the subject. The evil sect has been defeated by the true sect, and though it may take time, now I want you all to listen to what I have to say.

"First, on the top of the Grdhrakūta Mountains in India, the Buddha Shaka preached to a gathering that included gods, the Dragon King, human beings, and lesser mortals.[57] At this time in India there was a great pestilence that was spreading far and wide, and no one was immune to it. Taking pity on the people, the Buddha carved with his own hands an image of Yakushi, the healing Buddha, and he told the people that if they worshipped the image saying *"Namu Yakushi Ruriko Buddha,"* they would be cured.[58] So they all did as they were told and prayed this way to the image, and every one of them was cured. So the god of the pestilence,

---

57. There is a line in the manuscript marking the beginning of Hakuo's sermon, though no such mark is inserted at the end.
58. The full name of this Buddha is Yakushi Ruriko.

realizing it could not stay in that land, crossed the border into Srāvasti, and there the disease began to spread. The king of this land was called Prasenajit, and one of his subjects was the millionaire Sudatta. This Sudatta was the richest man in the land, but his only daughter was also infected by the disease, and he was saddened to see her prostrated by it. He had heard that the Buddha was in the Gṛdhrakūta Mountains and that he had saved the people there, so he sent a servant to the Buddha to ask for help. Shaka's answer was to say the prayer to Yakushi Buddha. So father and daughter both earnestly prayed to Yakushi, and the daughter was cured.

"Sudatta's joy knew no bounds, and he wanted to show his gratitude to the Buddha, so he went to him and begged the Buddha to come to Srāvasti where he would build a monastery in his honor. The Buddha replied that he should build it, and he would come. Then the millionaire said there was a twenty-square-mile bamboo forest called Gidaen that was unparalleled on this earth and would become the place in which to form a bond with all living things. The Buddha told Sudatta to build the monastery in that place, and Sudatta returned home.

"The bamboo forest belonged to the son of King Sāriputra, Prince Jeta, so Sudatta went to the prince and asked him how he could make it his own. The prince replied, 'This is the best garden in the land, and I will not part with it easily. However, if you spread over the surface of all the land five-*sun* coins of silver and six-*sun* coins of gold, and spread them thickly enough that no earth shows through, then you may have the land in return for those coins.' Sudatta was overjoyed and, opening nine of his storehouses, he had cartloads of gold and silver brought to the land and spread over it every day. Then he said to the prince, 'I have spread the land with silver and gold as you asked. Now I give it to you, and ask that you give me the land.' But the prince replied, 'When I asked you to spread the land with gold and silver I was only joking. I did not ask you to do such a thing thinking you would actually go through with it!' But Sudatta said, 'Deception on the part of a person of rank is unlawful in our land. Meanwhile, what has been given cannot be taken back.' And Sudatta would not take back the gold and silver.

"Thus, a temple complex with three hundred nine buildings was built on the piece of land, and it became the summer residence of the Buddha and the residence of eighty-four thousand disciples during the winter. This was the first temple in India, and it was named the Jetavana Monastery. Now, when you add the denominations of the five-*sun* and six-*sun* coins that were brought by Sudatta, you get eleven-*sun*. And if you write eleven-*sun* in *kanji*, it forms the character for temple, and this is the origin of that character.⁵⁹ The prince still refused to accept the coins Sudatta had brought, and the millionaire told him to throw them in the fields or the ocean. But the prince was determined to find a way to give them back, so he had a large bell made out of the metal and donated it to the Buddha, and this was the origin of the temple bell.

"At the time that the Jetavana Monastery was being built, there lived in Srāvasti an adherent of a heretic sect named Anamidō. One day Anamidō said to King Prasenajit, 'The millionaire Sudatta is building a monastery with three hundred nine buildings, and he plans to offer it to Shaka Nyorai. But the teachings of Shaka are not widely known in this world. You should put a stop to this building.' The king had often seen the wonders performed by Anamidō and did not think that Shaka had teachings or anything else of any great value, so he was sure that the heretic sect had the greater power of the two. Clearly, Shaka had a very small following, and since the heretic sect had a great many members, if they battled the Buddha they would surely win, the king thought. Shaka, for his part, was sure Anamidō could not best those of his sect, and he decided to send his disciple Sharihotsu.

Sitting on his *zazen* stone, Sharihotsu contemplated nirvana right up to the moment agreed upon for the confrontation. And though the appointed place lay thousands of miles away, his uncommon strength allowed him to cover the distance in a moment, and he arrived at the appointed hour in a field of twenty square miles for the battle between the sects of Anamidō and Sharihotsu. Then the grass of the field sprang to life, as Anamidō created a huge lake there, with water the color of indigo and seven kinds of jewels lining the shores. But Sharihotsu stepped over to the lake, raised one finger of his right hand to the sky, and caused a great elephant to descend. This elephant drank up the water of the lake in one gulp, and crushed all of the jewels on the shores. Then Anamidō stamped the ground with his foot and a great iron bull appeared. It roared with a voice like thunder and brandished fearsome iron horns. Sharihotsu raised his finger to the sky, and a great lion descended to the field and killed the iron bull with one bite. Then Anamidō beat the earth and a large tree rose up, fifteen meters tall with grown limbs and in full bloom. But Sharihotsu took a deep breath, and with one blow created a typhoon that uprooted the tree and toppled it. Anamidō tried a number of different tricks, but he could not prevail against Sharihotsu.⁶⁰ Next he pointed to

---

59. The three characters of 十, 一, and 寸 all written vertically together form the three elements of the character 寺.
60. Starting with this sentence, the name of the heretic leader is written "Anamidara." This is likely due to a miscopied character at the end (in *kana* the names are written あなみだう and あなみだら).

the sky and called down a dragon thirty meters long that tried to swallow Sharihotsu. But the disciple protected himself with the Golden Winged Bird that he summoned from above. And again, Anamidō stamped the earth and brought forth a demon thirty meters tall that threatened the disciple with its long iron staff. But Sharihotsu again beckoned to the sky, and down came the guardian deity Skanda, brandishing his pike, and the evil demon vanished like a shadow. Anamidō used many different spells, but each one was neutralized by Sharihotsu. Then, just as he began to lose hope, from the shoulder of Sharihotsu there appeared a flame thirty miles high. As Anamidō watched in fear, the flame blew over to his own shoulder, and with that he conceded, realizing he could not prevail against the power of Buddha. Then thirty-seven hundred of his disciples all turned at once to face Sharihotsu, and they bowed to him and became disciples of Buddha. In this way, the construction of the Jetavana Monastery led many to the correct path. And the tolling of the bell at the twelfth hour announces that 'all conditioned things are impermanent/ It is their nature to be born and die/ When birth-and-death itself disappears/ nirvana is our lasting bliss.'[61] All of these events occurred in India.

"At the time of Emperor Mei, Mato and Jikuhoran loaded the Buddhist canon onto a white horse and brought it to China. This coincided with the second year of the rule of Japan's twelfth emperor, Keikō. In China at the time, there was a heretical sect called the Rōdōsha, and they tried to do harm to the two priests. The emperor had seen the Rōdōsha perform wondrous feats any number of times, when they had held the sun and the moon in their hands, or caused the earth to shake beneath them. Because of this, the emperor himself had prayed to them, and though he believed the Rōdōsha could never lose, he decided he should see which of the two could perform the greatest wonders. When the two priests arrived, the Rōdōsha set about performing their feats in an attempt to defeat the Buddhists. They decided to do their easiest trick, to hold the sun and the moon in their hands, but try as they might, they could not make it work. Then the two Buddhist priests placed the bones of Shaka in a bowl of lapis lazuli and raised it high in their hands. Though it rose one hundred miles into the air, their feet did not touch the earth, nor did their heads touch the

---

61. This four-line verse from the *Nirvana sutra* is known as the *Shogyō-mujōge*, or "verse on the impermanence of all things." The message forms part of the famous "*I-ro-ha*" poem that showed the old organization of the *kana* system before the introduction of the modern fifty-syllable one. The English translation here is by Robert E. Morrell in his translation of the *Shasekishū*. Mujū Ichien, Robert E. Morrell, *Sand and Pebbles (Shasekishū); The Tales of Mujū Ichien, a Vvoice for pPluralism in Kamakura Buddhism* (Albany: State University of New York Press, 1985), 322.

heavens, but they remained suspended in the middle for a time. The light from the bones shone throughout the emperor's palace, and he gave in to that golden light and, without a thought for his own will, descended from his palace and bowed to the bones of Buddha. The best tricks of the Rōdō-sha were no match for the strength of the Buddha, and all of their disciples became disciples of the Buddha, just as they did in India. After that, White Horse Temple, the first temple in China, was built there."

When Hakuo had finished his sermon, the Shuri's mother and all of the spectators were moved to tears and deeply grateful. Then Hakuo returned to his dwelling, and his audience also dispersed to their own homes. As they spoke to each other of what they had seen and heard, they agreed that the sure sign of a heretical sect was one that offered alms and made people desire them.

Soon after, the Master Carpenter was given leave to return to his home, where he was able to spend time with his mother. There he heard about the things that the novice Babian from the Nanbanji had said and done, and he thought it all very strange. When he returned to the castle, he reported the incident to Hideyoshi. The leader said, "Nobunaga also thought this sect was no good and was talking about destroying it. I was present the day he said this, so I know all about it. But it was during the same audience that the declaration of war arrived from Araki Murashige, governor of Settsu, so he became distracted by other things. That is why this sect still exists. Since it is clearly an evil sect, it should be destroyed. As for most of the priests of the Nanbanji, since they are all quite young, they should have all of their property confiscated. But Padre Urugan, Padre Buraten, Yariisu, and Gerikori, these four deserve death." Then Hideyoshi was asked how that should be done. Should they be beheaded, and their heads displayed at the prison gates? Should they be crucified upside down, or right side up? Hideyoshi replied, "Any of those would be correct. Because theirs is a serious crime, drawing and quartering or crucifixion would be the most appropriate. However, doing so would be going too far. Because they have all come from another country, if they are killed in Japan it will only invite trouble.

"There is precedent for this. In the reign of Retired Emperor Kameyama, the eighty-ninth emperor, in the ninth year of Bun'ei, the Barbarian hordes began to make forays to try to invade Japan.[62] Then, in the second year of Kenji, during the time of the ninetieth emperor Go-Uda, hundreds of thousands of barbarians in five hundred large ships landed on the coast

---

62. This would have been 1273. Though Hideyoshi calls them the people of "Ebisu," or barbarians, he is referring to a Mongol invasion.

of Kyushu.[63] The Western daimyo came out in force and finally prevailed, taking prisoner the enemy commander, Ajirō. The prisoner was sent to Kamakura for judgment, and there Hōjō Tokimune made an error when he decided to have the commander beheaded on the beach at Yuigahama. News of Ajirō's death so angered the enemy that in the fourth year of Kōan, a force of forty thousand ships and 3,700,000 men crossed over to Japan and invaded Kyushu.[64] Armies from Shikoku and Chūgoku joined in the battle and tried to beat them back, but the enemy gave no heed to the number of dead and fought on in desperation. When they continued to gain ground and it seemed they would overcome the Japanese and reach the capital, Emperor Go-Uda became alarmed and sent an imperial messenger to the inner and outer shrines at Ise.[65] The emperor composed the following poem:

> Evil rides the waves
> that approach from foreign lands
> raise the wind's fury
> blow them back to their home
> Oh God of the Wind at Ise!

"After writing it out in an elegant hand and affixing his seal, he sent it by messenger into the Shrine of the God of the Wind. Then a puff of smoke seemed to come from inside the shrine, and all at once a great wind arose in the west that was so strong it blew huge boulders about as if they were fallen leaves. It tossed the waves of the great ocean so that all the ships on it were thrown about, broken up, and scattered. Thus, the wind of the gods was so strong that the barbarians' attempt to take over Japan was in vain.

"Bearing these events in mind, we can assume that if we kill the four Southern Barbarians, there will be retaliation, and that would endanger our people. Better to send them back to their country." Then Hideyoshi

---

63. This was in 1277.
64. This date is 1282. The Mongol invasions of Japan took place in 1274 and 1281 with forces that are traditionally estimated to have numbered about thirty thousand and one hundred thousand, respectively. However, in his study of the medieval picture scrolls on the Mongol invasion, Thomas Conlon cites a number of sources that point to much smaller numbers of two to three thousand in the first invasion, and no more than ten thousand in the second. For traditional estimates see George Sansom, *A History of Japan to 1334* (Stanford, Calif.: Stanford University Press, 1958), 442–50. See also Thomas D. Conlon, *In Little Need of Divine Intervention: Takezaki Suenaga's Scrolls of the Mongol Invasions of Japan* (Ithaca, N.Y.: Cornell East Asia Series, 2001), 261–64.
65. Ise Shrine is the ancestral shrine of the imperial family.

ordered Masada Emon and Nakatsuka Ōkura to lead three thousand men and take over the Nanbanji. At that time, the administrator Ishida Konishi, governor of Settsu, and Takayama Ukon, along with twenty-three others were all adherents of the Nanbanji. When they heard of Hideyoshi's plan, they sent word to the temple, where the news turned that peaceful world upside down. Babian, Cosmo, and Simon all managed to disappear before Hideyoshi's men arrived. But Masuda and Nakatsuka soon entered the Nanbanji and took Urugan, Buraten, Gerikori, and Yariisu back to Fushimi Castle. Then the four were put on a Dutch trading ship and promptly sent back to Nanban. Their followers were urged to apostatize, and those who did not were condemned as criminals.

Babian traveled down to the province of Hizen, where he preached about the sect in Amakusa. Cosmo went down to Tōtōmi Province where he stayed for four years before moving on to a place called Nakanohama in the town of Ebisu in Izumi Province.[66] There, he changed his name to Ichibashi Shosuke and began to practice medicine. Simon went to Echizen where he stayed for four years before moving on to a place called Sakai Higashiminato. He changed his name to Shimada Seian and also began to practice medicine.

On the fourteenth day of the ninth month in the sixteenth year of Tenshō, Tennojiya Shuchin and Aburaya Jōyū of Sakai in the province of Izumi visited Fushimi Castle.[67] Hideyoshi was in the castle at the time, so he received them. The two men were masters of the tea ceremony, and they spoke with the leader on a wide range of topics. At one point, Hideyoshi asked them to tell him about any unusual things they had seen in Sakai. They said that they had heard a strange story, though they had not witnessed it themselves and could not be sure it was true. The story was that two doctors, Ichibashi Shosuke of Ebisu and Shimada Seian of Higashiminato, were able to perform magic, and that they could do amazing things that no normal person could do. When Hideyoshi heard this, he was eager to see it, and he ordered Sasaki Heisaemon to have the two brought to him. The two were brought to the castle and told to prepare a performance for the next day.

The following day they were brought before Hideyoshi, and he said, "Now show me what you can do." They replied, "We will do our best to amuse you." Then they had a large bowl filled with water brought to them, and into it they scattered pieces of paper cut in diamond shapes. Suddenly,

---

66. Tōtōmi Province was in the western part of present-day Shizuoka Prefecture. Izumi Province was in the southern part of present-day Osaka Prefecture.
67. The year was 1589.

the pieces of paper turned into tiny carp and other kinds of fish and began to swim around in the bowl. Hideyoshi said, "Change them back," and the men said, "As you wish, " and immediately the fish turned back into pieces of paper. There were a number of ladies-in-waiting in attendance, and thinking they should do something to entertain them, the men said, "I hope this doesn't alarm you too much." Then one of them took from his breast pocket a twisted paper string two or three feet in length. He blew on the end, and it became a thick rope. Then he threw it on the ground and muttered a spell under his breath, and it immediately turned into a large snake. The ladies made a great commotion, and since it was an ugly sight in a formal reception room, Hideyoshi told him to change it back. The man uttered a spell, and it became a twisted paper string once more. Then they put sand in a dish and spread grain over it, and suddenly the grain became tiny ants crawling about in the sand. They performed many other tricks as well. When asked if they could make an egg crow like a rooster, they said they most definitely could. Then one man took an egg in his hands and said a spell over it, and when he opened his hands it had cracked open and there was a young chick there. Then, even as they watched, it grew into a rooster and crowed as if it were morning. When he was told to make it an egg again, the man uttered a secret spell, and it became an egg once more.

Because the ladies had never seen Mt. Fuji, they asked if the men could show it to them, and the latter said it would be too large for the reception room, but they would conjure it up in the garden. Then screens were set up, and the two men went outside and chanted a spell. When the screens were removed, the audience could see that Mt. Fuji had appeared in the garden. All agreed that it was truly an impressive sight, just as they had always been told. When they were ordered to make it disappear, the screens were set up again and the men chanted the spell. And when the screens were removed, the garden appeared as it had before. Then they were asked to conjure the eight most beautiful views in Ōmi. The screens were set up once more, and the men chanted their spells. When the screens were removed, the audience could see all eight views, including Mii, Mt. Hiei, Zeze Castle, Katata, and Hira. Everyone was very impressed with the sight.[68] When ordered to change it back, they raised the screens,

---

68. Mt. Hiei is on the border between Kyoto and Shiga Prefectures, near the former province of Ōmi, but it was not actually considered one of the eight views. Zeze Castle was also not included in the eight views, although it was in the province of Ōmi. The famous eight views of Ōmi are the evening snow at Hira, the autumn moon on Ishiyama, the setting sun at Seta, the tolling of the bells in the evening at Mii Temple, the arrival of the geese at Katata, the evening rains at Karazaki, the returning ships at Yabase, and the extremes of weather at Kuritsu.

uttered the spell, and lowered the screens again, and the garden was back to normal. When they were asked for views of Suma and Akashi in the province of Senshu, they made them appear in the same way as before.

Then Hideyoshi said, "I have heard about ghosts but have never seen one before. Can you make a ghost appear?" The men replied that they could easily do that, but that ghosts never appeared during the day, and they would have to wait until evening to conjure one. Hideyoshi understood that to be a reasonable request, and he ordered food for the men so that they could take a break. All waited impatiently for night to come, and when the sun finally set, many lamps were lit so that the reception room was as bright as day. But the two men said, "It will be difficult to conjure a ghost in this bright a room. Ghosts have always only appeared in dark places." So all of the lamps in the reception room were extinguished. It was the seventeenth day of the ninth month, and there was a moon that night, but in the reception room it was still very dark. The men set up the screens and went out onto the porch, where they chanted a spell. Then they returned and sat in the reception room. Suddenly, the moon clouded over and a strong wind began to blow, and all was pitch black. From a gap in the trees above the garden, a ghost appeared. It was wraith-like, with bony arms and legs and disheveled hair, and it began to approach the reception room. It continued to draw near and stopped on the step leading to the room. It was the eighteenth day, and though it was cloudy, there was still a moon.[69] When he looked more closely at the ghost, Hideyoshi realized it was a servant whom he had kept as a mistress when he was still known as Kinoshita Tōkichi.[70] Her name was Kiku. When Hideyoshi had risen to power, she had come to him and begged him to take her back into service. But she had previously spoken badly of him, so he refused to take her back. She became angry, and thus he had her executed. Hideyoshi realized that these men must have known of this and intentionally called up this ghost. In a bad temper, he told them it was an evil ghost and they should get rid of it, which they readily did by saying the same spell.

Hideyoshi then called the two men to another room. They gladly went, thinking they were to be praised and perhaps rewarded for their performance. Instead, Hideyoshi summoned his guards and ordered that the two be bound. The guards quickly tied up the two men, and Hideyoshi said, "These men are no ordinary fellows. I've heard that Babian went down to the province of Hizen, and we have been trying to find Cosmo and Simon, and now it seems these two are them." As a result, on the

---

69. The different date appears to be a mistake in the text.
70. Hideyoshi's original name was Kinoshita Tōkichiro 木下藤吉郎.

nineteenth day of the ninth month in the sixteenth year of Tenshō, the two men were crucified at Awataguchi. They had been performing magic only the day before on the eighteenth. If they had not called up the ghost of Kiku, Hideyoshi would not have gotten so angry, and things would not have gone so far. But because Kiku was the ghost, Hideyoshi grew angry and realized that the two men must have been members of the evil sect, and because of that they ended up dead.

After that, people were examined more closely, and it turned out that many had been secretly keeping images of Jesus and uttering incantations. All of these people were told that if they apostatized, they would be spared, but those who did not would be condemned. Those who did leave the sect were called "the fallen," and there were many of these.[71]

Twenty-four years after that, in the sixteenth year of Keichō, Katō Kiyomasa, governor of Higo, died.[72] Some disciples of Babian were encouraged by this and began to preach about the sect in the districts of Uto and Yayo in the province of Hizen.[73] In the town of Funai in Uto, they destroyed the Zen temple Jikkōji and drove out the priest of the temple who was named Shizōsu. This priest then traveled to Edo to complain to the government of Hidetada.[74] An administrator was sent down to the area and took charge of the matter, and eventually peace was restored to the district of Uto.

Then, sixteen years after that, there was a man who appeared to be on a pilgrimage, but who traveled through the areas of Tanba and Ōmi showing people there a special mirror. The administrator of that area pursued followers of this man unmercifully. Anyone found to be a follower was put into a sack. Then, at Sanjogawara in Kyoto, Goshironobaba in Osaka, and Shichidonohama in Sakai, fifty sacks at a time were thrown into a pile, and no matter how much they cried, those who would not apostatize were set on fire and burned to death. Those who agreed to apostatize were told they would be spared, and they begged for mercy and to be able to recant. These were taken out of the sacks and told to register as Buddhists and receive proof of that from the temple. This was the origin of the temple registration system.[75]

---

71. In Japanese they were called *korobi Kirishitan*, and there are extant manuscripts recording their confessions.
72. The year was 1611. Kiyomasa was a staunch Buddhist of whom the missionaries often complained in their letters.
73. Uto is a town in present-day Kumamoto Prefecture.
74. Hidetada was the son of Tokugawa Ieyasu, and the second shogun in the Tokugawa line.
75. Everyone was required to register at a temple and provide proof of that registration to show they were not Kirishitan. Though it began as a way to eradiate Kirishitan, it became an important administrative tool in the Edo period.

During this time, the sect began to grow in a place called Sumidake in the district of Fuji in Ōmi, where Cosmo had once stayed for a short time. This group was also strictly suppressed, and after that the sect died out. In Osaka there were three who would not apostatize. A jeweler named Shichibee was crucified upside down at Tobita. A farmer named Hachiemon was also crucified upside down, and a greengrocer named Sokichi was killed with the water torture.[76] In Kyoto there were four who would not apostatize, of which two were crucified and two were burned to death. In Sakai in the province of Senshu, there were three who would not apostatize. Two were crucified and one was drawn and quartered with oxen. The way this is done is ropes are tied to the neck, hands and feet of the condemned, and then these ropes are tied to five oxen. A fire is lit in the middle of the five oxen, and they become startled and run in five different directions, thus pulling the person into five pieces.

More than twenty years later, in the tenth month of the fourteenth year of Kan'ei, there was an uprising in Amakusa in the province of Hizen, which turned into the battle of Shimabara. In the time of the shogun Iemitsu, in the fifteenth year of Kan'ei, on the twenty-eighth day of the second month, the castle fell. General Shiro, the seventeen-year-old son of the commoner Shinbei of Oyada, was the opposition leader. He was killed by a soldier named Sozaemon who served in the house of Hosokawa, governor of Etchu.[77] The general Masuda Shiro Tokisada, took the castle in the year of the sheep. After this, the shogun restored peace to the entire country. The story of Amakusa is told in more detail in the *Amakusa gunki*, so there is no need to tell it here. The end.

Thirty-seven thousand Kirishitan died.

Where the original was considered to be unclear or in error, corrections and/or additions were made to this text.

Seventh month of the fifth year of Meiwa.[78]

---

76. In the water torture the condemned person was forced to lie down and had water poured continually on the face and down the throat until he died.
77. This is a reference to the legendary leader of the rebellion, later known as Amakusa Shirō.
78. These final sentences are the notes of the copyist, who apparently copied the text in 1771.

Appendix

Extant Copies and Variants of the *Raichō jikki* Narrative

The *Raichō jikki* narrative was not printed until the Meiji period, but the number of extant copies indicates that it circulated widely for one hundred and fifty years through the diligent efforts of many copyists. Under these circumstances, one might expect significant variations in the basic text over time. Though the more than eighty different manuscripts of the narrative examined for this study were surprisingly uniform, they did display a few noticeable deviations that helped divide them into the four categories of variants described below. The descriptions of the variants are followed by a discussion of *Shimabara jitsuroku*, a hybrid of *Raichō jikki* and *Kirishitan monogatari* that may have been a transitional text between the two, and by a chart detailing the titles, copy dates when available, variant names, and locations of each of the *Raichō jikki* manuscripts examined by the author.

KIRISHITAN SHŪMON RAICHŌ JIKKI AND NANBANJI MONOGATARI

The extant manuscripts with the most common title also belong to the most common variant, and it is for this reason that the *Kirishitan shūmon raichō jikki* is used to refer to the narrative throughout this study. However, there is a second variant that is also quite numerous. There is only one text in this group that bears the title *Nanbanji monogatari*, but I use this title to identify the category because this particular text has been included in the modern collection *Nihon shisō tōsō shiryō* and is the only one of these variants that is printed and easily accessible.[1] The original manuscript is

---

1. Washio Junkei, ed., "*Nanbanji monogatari,*" *Nihon shisō tōsō shiryō*, vol. 10 (Tokyo: Meichō Kankyōkai, 1969), 319–70. This text was used for the translation in this book.

held at the Diet Library in Tokyo, and an English translation of it accompanies this study.

The most recognizable difference between the *Nanbanji monogatari* and *Raichō jikki* variants is the inclusion in the former of a sermon by the Buddhist lay priest Hakuo after the religious debate. All versions include the debate between Hakuo and the Kirishitan convert Fabian, who is portrayed as a brash conman with a bag of tricks that are exposed by the wisdom and learning of Hakuo. Fabian is reduced to a mumbling, red-faced idiot who "scurries like a mouse" back to the Nanbanji in defeat. At this point in the *Raichō jikki* variant the narrative says that Hakuo told the onlookers some "Buddhist stories" and then returned home.[2] The *Nanbanji monogatari* variant, however, actually includes these stories as a kind of sermon that Hakuo gives to the crowd. There are three different stories included: one about the building of the first Buddhist monastery in India; a second about a battle waged between Sariputra, disciple of Shakyamuni, and Amidō, a follower of a heretical doctrine; and a third about how Buddhism was transmitted to China.[3] It is only after telling all of the onlookers these stories of the "correct path" that Hakuo returned to the capital. In the manuscript copy of *Nanbanji monogatari*, this sermon forms a considerable digression of nearly twelve pages from the main narrative.

Besides this rather large addition to the basic structure of *Raichō jikki*, the *Nanbanji monogatari* variant has some more subtle differences. The first is at the beginning. In *Raichō jikki*, the opening paragraph starts with a description of Oda Nobunaga's destruction of temples and shrines during his leadership, and it clearly places the blame for allowing the Kirishitan into the country onto him. This opening paragraph varies in length from four lines to approximately a full page, but in the *Raichō jikki* variant it clearly foregrounds Buddhism and Shinto as the religions of Japan that, because of the actions of Nobunaga, were threatened by a sect coming from Nanban. This paragraph is then followed by a description of the geographic location of Nanban before moving into the story of the king of Nanban and his plot to take over Japan. The *Nanbanji monogatari* variant, however, starts immediately with the geographic location of Nanban and leaves out the opening part about Nobunaga. It also contains a slightly longer speech by the king of Nanban, in which he goes into greater detail about how he would benefit from the riches of Japan.

2. Hiyane Antei, ed., *Kirishian monogatari hoka sanpen*, Kirishitan Bunko, vol. 1 (Tokyo: Keiseisha, 1926), 120.
3. All three are similar to ones found in the Buddhist tales section of the medieval *Konjaku monogatarishū* (Tales of Times Now Past).

In the section on the location of Nanban, all variants generally use the same description, with the only difference being in the name of the country to the south. That country is usually written as "Uba"(鳥馬) in the *Raichō jikki* variants, and as "Ume" in the *Nanbanji monogatari* variants. Most *Raichō jikki* variants use the Chinese characters 鳥馬, often glossed with the katakana ウバ. The *Nanbanji monogatari* variants usually write the name using the character 宇 for "U" (which is commonly used phonetically for the *u* sound and is also the first character in the name of Urugan Bateren) and the older *hentaigana* form of the *hiragana* character め.

Ibuki yomogi
The *Ibuki yomogi* (Mugwort of Mt. Ibuki) variant is distinguished from the others only by the addition to the standard text of a preface, and usually by the use of the words *Ibuki(yama)*, *yomogi*, and/or *mogusa* (moxa) in the titles.[4] The survey for this study found a total of ten texts using this title or containing the preface, including the oldest extant manuscript. While all of these contain the preface, the main text of the ten is sometimes the *Raichō jikki* variant and other times the *Nanbanji monogatari* variant, with the main difference being whether or not the sermon by Hakuo is included.

The preface tells of a thirty-year-old man who loses his wife and child and decides to leave his home and worldly concerns and take the tonsure. He departs from his home in Hiroshima in Genroku 2 (1689). One night, he is taken in at a temple on Mt. Ibuki, where he is told about the origins of the famous mugwort of that region and how it was brought by the people from Nanban.[5] Often the preface also includes the information about Nobunaga mentioned above as part of the opening of the *Raichō jikki* variant. In the cases where it occurs in the preface, the main text usually begins immediately with the description of Nanban, following the format of the *Nanbanji monogatari* variant. When the Nobunaga information is not in the preface, it is at the beginning of the text, as in the *Raichō jikki* variant. Though it is impossible to prove, it is possible that all of the variants originated in a single text that contained the preface and the sermon by Hakuo, and that later copyists rearranged and deleted those parts to create the prototypes of the variants described here.

References to Mt. Ibuki and the medicine can only be found in one brief mention in the body of the text. In two lines that appear in all

---

4. None of the variants with this preface is in print. I consulted the manuscript *Ibuki yomogi* held by the Kyoto University Library.
5. Mugwort was used in moxa treatments and was present in Japan long before the arrival of Western missionaries. One of the earliest mentions of mugwort in Japanese literature is in a poem in the eighth-century *Man'yōshu*.

variants of the main text, we learn that when the brothers Kerikori and Yariisu needed to grow medicines for healing the sick, they petitioned for and were given a tract of land on Mt. Ibuki, where they planted over three thousand varieties.[6] Among these plants are a few that the author maintains are still used "today," including the famous *Ibuki yomogi*. This is the extent of the reference to Mt. Ibuki in the text, but there are a number of reasons why this detail might have drawn such attention. The first is that healing was strongly associated with the foreign missionaries in the popular imagination and formed part of the portrayal of the padres as a kind of foreign *yamabushi*, or mountain ascetic. Another reason, however, may simply have been to disguise the narrative from the censors as something other than a story about the Kirishitan.

Nanbanji kōhaiki

Nanbanji kōhaiki is a later variant that was printed in Keio 4 (1868) using moveable type.[7] In fact, unlike the other variants, there are more extant copies of the Keiō 4 (1868) printing than there are manuscript versions of this variant.[8] The printed volume contains three sections: a preface by the compiler, Kiyū Dōnin, who produced a number of anti-Christian texts during this period; the main text of the variant; and Sessho's Shōhō 4 (1647) anti-Christian text titled *Jakyō tai'i* (Outline of the Evil Religion).[9]

The difference between *Nanbanji kōhaiki* and the *Raichō jikki* standard is the elimination from the former of the entire early section on Nanban and its King Gojimbi. The text instead begins from the moment that Urugan Bateren arrives in Japan. *Kirishitan monogatari* also started from that point, but the narrative is clearly that of *Raichō jikki* with one section edited

---

6. The Jesuits did run a hospital in Kyoto and had a presence in the province of Ōmi, where Mt. Ibuki is located, but there is no evidence in their records of any major project to grow medicinal plants, let alone one on Mt. Ibuki. Information on the hospitals and other charitable activities run by the Jesuits can be found in Ebisawa Arimichi, *Kirishitan no shakai katsudō oyobi nanban igaku* (Tokyo: Fuzanbō, 1944), 51–276. Reports on the earliest hospitals run by the Jesuits in Hirado and Bungo can also be found in the letters and reports sent back to Rome.
7. For more on the reintroduction of wooden moveable type in the eighteenth century, and a picture of a page from the *Nanbanji kōhaiki*, see Peter Kornicki, *The Book in Japan: a Cultural History from the Beginnings to the Nineteenth Century* (Honolulu: University of Hawai'i Press, 2001), 125–68 (photo on 141).
8. Of the four extant manuscripts listed in the *Sōmokuroku*, one is actually a *Raichō jikki* variant under the title *Nanbanji kōhaiki* (Ebisawa bunko), another was lost in a library that was destroyed (Koishikawa), and a third is a relatively recent copy (on printed lined paper) at the Tokyo University Library. The fourth is supposed to be at Kyushu University, but it is not listed in the catalog there.
9. See the chapter 1 for more on Sessho and this work.

out. A note at the end of the main text in the printed version gives a brief summary of the edited section and explains that it seemed to be fictional and was therefore left out. Information from Nishikawa Joken's works on foreign countries was inserted instead. Because the note is unsigned, it is unclear if it was written by the compiler of the 1868 printed edition, Kiyu Dōnin, or if it came with an earlier text for which we have no extant manuscripts. However, the lack of manuscripts does seem to point to its origin in the 1868 printing.

In the commentary for a modern reprint of *Nanbanji kōhaiki* edited by Ebisawa Arimichi, the scholar argues that this variant was compiled sometime in the middle of the eighteenth century by a well-educated reader who used the "seventeenth-century *Kirishitan kongenki*" and parts of the work of Nishikawa Joken 西川如見 called *Zōhō ka'i tsūshōkō* 増補華夷通商考, which was first published in Genroku 5 (1695) and then reissued in Hōei 5 (1708).[10] Ebisawa contends that the copyist removed the part about Nanban and King Gojimbi after reading Nishikawa's work on the various countries of the world, and, as a result, *Nanbanji kōhaiki* is a less vulgar variant. However, unless Ebisawa had access to manuscripts that no longer exist, it is difficult to understand why he would think that this variant originated any earlier than the 1868 printing, or that the change was not made by Kiyu Dōjin himself.[11]

The Hybrid Shimabara jitsuroku

In early commentaries on the different versions of the *Raichō jikki* narrative, scholars have suggested dates of origin that range from the mid-seventeenth century to the early eighteenth century. In his earliest article on *Kirishitan shūmon raichō jikki*, Ebisawa Arimichi says that it is impossible to pinpoint the date of origin.[12] Then, in reference to the variant *Nanbanji kōhaiki*, Ebisawa dates it to 1648 in his 1960 bibliography of Christian sources; yet four years later he does not mention that date in a preface to the reprinted text and speculates that the work was based

---

10. Ebisawa has argued that the *Raichō jikki* narrative is based on the earlier *Kirishitan kongenki*. See the discussion of *Shimabara jitsuroku* below for more on that text.
11. I should note that Miyatake Tobone includes *Nanbanji kōhaiki* in a list of works that were censored by the bakufu. The work is included in a section for books whose printing dates and censorship dates are unknown. Miyatake asserts that it is certain that all were printed before 1854, but he does not explain why that is so. Kornicki has pointed out that a number of censorship cases in Miyatake's study have proven to be wrong, and without more evidence to back it up, I'm inclined to think that this one is wrong as well. Miyatake Gaikotsu, *Hikkashi* (Chiba: Yamanosama shobō, 1974; reprint of the 1926 edition by Asakaya shoten), 163–64.
12. Ebisawa Arimichi, "*Kirishitan shūmon raichō jikki kō*," *Shūkyō kenkyū* 149 (1954): 156.

on an earlier one called *Kirishitan kongenki* and produced sometime after the appearance of Nishikawa Joken's *Ka'i tsūshōkō* in 1696.[13] Finally, in the revised version of his *Kirishitanshi no kenkyū*, he dates the appearance of the narrative to the Genroku period (1688–1704) and again links it to the earlier *Kirishitan kongenki*.[14] Unfortunately, he gives no details about that earlier text, nor are there any surviving documents to prove the link or its origins. Though the *Kokusho sōmokuroku* lists no extant copies of that text, a search of manuscripts in Japanese libraries turned up two of that name, of which one closely follows the *Raichō jikki* variant. The other is a copy of a text for which the more common title is *Shimabara jitsuroku*.[15] This latter work appears to be a transitional text and could be the *Kirishitan kongenki* to which Ebisawa refers. However, it does not bear a copy date, making it difficult to determine when it was written.

More recently, Kikuchi Yōsuke has estimated that the *Raichō jikki* variants date from the Kyōhō period (1716–35).[16] Though his analysis of them is from the perspective of trends in military tales and not the literary history of the *jitsuroku* genre, this date of origin would coincide with the early period of growth in that genre. In two articles that trace the origins of the Kirishitan *jitsuroku*, Kikuchi proposes that *Shimabaraki*, which itself derived from a number of accounts written by samurai involved in the fighting, is the source text for all of the later *jitsuroku* on the Kirishitan and the Shimabara Rebellion. In his analysis he includes a chart showing the divergence of the different variants and how they relate to each other, and he identifies the first variant to come from *Shimabaraki* as *Shimabara jitsuroku*. If the *Kirishitan kongenki* to which Ebisawa refers is, in fact, the text in Sophia University's Kirishitan Bunko, which is also a version of *Shimabara jitsuroku*, then Kikuchi and Ebisawa are in agreement on the origins of the Kirishitan *jitsuroku*. This conclusion is also supported by the hybrid nature of the text, which incorporates parts of both *Kirishitan monogatari* and the *Raichō jikki* narrative.

---

13. *Christianity in Japan: a Bibliography of Japanese and Chinese Sources* (Tokyo: Committee on Asian Cultural Studies, International Christian University, 1960), 38; *Nanbanji kōhaiki, Jakyō tai'i, Myōtei mondō, Ha Daiusu*, Toyo Bunko, vol. 14 (Tokyo: Heibonsha, 1964), 4.
14. Ebisawa Arimichi, *Zōtei kirishitanshi no kenkyū* (Tokyo: Shinjinbutsu juraisha, 1971), 153.
15. Both manuscripts are at the Kirishitan Bunko, Sophia University. See below for a more detailed analysis of *Shimabara jitsuroku/Kirishitan kongenki* as a transitional text.
16. Kikuchi Yōsuke, "Amakusa gunki mono jitsuroku no seiritsu—kanazōshi Shimabaraki kara Tamaru Kubō mono e," *Kinsei bungei* 66 (1997); Kikuchi Yōsuke, "Kirishitan jitsuroku gun no tanjō," *Shizudai kokubun* (Bulletin of the Shizuoka University Humanities Department) 44 (2005); Watanabe Kenji of Rikkyō University has also said in private conversation that the text seems to have originated in the Kyōhō period.

Shimabara jitsuroku tells the story of the Kirishitan and, in some versions, the Shimabara Rebellion, beginning with ten or twelve sections (depending on how they are divided) that include some parts that are identical to or resemble the *Raichō jikki* narrative, and others that are word-for-word copies of sections in *Kirishitan monogatari*. It begins with the arrival of Urugan Bateren in Nagasaki, as does *Kirishitan monogatari*, but while some details are closer to those in the earlier *kanazōshi* (specifically some elements of Urugan's physical description and the gifts he brings to Nobunaga), the narrative style is that of *Raichō jikki*, and the text often follows the *Raichō jikki* word for word. It omits the scene with King Gojimbi that opens the *Raichō jikki* tale, but the king appears later in a scene in which he writes to Urugan and urges him to use magic to take over the country. In the manuscript version at Tōhoku University Library, the next eight chapters follow the plot and style of the *Raichō jikki* narrative, with some areas that are more abbreviated and less detailed, ending with the scene at Hideyoshi's castle when the former *iruman* (brothers) perform magic and are discovered to be Kirishitan. From this point, however, the remaining four chapters are lifted word for word from *Kirishitan monogatari*, and they include the chapter describing the Kirishitan sect, the one in which a former brother accuses the foreign bateren of plotting for their king, and two chapters on the arrests and prosecution of Kirishitan.[17]

The *Kokusho sōmokuroku* states that the *Shimabara jitsuroku* text was written in 1730 (Kyōhō 14). This is based on a preface bearing that date that is attached to the copy at the Tōhoku University Library. However, in the preface, its author Ryūkō (隆好) clearly states that he copied it from the first part of a longer text titled *Seijū seibatsuki* (西戎征伐記, Punishment

---

17. The section titles in surviving manuscripts are often different, and they also differ greatly from the titles in *Kirishitan monogatari*, although the text itself is identical. For comparison, I will list the section titles as they appear in the Tōhoku University Library copy of *Shimabara jitsuroku* (A), and their equivalents in the original *Kirishitan monogatari* (B) (printed in *Kirishitan monogatari hoka sanpen*) and the translation by George Elison (C) (in *Deus Destroyed: the Image of Christianity in Early-Modern Japan*. [Cambridge, Mass.: Harvard University Press, 1973]): chapter 9 (A) *Nanbanjin buppō no koto* 南蛮人仏法の事 (B) *Kirishitan buppō no koto* 吉利支丹仏法の事 (C) On the Kirishitan Version of Buddhist Doctrine; chapter 10 (A) *Ieyasukō shūmon no kinsei no koto* 家康公宗門の禁制の事 (B) *Nanban yori nihon o shitagahen to suru sonin izuru koto* 南蛮より日本を従へんとする訴人いづる事 (C) How a Man Appeared to Accuse the Kirishitans of Desiring to Subject Japan to South Barbary; chapter 11 (A) *Jahō ikki* [illegible] 邪法一揆[illegible] (B) *Kirishitan ga shūtai domo tawara ni ireraruru koto* 吉利支丹が宗體ども俵に入らるる事 (C) How the Followers of the Kirishitan Religion Were Inserted in Straw Sacks; chapter 12 (A) *Teraukejōhō no koto* 寺請状法の事 (B) *Kirishitan no shūshi no goseibai no koto* 吉利支丹の宗旨の御成敗の事 (C) How the Kirishitan Religion Was Subjugated. Hiyane, *Kirishitan monogatari hoka sanpen*, 1–39; Elison, *Deus Destroyed*, 321–74.

of the Western Barbarians), indicating origins that are earlier than 1730.[18] There are at least five manuscripts of *Shimabara jitsuroku* extant, of which the three at Tōhoku University Library, Kanazawa Municipal Library, and Nagasaki Prefectural Library are listed in the *Kokusho sōmokuroku*. Another two that I have seen that are not in the *sōmokuroku* are one in the Vatican Library in Rome, and the aforementioned *Kirishitan kongenki* in the Kirishitan Bunko at Sophia University. Of the five, only those at the Vatican and at Kanazawa include the additional twenty-five sections on the Shimabara Rebellion, although the one at Nagasaki is the single remaining volume of a two-volume set, so the complete manuscript also likely included the battle tale. The copies at Tōhoku and Sophia, however, contain only the Kirishitan story, and both give every indication of being intact.[19] While the number of extant copies is much smaller than that of the *Raichō jikki* narrative, we know that it circulated at least until the 1770s and was popular enough to gain mention as one of the prohibited books in the 1771 *kinsho mokuroku* put out by the booksellers' guild.

There are a number of factors within the text that also support the idea that *Shimabara jitsuroku* is a transitional work that came between *Kirishitan monogatari* and the *Raichō jikki* narrative and not after the *Raichō jikki*. The first is simply the hybrid nature of it, containing as it does several complete chapters from *Kirishitan monogatari* while also including what would have been the newer material of the *Raichō jikki* narrative. This points to its production at a time when copies of *Kirishitan monogatari* were still readily available, perhaps before or soon after the second printing was banned in 1665. Another reason is that at least two of those chapters would have stood out to later censors and would have been harder to circulate freely, even in manuscript. These are the chapters discussing the Kirishitan sect and its beliefs and the chapter about a man accusing the foreigners of plot-

---

18. Of the five manuscript copies extant, only one, that of the Tōhoku University Library, has this preface. However, the preface also makes clear that the complete text consists of the twelve chapters on the Kirishitan. The other extant manuscripts that are longer and include the Shimabara Rebellion narrative could be copies of an earlier version. The *sōmokuroku* lists only one extant copy of a work titled *Seijū seibatsuki* at the Ise Shrine Library; however, that library was closed for renovations for over a year, and I was unable to visit and examine the text.
19. As mentioned earlier, the Tōhoku manuscript has a preface that confirms the complete text was only twelve chapters, while the Sophia manuscript has a table of contents in the first volume whose chapter headings are all included in the two extant volumes. I should note that the Kirishitan Bunko at Sophia has cataloged the two volumes as separate works (one titled *Kirishitan kongenki*, the other given the title of the first chapter in the volume, or *Nanbanji hakyaku no koto*), but I was able to demonstrate that they are two volumes of one work. I do not know if the cataloging has been corrected.

ting for their king, which contains the name of Tokugawa Ieyasu in the title. The former, with its description of the Kirishitan belief in Deus, *paraiso* and *inferno* (heaven and hell), is only mildly critical of the faith and would have come dangerously close to appearing to proselytize.[20] This section does not appear in the *Raichō jikki* narrative. And the latter, by actually naming Ieyasu in the title, blatantly contravened countless edicts prohibiting the mention of the ruling family in both printed and manuscript texts. If it appeared before *Raichō jikki*, perhaps in the mid- to late seventeenth century, it would have come out before the more explicit crackdown on printed and manuscript works about forbidden topics and would only have been replaced later by the slightly more sensational but also more politically safe *Raichō jikki* (which avoids any mention of the Tokugawa family). That would explain why, even though it was still circulating at the time of the *kinsho mokuroku*, there are considerably fewer copies extant.

Finally, there are some indications that the copy of *Shimabara jitsuroku* held in the Sophia University Library bearing the title of *Kirishitan kongenki* could be an older copy of the text. Though undated, it appears considerably older, not only because of its deteriorating condition, but also because of the large, flowing script using primarily *kana*, which closely resembles the style of the earlier, printed *Kirishitan monogatari*. Furthermore, though the title on the outer cover is written with the common eighteenth-century *kanji* for "Kirishitan" (切支丹), the inside cover page title is written with the older (吉利支丹). This latter way of writing the word is less pejorative and was used in the title for *Kirishitan monogatari*, but it is rarely seen on any of the *Raichō jikki* variants. Commentaries written on several *Raichō jikki* manuscripts noted that the change in the way Kirishitan was written was mandated in the first year of Tenna (1681) soon after Tokugawa Tsunayoshi came to power. This was because the first character in "Kirishitan" (吉) was also the character for *yoshi* in the shogun's name. To avoid any association between the two, it was ordered that the word "Kirishitan" henceforth be written with the character for *kiri* (切) or "cut."[21] Whether there was such an order or the explanation was made up to fit the circumstances, it is clear just by looking at the extant copies

---

20. This is identical to the chapter on the beliefs in *Kirishitan monogatari* and its second printing *Kirishitan taiji monogatari*. As the chapter that goes most deeply into the beliefs (however critically), it seems likely it was one of the elements that made the second printing so objectionable. And even though there is no evidence this text was printed, by the early eighteenth century some manuscript works were also drawing the censorship gaze of the bakufu.
21. A note about this change appeared in the margins of several of the manuscripts I examined. It also appears in Miyatake, *Hikkashi*, 9.

of *Raichō jikki* that by the mid-eighteenth century the old style of writing Kirishitan was extremely rare.[22] These indications of this particular manuscript's age, the commentary of Ebisawa and Kikuchi, and the content of the text itself, which combines the narratives of both *Kirishitan monogatari* and *Raichō jikki*, all point to the strong possibility that the *Shimabara jitsuroku* text is a transitional one.[23]

---

22. For a list of Japanese titles in *kanji*, see below.
23. There is another early text that may have had some influence on the *Raichō jikki* narrative and deserves mention. *Yaso seibatsuki* (耶蘇征伐記／耶蘇制罰記) survives in approximately four manuscript copies, with two at the National Archives in Tokyo, one at Tokyo University Library, and the other at the Ebisawa Bunko at Rikkyō University (a fifth copy also at the Ebisawa Bunko lacks the section about the foreigners that is relevant here). The Ebisawa Bunko manuscript has a copy date of Kyōhō 6 (1722), making it earlier than another other extant manuscript of the *Raichō jikki* narrative. The text is primarily an account of the Shimabara Rebellion, but it contains a few pages explaining the Kirishitan sect. In those pages, it explains that the Kirishitan sect first came to Luson (呂宋 glossed as ルソン) in the time of Go-Shirakawa (end of the Heian period), and at that time it was called the Horoboro or Kirishitan sect but later came to be known as Yaso. Then, in the reign of Go-Nara, in Tenbun 20 (1552), the sect came over to Japan and built a temple. In Tensho, the padre Xavier (シャビエル) came and brought gold and silver, precious jewels, medicine, and incense and gave them to Oda Nobunaga, who declared it a righteous sect and received the padres at Azuchi Castle. The padres also gave people food and clothing, so they flocked to the temple. There is mention of padres named Yayausu and Furate (similar to the Yarisu and Furaten of *Raichō jikki*). The text also explicitly states that the padres taught that the gods (仏神) are not outside of the heart, but inside of it, and that building temples and shrines is only a path to knowledge of them, not the place where they reside. But they also brought with them such sorcery (邪術) as a clock that kept time by itself. Ultimately, Tokugawa Ieyasu declared the sect foreign and dangerous to the teachings of Buddhism, Shinto, and Confucianism and expelled the padres from the country. There are a number of elements in this narrative that echo those in *Kirishitan monogatari* and *Raichō jikki*, so it should be considered a factor in their development. However, the portion on the Kirishitan is a very small part of the overall text and does not reproduce any of the text found in *Kirishitan monogatari* and *Raichō jikki*, as the *Shimabara jitsuroku* text does.

Table A1. Extant manuscripts of *Raichō jikki* variants found to date

Title	Location of examined copy	Copy date	Variant
Kirishitanki 切支丹記	Aoyama Gakuin	None	Raichō jikki
Kirishitan shimatsuki 切支丹始末記	National Archives	None	Nanbanji monogatari
Kirishitan shūmonki 切支丹宗門記	Kyoto Univ.	None	Nanbanji monogatari
Kirishitan hokki 切支丹発記	Tohoku Univ.	1843	Raichō jikki
Kirishitan jikki 切支丹實記	Tokyo Univ.	1789	Raichō jikki
Kirishitan jitsuroku 切支丹實録	Kanazawa City	None	Raichō jikki
Kirishitan kōhaiki 切支丹興廃記	Tokyo Univ.	1797	Raichō jikki
Kirishitan kongenki 切支丹根元記	Sophia Univ.	None	Nanbanji monogatari
Kirishitan denraiki 切支丹伝来記	Dōshisha Univ.	1766	Raichō jikki
Kirishitan raichō jikki 切支丹来朝實記	National Archives	None	Raichō jikki
Kirishitan raichō jitsuroku 切支丹来朝實録	Aoyama Gakuin	None	Raichō jikki
Kirishitan raichōki 切支丹来朝記	Sophia Univ.	1856	Raichō jikki
Kirishitan raichōki (variant) 切支丹来朝記（異本）	Sophia Univ.	None	Raichō jikki
Kirishitan raichōki (variant) 切支丹来朝記（異本）	Kyoto Univ.	1761	Nanbanji m. with Ibuki preface
Kirishitan shūmon raiyu 切支丹宗門来由	Sophia Univ.	None	Nanbanji monogatari
Kirishitan shūmon yurai 切支丹宗門由来	Waseda Univ.	1811	Nanbanji monogatari
Kirishitan yuraiki 切支丹由来機	Tōhoku Univ.	1835	Raichō jikki
Kirishitan yurai jikki 切支丹由来實記	Tokyo Univ.	None	Raichō jikki
Kirishitan sōraichōki 切支丹僧来朝記	Dōshisha Univ.	None	Raichō jikki
Kirishitan denrai hiroku 切支丹伝来秘録	Dōshisha Univ.	None	Raichō jikki
Kirishitan yurai Ibuki yomogi 切支丹由来伊吹蓬	Aoyama Gakuin	None	Raichō jikki
Kirishitan nanban jikki 切支丹南蛮寺記	Sophia Univ.	None	Raichō jikki

APPENDIX

Title	Location of examined copy	Copy date	Variant
Kirishitan shūmon raichōki 切支丹宗門来朝記	Sophia Univ.	1821	Raichō jikki
Kirishitanshū toraiki 切支丹宗渡来記	Kyushu Univ. Law Library	None	Nanbanji m. with Ibuki preface
Kirishitan shūmon jikki 切支丹宗門實記	Kyushu Univ. Literature Library	1851	Raichō jikki
Kirishitan shūmon ranshō 切支丹宗門濫觴	Aoyama Gakuin	1859	Raichō jikki
Kirishitan shūmon yurai kikigaki 切支丹宗門由来聞書	Kanazawa City	1765	Raichō jikki
Kirishitan shūmon tōrai jikki 切支丹宗門渡来實記	Tōhoku Univ.	None	Raichō jikki
Kirishitan shūmon raichō denki 切支丹宗門来朝伝記	Kyoto Univ. Literature Library	None	Raichō jikki
Kirishitan shūmon raichō jikki 切支丹宗門来朝實記	Tokyo Univ.	1767	Raichō jikki
Kirishitan shūkyō raichō jikki 切支丹宗教来朝實記	Dōshisha Univ.	None	Raichō jikki
Kirishitan shūmon raichō jitsuroku 切支丹宗門来朝實録	Sophia Univ.	1861	Raichō jikki
Kirishitan shūmon kongen seisuiki 切支丹宗門根元盛衰記	Kyushu Univ. Literatrure Library	None	Raichō jikki
Kirishitan honcho ni wataru koto 吉利支丹本朝に渡る事	Dōshisha Univ.	1841	Nanbanji monogatari
Kirishitan shūmon raichō jikkiroku 切支丹宗門来朝實記録	Seikadō Bunko, Tokyo	1760?	Raichō jikki
Kirishitan shūmon wachō ni wataru kongenki 吉利支丹宗門渡和朝根元記	Nagoya Tsurumi Central Library	1743	Nanbanji m. with Ibuki preface
Kirishitan nihon denrai ranshō 切支丹日本伝来濫觴	Dōshisha Univ.	None	Raichō jikki
Honchō kirishitan shūmon raichō jikki 本朝切支丹宗門来朝實記	Sophia Univ.	1755	Raichō jikki

Title	Location of examined copy	Copy date	Variant
Kirishitan metsubōki 切支丹滅亡記	Sophia Univ.	1830	Nanbanji monogatari
Kirishitan seibatsuki 切支丹征伐記	Sophia Univ.	None	Raichō jikki
Yasoshū ranshōki 耶蘇宗濫觴記	Kyushu Univ. Cultural History Lib.	None	Raichō jikki
Yaso kinparoku 耶蘇禁破録	Iwase Bunko	1761	Raichō jikki
Yaso shūmon kōhaiki 耶蘇宗門興廃記	Tokyo Univ.	1769	Nanbanji monogatari
Yaso shūmon kongenki 耶蘇宗門根元記	Iwase Bunko, Nagoya	1856	Nanbanji monogatari
Yaso shūmon shimatsuki 耶蘇宗門始末記	Seikadō Bunko, Tokyo	1764	Raichō jikki
Yaso shūmon raichō jikki 耶蘇宗門来朝實記	Kyoto Univ.	1846	Nanbanji m. with Ibuki preface
Yaso shūmon raichō genki 耶蘇宗門来朝元記	Osaka Pref. Library	None	Nanbanji m. with Ibuki preface
Yaso shūmon raichō jitsuroku 耶蘇宗門来朝實録	Kyushu Univ. Law Library	1801	Raichō jikki
Eshū ibukiyama yomogi no yurai kirishitan shūmon denki 江州伊吹山蓬の由来切支丹宗門伝記	Kyushu Univ. Literature Lib.	None	Raichō jikki with Ibuki preface
Ibuki yomogi kirishitan shūmon no yurai 伊吹蓬切支丹宗門の由来	Kyoto Univ.	None	Nanbanji monogatari
Kirishitan shūmon shimatsu/ Ibukiyama yomogi in'enki 切支丹宗門始末／伊吹山蓬因縁記	Diet Library	None	Raichō jikki with Ibuki preface
Ibukiyama yomogi no in'enki 伊吹山蓬の因縁記	Diet Library	1828	Raichō jikki with Ibuki preface
Ibukiyama mogusa ki 伊吹山艾記	Tokyo Univ.	1759	Raichō jikki with Ibuki preface
Kaisei Ibuki mogusa 改正伊吹艾	Tōhoku Univ.	1789	Raichō jikki with Ibuki preface

Appendix

Title	Location of examined copy	Copy date	Variant
Nanban jikki 南蠻實記	Iwase Bunko	1835 (from 1769 original)	Nanbanji m. with Ibuki preface
Nanbanji yurai 南蛮寺由来記	Tōhoku Univ.	1800	Raichō jikki
Nanbanji monogatari 南蛮寺物語	Diet Library	1771	Nanbanji m.
Nanbanji kōhaiki tan 南蛮寺興廃機單	Rikkyo Univ.	Printed 1868	Nanbanji kō.
Nanbanji kōhaiki 南蛮寺興廃記	Rikkyo Univ.	Printed 1885	Nanbanji kōhaiki
Nanbanji kōhaiki (variant) 南蛮寺興廃記（異本）	Rikkyo Univ.	None	Raichō jikki
Nanban yōhōki 南蛮妖法棄	Tokyo Univ.	None	Raichō jikki
Nanban metsubōki 南蛮滅亡記	Nagasaki City Museum	1782	Nanbanji monogatari
Nanban yaso raichō jitsuroku 南蛮耶蘇来朝實錄	Tokyo Univ.	None	Raichō jikki
Banshū seikinroku 蠻宗制禁錄	Dōshisha Univ.	None	Raichō jikki

Table A2. Longer texts that include the *Raichō jikki* narrative in full

Title	Location of manuscript or title of edited vol.	Copy/Print Date
Kinka keiranshō 金花傾嵐抄	Rikkyo Univ. Ebisawa Bunko	m. 1843
Amakusa sōdō 天草騒動	Amakusa sōdō shimabara amakusa gunkishū	p. 1970
Kirishitan amakusa gunki 切支丹天草軍記	Rikkyo Univ. Ebisawa Bunko	m. 1810
Kirishitan ikkan oboegaki 幾利支丹一巻覚書	Seikadō Bunko	m. 1839
Sankō amakusa gunki 参考天草軍記	Rikkyo Univ. Ebisawa Bunko	w.b. 1883
Sankō amakusa gunki 参考天草軍記	Rikkyo Univ. Ebisawa Bunko	w.b. 1885
Nanbanshi 南蠻志	Seikadō Bunko	None
Amakusa seibatsuki 天草征伐記	Rikkyō Univ. Ebisawa Bunko	None
Samidaresho 五月雨抄	Nihon shisō tōsō shiryō	
Sokkyohen 息距編	National Archives	m. Meiji

Table A3. Manuscripts of the *Shimabara jitsuroku* text

Title	Location	Copy Date
Kirishitan kongenki 切支丹根元記	Sophia Univ.	None
Shimabara jitsuroku 島原實録	Tōhoku Univ.	1778
Shimabara jitsuroku (variant) 島原實録（異本）	Vatican Lib.	1787
Hizen shimabara jitsuroku 肥前島原實録	Kanazawa City	1750

Bibliography

Aizawa Seishisai 会沢正志斎. *Shinron*. In *Mitogaku*, edited by Imai Usaburō et al. Nihon shisō taikei, vol. 53. Tokyo: Iwanami shoten, 1973.

_____. *Kikōben*, edited by Seki Giichiro. Nihon jurin sōsho, vol. 4. Tokyo: Ōtori shuppan, 1971.

Alcune lettere delle cose del Giappone Scritte da' Reverendi Padri della Compagnia Di Iesu Dell' Anno 1579 insino al 1581. Rome: Francesco Zanetti, 1584.

Anesaki Masaharu 姉崎正治. *Kirishitan shūkyō bungaku*. Tokyo: Dōbunkan, 1932.

_____. *Kirishitan dendō no kōhai*. Tokyo: Dōbunkan, 1930.

_____. *Kirishitan shūmon no hakugai to senpuku*. Tokyo: Dōbunkan, 1925.

Arai Hakuseki et al. *Arai Hakuseki*. Tokyo: Iwanami shoten, 1975.

_____. "Seiyō Kibun, Or Annals of the Western Ocean (part 2)," translated by S. R. Brown. *Journal of the North China Branch of the Royal Asiatic Society*, New series 3 (1866): 40–62.

_____. "Seiyō Kibun, Or Annals of the Western Ocean (part 1)," translated by S. R. Brown, *Journal of the North China Branch of the Royal Asiatic Society*, New series 2 (1865): 51–84.

Asai Ryōi 浅井了意. *Kirishitan hakyaku ronden*. In *Kaihyō sōsho*, vol. 1, edited by Shinmura Izuru. Kyoto: Kōseikaku shoten, 1927.

Asakura Haruhiko 朝倉治彦, ed.. *Kirishitan taiji monogatari*. Kanazōshi shūsei, vol. 25. Tokyo: Tokyodō shuppan, 1999.

Baddeley, J. F. "Father Matteo Ricci's Chinese World-Maps, 1584-1608." *The Geographical Journal* 50, no. 4 (1917): 254–70.

Banshū seikinroku (Record of the Suppression of the Barbarian Religion). MS. Dōshisha University Library, Kyoto.

Bentley, James. *A Calendar of Saints: the Lives of the Principle Saints of the Christian Year*. London: Macdonald & Co. Ltd., 1988.

Berry, Mary Elizabeth. *Japan in Print: Information and Nation in the Early Modern Period*. Berkeley: University of California Press, 2006.

Bhabha, Homi. *The Location of Culture*. London: Routledge, 1994.

Blacker, Carmen. "The Religious Traveler in the Edo Period." *Modern Asian Studies* 18.4, Special Issue: Edo Culture and its Modern Legacy (1984): 593–608.

_____. *The Catalpa Bow: A Study of Shamanistic Practices in Japan*. London: Allen & Unwin, 1975.

Boscaro, Adriana. "*I Kirishitan Monogatari*: Una Rilettura del 'Secolo Cristiano.'" In *Annali della Facolta' di Lingue e Letterature Straniere di Ca' Foscari* 18.3 (1979).

Boxer, Charles F. *The Christian Century in Japan 1549–1650*. Berkeley: University of California Press, 1951.

Brandon, James, and Samuel Leiter, eds. *Kabuki Plays on Stage: Darkness and Desire, 1804-1864*, vol. 3: *The Tale of Tokubei from India*. Honolulu: University of Hawai'i Press, 2002.

Cartas De Iapão Que Escreverão Os Padres E Irmãos Da Companhia De Jesus. Fascimile edition, vol. 2. Tenri Central Library, 1598.

Chau, Ju-Kua. *Chau Ju-Kua, His Work on the Chinese and Arab Trade in the Twelfth and Thirteenth Centuries, Entitled Chu-Fan-Chi/ Translated From the Chinese and Annotated By Friedrich Hirth and W.W. Rockhill*. St. Petersburg: Imperial Academy of Sciences, 1911.

Chikamatsu Monzaemon 近松門左衛門. *Keisei shimabara kaeru kassen*. Chikamatsu zenshu, vol. 11. Tokyo: Iwanami shoten, 1989.

Cieslik, Hubert. "The Great Martyrdom in Edo 1623." *Monumenta Nipponica* 10, no. 1/2 (1954): 1–44.

_____. "Nanbanji-Romane Der Tokugawa-Zeit." *Monumenta Nipponica* 6, no. 1/2 (1943): 13–51.

Conlan, Thomas. *In Little Need of Divine Intervention: Takezaki Suenaga's Scrolls of the Mongol Invasions of Japan*. Ithaca, N.Y.: Cornell East Asia Series, 2001.

Cooper, Michael. *The Japanese Mission to Europe, 1582-1590*. Kent: Global Oriental, 2005.

_____. *Rodrigues the Interpreter: an Early Jesuit in Japan and China*. New York: Weatherhill, 1974.

_____ et al., eds. *The Southern Barbarians: the First Europeans in Japan*. Tokyo: Kodansha International Ltd., 1971.

Dobbins, James, Kuroda Toshio, and Suzanne Gay. "Shinto in the History of Japanese Religions." *Journal of Japanese Studies* 7.1 (1981): 1—9.

Doi, Tadao 土井忠生. *Nippo jisho. Vocabvlario da lingoa de Iapam*. Tokyo: Iwanami shoten, 1960.
Dykstra, Yoshiko Kurata. *The Konjaku Tales*. Osaka: Intercultural Research Institute, 1986.
Ebisawa Arimichi 海老沢有道. *Zōtei kirishitanshi no kenkyū*. Tokyo: Shinjinbutsu juraisha, 1971.
_____ et al., eds. *Kirishitansho, haiyasho*. Nihon shisō taikei, vol. 25. Tokyo: Iwanami shoten, 1970.
_____. *Nihon kirishitanshi*. Tokyo: Hanawa shobō, 1966.
_____, ed. *Nanbanji kōhaiki, Jakyō tai'i, Myōtei mondō, Ha Daiusu*. Toyo Bunko, vol. 14. Heibonsha, 1964.
_____, ed. *Christianity in Japan: a Bibliography of Japanese and Chinese Sources*. Tokyo: Committee on Asian Cultural Studies, International Christian University, 1960.
_____. "'Kirishitan shūmon raichō jikki' kō." *Shūkyō kenkyū* no. 139, special edition (August 1954): 36–62.
_____. *Kirishitan no shakai katsudō oyobi nanban igaku*. Tokyo: Fuzanbō, 1944.
_____. *Kirishitanshi no kenkyū*. Tokyo: Unebi shobō, 1942.
_____. "Irmão Lourenço, the First Japanese Lay-Brother of the Society of Jesus and His Letter." *Monumenta Nipponica* 5, no. 1 (1942): 225–33.
Edwards, Mark. *Constantine and Christendom: the Oration to the Saints, the Greek and Latin Accounts of the Discovery of the Cross, the Edict of Constantine to Pope Silvester*. Liverpool: Liverpool University Press, 2003.
Elison, George. *Deus Destroyed: the Image of Christianity in Early-Modern Japan*. Cambridge, Mass.: Harvard University Press, 1973.
Eshū Ibukiyama yomogi no yurai kirishitan shūmon denki (Story of the Kirishitan Sect and the Origins of the Mugwort of Mt. Ibuki in Eshu Province). MS. Kyushu University Literature Department Library, Fukuoka.
Fanon, Frantz. *Black Skin, White Masks*. London: Pluto, 1986.
Frois, Luis, S.J. *Historia de Japam*. Edited by Joseph Wicki. Vols. 1-5. Lisbon: Biblioteca Nacional de Lisboa, 1976.
Gonoi, Takashi 五野井隆史. *Tokugawa shoki kirishitanshi kenkyū*. Tokyo: Yoshikawa kōbunkan, 1983.
Gunji Masakatsu 郡司正勝, ed. *Tsuruya Nanboku zenshu*. Tokyo: Kabushiki gaishi san'ichi shobō, 1971.
Hammond, Dorothy. "Magic: a Problem in Semantics." *American Anthropologist*, New series 72 (1970): 1349–56.
Harootunian, H. D. *Things Seen and Unseen: Discourse and Ideology in Tokugawa Nativism*. Chicago: The University of Chicago Press, 1988.

Hayashi Razan 林林羅山. *Haiyaso*. In Ebisawa Arimichi et al., eds. *Kirishitan-sho, haiyasho*. Nihon shisō taikei, vol. 25. Tokyo: Iwanami shoten, 1970.

Hayashi, Senkichi 林鉄吉, ed. *Shimabara hantōshi*. Vols. 1-2, Shimabara: Nagasaki-ken Minami Takaki Gunshi Kyōikukai, 1954.

Higashibaba, Ikuo. *Christianity in Early Modern Japan: Kirishitan Belief & Practice*. Leiden: Brill, 2001.

Hiyane Antei 比屋根安定, ed. *Kirishitan monogatari hoka sanpen*. Kirishitan bunko, vol. 1. Tokyo: Keiseisha, 1926.

———. *Nanbanji kōhaiki hoka nihen*. Kirishitan bunko, vol. 2. Tokyo: Keiseisha, 1926.

Hizen shimabara jitsuroku (True Account of Shimabara in Hizen). MS. Kanazawa City Library.

Honchō kirishitan shūmon raichō jikki (Record of the Arrival of the Kirishitan in Japan). MS. Sophia University, Tokyo.

Howell, David L. *Geographies of Identity in Nineteenth-Century Japan*. Berkeley: University of California Press, 2005.

Hutchinson, Rachael, and Mark Williams. *Representing the Other in Modern Japanese Literature: a Critical Approach*. London and New York: Routledge, 2007.

Ibukiyama mogusa-ki (Mugwort of Mt. Ibuki). MS. Tokyo University Library.

Ibukiyama yomogi in'enki (Origins of the Mugwort of Mt. Ibuki). MS. Diet Library, Tokyo.

Ibukiyama yomogi no in'enki (Origins of the Mugwort of Mt. Ibuki). MS. Diet Library, Tokyo.

Ibuki yomogi (The Mugwort of Ibuki). MS. Kyoto University Library.

Ibuki yomogi kirishitan shūmon no yurai (The Mugwort of Ibuki and the Origins of the Kirishitan Sect). MS. Kyoto University Library.

Ichikawa Hirofumi 市川浩史. *Nihon chūsei no hikari to kage: 'uchinaru sangoku' no shisō*. Tokyo: Perikansha, 1999.

Ikoku nanbanji yurai (Origins of the Foreigners' Southern Barbarian Temple). MS. Tōhoku University Library, Sendai.

Inoue Akira 井上章, ed. *Amakusa-ban isopo monogatari*. Tokyo: Kazama shohō, 1964.

Jennes, Joseph. *A History of the Catholic Church in Japan*. Tokyo: The Committee of the Apostolate, 1959.

Kaisei ibuki mogusa (Revised Mugwort of Mt. Ibuki). MS. Tōhoku University Library, Sendai.

Kaisei ibuki yomogi (The Mugwort of Ibuki, Revised). MS. Tōhoku University Library, Sendai.

Kamei, Takanyoshi 亀井高孝, ed. *Kirishitan-ban amakusa-bon Heike monogatari*. Tokyo: Yoshikawa Kōbunkan, 1969.

Kanazōshi kokusenya jitsuroku. Kabuki daichō shūsei, vol. 13. Edited by Tsuchida Mamoru 土田衛 and Matsuzaki Hitoshi 松崎仁. Tokyo: Benseisha, 1987.

Katō Atsuko. *"Nihon kinsei engeki ni miru 'Kirishitan' no imēji no hen'yō."* Panel presentation at symposium, *Kirishitan bunka to nichiō kōryū,* Strasbourg, France. March 27, 2007.

Kawatake, Shigetoshi 河竹繁俊. "Jitsuroku no enkaku." Pp. 1–45 in *Kinsei jitsuroku zensho,* vol. 1. Tokyo: Waseda University, 1929.

Keisei sato no kawazu. Kabuki daichō shūsei, vol. 10. Edited by Tsuchida Mamoru 土田衛 and Matsuzaki Hitoshi 松崎仁. Tokyo: Benseisha, 1986.

Keisei takasago ura. Kabuki daichō shūsei, vol. 18. Edited by Tsuchida Mamoru and Matsuzaki Hitoshi. Tokyo: Benseisha, 1989.

Keisei to kakugedai no hajimari. Kabuki daichō shūsei, vol. 38. Edited by Tsuchida Mamoru and Matsuzaki Hitoshi. Tokyo: Benseisha, 1999.

Kikuchi, Yōsuke. "Kirishitan jitsuroku gun no tanjō." *Shizudai kokubun* (Bulletin of the Shizuoka University Humanities Department) 44 (2005).

———. "Amakusa gunki mono jitsuroku no seiritsu—kanazōshi Shimabaraki kara tamaru kubō mono e." *Kinsei Bungei* 66 (1997).

Kimbrough, R. Keller. *Preachers, Poets, Women, and the Way: Izumi Shikibu and the Buddhist Literature of Medieval Japan.* Michigan Monograph Series in Japanese Studies, no. 62. Ann Arbor: Center for Japanese Studies, The University of Michigan, 2008.

Kinka keiranshō (Tales of Storm and Splendor). MS. Ebisawa Bunko, Rikkyo University Library, Tokyo.

Kinka keiranshō (Tales of Storm and Splendor). MS. Seikadō Bunko, Tokyo.

Kinsei jitsuroku zensho. Tokyo: Waseda Daigaku shuppanbu, 1929.

Kirishitan amakusa gunki (Account of the Kirishitan Amakusa Battle). MS. Ebisawa Bunko, Rikkyo University Library, Tokyo.

Kirishitan denrai hiroku (Secret Record of the Introduction of Kirishitan). MS. Dōshisha University Library, Kyoto.

Kirishitan denraiki (Record of the Arrival of the Kirishitan). MS. Dōshisha University Library, Kyoto.

Kirishitan hokki (Record of the Rise of the Kirishitan). MS. Tōhoku University Library, Sendai.

Kirishitan honchō ni wataru koto (On the Arrival of the Kirishitan). MS. Dōshisha University Library, Kyoto.

Kirishitan ikkan oboegaki (One Volume of Memories of the Kirishitan). MS. Seikadō Bunko, Tokyo.

Kirishitan jikki (The True Account of the Kirishitan). MS. Tokyo University Library.

Kirishitan jitsuroku (True Record of the Kirishitan). MS. Kanazawa City Library.

Kirishitanki (Record of the Kirishitan). MS. Aoyama Gakuin University, Tokyo.

Kirishitan kōhaiki (Account of the Destruction of the Kirishitan). MS. Tokyo University Library.

Kirishitan kongenki (Account of the Origins of the Kirishitan). MS. Sophia University Library, Tokyo.

Kirishitan kongenki (Account of the Origins of the Kirishitan). Variant. MS. Sophia University Library, Tokyo.

Kirishitan metsubōki (Account of the Destruction of the Kirishitan). MS. Sophia University Library, Tokyo.

Kirishitan nanban jikki (Account of the Southern Barbarian Kirishitan). MS. Sophia University Library, Tokyo.

Kirishitan Nihon denrai ranshō (The Origins of the Arrival of the Kirishitan to Japan). MS. Dōshisha University Library, Kyoto.

Kirishitan raicho jikki (Account of the Arrival of the Kirishitan). MS. National Archives, Tokyo.

Kirishitan raichō jitsuroku (Account of the Arrival of the Kirishitan). MS. Sophia University Library, Tokyo.

Kirishitan raichōki (Account of the Arrival of the Kirishitan). MS. Sophia University Library, Tokyo.

Kirishitan raichōki (Account of the Arrival of the Kirishitan). Variant. MS. Sophia University Library, Tokyo.

Kirishitan raichōki (Account of the Arrival of the Kirishitan). Variant. MS. Kyoto University Library.

Kirishitan ranshōki (Origins of the Kirishitan). MS. Diet Library, Tokyo.

Kirishitan seibatsuki (Subjugation of the Kirishitan). MS. Sophia University Library, Tokyo.

Kirishitan shimatsuki (The Rise and Fall of the Kirishitan). MS. Diet Library, Tokyo.

Kirishitan shimatsuki (The Rise and Fall of the Kirishitan). Variant. MS. National Archives, Tokyo.

Kirishitan shūkyō raichō jikki (Record of the Arrival of the Kirishitan Religion). MS. Dōshisha University Library, Kyoto.

Kirishitan shūmon jikki (Record of the Kirishitan Sect). MS. Kyushu University Literature Department Library, Fukuoka.

Kirishitan shūmonki (History of the Kirishitan Sect). MS. Kyoto University Library.

Kirishitan shūmon kongen seisuiki (Record of the Origins and the Rise and Fall of the Kirishitan Sect). MS. Kyushu University Literature

Department Library, Fukuoka.
Kirishitan shūmon no koto (On the Kirishitan Sect). MS. Ise Jingū Library, Ise Shrine.
Kirishitan shūmon raichō denki (Story of the Arrival of the Kirishitan Sect). MS. Kyoto University Literature Department Library.
Kirishitan shūmon raichō jikki (A True Account of the Arrival of the Kirishitan Sect in Japan). Printed in Hiyane Antei, ed. *Kirishitan monogatari hoka sanpen.* Kirishitan bunko, vol. 1. Tokyo: Keiseisha, 1926.
Kirishitan shūmon raichō jikki (A True Account of the Arrival of the Kirishitan Sect in Japan). MS. Sophia University Library, Tokyo.
Kirishitan shūmon raichō jikki (A True Account of the Arrival of the Kirishitan Sect in Japan). MS. Tokyo University Library.
Kirishitan shūmon raichō jikki (A True Account of the Arrival of the Kirishitan Sect in Japan). Translated into English: Paske-Smith, M., ed. *Japanese Traditions of Christianity, Being Some Old Translations From the Japanese, With British Consular Reports of the Persecutions of 1868-1872.* Kobe: J. L. Thompson & Co., 1930.
Kirishitan shūmon raichō jikkiroku (Record of the Arrival of the Kirishitan). MS. Seikadō Bunko, Tokyo.
Kirishitan shūmon raichō jitsuroku (A True Account of the Arrival of the Kirishitan Sect in Japan). MS. Sophia University Library, Tokyo.
Kirishitan shūmon raichōki (Account of the Arrival of the Kirishitan Sect). MS. Sophia University Library, Tokyo.
Kirishitan shūmon raiyu (Origins of the Kirishitan Sect). MS. Sophia University Library, Tokyo.
Kirishitan shūmon ranshō (The Source of the Kirishitan Sect). MS. Aoyama Gakuin University Library, Tokyo.
Kirishitan shūmon torai jikki (Record of the Crossing of the Kirishitan Sect). MS. Tōhoku University Library, Sendai.
Kirishitan shūmon wachō ni wataru kongenki (Record of the Origins of the Crossing of the Kirishitan Sect). MS. Tsurumi Central Library, Nagoya.
Kirishitan shūmon yurai (Origins of the Kirishitan Sect). MS. Waseda University Library, Tokyo.
Kirishitan shūmon yurai kikigaki (Reports on the Origins of the Kirishitan Sect). MS. Kanazawa City Library.
Kirishitan sōraichōki (Account of the Arrival of the Kirishitan Priests). MS. Dōshisha University Library, Kyoto.
Kirishitan taiji mongatari (Tale of the Defeat of the Kirishitan). Kyoto University Library copy of Edo-period woodblock-printed text. The volume bears no colophon indicating date of publication, but library notes that it was published in the eighth month of Kanbun 5

(September 1665) in the shop of Nakano Tarōzaemon 中野太郎佐衛門 in Kyoto.

Kirishitan taiji monogatari 吉利支丹退治物語. Kanazōshi shūsei 仮名草子集成, vol. 25. Edited by Asakura Haruhiko. Tokyo: Tokyodō shuppan, 1999.

Kirishitan tokai kongenki (Account of the Original Crossing of the Kirishitan Sect). MS. Christian Central Library, Chiba.

Kirishitan tōraiki (Account of the Crossing of the Kirishitan). MS. Kyushu University Law Library, Fukuoka.

Kirishitan yurai ibuki yomogi (Ibuki Mugwort—The Origins of the Kirishitan). MS. Aoyama Gakuin University Library, Tokyo.

Kirishitan yurai jikki (True Account of the Origins of the Kirishitan). MS. Tokyo University Library.

Kirishitan yuraiki (Account of the Origins of the Kirishitan). MS. Tokyo University Library.

Kirishitan yuraiki (Account of the Origins of the Kirishitan). Variant. MS. Tohoku University Library, Sendai.

Kokuritsu gekijō geinō chōsashitsu, ed. *Tenjiku Tokubei ikoku banashi*. Kokuritsu gekijō jōen shiryōshu, vol. 248. Tokyo: 1986.

Kokusho sōmokuroku (Bibliography of National Literature). 9 vols. Tokyo: Iwanami shoten, 1963–76.

Konjaku monogatarishū. Edited by Mabuchi Kazuo 馬淵和夫, Kunisaki Fumimaro 国東文麿, and Konno Tōru 今野達. Nihon koten bungaku zenshū, vols. 21–24. Tokyo: Shogakukan, 1971.

Konta, Yōzō 今田洋三. *Edo no kinsho*. Tokyo: Yoshikawa kōbunkan, 1981.

Kornicki, Peter. "Edo jidai no shahon no kanōsei" (The Potential of Manuscripts in the Edo Period). *Bungaku gogaku* 186 (2007): 11–14.

⸺. "Manuscript, Not Print: Scribal Culture in the Edo Period." *Journal of Japanese Studies* 32, no. 1 (2006): 23–52.

⸺. *The Book in Japan: a Cultural History From the Beginnings to the Nineteenth Century*. Honolulu: University of Hawai'i Press, 2001.

⸺. "The Enmeiin Affair of 1803: the Spread of Information in the Tokugawa Period." *Harvard Journal of Asiatic Studies* 41, no. 2 (1981): 461–82.

Kumazawa Banzan. *Kumazawa Banzan*. In *Nihon shisō taikei*, vol. 30. Edited by Gotō Yōichi 後藤陽一, Tomoeda Ryūtarō 友枝龍太郎, and Iwanami Yūjirō 岩波雄二郎. Tokyo: Iwanami shoten, 1971.

Kuroda Toshio, James C. Dobbins, and Suzanne Gay. "Shinto in the History of Japanese Religions." *Journal of Japanese Studies* 7, no. 1 (1981): 1–9.

Lamers, Jeroen Pieter. *Treatise on Epistolary Style: João Rodrigues on the Noble Art of Writing Japanese Letters*. Michigan Monograph Series in Japanese

Studies, no. 39. Ann Arbor: Center for Japanese Studies, University of Michigan, 2002.

Laures, Johannes, S.J. "Takayama Ukon: A Critical Essay." *Monumenta Nipponica* 5, no. 1 (1942): 86–112.

Matsuda Kiichi 松田毅一. *Kinsei shoki nihon kankei nanban shiryō no kenkyū*. Tokyo: Kazama shobo, 1967.

———. *Taikō to gaikō*. Tokyo: Tōgensha, 1965.

———. *Nippo kōshōshi*. Tokyo: Kyōbunkan, 1963.

McBrien, Richard P. *Lives of the Saints: From Mary and St. Francis of Assisi to John XXIII and Mother Theresa*. San Francisco: HarperCollins, 2001.

Mills, D. E. *A Collection of Tales From Uji; a Study and Translation of Uji Shūi Monogatari*. Cambridge: Cambridge University Press, 1970.

Mitamura Engyō 三田村鳶魚. "Bungakushi ni habukareta jitsurokutai shōsetsu." Pp. 299–342 in *Mitamura Engyō zenshū*, vol. 22. Tokyo: Chūo kōronsha, 1975.

Miura Baien 三浦梅園. "Samidare-Shō (Musings During the Early Summer Rain)." *Monumenta Nipponica* 9, no. 1/2 (1953): 330–56.

———. "Samidare-Shō (Musings During the Early Summer Rain)." *Monumenta Nipponica* 8, no. 1/2 (1952): 289–326.

———. *Samidareshō*. Baien zenshū, vol. 1. Tokyo: Butsudōkan, 1912.

Miura, Kunio. 三浦邦夫. *Kanazōshi ni tsuite no kenkyū*. Tokyo: Ōfūsha, 1996.

Miyatake Gaikotsu 宮武外骨. *Hikkashi*. Chiba: Yamanosama shobō, 1974. Reprint of 1926 edition published by Asakaya shoten.

Miyazaki Seishin 宮崎成身. *Shichōsō* (Writings on Things Seen and Heard). MS. National Archives, Tokyo.

Mizuta Jun 水田潤. *Kana-zōshi no sekai—mibunka no seifu*. Tokyo: Sakuradaede, 1981.

Mori, Ōgai 森鴎外. *Saiki Kōi and Other Stories*. Edited by David Dilworth and J. Thomas Rimer. Honolulu: University Press of Hawai'i, 1977.

Mori, Tokuichirō 森徳一郎. *Binō kirishitan nenpyō*. Privately published, 1935.

Morley, Carolyn Anne. *Transformation, Miracles, and Mischief: The Mountain Priest Plays in Kyōgen*. Ithaca, N.Y.: Cornell East Asia Series, 1993.

Morris, Ivan. *The Nobility of Failure: Tragic Heroes in the History of Japan*. New York: Meridian, 1975.

Mujū Ichien and Robert E. Morrell. *Sand and Pebbles (Shasekishū); The Tales of Mujū Ichien, a Voice for Pluralism in Kamakura Buddhism*. Albany: State University of New York Press, 1985.

Mulhern, Chieko Irie. "Cinderella and the Jesuits. An Otogizoshi Cycle as Christian Literature." *Monumenta Nipponica* 34, no. 4 (1979): 409–47.

Munemasa Isō 宗政五十 and Wakabayashi Seiji 若林正治, eds. *Kinsei Kyōto shuppan shiryō*. Tokyo: Nihon Kosho Tsūshinsha, 1965.

Murai, Masahiro 村井昌弘. *Yaso tenchūki*. MS. Tokyo University Library.

Muroga Nobuo and Unno Kazutaka. "The Buddhist World Map in Japan and Its Contact With European Maps." *Imago Mundi* 16 (1962): 49–69.

Nagatomo Chiyoji 長友千代治. *Kinsei kashihonya no kenkyū*. Tokyo: Tokyodō shuppan, 1982.

Nakamura Yukihiko 中村幸彦. *Nakamura Yukihiko chojutsushū*. 15 vols. Tokyo: Chūō kōronsha, 1982–89.

———. "Kinsei no dokusha." *Osaka furitsu toshokan kiyō* 9 (1973): 80–98.

Nanba Matsutarō 南波松太郎, Muroga Nobuo 室賀信夫, and Unno Kazutaka 海野一隆. *Nihon no kochizu*. Tokyo: Sōgensha, 1969.

Nanban jikki (Record of South Barbary). MS. Iwase Bunko, Nagoya.

Nanbanji kōhaiki (The Rise and Fall of the Southern Barbarian Temple). Preface by Kiyū Dōjin 杞憂道人. Edo (Tokyo), 1868.

Nanbanji kōhaiki (The Rise and Fall of the Southern Barbarian Temple). Preface by Kiyū Dōjin 杞憂道人. Edo (Tokyo), 1885.

Nanbanji kōhaiki (The Rise and Fall of the Southern Barbarian Temple). MS. Variant. Ebisawa Bunko, Rikkyo University, Tokyo.

Nanbanji mongatari (The Tale of the Southern Barbarian Temple). MS. Diet Library, Tokyo.

Nanbanji yurai (Origins of the Southern Barbarian Temple). MS. Tōhoku University Library, Sendai.

Nanban metsubōki (Destruction of the Southern Barbarians). MS. Nagasaki Metropolitan Museum.

Nanbanshi (Record of South Barbary). MS. Seikadō Bunko, Tokyo.

Nanban yaso raichō jitsuroku (Record of the Arrival of the Southern Barbarian Jesus [Sect]). MS. Tokyo University Library.

Nanban yōhōki (Account of the Southern Barbarian's Heretical Sect). MS. Tokyo University Library.

Nei Kiyoshi 根井淨. *Shugendō to kirishitan*. Tokyo: Tokyodō shuppan, 1988.

Nihon bungaku daijiten. Edited by Fujimura Tsukuru 藤村作. Tokyo: Shinchōsha, 1963.

Nunn, Raymond G. "On the Number of Books Published in Japan From 1600 to 1868." In *East Asian Occasional Papers (1)*. Edited by Harry Jerome Lamley. Honolulu: University of Hawaii, 1969.

Ōtsuka, Mitsunobu 大塚光信, ed. *Kirishitan-ban esopo monogatari*. Kadokawa Bunko 2632. Tokyo: Kadokawa, 1971.

Pacheco, Diego. "Diogo De Mesquita, S.J. and the Jesuit Mission Press." *Monumenta Nipponica* 25, no. 4 (1971): 431–43.

Paramore, Kiri. *Ideology and Christianity in Japan*. London: Routledge, 2009.

———. "Hayashi Razan's Redeployment of Anti-Christian Discourse: The Fabrication of Haiyaso." *The Japan Forum* 18, no. 2 (2006): 185–206.

Paske-Smith, M., ed. *Japanese Traditions of Christianity, Being Some Old Translations From the Japanese, With British Consular Reports of the Persecutions of 1868-1872*. Kobe: J. L. Thompson & Co., 1930.
Pickering, Michael. *Stereotyping: the Politics of Representation*. New York: Palgrave, 2001.
Pratt, Mary Louise. *Imperial Eyes: Travel Writing and Transculturation*. London: Routledge, 1992.
Rodrigues, João. *Arte Da Lingoa De Iapam*. Facsimile edition. Tokyo: Bunka shobō hakubunsha, 1969 edition. Nagasaki: Collegio de Iapao da Companhia de Iesu, 1604.
Ruiz de Medina, Juan G., ed. *Monumenta Historica Japoniae*, vol. 2. Rome: Instituto Historico de la Compania de Jesus, 1990.
Said, Edward. *Orientalism*. New York: Penguin, 2003.
Sankō amakusa gunki (Information on the Battle of Amakusa). Printed copy in Ebisawa Bunko, Rikkyo University, Tokyo.
Sankō amakusa gunki (Information on the Battle of Amakusa). Printed copy in Ebisawa Bunko, Rikkyo University, Tokyo.
Sansom, George. *A History of Japan*, vol. 1: *A History of Japan to 1334*. Stanford: Stanford University Press, 1958.
Satow, Ernest Mason. *The Jesuit Mission Press in Japan*. Tokyo: Privately published, 1888.
Schurhammer, Georg, S.J. *Das Kirchliche Sprachproblem in Der Japanischen Jesuitmission Des 16. Und 17. Jahrhunderts*. Tokyo: Deutsche Gesellschraft für Natur- und Völkerkunde Ostasiens, 1928.
Schutte, Josef, S.J. *Valignano's Mission Principles in Japan*. Translated by John J. Coyne. Vol. 1. St. Louis: The Institute of Jesuit Sources, 1985.
_____, ed. *Il Ceremoniale per I missionary del Giappone: Advertimientos e avisos acerca dos costumes e catangues de Jappão, di Alexandro Valignano*. Rome, 1946.
Screech, Timon. *The Lens Within the Heart: The Western Scientific Gaze and Popular Imagery in Later Edo Japan*. Honolulu: University of Hawai'i Press, 2002.
Shapiro, James. *Shakespeare and the Jews*. New York: Columbia University Press, 1996.
Shimabara jitsuroku (True Account of Shimabara). MS. Vatican Library, Rome.
Shimabara jitsuroku (True Account of Shimabara). MS. Variant. Tōhoku University Library, Sendai.
Shibata Mitsuhiko 柴田光彦, ed. *Daisō zōsho mokuroku to kenkyū*. 2 vols. Tokyo: Seishōdō shoten, 1983.
Shima, Masakazu 島政三, ed. *Amakusa-bon Heike monogatari ken'an*. Tokyo: Ōfūsha, 1967.

Shinbō Kazuya 神保五彌 et al., eds. *Kanazōshishū, ukiyozōshishū*. Nihon koten bungaku taikei, vol. 37. Tokyo: Shogakkan, 1971.

Shinmura Izuru 新村出, ed. *Kaihyō sōsho*, vol. 1. Tokyo: Kōseikaku shoten, 1927.

———. *Kaihyō sōsho*, vol. 2. Tokyo: Kōseikaku shoten, 1927.

Shirahara, Yukiko, ed. *Japan Envisions the West: 16th-19th Century Japanese Art From Kobe City Museum*. Seattle: Seattle Art Museum, 2007.

Shirane, Haruo, ed. *Early Modern Japanese Literature: An Anthology, 1600-1900*. New York: Columbia University Press, 2002.

Shisō zasshiki. National Archives, Tokyo.

"Shutendōji." In Nihon koten bungaku zenshu, vol. 36: *Otogizōshishu*. Edited by Ōshima Tatehiko 大島建彦. Tokyo: Shogakkan, 1974.

Sokkyohen. Mito Domain, 1855. MS. National Archives, Tokyo.

Suzuki, Keiko. "The Making of Tōjin Construction of the Other in Early Modern Japan." *Asian Folklore Studies* 66, no. 1/2 (2007): 83–105.

Takagi Gen 高木元. *Edo yomihon no kenkyū—jūkyūseiki shosetsu yōshiki kō*. Tokyo: Pelican, 1995.

Takahashi, Keiichi 高橋圭一. "Jitsuroku no hen'yō, 'Nanba Senkimono' wo daizai ni." *Bungaku gogaku* 186 (2007).

———. *Jitsuroku kenkyū: Suji wo tōsu bungaku*. Osaka: Seibundō, 2002.

Takayanagi Shinzō 高柳眞三 and Ishii Ryōsuke 石井良助, eds. *Ofuregaki tenpō shūsei*. Tokyo: Iwanami shoten, 1937.

Temma ibun (Strange Record of the Amakusa Rebellion). MS. Ebisawa Bunko, Rikkyo University, Tokyo.

Tenjiku Tokubei banri no irifune. In Tsuruya Nanboku zenshu, vol. 1. Edited by Gunji Masakatsu 郡司正勝. Tokyo: San'ichi shobō, 1971.

Toby, Ronald P. "Three Realms/Myriad Countries: an 'Ethnography' of Other and the Re-Bounding of Japan, 1550-1750." Pp. 15–45 in *Constructing Nationhood in Modern East Asia*. Edited by Kai-wing Chow, Kevin M. Doak, and Poshek Fu. Ann Arbor: The University of Michigan Press, 2001.

———. "The 'Indianness' of Iberia and Changing Japanese Iconographies of Other." Pp. 323–51 in *Implicit Understandings: Observing, Reporting, and Reflecting on the Encounters Between Europeans and Other Peoples in the Early Modern Era*. Edited by Stuart B Schwartz. Cambridge: Cambridge University Press, 1994.

———. *State and Diplomacy in Early Modern Japan*. Stanford: Stanford University Press, 1991.

———. "Contesting the Centre: International Sources of Japanese National Identity." *The International History Review* 7, no. 3 (1985): 347–63.

Tyler, Royall. *Japanese Tales*. New York: Pantheon, 1987.

Ury, Marian. *Tales of Times Now Past: Sixty-Two Stories From a Medieval Japanese Collection*. Michigan Classics in Japanese Studies, no. 9. Ann Arbor: Center for Japanese Studies, The University of Michigan, 1993 reprint.

Valignano, Alexandro, S.J. *Sumario De Las Cosas De Japon*. Edited by Jose Luis Alvarez-Taladriz. Monumenta Nipponica Monographs, vol. 9. Tokyo: Sophia University, 1954.

Vega, Lope de. "Triunfo De La Fe En El Japon." Pp. 928–60 in *Obras Escogidas*, vol. 2. Edited by Federico Carlos Sainze de Robles. Madrid: Aguilar, 1967.

Wakabayashi, Bob Tadashi. *Anti-Foreignism and Western Learniing in Early-Modern Japan: the New Theses of 1825*. Cambridge, Mass.: Harvard University, 1986.

Wakaki Taiichi 若木太一. "'Shimabaraki' no seisei to sono tenkai." *Bungaku* 54, no. 12 (1986): 142–51.

Waley, Arthur. *The Nō Plays of Japan*. Rutland, Vt.: Charles E. Tuttle Co, 1976.

Washio Junkei 鷲尾順敬, ed. *Nihon shisō tōsō shiryo*. Vol. 10. Tokyo: Meichō kankyōkai, 1969.

Watanabe Kenji 渡辺憲司. "*Kirishitan to bungaku to nonfikushon bungaku: Shimabara no ran wo chūshin ni*. Paper presented at the *16 seiki ikō no nihon to higashi ajia no Kirishitan bungaku no eikyōdo wo meguru sōgōteki hikaku kenkyū*, Tokyo, 2008.

――――. "Kanazōshi to nonfikushon: Ōsaka no yaku to Shimabara no ran." Pp. 25–50 in *Edo No Nonfikushon* (Nonfiction of the Edo Period). Edited by Shiraishi Yoshio, Norizuki Toshihiko, and Watanabe Kenji. Tokyo: Tokyo shoseki, 1993.

Yamazaki Fumoto 山崎麓, ed. *Nihon shōsetsu shomoku nenpyō*. Tokyo: Shoshi kenkyūkai, 1977.

Yaso kinparoku (Record of the Outlawing and Destruction of the Jesus Sect). MS. Iwase Bunko, Nagoya.

Yasoshū ranshōki (Account of the Origins of the Jesus Sect). MS. Kyushu University Cultural History Library, Fukuoka.

Yaso seibatsuki (The Subjugation of the Jesus Sect). MS. Ebisawa Bunko, Rikkyo University Library, Tokyo.

Yaso shūmon kōhaiki (The Rise and Fall of the Jesus Sect). MS. Tokyo University Library.

Yaso shūmon kongenki (Account of the Origins of the Jesus Sect). MS. Iwase Bunko, Nagoya.

Yaso shūmon raichō jikki (Record of the Arrival of the Jesus Sect). MS. Kyoto University Library.

Yaso shūmon raichō jitsuroku (Record of the Arrival of the Jesus Sect). MS. Kyushu University Law Department Library, Fukuoka.

Yaso shūmon raichō kongenki (Account of the Origins and Arrival of the Jesus Sect). MS. Osaka Prefectural Library, Osaka.

Yaso shūmon shimatsuki (Account of the Origins of the Jesus Sect). MS. Seikadō Bunko, Tokyo.

Yaso yurai jikki (Record of the Origins of Jesus). MS. Kyushu University Law School Library, Fukuoka.

Yōkyokushū. Nihon koten bungaku taikei, vol. 41. Edited by Yokomichi Mario 横道萬里雄 and Omote Akira 表章. Tokyo: Iwanami shoten, 1960.

Yokoyama Shigeru 横山重 et al., eds. *Amakusa monogatari*. Kojoruri shohonshu, vol. 3. Tokyo: Kadokawa shoten, 1964.

Yonemoto, Marcia. *Mapping Early Modern Japan: Space, Place, and Culture in the Tokugawa Period (1603-1868)*. Berkeley: University of California Press, 2003.

Yosano Tekkan 沢野忠庵, Masamune Atsuo 正宗敦夫, and Yosano Akiko 与謝野晶子, eds. *Giya Do Pekadoru Gekan, Myōtei mondō, Ha Daiusu, Kengiroku*. Nihon koten zenshū. Tokyo: Nihon koten zenshu kankokai, 1927.

Zokuzoku gunsho ruijū. Vol. 12. Tokyo: Kokusho kankōkai, 1907.

Index

A
Abaran, 151n48
abito, 168n19
Account of the Arrival of the Kirishitan (Kirishitan raichōki), 77n27
Account of the Bishū Kirishitan (Bishū Kirishitan shimatsu), 133
Advertimientos e avisos acerca dos costumes e catangues de Jappão (Observations and Advice on the Customs and Ceremonies of Japan) (Valignano), 18–19n45
aito, 168
Aizawa Seishisai, 107, 127–31, 133
Akechi Mitsuhide, 182
Almeida, Luis de, 13, 18–19n45, 81n36; arrival, 172–73; fate, 194; monuments honoring, 13n29, 58n63; Yari-isu, 16, 173n30
Amakusa gunki, 198
Amakusa monogatari (Tale of Amakusa), 45n29, 110n10, 114n16
Amakusa Rebellion, 113. *See also* Shimabara Rebellion
Amakusa Shirō, 109, 198n77
Anamidara, 190n60
Anamidō, 190
Anesaki Masaharu, 78
animals and demons, 10–12, 14
Anointing the Sick, 34n8, 140n17
anti-Western discourse, 124–31; Aizawa Seishisai, 127–31; Miura Baien, 124–27
appearance of the Kirishitan, 9–12, 147–48, 166, 168, 173
Arai Hakuseki, 19, 125
Araikitsu, 117
Aristotle, 42, 146
Ashikaga Yoshiteru, 95, 119, 166–67
Avatamsakra sutra (Kegonkyō) (Flower Sutra), 25n58

B
Babian, 178, 178n42, 182–88, 192, 194, 196, 197. *See* Fabian Fucan
Baien, Miura, 98, 124–25
bankoku, 117
Bankoku shōho (World Map), 103, **104**
Bankoku sōzu (Map of the Myriad Realms), 6n13
baptism, 34n8, 137–38
bateren (padre), 15, 16, 32n1, 80–81, 81n35, 163n7
Bateren Dorozō, 116
baterenki, 99
Baterenki (History of the Padres) (anonymous), 2, 137–60; arrival of Kirishitans, 37–39, 145–60; authorship and period, 32–34, 42, 43–44, 55n52, 137n1; earliest extant

chronicle of arrival and expulsion, 32, 32n1; king cured of leprosy account, 37, 143–45; sacraments described, 34, 137–40; St. James, 142; St. Lucy account, 34–37, 140–42
Battles of Coxinga (Chikamatsu) (play), 116n21
behavior, uncivilized of the foreigner, 10, 20–21, 92, 93, 94, 168–70
believers, persecution, 132–33, 194–98; *Baterenki* accounts of, 38–40, 146, 160; first Japanese, 38; a hidden threat, 23; national campaign, 65–66; recognizing, 132, 163n6, 197–98; sacks, followers thrown into, 197; torture, 58; torture to Buddhahood, 56
Benzaiten, 118
Bernanto, 143–45
Berry, Mary Elizabeth, 65, 72
Bishū Kirishitan shimatsu (Account of the Bishū Kirishitan), 133
Blacker, Carmen, 14, 15n34
blood, corruption of, 18, 22–23, 55–56
Bo Juyi, 89–90
book audiences, 71
Book in Japan, The (Kornicki), 71n2, 71n4, 73n11
book reading audience, 71, 96–97n66
booksellers' guilds, 72–73
book shops, 74–75
bowing custom, 10, 92, 93, 94, 168–70
Boxer, Charles, 58n63
Buddha Deus, 18–19n45, 19, 56n55
Buddhahood, 56
Buddhism: Kirishitan sect, 9–10, 18–24, 108; *Nanbanji monogatari* debate, 185–92; transmission to Japan, 94, 96–97, 112n12; virginity as a virtue, 36
Buddhism, Confucianism, Shinto, linked, 92–93, 112
Buddhist Map of the World (Nansenbushū bankoku shōka no zu), 101, **102**
Buddhist maps, 101, 101n73, 102. *See also* maps
Buddhist rituals and ceremonies, 25, 28
Bunkyōin Hokkyō, 92–95, 169–71
Buraten, Padre, 163–65, 172–76. *See* Furaten, Padre

Buraten Bateren, 15–16

C
cannibalism, 11, 57n58
Catholic Church: origin, 37, 143n25
censorship, 2, 71–74; ban on imported books *vs.* Japanese books on Christianity, 72; earliest documented case of, 72; of *jitsuroku*, 76–77; of *Kirishitan monogatari*, 71, 72n7; of *Kirishitan taiji monogatari*, 68; military books, 72; under Tokugawa Yoshimune, 72
Cerqueira, Luis de, 45, 45n28
Cespedes, Gregorio de, 13, 16, 81n36, 153n53, 172–73, 173n30
chants and incantations, 117, 118, 186, 188; in plays, 119, 120–21
Chau Ju-Kua (Shapinsky), 98n68
Chijiwa Seizaimon, 39, 62n73, 160
Chikamatsu Hanji, 119
Chikamatsu Monzaemon, 108, 112
China, 24–25, 38, 42, 161–62n3
Chinese Others, 66
Chrismo, 138–39, 138n8
Christian century, 2, 29n61
Christian Century in Japan, The (Boxer), 29n61
Christianity. *See also* believers, persecution: 1889 ban lifted, 23; banning, 1–3, 45, 133; Japanese view/Western view, 1n2
Christianity in Japan (Ebisawa Arimichi), 78n30
civility, views of, 93–94, 94–95n62
civilizations, levels of, 6–7n13, 97
Coelho, Gaspar, 155n56
Collection of Ten Thousand Leaves (Man'yōshu), 17n41
commercial printing, 4n8, 65, 71
communion, 139–40
Confession *(confissão)*, 34n8, 55, 138
confirmation, 34n8
confissão (confession), 55, 138
Confucianism, Buddhism, Shinto, linked, 92–93, 112
Confucian principles, 126–27
Conlon, Thomas, 193n64
conquest, 80, 124–25, 128–31, 145,

162–63; by conversion, 174; Donation of Constantine possible origin, 37, 143n25; plans admitted to under torture, 125; by the praying hands of converts, 105–6; symbolized by fallen pine trees, 88–91, 105–6, 167
Constantine, Emperor, 37
contas (rosary), 18n43, 165n11. *See also* rosary *(gondatsu)*, Kirishitan
Cooper, Michael, 29n61, 45n28, 158n63, 160n70
Cosme. *See* Torres, Cosme de
cross *(cruz)*, 55, 81
crucifixions, 198
cruz (cross), 55, 81

D
duinichi, 18n45, 168–69n20
Daisō lending library, 110n9, 116, 121
date dōgu (newfangled bric-a-brac), 57n60
Deceit Disclosed (Kengiroku) (Ferreira), 40n24
dei dei paraiso (Deus, Deus, paradise), 107–8, 119, 121
deikō, 117
deisumaru, 117
demons and animals, 10–12, 14
Deus, 38, 56n55, 68n91, 83, 108, 108n2, 109, 117, 117n22, 118, 119, 121, 122, 138n5, 140, 154, 179, 186; Buddha Deus, 18, 19, 186; creator of the world, 60–61; money and health as power of, 85–86, 105. 175, 176–78, 187, 188, 207; translation errors, 18–19n45, 19, 168–69n20. See also *dei dei paraiso*
Deus Destroyed (Elison), 18–19n45, 56n54, 57, 92n54, 163n6, 168–69n20
dharani, 16, 16n38, 17–18, 117
Dialogue of Myoshu and Yutei, The (Myōtei mondō) (Fabian Fucan), 40n24, 60–61, 60n68
disciprinas (self-flagellation), 18, 18n44, 55–56
Dochiriina kirishitan (Jesuits), 34
Dōjōji tale, 11, 11n24
dōjuku, 156n60

domain lords, 96–97n66
Donation of Constantine, 37, 143n25
Dōnin, Kiyu, 99
Dorozō, Bateren, 116
Dutch medicine, 17n42

E
Ebisawa Arimichi, 18–19n46, 32n1, 33, 78n30
ebisu, 10n22, 92n55
edict of censorship, 73
edict of Constantine to the pope, 37, 143n.25
edict of expulsion, 1–2, 28–29, 29n61
eggs, 132, 195
Eight Sages of Chinese folklore, 114
Elison, George, 58, 92n54, 163n6, 168–69n20
Encyclopedia Primer (Kinmōzui) (Nakamura Tekisai), 6–7n13
encyclopedias, 6–7n13
Englishness/Jewishness, 7, 8
Enmeiin affair manuscript texts, 77
En no Gyōja, 15n33, 25n58
E no Ozuno, 15n33
E no Ubasoku, 14n31, 15
Enryakuji temple, 170–72
Eucharist, 34n8
excommunication, 145
expulsion, 32, 32n1; rewards for leads, 62–63
expulsion edicts, 1–2, 28–29, 29n61
Extreme Unction, 34n8, 139–40
eyeglasses *(megane),* 50n43
Ezo, 92n55

F
Fabian Fucan, 158, 158n62, 178n42, 179, 183, 194; about, 40, 40n24, 123; debate with Hakuo, 18, 20–22, 59–64, 60n68, 95–96, 125n37, 126, 161n1, 185n51, 186–92, 200; finery of, 20–21; *Ha Daiusu,* 40, 40n24, 62n73, 129–30, 178n42; portrayed by *Kirishitan monogatari* and *Raichō jikki,* 60, 79–86. *See* Babian
farming guides, 71n2
Fernandez, João, 56n53

Fernandez, Juan, 57n58
Ferreira, Christovão, 40n24, 158n63
filosofia, 80n34, 163n6
Flower Sutra (Kegonkyō) (Avatamsakra sutra), 25n58
fly, power to, 16, 32n1, 163
foolish *(gujin)*, 57
forty-two provinces: forty-two beads, 105–6, 165, 176
Four Guardian Kings of the Dharma, 15n34
foxes, 11
Franciscans, 13; work with poor and sick, 58–59, 163n6
Francisco Tōan, 159, 159n68
fratrum *(furaten)*, 59, 81n36, 163n6
frogs, 114. *See also* toad magic
Frois, Luis, 81n36, 98n68, 161n3
"from the temple to the supplicant," 21
Fujita Yūkoku, 128
fumie, 2n5, 119
Furaten, Padre 59, 81, 81n36, 84, 163, 163n6, 208n23
furaten (fratrum), 59, 59n67, 81n36, 163n6

G

gai'i jinbutsu (outer barbarian peoples), 94–95n62
gaikoku no jōkyōtō (situations in foreign countries), 73
Gama Sennin. *See* Toad Hermit
gedō (mistaken path), 20, 57
Genso Komei Kotei, 94
Gerikori, Brother: fate, 194
gesshi tribe, 112n12
gift giving, 57–58, 129–30, 148, 162–63, 165, 173
Gnecchi-Soldo, Organtino, 50–51n44
Goa, 38, 42n26
gods: Buddhist absorption of Shinto, 28; shift from protector to protected, 28–30; translation errors, 18–19n45
Gogi, Lord, 162–65
Gojimbi (Nanban king), 15, 98, 126, 161
Gokinai, 175n35
golpes de pecho (pounding of the chest), 56n53
Go-Nara, 50n41

gondatsu (rosary). *See* rosary *(gondatsu)*, Kirishitan
Good Friday, 149n46
Goshōten haraisō zensumaru, 176, 176n37, 186, 188
Gōshū, 174
Gotenjiku zu (Map of the Five Indies), 101
"gozan" Zen system, 18–19n45
Gregory, Pope, 35
gujin (foolish), 57

H

Ha Daiusu (Deus Destroyed) (Fabian Fucan), 40, 40n24, 62n73, 129, 178n42. *See also* Fabian Fucan
Hayashi Razan, 60n68
Haiyaso (The Anti-Jesus) (Hayashi Razan), 60n68
Ha Kirishitan (Christians Countered) (Suzuki Shōsan), 68n91
Hakuo Koji, 60; and Fabian debate, 18, 20–22, 59–64, 60n68, 95–96, 125n37, 126, 161n1, 185n51, 186–92, 200; opposite of Fabian finery, 21; sermon denouncing Kirishitan discussed, 60–62, 95–96n63–66, 95–97
Hakurakuten (Zeami), 89
Hara Castle, 112, 113
haraisō, 16, 16n38, 81, 81n37, 120, 121, 176, 176n37, 186, 188. See *paraiso*
Hashiba Hideyoshi, 182. *See also* Toyotomi Hideyoshi
Heian, 88n45
hiden (secret transmissions), 73
Higashibaba, Ikuo, 13
hisōjō (magic), 15, 80n34, 115, 163, 163n6
Historia de Japam (Frois), 98n68, 161n3
History of the Kirishitan Sect (Kirishitan shūmonki), 77n27
History of the Nanban (Nanbanshi), 127n39
History of the Padres. See *Baterenki* (History of the Padres) (anonymous)
Hitō senki (Military History of the Islands of Hizen), 125n36
Hiyane Antei, 33

Holy Orders, 34n8
honji suijaku, 92–93
hospitals, 13n29, 58n63–64
Hōtan, 101, 102
hotoke, 56n55
Hsüan-tsang, 101

I
Iberian Irruption, 3, 66
Iberians, 99
Iberian ships: prohibition, 2
Ibuki mogusa variant, 125–27
Ibuki mugwort, 16–17
Ibukiyama mogusaki (Tale of the Mugwort of Mt. Ibuki), 79
Ibuki yomogi, 95–96, 95n63
Ichibashi Shosuke, 194–97
ikoku, 94–95n62
ikyō (barbarian teachings), 129
Imago Mundi, **100**
India, 24–25, 42, 98n68, 99, **100**, 101n73, 161n3
inferno (hell), 55
Inoue Masashige, 163n6
interpreter *(tsūji)*, 159n64
irmão. See *iruman (irmão)*
I-ro-ha poem, 191n61
iruman (irmão), 32n1, 81n36, 146n35, 163n8
Ise Shrine, 193
Ishida Konishi, 194
Islam, 20; misguided version of Christianity, 9, 18–19n47; threat to Europe, 8–9

J
jahō, 115
jakyō (evil religion), 128
Jakyō tai'i (Extermination of the Evil Religion) (Sesshō), 40n24. See *Taiji jashūron*
Japan, 155n57
Japanese identity, 1–5, 8, 30–31, 65–67
Japanese mission to Europe, 38, 39, 158n63, 160, 160n69
Japanese Mission to Europe, The (Cooper), 158n63
Japon (Japan alt.), 38, 43, 44n27, 155n57

Jesuits (Society of Jesus), 18–19n45, 163n8; *Dochiriina kirishitan*, 34; establishment in Japan, 1n1, 161n2; less active with ministry to sick, 13; locations of major missions, 38; *Nippo jisho* (dictionary), 50n43, 108n2; noted as differing from *furaten*, 59; views on *shugenja*, 13n27
Jetavana Monastery, 189–90
Jewishness/Englishness, 7, 8
Jikkōji temple, 197
jitsurokutai shōsetsu (true accounts), 75–77, 75n21, 76n23
jōruri puppet plays, 107, 118
Justo Ukondono, 143n.25

K
kabuki plays, 118
Ka'i jinbutsu zu (A Map of the Peoples of Barbarian and Civilized Countries), 103
Ka'i tsūshō kō (Thoughts on Trade between China and Barbarians) (Nishikawa Jōken), 6–7n13
ka'i worldview, 93, 94
kakihon, 75
Kakuken, 25, 112n12
kami (gods), 28
Kanazōshi kokusenya jitsuroku (True Account of Kokusenya) (play), 116–18
kanbun, 127
Kanō Motohide, 170n24
karma, 11–12, 22, 187
kashihon'ya (lending library). See lending library *(kashihon'ya)*
Katō Atsuko, 101, 108n1, 114n16
Katō Kiyomasa, 197
Katsuragisan (mountain), 25
Keene, Donald, 116n21
keisei, 112
Keisei shimabara kaeru kassen (Pillow Wars Tales) (Chikamatsu), 116
Keisei takasago ura (play), 108n1
Kerikori, Brother. See Cespedes, Gregorio de
kijin, 167n16
kijutsu (trickery), 129
Kingoku, 175n35

Kinka keiransho (Tales of Storm and Splendor), 45n29
Kinmei, Emperor, 94
Kinmōzui (Encyclopedia Primer) (Nakamura Tekisai), 6–7n13, 6n13
Kinoshita Tōkichi, 126, 196–97
Kinoshita Tōkichiro, 196n70. *See also* Toyotomi Hideyoshi
Kinsho mokuroku (List of Banned Books), 73
Kirishitan, haiyasho (Ebisawa Arimichi et al.), 18–19n46
Kirishitan, the, 5–10, 131, 133; animals and demons of, 10–12, 14; appearance, 9–12, 50–55, 147–48, 166, 168, 173; association with blood and disease, 22–23, 56–57; construct development, 3–5; magic and medicine, 12–18; plays featuring Kirishitan villain (table), 107–22; portrayed as villains, 44, 107–22; preoccupation with wealth and money, 20–21, 23, 57–58, 175, 180, 182; uncivilized behaviors, 20–21; Western/Kirishitan Other, 127, 134; as *yamabushi* type, 16–18
Kirishitan buppō, 19–20, 56, 168–69n20
Kirishitan jikki (True Account of the Kirishitan), 79
Kirishitan monogatari (Tales of the Kirishitan): about, 2, 45–49, 63–69; converts, 62–63; debate, 49, 59–62; Kirishitan beliefs, 49, 55–57; meetings in the capital, 52–55, **53, 54**; physical description of Kirishitan, 50–55; preoccupation with wealth and money, 57; printings, 2; Shimabara Rebellion events, 49, 63, 65; structural differences from *Baterenki*, 49–50; "subjugation of Japan," 62
Kirishitan raichōki (Account of the Arrival of the Kirishitan), 77n27
Kirishitan sect of Buddhism, 9–10, 18–24, 108
Kirishitanshū (Kirishitan sect), 73
Kirishitan shūmonki (History of the Kirishitan Sect), 77n27
Kirishitan shūmon raichō (A True Account of the Kirishitan Sect), 2
Kirishitan shūmon raichō jikki (A True Account of the Arrival of the Kirishitan Sect in Japan), 2, 161–98, 161n1; censored, 68, 70–71, 90n50; earliest manuscript, 79; extant copies, 78–79; long-standing popularity of narrative, 130–31, 133; *Nanbanji kōhaiki*, 70n1; padre magician of, 79–86; three-realms and sacred Japan, 86–97; three-realms in the world, 97–106; title variants, 16–17, 76n22, 77–79, 77n27, 78n30, 95; Toyotomi Hideyoshi a hero, 90–91. See also *Nanbanji monogatari* (Tale of the Southern Barbarian Temple) (anonymous)
Kirishitan shūmon wachō wataru kongenki (Record of the Origins of the Crossing of the Kirishitan Sect), 79n32
Kirishitan taiji monogatari (Tale of the Defeat of the Kirishitan): banning, 71, 72; illustrations, **53, 54**; printings, 2n3
Kirishitan yuraiki (Origins of the Kirishitan), 79
Kirisutoki (Inoue Masashige), 163n6
Kokusenya, 116, 117
Kokusho sōmokuroku, 78n30
Konjaku monogatarishū (Tales of Times Now Past), 11n24–25, 14, 96
Korea, 109–10
Kornicki, Peter, 71, 72, 73
korobi Kirishitan, 197n71
kowtow ritual. *See* bowing custom
Kumazawa Banzan, 18–19n47, 19
Kyōōgokuji temple, 88–89, 88n45, 167, 167n15
Kyoto guild, 72–73

L
Latin terms, 41n25
Law of Buddha, 93, 171, 171n25
Legend of Tenjiku Tokubei, The (Tenjiku Tokubei kikigaki ōrai) (Namiki Shōzō), 119–22
lending library *(kashihon'ya)*, 71, 74–77, 74n15, 110

Lens Within the Heart, The (Screech), 5n12
Lent *(Quaresma)*, 55
leprosy, 58, 145n31; believers cured, 39; king cured of account, 37, 143–45
Lião, 156–57
List of Banned Books (Kinsho mokuroku), 73
Lives of the Saints (Sanctos no gosagyō) (McBrien), 35n9
Lourenço, Brother, 38–39, 38n20, 154, 154n55

M
Macao, 5
magic *(hisōjō)*, 12–18, 15, 80n34, 163, 163n6; toad magic, 109, 112–16, 119
maho (magic), 57, 115, 117
Manila, 5, 162n4
manuscript copies *(shahon)*, 2, 74, 77n24
manuscript culture, 73–74
manuscripts, copied by lending libraries, 74–75
Man'yōshu (Collection of Ten Thousand Leaves), 17n41
Map of the Myriad Realms, 6n13
Map of the Peoples of Barbarian and Civilized Countries, A (Ka'i jinbutsu zu), 103
maps, 6–7, 6–7n13, **100**, 101n73, **102**; "fixing" a foreign image, 23; new world, 3; screen map of Nanban, 99n71; three-realms, 3, 24–27, **26, 27,** 30–31, 42; *World Map (Bankoku shōho)*, 103
Mashida Hisayoshi, 116
Masuda Tokisada, 109
Mato, 94
Matrimony, 34n8, 139
McBrien, Richard, 35n9
medicine, practice of: attracts converts, 58–59, 81, 174–80; Dutch, 17n42; Jesuits known for, 13–14, 163n6
megane (eyeglasses), 50n43
mikoshi nyūdō, 10
military books, 72
Military History of the Islands of Hizen (Hitō senki), 125n36
military tales (oral), 76
Mito scholars, 127–28, 133
Mohammed, 9
mōko, 10n22, 92n55
money and wealth, 20–21, 23, 57–58; handed out, 126, 175, 180, 182
Mongol defeat, 25–26, 43, 162
Mongolia, 170n23
Mongol invasions, 89, 90–91, 192–94, 192n62; frog omen, 114–15; number of invaders, 193n64
Monmu, Emperor, 15
Monte Plata (Japan alt.), 38n21, 42, 43, 44n27, 146–60
Morales, Francisco de, 45
Morely, Carolyn, 14n32
moretto (black man), 51n46
Mori Ōgai, 75
Morris, Ivan, 109, 109n3
Mt. Hiei, 195n68
Mt. Ibuki, 16, 17, 174
Mt. Sumeru, 25
mugwort, 16–17, 17n41, 174, 174n34
Muroga Nobuo, 101
Musings During the Early Summer Rain (Samidareshō) (Baien), 98, 124–25
Myōtei mondō (The Dialogue of Myoshu and Yutei) (Fabian Fucan), 40n24, 60–61, 60n68

N
Nagasaki, 39, 45n28, 158, 160n70
Nakamura Tekisai, 6–7n13
Nakamura Yokihiko, 75
Namiki Shōzō, 119
Nanagusa Shirō (character), 109, 113, 116
Nanban, 5–6, 24, 97–106, **98**; described, 97–98; forty-two provinces, 105–6, 165, 176; king of, 5n12, 15
Nanbanji kōhaiki, Jakyō tai'i, Myōtei mondō, Ha Daiusu (Ebisawa Arimichi), 32n1, 133–34
Nanbanji monogatari (Tale of the Southern Barbarian Temple) (anonymous), 79, 95–96, 161–98, 161n1; appearance of the foreigner,

166, 168, 173; Bunkyōin and Nobunaga discussion, 169–71; care to the poor and sick, 174–80; Fabian and Hakuo debate, 60–63, 186–92; forty-two bead rosary, 176; Kerikori and Yariisu arrive, 172–73; manners of the foreigner, 169; not Enryakuji temple but Nanbanji temple, 169–72; seven-day period of indoctrination, 177–78; Shuri's mother, 182–85, 188; sixty-six fallen pines, 167
nanbanjin, 98, 99
Nanbanjin (Southern Barbarians), 5n12; compared to Kirishitan, 5, 5n12; first use of term, 44, 155, 155n59
Nanbanji temple, 81, 169–72; beauty of, 20; Our Lady of the Assumption, 170n24; taken over, 194
Nanbanshi (History of the Nanban), 127n39
Nansenbushū bankoku shōka no zu (Buddhist Map of the World), 101, **102**
Nihon (Japan alt.), 38n21, 150
Nihon akitsushima (Japan alt.), 44n27
Nihon chūsei no hikari to kage (Ichikawa), **26, 27**
Nippo jisho (dictionary), 50n43, 108n2
Nirvana sutra, 191n61
Nishikawa Jōken, 6–7n13, 98, 103
Nobility of Failure, The (Morris), 109n3
northeast direction, 164n9, 171n26
Nunn, Raymond G., 71n4

O
Observations and Advice on the Customs and Ceremonies of Japan (Advertimientos e avisos acerca dos costumes e catangues de Jappáo) (Valignano), 18–19n45
Oda Nobunaga: Buddhism itself came from abroad, 18, **54,** 95, 116, 129–30, 159n64, 169–71, 192; death, 182; role played in *Nanbanji monogatari*, 166–82
Ōgimachi, Emperor, 97, 161
Ogyū Sorai, 73
Ōhara Sakingo, 128

okushū, 114, 118
Ōmi, 174, 195
Ōmura region, 2, 39, 44, 45n28
Ōmura Sumitada, 160
Onoe Matsusuke I, 121n26
Ordo Fratrum Minorum, 59n67, 163n6
Organtino, Gnecchi Soldo, 161n2, 163n6. *See also* Urugan, Padre
Orientalism (Said, Edward), 8, 18–19n47
Origins of the Kirishitan (Kirishitan yuraiki), 79
Our Lady of the Assumption, 170n24. *See also* Nanbanji temple
Owari/Mino area, 75n18, 133

P
padre, 7, 10, 11, 20, 28, 32n1, 39–41, 57–59, 81–84, 95, 124, 126, 163, 163n7; and Baterenki, 137–60; delegation to Siam, 38; Kirishitan padres *vs.* Baterenki padres, 63; narrator of Baterenki, 43; as *yamabushi*, 12–18, 52n49, 115
painting of *tenjikujin*, 98n68, 161n3
paradise *(paraiso)*, 55, 81n37, 107–8
paraiso (paradise), 55, 81n37, 107–8, 117, 117n22, 118, 119, 122, 176n37, 207. See *haraiso*
Pasio, Francisco, 45
Peacock King, 15, 15n34
Penance, 34n8, 81n38
penitence *(penteisha)*, 55, 81n38
penteisha (penitence), 55, 81n38
Pillow Wars Tales (Keisei shimabara kaeru kassen) (Chikamatsu), 116
pine trees, fallen, 88–91, 105–6, 167
plays featuring Kirishitan villain (table), 107–22, 111
Portuguese, 23; terms, 33n3, 41n25; trade with, 2, 29, 45
pounding of the chest *(golpes de pecho)*, 56n53
printing, commercial: and manuscript culture, 71–73; not distinguished from narratives by readers, 4n8; power of, 4n8, 65
puppet plays, 107

Q
Quaresma (Lent), 55

R
raichō (embassy), 55n51
Raichō jikki. See *Kirishitan shūmon raichō jikki* (A True Account of the Arrival of the Kirishitan Sect in Japan)
Ran, 4
rangaku, 17n42
Ranjin, 5n12
Record of the Origins of the Crossing of the Kirishitan Sect (Kirishitan shūmon wachō wataru kongenki), 79n32
Record of the Transmission of the Law in the Three Realms (Sangoku dentōki) (Kakuken), 25, 112n12
Regional Maps with Pictures of Forty-eight Peoples (Sekai yondaishū zu / Yonjūhachi-ka-koku jinbutsu zu), 99n71
Revised Treatise on Relations with Chinese and Barbarian Countries (Zōhō ka'i tsūshōkō) (Nishikawa Joken), 98
Ricci, Matteo, 73
Roba, 98n68, 161–62n3
Rodrigues the Interpreter (Cooper), 45n28
Roman, Brother, 35–36
Romance of the Three Kingdoms (Tsūzoku sangokushi), 114
Rome, 162n4
Romé, 161–62n3
rosary, Japanese: 108; beads, 105; praying with, 13n27
rosary *(gondatsu)*, Kirishitan, 17–18, 18n43, 176; forty-two beads, 105–6, 165, 176; praying with, 13n27
Russia, 23
Ryōsei. See Lourenço, Brother
Ryū Kai Sen, 114
Ryūzōji Takashige, 166–67

S
sacks, followers thrown into, 197
sacraments, 13, 32–34, 137–40
Said, Edward, 8, 18–19n47
Saiji (Western Temple), 88n45

Saiki kōi (Mori Ōgai), 75, 75n20
salt, 138
salvation, 36, 39, 56, 86, 92, 106
Samidareshō (Musings During the Early Summer Rain) (Baien), 98, 124–25
samurai reading audience, 71, 96–97n66
Sanctos no gosagyō (Lives of the Saints), 36
sandamaru (Saint Mary), 108, 117
Sangoku dentōki (Record of the Transmission of the Law in the Three Realms) (Kakuken), 25, 112n12
Sangokushi (Romance of the Three Kingdoms), 114
santamaro, 117n22. See also chants
Santiago Hospital, 58n64
Santō Kyōden, 75
Schutte, Josef, 18–19n45
Screech, Timon, 4, 5n12
Sekai yondaishū zu / Yonjūhachi-ka-koku jinbutsu zu (Regional Maps with Pictures of Forty-eight Peoples), 99n71
self-flagellation, 18–19n45, 22, 55–56, 81n38
senjutsu, 115
Sesshō, 19, 34
setsuwa literature, 12–13; *yamabushi* of, 14, 22; demons in, 10–11
seven-day period of indoctrination, 16, 177–78
shahon. See manuscript copies *(shahon)*
Shapinsky, Peter, 98n68
Shapiro, James, 7, 8
shigo shōten, 16n38, 108, 117n22
shigo shōten dei, 117
Shigo shōten haraisō zensumaro, 16, 16n38, 81, 81n37, 121
Shijō Bōmon, 170, 170n24
Shijūnikoku jinbutsu zusetsu (The Peoples of the Forty-two Countries) (Nishikawa Jōken), 6–7n13, 103
Shimabara jitsuroku (True Account of Shimabara), 74, 74n15, 79n31
Shimabara kaeru kassen (Frog Battle of the Shimabara Beauties) (Chikamatsu Monzaemon), 112
Shimabara-ki (Record of Shimabara),

109n3; title variants, 45n29, 79n31
Shimabara Rebellion, 2, 109, 112, 198; left out of some *jitsuroku*, 77–78; literature on, 45n29, 79n31; missionaries after, 67; number of marchers, 63; uprising and defeat, 2
Shimada Seian, 194–97
Shinron (New Theses) (Aizawa Seishisai), 107, 127–31
shinsei, 140
Shinto, Buddhism, Confucianism, linked, 92–93, 112
Shinto gods, 92n54
Shinto Yoshida diary, 57n58
Shisō zasshiki, 132
Shogyō-mujōge, 191n61
Shoku, 98n68
Shōtei Kinsui, 75
Shūgaihō, **100**
Shugendō, 12, 15
shugenja (yamabushi), 12. See also *yamabushi*
Shutendōji (demon), 17
Siam, 38
Sidotti, Giovanni Battista, 125
Simon, Padre, 146, 153, 194
Society of Jesus (Jesuits). *See* Jesuits (Society of Jesus)
Sokkyohen (Anthology of Heretical Texts) (Mito school), 129
South Barbary, 159, 159n66, 161; forty-two provinces of, 105–6, 165, 176
Southern Barbarians, The (Cooper et al.), 29n61
Spanish, the, 2, 5, 23
St. James, 142, 142n24
St. John the Evangelist, 140
St. Lucy, 35–37, 140–42
St. Peter, 34
storytelling traditions, 76n23
Subjugation of the Jesus Sect, The (Yaso seibatsuki), 125n36
Sugiya Yukinao, 103
Sumario de las Cosas del Japon (Summary of Things Japanese) (Valignano), 18–19n45
Sumidake, 198
Sumiyoshi Shrine, 88–91

Summary of Things Japanese (Sumario de las Cosas del Japon) (Valignano), 18–19n45
Suzuki Shōsan, 68n63
Sylvester I, Pope, 37, 143n.25
symbolism and symbols, 13; *gondatsu*, 17–18

T
Taiji jashūron (On the Extermination of the Evil Religion) (Sesshō), 19, 34, 40n24. See *Jakyō tai'i*
Takagi Gen, 114
Takaura Julian, 158n63
Takayama Ukon, 143n.25
Takemoto Saburobee, 119
Tale of Amakusa (Amakusa monogatari), 45n29, 110n10, 114n16
Tale of the Defeat of the Kirishitan (Kirishitan taiji monogatari): banning, 71, 72; illustrations, **53, 54**; printings, 2n3
Tale of the Mugwort of Mt. Ibuki (Ibuki-yama mogusaki), 79
Tale of the Southern Barbarian Temple (Kirishitan shūmon raichō jikki). See *Nanbanji monogatari* (Tale of the Southern Barbarian Temple) (anonymous)
Tales from Uji (Uji shūi monogatari), 14
Tales of Storm and Splendor (Kinka keiransho), 45n29
Tales of the Kirishitan (Kirishitan monogatari). See Kirishitan monogatari (Tales of the Kirishitan)
Tales of Times Now Past (Konjaku monogatarishū), 14, 96
Tamenaga Shunsui, 75
Tçuzzu, Rodrigues, 159n64
temple registration system, 2–3n5, 197–98, 197n75
temple schools *(terakoya)*, 71
tengu, 10, 14
Tenjiku (India alt.), 42
tenjikujin, 98n68
Tenjiku shinadakoku, 98n68, 161n3
Tenjiku Tokubei (character), 109, 118–22

Tenjiku Tokubei ikoku banashi (play), 110n10, 120n24
Tenjiku Tokubei kikigaki ōrai (The Legend of Tenjiku Tokubei) (Namiki Shōzō), 119–22
tenshu (Deus), 108n2
tenshukyō (teachings of the Lord of Heaven), 108
tentai (Deus), 108, 175n36. *See also* tentei
tentei (Deus), 108n2, 175n36. *See also* tentai
Terajima Ryōan, 6–7n13, 94–95n62
terakoya (temple schools), 71
terms, translation: errors in, 18–19n45, 19, 168–69n20; Portuguese or Latin, 33n3, 34, 41n25; untranslated, 41
Thoughts on Trade between China and Barbarians (Ka'i tsūshō kō) (Nishikawa Jōken), 6–7n13
three-realms maps, 5, 24–27, **26, 27,** 30–31; about, 24–25; challenges, 3; as presented in the *Baterenki*, 42
three-realms worldview, 93, 94
three-worlds mirror, 16, 172, 175
Toad Hermit, 112–16; Gama Sennin, 113n13
toad magic, 109, 112–16, 119
Toby, Ronald, 66, 103, 110
Tōji (Eastern Temple), 88–89, 88n45
tōjin, 109–10, 110n7
Tokugawa Ieyasu, 30, 30n62, 159n64, 160n70
Tokugawa Mitsukuni, 127
Tokugawa Yoshimune, 73
Torres, Cosme de, Padre, 43, 153–54, 153n52, 154n55, 194, 198
Toyotomi Hideyoshi: banishes foreign missionaries, 95, 192–98; books about banned, 72; Hashiba, 182n45; interpreted by Rodrigues, 159n64; portrayal in *Raichō jikki*, 90–91; portrays gods as needing protection, 28–30
Tōzai, 175n35
trade, 2; Portuguese, 2, 29, 45; with West, 23, 133–34
Transformation, Miracles, and Mischief (Morely), 14n32
translation errors: errors in, 18–19n45
True Account of Kokusenya (Kanazōshi kokusenya jitsuroku) (play), 116–18
True Account of the Arrival of the Kirishitan Sect in Japan, A. See Kirishitan shūmon raichō (A True Account of the Kirishitan Sect)
Tsuchizō, Iruman, 116
Tsuji, Father, 158n63
Tsuruya Nanboku, 108, 118
Tsūzoku sangokushi (Romance of the Three Kingdoms), 114

U
Uba, 98n68, 161–62n3
Uji shūi monogatari (Tales from Uji), 14
Ume, 98n68, 161–62n3
Unno Kazataka, 101, 102
Urakami, 160n70
Urugan, Padre, 18, 50–51n44, **53, 54,** 163–70, 172–76; coming preceded by divine warning, 88; fate, 194; Organtino, Gnecchi Soldo, 163n6
Urugan Bateren, 15–16
Uto, 197

V
Valignano, Alexandro, 18–19n45, 51, 58, 145n31, 158n63
Valignano's Mission Principles in Japan (Schutte), 18–19n45
Vicente, Paulo, 36
Vicente, Tōin, 36, 142n24
Vietnam, 98, 98n68, 153n50, 161–62n3
Vilela, Gaspar, 154n55, 155n56
virginity, 36–37

W
wagachō, 155n57
Wakan sansai zue (Sino-Japanese Encyclopedia of the Three Realms) (Terajima Ryōan), 6–7n13
wakō dōjin, 92n54, 169n22
Waley, Arthur, 89
wandering stranger, 14. *See also yamabushi*
water torture, 198, 198n76

Western/Kirishitan Other, 5, 67, 124–27, 134. *See also* anti-Western discourse; Kirishitan, the
White Horse Temple, 192
winds, divine, 25–26, 29, 43, 147, 151, 152, 193; *Baterenki* account of, 37, 147, 150–51, 152
World Map (Bankoku shōho), 103
Wu Ma Pa, 98n68, 161–62n3

X
Xavier, Francis, 57n58, 161n2; and Lourenço, 38n20, 154n55; mission establishment, 1n1, 153n52; painting of, 93; uses term *dainichi* and Deus, 18–19n45

Y
Yajirō (interpreter), 18–19n45
Yakushi Ruriko, 188n58
yamabushi, 9, 12–15, 16–18

yaso (Jesus), 108n2
yasokyō (teachings of Jesus), 128–29
Yaso seibatsuki (The Subjugation of the Jesus Sect), 125n36
yaso shūmon (the Jesus Sect), 108
yōjutsu (magic), 117
yōkyō (occult teachings), 129
Yuima, 21
Yuima sutra, 21n50

Z
Zeami, 89n47
Zen, 18–19n45
zensumaro (*zensumaru* var.) (Jesus Mary), 16, 16n38, 58, 81, 81n37, 108, 117n22, 121, 176, 176n37, 186, 188. *See also* chants
Zōhō ka'i tsūshōkō (Revised Treatise on Relations with Chinese and Barbarian Countries) (Nishikawa Joken), 98

ABOUT THE AUTHOR

Jan C. Leuchtenberger is Associate Professor of Japanese and Director of the Asian Studies Program at the University of Puget Sound in Tacoma, Washington. Her research interests include representations of Japan and the West in early modern Japanese discourses and the earliest representations of Japan in Europe.